A HISTORY
OF ARCHITECTURE

HARPER'S FINE ARTS SERIES

A HISTORY OF
ARCHITECTURE

BY

FISKE KIMBALL, M.Arch., Ph.D.

AND

GEORGE HAROLD EDGELL, Ph.D.

ILLUSTRATED

GREENWOOD PRESS, PUBLISHERS
WESTPORT, CONNECTICUT

The Library of Congress has catalogued this publication as follows:

Library of Congress Cataloging in Publication Data

Kimball, Sidney Fiske, 1888-1955.
   A history of architecture.

    Original ed. issued in series: Harper's fine arts
series.
   Includes bibliographical references.
    1. Architecture--History. I. Edgell, George Harold,
1887-1954, joint author. II. Title. II. Series.
NA200.K5 1972   720'.9   72-169847
ISBN 0-8371-6243-2

Originally published in 1946 by Harper & Brothers, Publishers,
New York

Reprinted with the permission of Harper & Row, Publishers

Reprinted by Greenwood Press, Inc.

First Greenwood reprinting 1972
Second Greenwood reprinting 1977

Library of Congress catalog card number 72-169847

ISBN 0-8371-6243-2

Printed in the United States of America

CONTENTS

ILLUSTRATIONS

EDITOR'S INTRODUCTION

Harper's Fine Arts Series is intended to provide for the student and the general reader concise but authoritative histories of architecture, sculpture, and painting. During the last twenty years the study of the monuments of the past has been pursued with constantly increasing thoroughness by a great number of well-trained scholars. Hundreds of books and articles devoted to individual artists, to single monuments or groups of monuments, or to special periods have appeared, which have greatly modified the generalizations and theories of a generation or even a decade ago. The spade of the excavator has added many new and important monuments to those already known, and brought to light new evidence on disputed points. Most of the older handbooks, therefore, are "out of date" in many respects, and some of those more recently published repeat traditional statements which have, in many cases, been proved incorrect. It has been the endeavor of the writers of this series to consider all the results of modern investigation and to summarize them as clearly as possible. The need for such summaries of the results of research seems to be better met by single volumes than by more elaborate treatises, which can have no compensating gain in authoritativeness unless they are the work of many collaborators.

In every case of conflicting theories the writers have tried, after weighing all the evidence, to present the view which seems to them most probable, and then to give, in selected bibliographies, the titles of books which will be found helpful for further study. They have not attempted to discuss a large number of monuments of any given period, but have chosen rather to emphasize important and characteristic works and to show their relation to the whole development. In some cases, also, they have emphasized certain aspects of their subjects at the expense of others. The development of American art has been discussed at rather greater length than has been customary in similar books, since it seems to the writers that American art merits fuller treatment than it has usually received at the hands of critics and historians. As the books are intended for Occidental readers, Eastern art, in spite of its historical importance and intrinsic value, is treated in a single chapter. Throughout, the endeavor has been to consider the art of the past in the light of the present, to try to show how modern art is related to that which has preceded it.

In the arrangement of the material the use of the books by classes has been constantly kept in mind, and headings for sections or paragraphs have been freely introduced throughout the three volumes.

One other principle the writers have constantly kept before them. The office of the historian is to trace development, to show how the art of any period grew out of that of earlier times and in turn conditioned that of later days. Too many of the older histories were written to uphold a particular system of æsthetics or to glorify a particular phase of artistic development, frequently in a particular country. Many of these books are valuable as expressions of the judgment of a critic or as records of the taste of an age. But for the beginner and the general reader they are often confusing. They place him at an unfair disadvantage and tend to warp his judgment. Discussions of æsthetic principles and statements of the consensus of critical opinion may properly find place in an elementary book, but expressions of purely personal judgments and theories which have not been generally accepted should be eliminated so far as possible. The aim of the writers of this series has been to point out the qualities in the works of any period which have appealed most strongly to the creators of those works and to endeavor to emphasize what has enduring value. It is hoped that the resulting "objectivity" of the books will add materially to their usefulness.

The problem of illustration is always difficult. In recent years, histories of art and similar books have exhibited two opposite tendencies, the one toward a large number of illustrations on a very small scale, the other toward few illustrations, but those of large size. The former system has the advantage of bringing before the reader most of the buildings or statues or paintings mentioned in the text, the latter that of showing more clearly the details of individual works. In this matter the writers have tried, with the co-operation of the publishers, to steer a middle course, providing a considerable number of full-page illustrations for especially important monuments and a much larger number of small cuts for others. They hope that they have hit upon a "golden mean."

GEORGE H. CHASE.

HARVARD UNIVERSITY,
     1917.

AUTHORS' PREFACE

During the last twenty years the origins of architecture have been pushed back another millennium, and its later development has been enriched by wholly new chapters. Minute research on a multitude of special points has modified or overthrown generalizations of the nineteenth century which are still too often repeated. Scholars have been forced, for instance, to abandon the suppositions that Assyria and Etruria made any advance over Egypt and Greece in the use of the arch, that the proportions of the Greek orders evolved uniformly in a given direction, that the characteristic feature of Roman architecture was an inconsistent application of the orders to arched constructions. Similar instances from mediæval and modern architecture could be cited, where new agreements have been reached on questions of fact.

Equally important have been the changes of attitude on many questions of interpretation. The part of spiritual influences and spontaneous creation in the formation of styles is now emphasized, to balance the one-sided affirmation, by nineteenth-century writers, of the influence of material environment. The *raison d'être* of many forms is sought in a purely formal expressiveness, rather than in a supposed structural necessity. The idea of an analogy between the history of styles and the growth and inevitable decay of organic life is now generally abandoned, and it is understood that the material must not be forced into conformity with any other misleading analogy. Most important of all, it is recognized that in the history of art, as in other branches of history, subjective criticism must give way to the impartial study of development—in which historical influence is the criterion of importance. Freed from dogmatic appraisal, Roman architecture, Renaissance and baroque architecture, and, especially, modern architecture, can receive the exposi-

tion to which their influence and their diffusion entitle them.
The modern historian, like Chesterton's modern poet, gives
his subjects not halters and halos, but voices.

In the apportionment of space in this book there is a departure from the tendency of older works to discuss ancient
styles at great length and pass over recent developments with
few words. Here it has been thought better to give progressively greater emphasis and space as modern times are approached. No date is suggested as marking a supposed
death of traditional art; on the contrary, the development
is followed to the present day, in a belief in unending creative
vitality. Thus it is hoped that the professional architect and
others already familiar with the subject may still find new
matter of interest to them.

In accordance with the usage of most recent writers, the
term Renaissance architecture is confined to buildings of the
Renaissance in its more restricted sense (to about 1550 or
1600), and is not extended to cover the later developments
of classical forms. The need of a general designation for all
of the works of the following period, whether academic or
free in character, is a strong one. German and Italian
scholars have attempted to include them all by an extension
of the term baroque architecture, but such an extension is
a departure from the original sense of *baroque* and a viola-
tion both of French and of English usage. In consequence
the authors have ventured to propose a new term which is
self-explanatory: post-Renaissance architecture.

The attempt has been made to present each style as a thing
of growth and change, rather than as a formula based on the
monuments of some supposed apogee, with respect to which
the later forms have too often been treated as corrupt.
The general development of the style is first sketched
with little description of individual monuments, and these are
then illustrated and discussed more at length in sections
devoted to the development of single forms and types.

A chronological outline is added to each chapter, with a
bibliographical note, including references to more extended
guides to the literature of the subject.

The illustrations have been selected, in conformity with
recent tendencies both in architecture and in archæology, to

show not merely isolated details and monuments, but the ensemble. Those which are not from photographs are reproduced, so far as possible, from the original sources, as noted in the list of illustrations. To the owners of copyrights who have courteously permitted the use of their material the authors extend cordial thanks; also to Messrs. B. T. Batsford, Ltd., G. P. Putnam's Sons, Doubleday, Page & Co., and the Macmillan Co., for permission to reproduce other material. Messrs. Cram and Ferguson, Charles A. Platt, and Frank Lloyd Wright, as well as the American Academy at Rome and the Metropolitan Museum, have kindly furnished photographs which would otherwise not have been obtainable. Certain plates which could not be reproduced directly have been drawn by Mr. M. B. Gulick and Mr. A. P. Evans, Jr.

The portion of the book which deals with the Middle Ages (Chapters VI to IX) has been written by Mr. Edgell; the portion which deals with ancient and modern times, together with the chapters on Eastern architecture, by Mr. Kimball.

F. K.
G. H. E.

PREFACE TO THE SECOND EDITION

In the decade since the publication of this book research in the history of architecture has been particularly active. Many of its results have been incorporated in successive printings of this work.

In the present edition a multitude of revisions, involving very extensive resetting, have been made to keep it abreast of the advance of knowledge. The wealth of new publications is noted separately in the bibliographies, which may thus give a convenient guide for new purchases by libraries and individuals.

F. K.
G. H. E.

A HISTORY
OF ARCHITECTURE

A HISTORY
OF ARCHITECTURE

CHAPTER I

THE ELEMENTS OF ARCHITECTURE

From the beginning of its history architecture has had a threefold problem or aim: to build structures at once commodious, strong, and satisfying to the artistic sense. Each of the phases of the problem offers its own possibilities and difficulties, rooted in natural conditions and universal human traits, and thus to a certain degree constant. As an introduction to the study of the varied historical solutions of the problem of architecture these constant factors deserve a brief discussion.

The primary, compelling need, which brought and still brings the majority of buildings into existence, is of course the need of inclosed space sheltered from the weather. A roofed area, surrounded by walls, requires also certain other elements for practical usefulness—doors, windows, chimneys. In all but the simplest buildings there must be interior partitions, separating rooms intended for various uses, and accommodated to these uses in their sizes and relationships. When these rooms are numerous, or occupy several stories, the provision of light and of intercommunication becomes complicated. To secure good light throughout the interior, the masses of building must be kept relatively thin or the rooms must be grouped about interior courts of greater or less area. In primitive buildings there may be no strict division of the functions of different rooms and courts, and it may be necessary to pass through a number intended for one use to reach one intended for other uses. In more advanced construction the functions become specialized, and a distinct class of elements of communication is created. Corridors and stairhalls provide means of circulation which do not disturb the privacy of individual apartments. The provisions for the reception of strangers and for the carrying on of the service of the establishment are then also separated from the private portions of the building.

Like these gradations in complexity of function, there are also gradations in geometrical organization, which affect convenience as well as appearance. The elements of the plan—rooms and courts—may be of quite irregular shape, juxtaposed without attention to their mutual relationships or to the resulting general outline. Elsewhere they may be made predominantly rectangular, the outline may be brought to some regular geometrical form, and communications between the elements may be provided at points on their several axes. A further degree of organization may result from the carrying through of a general axis of symmetry common to the principal elements of the building, or possibly from the establishing of two or more important axes, usually at right angles.   In the most highly developed buildings there may be a multitude of minor axes, related to these main axes and forming with them a complex but orderly system. Such schemes permit a clear oversight of the components of the whole, and a mental grasp of the arrangement, without which it might prove only a confused labyrinth.

Essential even to mere provision of inclosed space, as well as to resistance against the various forces of disintegration, is a sufficient measure of strength. In the simplest of all forms of construction, a solid wall, the only tendency is for weight above to compress or crush the material below or to force it out at the sides. The remedy is to increase the surface over which a given pressure acts by thickening the wall until safety is amply attained. With foundations, where the soil is compressible, it is equally essential that the pressure shall everywhere have the same relation to the bearing power of the soil, otherwise unequal settlements and cracks will result. As in any wall or pier the stones at the bottom have manifestly more weight to sustain than those above, there is a logical satisfaction and often a real necessity for making a wall thicker at the bottom than at the top, either by occasional increases or by a constant slope. Ordinarily the margin of safety allowed is so great that the mere weight of the material itself, except in very high walls, does not actually necessitate a slope, and other considerations, practical or artistic, may render it undesirable. Thus it is more usual to find vertical surfaces with increases of thickness only where concentrated weights, such as those of floors, must be upheld. Another occasion for increasing the thickness occurs when a material of greater compressive strength rests upon a weaker material, as when a story of cut stone rests on a basement of rubble or a foundation wall upon ordinary soil. These conditions are frequently responsible for the existence and the forms of horizontal moldings—string courses or belt courses as they are called—at the level of floors or at the junction of different materials and at the base.

Instead of a continuous wall there may be a series of isolated supports—circular columns or piers of other forms. With columns even more than with walls it is usual to find an increase of diameter toward the base or a "diminution" toward the top. Here, also, it is common to find transitional members, the capital supporting the load above, the base spreading the weight on the substructure.

Where openings are to be spanned, either in a wall or between isolated supports, new problems arise. In a beam or lintel supported only at its ends the action of gravity produces not only the usual crushing tendency upon those portions which bear on its supports, and which must be made large enough to resist this, but also produces a tendency to shear the beam across just at the point where the support ceases and a tendency to bend and finally to break it in mid-span. Against both these tendencies, stone, with its crystalline or granular structure, offers a resistance very feeble relatively to its weight. The tendency to break increases much more rapidly than the distance spanned, and the difficulty and cost of getting larger blocks likewise increases beyond all proportion. Thus stone lintels can be used but rarely for spanning intervals of more than ten feet, and a clear span of twenty-four feet is the extreme instance. The lightness and fibrous nature of wood, on the contrary, make it well fitted to span long distances, provided the weight above be not too great. Iron and steel have in modern times made possible beams of immensely greater strength and span at relatively small cost.

When masonry is to be used to bridge wide openings, or in any case when only small stones or brick are at command, some form of arch must be employed, and a new element of disintegration, horizontal thrust, appears. A rudimentary form of arch is the corbeled arch, built up in horizontal courses, each projecting somewhat in front of the course below, finally meeting over the center of the opening. The true arch differs from this in having radiating joints, being composed, in principle, of wedge-shaped blocks called voussoirs. It may be semicircular, elliptical, or pointed—of tall or squat proportions. The weight of the crown of the arch tends to push the two sides apart with a force which is relatively greater in broad, low arches than in tall, narrow ones. The sides require to be abutted by masses of earth or masonry, to be brought into equilibrium by the counter thrust of other arches, or, failing these methods, to be connected by a tie-rod. In a continuous arcade, or series of arches resting on piers or columns, the thrusts neutralize each other and produce merely vertical pressure on all the intermediate supports. A massive abutment is thus needed only at the ends, and the intervening piers may be more slender.

Covering the spaces inclosed by the walls are the roofs, which take on a multitude of forms influenced by the climate, the materials, and the shapes below. Only in a rainless climate can roofs be perfectly flat and joints penetrate them without any overlapping protection. Under all other conditions there must be a slope of greater or less degree to carry off the water from rain or melting snow. If there is a continuous impervious covering like clay, tar, or soldered metal, the slope may be almost imperceptible, and the roof may still form a terrace, reasonably flat. If the covering material is of small, overlapping pieces like shingles, slate, or tiles, the roof, to insure the shedding of water, must have a

pronounced inclination.   Where there is a deep fall of snow
it is necessary either to make the roofs strong enough to support a great weight or steep enough to throw off the snow
before it accumulates dangerously.   To assume merely that
southern climates demand flatter roofs and northern ones
steeper roofs is obviously too inaccurate a generalization.
The climate, in most cases, is a less important factor than the
covering material.   The form of the roof may also be influenced by the shape of the areas to be covered or, con-
versely, the form of roof once adopted may govern the arrangement of the plan.   A pitched or sloping roof requires
relatively narrow and uniform buildings if the ridge is not to
rise wastefully high and the form is not to become over-
complex.   A terraced roof permits the masses of building to
be of any shape and size.   In either case there are practical
as well as artistic reasons for a special treatment where roof
and wall meet   With a terraced roof there is need of a
parapet, breast-high; with a sloping roof there is need of a
projecting cornice, to support a gutter or to keep the drip
from the eaves clear of the walls.

   The support of the roof and its form on the interior raise
further questions.   If the width is small, beams may span
directly from wall to wall, or two sets of inclined rafters,
resting on the walls, may meet at the ridge.   With greater
widths there must either be intermediate supports, or trusses
of wood or metal members so framed and braced as to be self-
supporting over a wide span; or else, instead of either, there
must be vaults of arched masonry.   Vaults have the advantage
of resisting fire, but they have horizontal thrusts which require suitable abutment.   Vaults of continuous hemispherical
or semi-cylindrical form—domes or barrel vaults—necessitate
a continuous abutment by thick walls.   Vaults composed of
intersecting surfaces or resting on arches, however, may
have their thrusts concentrated at a few points, where they
may be met by walls or projecting buttresses which are more
efficiently disposed.   Sometimes there is but a single covering
to the building: a roof construction of beams and trusses
appears on the interior, or vaults show their forms directly
on the exterior.   More often, however, greater freedom is
desired to adapt exterior and interior coverings to their dif-

ferent functions.   Thus ceilings may be introduced below the
roof beams, or independent roofs constructed above the
vaults.

Along with the desire for strength and practical usefulness
goes often a conscious striving for artistic effect.   Even in the
most utilitarian buildings, indeed, there must always be a
certain measure of choice in the selection of materials or of
forms.   Thus there is inevitably some expression of preferences which are, consciously or unconsciously, artistic.   It
is the sum of such expressions, partly of conscious preference,
partly of traditional usage, partly of natural conditions and
practical necessity, which constitutes the artistic character of a
structure.

The artistic ideas which may be thus expressed are of many
different sorts.   The adaptation of the building to its practical
functions, the purpose and relationships of its various parts,
may be made clear.   The specific character—religious, civic,
military, commemorative—may be emphasized.   The nature
of the environment may be mirrored in picturesqueness or
formality of design.   The size or "scale" of the building may
be unmistakably declared through features the size of which
bears a necessary relation to the materials used or to the
human figure.   The treatment of the materials themselves
may be such as to bring out all their characteristic possibilities
of color, texture, or veining.   The principles of the structural
system may be revealed and the *raison d'être* of every detail
made evident.   Finally there are the ideas of pure form,
expressed in the mere sizes, shapes, colors, and light and
shade.   This domain of pure form is the one which architecture shares with painting and sculpture.   In architecture,
however, the forms are not representative, but abstract and
geometrical, and there is, besides, one possibility which none
of the other arts possesses.   It is that of creating forms of
interior space, within which the observer stands.   In all these
architectural expressions and in their mutual relationships
there may be a greater or a less degree of consistency, harmony, and interest.   Certain expressions are even incompatible with others, and each fusion of expressions in a single
building involves the sacrifice of many others, and is a unique
creation

At a given period or in a given region, however, many of the elements remain constant. The use of certain materials or constructive systems may be imposed by the geologic formation, by climatic conditions, or by the isolation of the inhabitants. Even if there are few restrictions of this sort, there will be the force of custom, perpetuating a thousand peculiarities and methods of varied origin. Often there will be also the influence of older and of neighboring civilizations, steadily exercised in definite directions. Thus it comes about that, in the expression of their artistic instincts, the men of one time and one place have a common vocabulary of forms and tend to speak a common architectural language, in the same way that they tend to employ a common spoken language. It is these architectural languages, varying in every country and province and in every generation, which we mean when we speak of the historic styles of architecture.

BIBLIOGRAPHICAL NOTE

Works dealing with the elements and theory of architecture

A popular work in English is J. Belcher's *Essentials in Architecture*, 1907. Others addressed to a more professional audience are J. B. Robinson's *Architectural Composition*, 1908, and J. V. Van Pelt's *Essentials of Composition*, 2d ed., 1913. Systematic and fundamental discussions occur in J. Guadet's *Eléments et théorie de l'architecture*, 4 vols., 3d ed., 1909, and L. Cloquet's *Traité d'architecture*, 5 vols., 1898–1901. The *Handbuch der Architektur* contains similar material : pt. I, vol. 2, *Die Bauformenlehre* by J. Bühlman, 2d ed., 1901 ; and pt. IV, vol. 1, *Architektonische Komposition* by H. Wagner and others, 3d ed., 1904. Recent books emphasising the element of form are N. C. Curtis' *Architectural Composition*, 1923, and Arthur Stratton's *Elements of Form and Design in Classic Architecture*.

CHAPTER II

PREHISTORIC ARCHITECTURE

From the origins of mankind in the mists of the preglacial period down to the beginnings of recorded history there was a gradual development lasting over great periods of time. The steps in the development were much the same among different peoples, although their degrees of advancement at a given time varied greatly. Men passed through successive ages in which stone, bronze, and iron were used for tools and weapons, and in which corresponding advances were made in other branches of culture. The Egyptians and the peoples of Mesopotamia had already completed this development while the inhabitants of central Europe were still in the stone age, and Europeans in their turn have found the American Indians and other peoples still ignorant of bronze and iron. It is thus in central Europe that we are best able to trace the changes which, in more favored regions, took place at a much earlier time, and which in less favored regions are still incomplete.

The stone age. During the earlier stone age, the paleolithic period, when instruments were still crudely chipped, men lived by hunting and fishing. They dwelt in caves or dugouts, or in tents of poles and hides. In the later stone age, or neolithic period, when they had learned to polish stone implements, to raise cattle, and till the soil, new methods of housing were added. Huts were built of poles and reeds plastered with clay, with thatched roofs. Sometimes the floors of these were raised above the ground on piles, for protection against hostile attack, as well as against animals and vermin. Sometimes the huts were even built on piles over the water. In the Swiss and Italian lakes there were whole villages of these pile dwellings, the remains of which show the rudimentary beginnings of carpentry. The dwellings were already surpassed in importance at this time, however, by sepulchers of the dead and religious monuments. These were of stone, usually not composed of many small pieces, but "megalithic"—of enormous blocks which singly sufficed for a wall or roof. Tomb chambers were made of a pair of such blocks with a covering slab—constituting what

FIG. 1—STONEHENGE. (RESTORED BY HARTMANN)

are called dolmens. Sometimes these were buried beneath a mound of earth, or were preceded by a covered corridor. Other monuments, which may well have had a religious significance, are the menhirs, or single standing pillars, and the cromlechs, or circles of stones. A menhir in Brittany had the extreme height of seventy feet. The most famous of the cromlechs is at Stonehenge near Salisbury in England (Fig. 1). It had two concentric circles of tall standing stones, with lintels resting on them, minor circles of smaller stones just inside of each, and a great "altar stone" within.

The ages of bronze and iron. With the discovery of the art of working metals began the bronze age, which made possible more advanced works of carpentry and masonry. This oc-

curred in central Europe about 2000 B.C. Following villages
of improved pile dwellings on land, such as the terramare
of Italy with their walls and moats, came huts once more
resting on the ground. These were at first circular or oval,
but they gradually assumed a rectangular shape. The
conical or domical roofs of the earliest huts were later replaced, in northern climates, by a pitch roof with a longitudinal ridge. The introduction of iron, which took place
in central Europe about the seventh century B.C., made but
little change in the manner of building. Architecture there
remained essentially primitive until it was influenced by offshoots of the highly developed styles which grew up about the
eastern Mediterranean. To study their rise will be the
object of the following chapter.

BIBLIOGRAPHICAL NOTE

A comprehensive and authoritative work on prehistoric architecture is lacking. Monographs on individual sites and monuments
abound, too numerous to be listed here. Reference must be made
to certain general works covering the prehistoric period, such as
Sir John Lubbock's *Prehistoric Times*, 7th ed., 1913; H. H. Wilder's
Prehistoric Man, 1923; M. Hoernes's *Primitive Man*, English translation, 1900 (Temple Primers); and *Urgeschichte der Kultur*, 3 vols.,
1912 (Sammlung Göschen); or to works which cover limited regions.
Hoernes's *Urgeschichte der bildenden Kunst*, 2d ed., 1915, and E. A.
Parkyn's *Prehistoric Art*, 1915, unfortunately do not include architecture. For the development in prehistoric Europe, principally
dealt with in this chapter, see, above all, J. Déchelette's *Manuel
d'archéologie préhistorique, celtique et gallo romaine*, 4 vols., 1913–24
(primarily on France, but with some references to other countries and
full bibliographical notes), and S. Müller's *Urgeschichte Europas:
Grundzüge einer prähistorischen Archäologie*, translated from the
Danish, 1905; French translation: *L'Europe préhistorique*, 1907. For
England consult R. Munro's *Prehistoric Britain*, 1914 (Home University Library), T. R. Holmes's *Ancient Britain*, 1907, or B. C. A.
Windle's *Remains of the Prehistoric Age in England*, 1904. On the
pile dwellings see R. Munro's *The Lake Dwellings of Europe*, 1890.

CHAPTER III

PRECLASSICAL ARCHITECTURE

EGYPT

The first notable development of architecture was reached
in the fertile valley of the Nile. At the beginning of the
third millennium before Christ, when the earliest of the great
Egyptian royal tombs were building under a strong centralized rule, the valley of the Tigris and the Euphrates seems
not yet to have possessed any monuments comparable to
them in workmanship or magnitude. The Great Pyramid,
built by Khufu as his own burial-place in the years following
2800 B.C., is not only the most considerable of all architectural
works in bulk, but one of the most perfect in execution.
Although over seven hundred and fifty feet on a side, it was
laid out with such accuracy that Petrie reports its diver-
gencies from exactness in equality of sides, in squareness, and
in level, no greater than his own probable error in measuring
it with the most modern surveying instruments.

General characteristics. The course of excavations has revealed a variety in Egyptian art, during its three thousand
years of active life, quite different from the uniformity which
was at first supposed to exist, yet it is possible to summarize
certain enduring characteristics of its architecture. This
was largely conditioned by religious beliefs, which demanded
the utmost grandeur and permanence for tombs and temples,
the residences of the dead and of the gods, in contrast with the
light and relatively temporary houses which sufficed for even
the greatest of the living. Such permanence was sought by
the almost exclusive employment of fine stone, which the
cliffs of the Nile Valley furnished in abundance, and by the
adoption, as the dominant constructive types, of the simple

mass, and of the column and the lintel. The arch, occasionally used from the earliest times, was confined to substructures
where it had ample abutment and was little in view. The
architectural members, moreover, were generally of great
size and massiveness, although sometimes of extreme refinement and in certain cases even of delicacy. Traditional elements of composition in plan recurred in many types of
buildings. These were the open court, often surrounded by a
continuous interior colonnade or peristyle, and the rectangular
room opening on its broader front, with its ceiling supported
by columns. With the flat roofs which the rainless climate
permitted, rooms could be juxtaposed without any other
restraint than the necessity of light. Partly as a consequence
of religious beliefs, partly doubtless from natural preference,
the architectural members were usually covered with sculpture
in relief, everywhere blazing with harmonious color. Architecture formed an equal union with sculpture and painting.
The rich flora of the Nile, especially the lotus and the papyrus,
furnished the principal motives of ornament, and even suggested the form of structural members.

Development. The architecture of Egypt, from its earliest
traces to the Christian era, shows a continuity of character
never destroyed and scarcely interrupted by any foreign influence. The early Semitic invasion from Asia by which the
structure of the Egyptian language is explained must have
taken place long before our remotest knowledge. The varied
development of Egyptian art was essentially a native one,
resulting from the interaction and successive supremacy of a
number of local schools, raised to prominence by the political
importance of their centers.

Thinite period. The earliest of these schools to attain a
general predominance was that of This, a city about two-
thirds of the way from the Delta to the First Cataract. This
became the capital of Menes, who first succeeded in bringing
under one rule the earlier kingdoms of the north and the
south about 3400 B.C. His successors of the First and
Second Dynasties, so-called, lived here for perhaps four
hundred years. The slight remains of architecture preserved
from this period indicate a primitive condition. Sun-dried
brick was the principal material, although stone masonry and

even the arch were soon introduced. The rudimentary forms of the tomb and of the temple display a similarity to the form of the house which persists fundamentally even in later times and indicates a common derivation from the simple dwellings of the people.

Memphite period, or "Old Kingdom." With the transference of the seat of government to Memphis, a little south of modern Cairo, began the first of the great flowerings of Egyptian art. Under the kings of the Third Dynasty the royal tombs gradually took the form of pyramids, and with the first king of the Fourth Dynasty, Khufu, came the culmination of Memphite architecture in the Great Pyramid at Gizeh (Fig. 2). The buildings of this king and his immediate successors of the "Old Kingdom" set a standard of size and workmanship never afterward equaled. The architectural forms, though simple, were of the greatest refinement. The colonnade was employed in the courts and the halls of temples, and the characteristic and beautiful "papyrus" or "lotus bud" column first made its appearance. After a gradual decline Memphis lost its importance with the close of the Sixth Dynasty. A period of relative barrenness ensued, from which emerged about 2160 B.C. the powerful monarchs of the eleventh and later dynasties whose reigns constitute the "Middle Kingdom." Their seat was Thebes, again in Upper Egypt, a little south of This.

Theban period: "Middle Kingdom" and "Empire." With them began the long supremacy of Theban art, which dominated the development of Egyptian architecture, directly or indirectly, to the end of its history under the Romans. The invasion of the Asiatic "Hyksos" who overran the country caused an interim from about 1675 to 1575, but the empire which followed picked up the thread almost at the point where the Middle Kingdom had dropped it. Though the buildings previous to the invasion have been mostly swept away by subsequent rulers, they apparently furnished the prototypes of the temple and other buildings in their later form. On the expulsion of the invaders followed the age of greatest splendor, under the monarchs of the Eighteenth and Nineteenth Dynasties, whose monuments, reaching from the Fourth Cataract to the Euphrates, furnish the usual idea of

FIG. 2—GIZEH. THE PYRAMIDS OF KHAFRE AND KHUFU. (RESTORED BY HÖLSCHER)

Egyptian architecture. In the three hundred and fifty years following 1500 B.C. were built the great temples of Der-el-Bahri, of Abu Simbel, and of Medinet Habu, the delicate shrines of Elephantine, the superb halls and courts of Karnak and Luxor, the tombs of the valleys behind Thebes—half, perhaps, of all that has been saved of Egyptian architecture. Columnar architecture was magnified to a scale seldom equaled. Columns sixty to seventy feet high in a few instances, with lintels of a clear span of twenty-four feet, were among the structural triumphs of this relatively brief period of world empire and artistic magnificence. At its close the artistic impulse had spent itself. The buildings of Ramses III., last of the great imperial Pharaohs, already show heaviness of design and carelessness of execution. Under the kaleidoscopic usurping dynasties that shortly followed—Tanite, Libyan, and Nubian—only an isolated monarch now and then had power to attempt a revival of the splendors of the imperial architecture.

Saite period. In the midst of political decadence, however, a new artistic fermentation was beginning. After the expulsion of Assyrian conquerors, about 660 B.C., under the rulers of Sais in the Delta, art sprang again into vigorous activity such as it had not known for five hundred years. Although the policy of these astute monarchs was everywhere to restore the Theban culture, even to revert to the style of the Old Kingdom, the originality of their artists was not to be denied, and new and beautiful modifications resulted. Persian domination followed, and the architecture of the period suffered almost complete destruction; but we can trace its innovations in the elaborate and diverse columns of the temples built by the Ptolemies and the Romans.

Ptolemaic and Roman periods. It was the character impressed upon it by the Saite builders that Egyptian architecture retained till it finally succumbed before the advent of Christianity. Greeks and Romans alike brought their own national forms, but these were unable to effect any substantial change outside of the cities of the Delta. The native architecture was adopted by the conquerors themselves, at least for the temples of the traditional religion. Under the prestige of Alexandria, Egyptian dispositions, clothed in

Greek detail, spread beyond the boundaries of Egypt. The peristylar court and hall, the clerestory, and other characteristic elements, became henceforth international.

The tombs. Throughout this long history the most important monuments were the tombs and the temples. Egyptian religious beliefs demanded shelter and sustenance for the dead as well as for the living. Hence, in the tomb, elaborate precautions were taken for the preservation of the body, and for the nourishing of the "ka," or vital force, now dissociated from it. The forms of the tomb varied in different districts, though they tended in every period to take the form customary in the region which was dominant politically. In Lower Egypt the preference was for masonry structures erected on the plain; in Upper Egypt, for chambers and passages excavated in the rock of the valley walls. The masonry tombs were alike in presenting on the exterior a simple mass rectangular in plan and almost unbroken by openings; they differed in geometrical form and in interior arrangement.

Mastabas. The form of most frequent occurrence in the Old Kingdom was the one employed for the Memphite nobles, the so-called "mastaba." It was a low, flat-topped mass, varying in size with the importance of the occupant, and having its faces sloped back at an angle of about seventy-five degrees. The solid bulk of the mastaba contained at first merely the filled-up shaft to the tomb chamber below, and a small chapel for offerings. Later the upper chambers were multiplied for ceremonial and for the storage of provisions and household utensils.

Pyramids. From the beginning of the Memphite dynasties the kings adopted distinctive forms which approached the pyramid. The first king of the Third Dynasty, Zoser, built his tomb at Sakkara in seven great receding steps; its last king, Snefru, erected one at Medum in three steps, another at Dahshur in true pyramidal shape, fixing the type for the rest of the period. The most striking group of the pyramids is that of the Fourth-Dynasty necropolis at Gizeh. Here stands the familiar group of three built by Khufu, Khafre, and Menkure—the Cheops, Chephren, and Mycerinus of classical writers. Around them are the smaller pyramids of royalty and serried lines of mastabas built by the nobles. In the pyramids, as in the mastabas, the interior arrangements differ. They are alike in having the tomb chamber elaborately safeguarded by granite portcullises and misleading passages. These, however, uniformly failed to protect the bodies against despoilers, often only a few generations later. The pyramids were preceded by massive chapels for services and offerings and approached by causeways of stone leading up

FIG. 3—BENI HASAN. PORTICO OF A TOMB

from the river. By size and by the very simplicity of their form these greatest of Egyptian monuments make an unrivaled impression of grandeur and power.

Rock-cut tombs. Under the Theban monarchs of the Middle Kingdom the existing local types of Middle and Upper Egypt were developed—the pyramid-mastaba, a mastaba with a small pyramid on top; and the tomb cut in the western cliffs (Fig. 3). Under the Empire this last type, adopted by the kings, became by far the most employed. Every wealthy Theban family had its concealed vault, preceded by a small rock-cut chapel. To protect their bodies, the Pharaohs carried passages, gradually descending and interrupted by small chambers, for hundreds of feet into the cliffs. Their funerary chapels, however, became separated from the tombs themselves. They were erected on the plain before the cliffs fronting the river, and in time became comparable to the temples of the gods on the opposite bank.

The first of such chapels, built by Queen Hatshepsut in the years from 1500 to 1480, is one of the most original and most refined of all Egyptian monuments (Fig. 4). It lies in the valley known as Der-el-Bahri, and rises in three great colonnaded terraces to the sanctuaries cut in the rock. The architectural forms are of the simplest—square or sixteen-

FIG. 4—DER-EL-BAHRI.   MORTUARY TEMPLE OF HATSHEPSUT.
(RESTORED BY BRUNET)

sided columns in long ranks—but the proportions are so just, the effect so pure, as to suggest Greece in the days of Pericles.

The temples.   In the form finally reached under the Ramessid Pharaohs of the Nineteenth and Twentieth Dynasties, the mortuary temples closely resembled the temples of the gods, likewise the product of a long evolution. The gods, like the dead, required shelter and food. They were housed with solidity and splendor, and served by the provision of meat and drink and diversion, all presented with increasing ceremonial. As it was the Pharaoh who provided the revenue for all this, so it was he who in theory made the presentation. It was made, in fact, by the priests, his representatives, the people participating only when, on feast-days, the offering

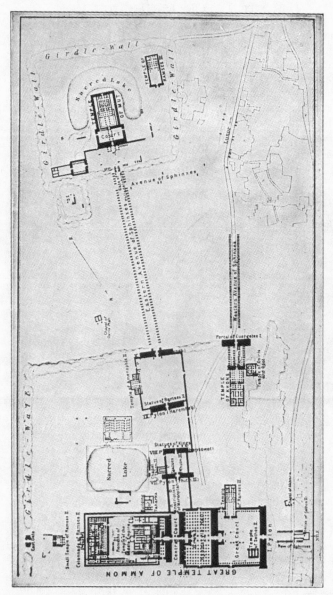

FIG. 5—KARNAK. PLAN OF PRINCIPAL TEMPLES. (BAEDEKER)

was distributed in the temple court after being presented to the god.   Though many of the elements of the temple seem to have been in use from the time of the Old Kingdom, and, already in the Middle Kingdom to have assumed somewhat their final relations, it is only the temples of the Empire and later times that are sufficiently preserved to give a visual idea of the whole.

Imperial temples.   At the great national center of Amon-worship at Karnak in Thebes (Fig. 5) there are many temples, the product of long growth.   Several of the relatively smaller

FIG. 6—KARNAK.   CENTRAL AISLES OF THE HYPOSTYLE HALL OF THE
GREAT TEMPLE OF AMON.   MODEL IN THE METROPOLITAN MUSEUM

ones well display the similarities, as also the minor diversities, found in the temples of the Theban period.   Each consists essentially of a small sanctuary at the back, flanked by cells for the minor divinities of the religious triad, by chapels and store chambers, and preceded by a colonnaded hall, the so-called "hypostyle hall" (Fig. 6) which turned its broad side to a square court surrounded by columns.   The façade was composed of a great doorway between two tall quadrangular towers, their faces sloping back from the perpendicular, together constituting a "pylon."   Before the pylon

stood obelisks, colossal statues of the king or the divinity,
and wooden masts carrying long streamers; before these,
again, were often long avenues of approach, lined with sculptured rams or sphinxes.   As one passed inward from the sun-
lit court, through halls successively smaller and lower, the
light diminished till the sanctuary was in almost total dark-
ness, admirably calculated to heighten the effect of religious
mystery and awe.

Special types.   At the most important temples, such as those
of Amon at Karnak and Luxor, successive monarchs vied in
multiplying the elements.   They built new and larger hypostyle
halls and courts in front of the earlier pylons, until in the
great temple at Karnak, under the Ptolemies, a seventh
pylon was under construction.   In a similar way at Philæ,
their favorite shrine, the Ptolemies and the Roman monarchs
built many courts, pavilions, and the accessory buildings demanded by the late religious cults.   Here the irregularity of
the island site forced departures from the usual formality,
but, as elsewhere in Egypt in such cases, ingenious adaptation
produced a composition of the greatest charm.   An effect
still further removed from the heaviness and solemnity usually
associated with Egyptian architecture is found in the smallest
temples.   One of these, built by Amenhotep III. at Elephantine, now destroyed, is especially famous for beauty of proportion and dignified grace.

Dwellings.   The Theban palace is still too little known for
safe generalization.   The Pharaohs seem to have preferred
not to live in dwellings previously occupied, and the practice
of abandoning old palaces for new ones, hastily improvised,
led to the employment of a construction which has left but
few remains.   The villa of Amenhotep III. at Thebes has a
rectangular outer wall inclosing a labyrinth of small courts,
columned rooms, and dark cells, all built of sun-dried brick,
plastered and richly painted.   Wall paintings elsewhere show
the houses of the wealthy, surrounded by shaded gardens.
The quarters of the poorer classes were closely built in blocks,
often on a regular plan.   Their houses, reduced to lowest
terms, comprised a small, square court, along the back of
which lay a rectangular room with the entrance on its broad
side.

The column: origins.   Interest in the details of Egyptian architecture centers in the development of the column, which the Egyptians were the first to employ, and which they treated with great mechanical skill and artistic taste.   In the Fourth Dynasty we find square monolithic piers, without division or ornament of any kind—the system of support and lintel at its lowest terms.   The so-called Temple of the Sphinx, a waiting-hall at the foot of the causeway leading to the pyramid of Khafre, thus constructed, is effective by its proportions and by the perfection of its workmanship.   By the Fifth Dynasty we find the first circular columns, of types common throughout later Egyptian architecture. The motives of their designs were taken from the palm and from the papyrus or the lotus, palm leaves being carved upright about the top of the shaft, bending gracefully under the weight of the abacus, or the shaft itself being made in the form of several lotus or papyrus stems bound together, the buds swelling at the top to form the capital.

Later forms.   Under the Middle Kingdom the most popular form was a column abstractly geometrical—polygonal in plan, or with concave vertical flutings.   In either case it was crowned by a simple square abacus.   Such columns, as at Beni Hasan and later Der-el-Bahri, have a rough resemblance to the Doric columns of Greece, which may indeed have been suggested by them.   Under the Empire all these types were still employed, the papyrus or lotus-bud form leading in popularity, but a new type was given the place of honor in the tall central aisles of the hypostyle halls (Fig. 6).   This was the column with a capital like an inverted bell, imitative of the flower of the lotus.   A capital with heads of the cow-goddess, Hathor, was used in her shrines, and piers fronted by standing colossi were frequent, especially under the great Ramessids.   The Saite and Ptolemaic architects elaborated the capitals, especially the bell capital, by applying to the smooth surfaces motives drawn from native flora—leaves, flowers, buds, in gracefully ordered profusion. They even employed different varieties in the same colonnade, though always in pairs, placed at equal distances on either side of the axis.   No attempt was made to develop a separate system of forms to accompany each type of column.   The same type of cornice is found with all, a quarter-hollow, or cavetto, making transition from the vertical members to the horizontal projecting line of the roof.

The peristyle. Although many Egyptian halls were subdivided by ranges of columns extending the full depth of the room, an equally characteristic arrangement was that of an interior peristyle, or continuous surrounding file of columns. This arrangement, which was preferred in the case of open colonnaded courts, is a typically oriental disposition, being found also in Mesopotamia and throughout the East. Owing perhaps to the guarded nature of Egyptian life and Egyptian cults, a similar surrounding peristyle was rare on the exterior. A single instance was the little temple of Elephantine.

The arch. The arch form was used sometimes in tombs and notably in the sanctuaries of the temple of Seti 1. at Abydos, but in all such important works it was merely a corbeled arch, cut out of projecting stones in horizontal courses. True arches abound in subterranean tomb chambers from the time of the Third Dynasty, apparently as early as any in Mesopotamia. The store chambers of the Ramesseum, the mortuary temple of Rameses II. at Thebes, present an extensive series of parallel barrel vaults resting on light intermediate walls. For use in the superstructure, however, the true arch seems to have been thought too insecure.

The clerestory. A device first invented by the Egyptians, destined to play an important rôle in later architecture, is the clerestory, introduced under the Empire. To light the wide hypostyle halls, unprovided with windows at the outside, the roof was raised over the three central aisles, admitting light through grated openings over the lower roofs at the sides (Fig. 6).

Methods of construction. The Egyptian roofs were flat, as the rainless climate permitted. Those of the temples were constructed of slabs of stone resting directly on the lintels, dispensing with all wood. The compact soil rendered deep foundations unnecessary. Piers and columns, originally monolithic, were perforce, in the largest examples, built up like towers with rough filling, often none too solid. The masonry gradually lost the precision of the earliest monuments in the vast and hasty erections of the later Empire, but the constructive methods remained nearly constant.

Decoration. The elements of decorative expression likewise remained substantially the same in different periods. They were based on natural forms, like the lotus and palm, or on conventional geometric lines, such as the spiral. The god's house, conceived as the world, had its walls painted with conventional landscapes, its ceiling spangled with stars. The legends of the gods and the exploits of the kings filled every available space, proclaiming in no modest way the glories of the builders, of the restorers, and of usurping monarchs who wished to shine by reflected light.

The architect. During the whole of Egyptian history the architect was a man of importance, as might be expected when building formed so large a part of the monarch's activity. Inscriptions in tombs of the Fifth Dynasty show that in two cases, at least, the functions of prime minister, chief judge, and royal architect were combined. The mortuary inscription of the prime minister of Thothmes III., in recounting his duties, includes personal inspection of monuments under construction. Whoever the real designers were, they were far from being mere slaves of tradition, and some of them, like Sen-Mut, the architect of Der-el-Bahri, showed themselves men of the highest genius.

It is to its strength and dignity, above all, that Egyptian architecture owes its effect. Less structural than sculptural in many of its forms, it nevertheless has breadth and monumental quality. At its best pure and subtle, it is seldom lacking in magnificence or even in some touch of sublimity, which is universally recognized in its major creations.

MESOPOTAMIA

The Tigris and the Euphrates supported a civilization perhaps even more ancient than that of Egypt. It is impossible to date the most primitive monuments of either country accurately enough to decide priority of origins. In the formation of a developed style and the execution of monuments of the first magnitude, however, the peoples of the Mesopotamian valley lagged many centuries behind the Egyptians.

PRECLASSICAL ARCHITECTURE

Natural conditions and modes of construction. The natural
conditions were in many respects less favorable than in
Egypt. The absence of any good native building-stone or
abundance of wood left sun-dried mud brick the best material available in large quantities. Torrential rains and
frequent floods rendered constructions relatively imperma-
nent, even though the walls were faced with burnt brick and
the buildings were raised on huge platforms. In Babylonia
in early times stone was almost impossible to secure. Even
in Assyria the difficulty of bringing it from the mountains was
so great as to prevent its being used ordinarily even for lintels.
Wood, itself hard to obtain, had to be used for columns and
for ceiling beams, to support the thick roofs of clay. With
the materials available, the only device which could have
furnished a permanent covering of voids with great weight
above was the arch. Its principle was known in Mesopotamia from the earliest times, and was employed frequently
in subterranean vaults, in gateways and doors, where there
was no lack of abutment. Whether spanned by wooden
beams or by barrel vaults, the rooms were given by preference a long, rectangular form. Tradition dictated, as in
Egypt, that the entrance to such rooms should be on the
longer side; in other words, the rooms were broad and shallow, rather than narrow and deep. Terraced roofs permitted the rooms to be massed in any convenient arrangement, without complicating the disposal of rain-
water. Thus, as in Egypt, great aggregations of rooms
and courts, rather than isolated blocks, were the rule. The
ornamentation of buildings, like the construction, had to be
largely of clay.

Prevailing types. As with most early peoples, the temples
were of great importance. A rather gloomy view of a future
life, on the other hand, gave no encouragement to the building of elaborate tombs. The palaces of the Assyrian kings
were more massive in construction than those of Egypt, as
befitted the greater relative importance of the life on earth.
Constant exposure to invasion gave military architecture a
development for which there was no occasion in Egypt.

Development. In the history of Mesopotamian architecture
four principal periods of activity may be distinguished, suc-

cessively in Chaldea, in the "Old Babylonian" kingdom, in Assyria, and in reincarnated Babylon.

Origins. The earliest Mesopotamian culture seems to have developed near the mouths of the rivers, in Chaldea, spreading over the lower half of the valley to embrace what later became Babylonia. The struggle between the primitive city states lasted much longer in this region than in Egypt, and unification was postponed till a full millennium after Menes had brought about the union of the Two Lands of the Nile. A difference of language in the cuneiform script has lent color to ancient tradition of a Sumerian population, perhaps native, gradually giving way before a Semitic people which borrowed its civilization and its arts. The two existed side by side in the formative period and possibly may be but two branches of a single stem.

Chaldea. Remains at the Sumerian center of Lagash, the modern Tello, include a building of the king Ur-Nina—the oldest structure yet found in Mesopotamia which can be dated —built perhaps 3000 years before Christ. There is also a fragment of the staged tower built by Gudea about 2450 B.C. incorporated in a later palace. The early Semitic religious center was at Nippur, where the ruins of the temple precinct include superposed remains of several staged towers, dating from the very earliest times. The general similarity of these buildings to the later buildings of Assyria and Babylon establishes the essential continuity of Mesopotamian architecture.

Old Babylonian Kingdom. Although as early as 2650 B.C. the Semitic kings of Agade had extended their rule to the Mediterranean, the internal consolidation of Babylonia itself was not accomplished till about 2100, under the great king Khammurabi of Babylon. His city, hitherto relatively unimportant, now became the center of a powerful state, the so-called Old Babylonian Kingdom. Plans of dwelling-houses from this period show already the characteristic Babylonian scheme of a square court with the principal room along its southern side. The streets and blocks then established remained unchanged throughout the history of the city. The kingdom flourished till about 1750 B.C., when it was overrun by Kassite invaders.

Assyrian supremacy. The leadership next fell to Assyria, the northern half of the valley, which had been colonized by the Semites of the south about 2000, and which now began an independent career. The Asiatic conquests of Thothmes III. and his great successors in the fifteenth and fourteenth centuries brought both Assyria and Babylon in contact with Egypt, to which their kings sent gifts. By 1100 Assyria was strong enough to eject the Kassites from the south and for a

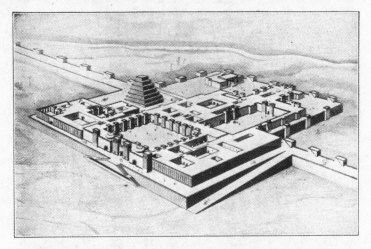

FIG. 7—DUR-SHARRUKIN (KHORSABAD) THE PALACE OF SARGON. (RESTORED BY PLACE)

brief period to rule over a united country. After an interruption of two centuries she again assumed her aggressive policy, and under a series of strong kings had conquered all western Asia by 700. The capital, first at Ashur, was later more usually at Calah, though royal residences were often maintained in both places and in Nineveh as well. Sargon II., who ruled from 722 to 705, founded for his capital a new city, Dur-Sharrukin, the modern Khorsabad. His successor, Sennacherib, raised Nineveh to the primacy, which it retained to the downfall of the Empire. He was driven to destroy rebellious Babylon, which, however, was restored by his son, Esarhaddon. Under Esarhaddon even Egypt was brought

beneath the Assyrian yoke for a brief period.   The culmination
followed in the peaceful days of Ashurbanipal (668–626).   His
palace at Nineveh, inferior only to that of Sennacherib, was

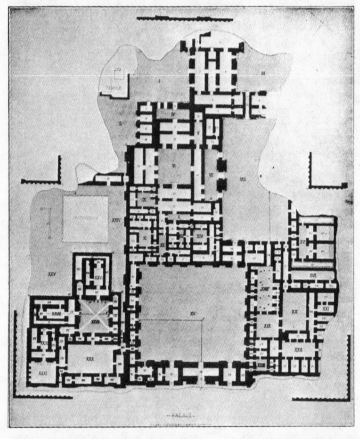

FIG. 8—DUR-SHARRUKIN.   THE PALACE OF SARGON.   PLAN.   (PLACE)

adorned with bas-reliefs of remarkable animation and naturalness.

Dur-Sharrukin.   The best preserved of all Mesopotamian
monuments, the one which gives the most vivid idea of Assy-

rian architecture in its maturity, is the palace of Sargon at
Dur-Sharrukin, the modern Khorsabad (Figs. 7 and 8). The
city, of which it was an integral part, formed a rectangle a little
over a mile on each side, inclosed by a wall one hundred and
fifty feet wide and sixty feet high, with battlements, towers,
and outworks. Like most Mesopotamian structures, it had
its corners toward the points of the compass, contrary to the
practice in Egypt, where the sides faced the cardinal points.

The palace of Sargon. The palace itself, on a huge platform in the middle of the northwest wall, covered an area
of twenty-five acres. The platform was faced with massive
blocks of limestone, here accessible, and limestone was also
used as a plinth for the crude brick walls. A ramp and a
monumental staircase led up from the city, through arched
and towered gateways, to two great courts, about which the
main divisions of the palace were grouped. The state apartments in the center, and the khan, or service, division at the
eastern corner, can be identified with certainty. The walls
were very thick, one story high, and at right angles. The
rooms were relatively small and dark, opening through one
another to minor courts, irregularly placed. Although the
plan was very complex, and its chief quarters were kept
separated, it lacked any highly organized system of communications and any extended symmetry or expression of the
internal arrangements.

The temples. On the same platform with the palace stood
a second block of buildings, a group of temples, in close association with the *ziggurat*, or lofty staged tower, "the link of
heaven and earth," which was the most striking feature of
Mesopotamian religious groups. In the temple block are three
distinct suites, dedicated evidently to different divinities,
each suite consisting essentially of a square court, a broad
vestibule, and a long hall with a cell at the end, apparently
the sanctuary proper. In these suites the household of the god
was established, here sacrifices were offered, and here the
most valuable votive offerings of the kings were deposited.

The ziggurat. The special residence of the god himself and
his consort was the chamber which crowned the ziggurat,
"the house of the mountain." At Dur-Sharrukin the tower
which supported this was formed of a single continuous ramp,

square in plan, rising like a screw with seven turns. The walls were enameled successively white, black, purple, blue, vermilion, silver, and gold, symbolizing the heavenly bodies. The mass was one hundred and forty feet square at the base and rose twenty feet at each turn. Some Assyrian ziggurats seem to have had three or five stages; sometimes each of these was a level terrace connected with the others by stairs. The plans were now square, now rectangular.

New Babylonian Kingdom. Within twenty years of the death of Ashurbanipal his empire had succumbed to the Medes. Babylon, which had assisted them, was left independent and entered on a splendid renaissance. In the reign of her great king, Nebuchadnezzar, especially, from 604 to 561, were built the magnificent walls, the temples, the palaces, the so-called "Hanging Gardens" which excited the admiration of Herodotus and other travelers, and the great ziggurat. The wealth of the Babylonian kings enabled them to burn brick and to bring stone from a distance, yet the fundamental constructive system remained unchanged. The palace plans show a somewhat more regular disposition than those of Assyria, with recurring suites of similar form for the living-apartments and access facilitated by corridors. The temples, which are square or nearly square in plan, have a central court, with the sanctuary and its vestibule lying usually along the southern side (Fig. 9), much as in the plan of the Babylonian dwelling. The ziggurat of Babylon, like the one at Nippur, stands in a vast walled inclosure, preceded by minor courts. In the palace of the citadel is a massive substructure with two series of parallel rooms, which retain unmistakable traces of having been vaulted in brick. The excavators have sought to recognize in this unfamiliar arrangement the foundation of the Hanging Gardens, which would accordingly have obtained their sobriquet through astonishment at a method of support so novel to its observers. The revival of Babylonian glory was brief. In 538 the city fell before the all-conquering Persian, Cyrus, and the supremacy of its native art came to a close.

Roofs and vaulting. Throughout ancient times, as now, the normal method of roofing in Mesopotamia was by wooden beams supporting a mat of reeds, and then a thick bed of clay graded with a slight inclination to permit water to run off. Inscriptions tell of the bringing of beams of cedar, pine, and oak from Amanus and Lebanon to form the ceilings of temples and palaces. The earliest investigators made the unwarranted assumption that barrel vaults were employed in most of the rooms of the Assyrian palaces, an inference from their generally elongated shape and thick walls, and from the absence of any vestige of ceiling beams. A famous bas-relief at Nineveh, furthermore, shows houses covered externally with egg-shaped domes, similar to those of the Sassanian buildings of Persia many centuries later. Remains of at least one such dome have been found which is thought to date from Sumerian times. It is now generally admitted,

FIG. 9—BABYLON. PLAN OF THE TEMPLE OF NINMAH. (AFTER KOLDEWEY)

however, that even single vaulted rooms in Mesopotamian buildings were exceptional, and that the group of free-standing vaults in the palace at Babylon is, as far as we know, unique in the country. On the other hand, vaulted drains below-ground abound in both Assyrian and Babylonian times. These, which are sometimes semicircular, sometimes pointed in section, are remarkable in being built in successive rings, which are not vertical, but inclined. By means of this inclination the builders were enabled to carry their vault along over the void, without any necessity for wooden false-work or centering. Each course adhered to the preceding one and was supported by it. It was merely necessary to have a wall or arch to start against.

Columns. Columns were used but sparingly, as supports for light, isolated structures, and in porticos along the sides of a court. They were, for the most part, apparently, of wood, painted or covered with metal plates. Some fragments of stone columns have been found in Assyria with carved capitals and bases, usually of cushion form. A relief from Nineveh shows a small columned shrine having capitals with two pairs of scrolls or volutes, one above another. These are very similar to those of the later Ionic capital of the Greeks, and doubtless exercised an influence on it.

Ornament. Winged bulls of stone carved in high relief were used to decorate the jambs of arched gateways and the bases of towers. Friezes in low relief representing historical subjects or hunting scenes ornamented the state apartments of the palaces. Brick enameled in colors was also a favorite mode of surface decoration. At Dur-Sharrukin broad bands were placed around the arches; at Babylon a frieze of stalking lions followed the processional street and representations of columns lined the walls of the palace.

The assumption of all credit for Mesopotamian buildings by the monarch has kept in obscurity the men who built them. Their work is indeed less individual than official in character. By the very repetition of the great rectangular masses with their endless towers and battlements it gives a powerful expression of the size and grandeur of the Oriental monarchies.

PERSIA

The architecture of the Persians, who next succeeded to the domination of western Asia under Cyrus and other Achæmenian kings, borrowed certain forms from the conquered regions—Mesopotamia, Ionia, and Egypt. Nevertheless, it retained a large native element, suggestive of a primitive columnar architecture of wood. Similar reminiscences of wooden construction can be traced in Ionia and especially in Lycia, but it seems less probable that the Persian forms were merely imitative of these than that all were descended from a more or less common type, the product of similar conditions. Wood and stone were both obtainable on the plateau of Iran, as on the coast of Asia Minor; wood was naturally used in early days, stone after the growth of wealth and power. In Persia the entablatures and roof framing remained of wood throughout the Achæmenian period, making possible the unusual slenderness and the wide spacing of the columns. As in Assyria and early Greece, the roof itself was a thick mass of clay, terraced, with a very slight inclination. Though the Persians drew some decorative forms from other countries, their chief source for them was Assyria. The winged bulls and bas-reliefs are but clumsily imitated; and even the polychrome friezes of enameled brick from Susa, the masterpieces of Persian art, are relatively crude beside their prototypes at Babylon.

Development. The development of Achæmenian art follows the dramatic history of the dynasty. It appeared suddenly with Cyrus about 550 B.C., absorbing Mesopotamian and Ionian elements as he conquered those countries, and Egyptian motives after the conquests of Cambyses. It disappeared as suddenly before Greek civilization on the collapse of the vast empire in its struggle with Alexander.

Types of buildings. Zoroastrianism, the ancient religion of Persia, had no images and required neither true temples nor sepulchers. The Achæmenian kings, however, did not observe the custom of exposing their bodies after death, as prescribed by the Avesta, and their monumental tombs are among the chief remains of Persian architecture. Still more important are the palaces, which reflect the proud absolutism of the Great King.

Palaces. The Persian palaces at Pasargadæ and Persepolis stood on great platforms like those of Assyria. Here these were built of stone and served at once to give military security and monumental setting (Fig. 10). At Persepolis a vast double staircase leads up from the plain, giving access to the platform through a tall columnar porch flanked with winged bulls.

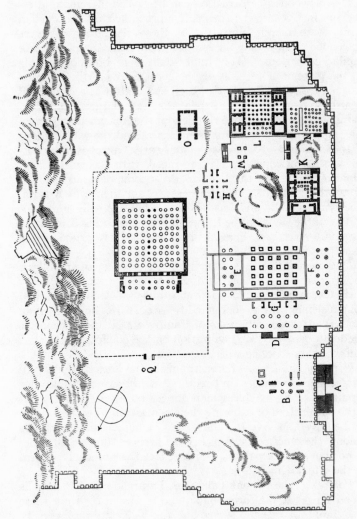

FIG. 10—PERSEPOLIS. PLAN OF THE PALACE PLATFORM

On low platforms resting on the larger one stand three palaces, those of Darius, Xerxes, and Artaxerxes III.   They are similar in general arrangement, with a large, square, columned hall, preceded by a deep portico and surrounded by minor rooms.

Audience-halls.   Independent of the palaces are the magnificent audience-halls of Darius and of Xerxes, each cover-

FIG. II—PERSEPOLIS.   TOMB OF DARIUS, NAKSH-I-RUSTAM.   (JACKSON)

ing more than an acre.   In disposition they reproduce the central feature of the palaces, but on a greater scale.   The hall of Darius has ten columns each way, inclosed by massive walls. A portico eight columns wide and two deep is flanked by colossal winged bulls. The hall of Xerxes has but six columns each way in the central portion, but has porticos the full width of this on three sides. With its columns thirty feet apart and almost seventy feet high, this building takes rank with the greatest columnar buildings of Egypt and of Greece.

Tombs. The earliest royal tomb, supposed to be that of Cyrus—a small gable-roofed cella mounted on seven great steps—is obviously imitative of Ionian architecture. Those of later monarchs seem to have been inspired by the rock-cut tombs of Egypt. They are found in the cliff at the back of the palace platform at Persepolis, and near by in the rock now known as Naksh-i-Rustam (Fig. 11). All are substantially similar, with a portico of four engaged columns carved about the door, a great bas-relief above, and a blank space of equal size below. Their chief interest lies in their representation of the Persian entablature of wood. With its architrave of three superposed bands, its projecting beam-ends above, this is clearly related in its origin to the forms of the Ionic entablature in Greece.

Religious buildings. Though the ancient Persians had no true temples, their sacred fire needed a small inclosed shrine where it could be kept continually burning, and altars in the open air where it could be occasionally kindled for sacrifice. These may be recognized, perhaps, in the small square towers with blank windows, still preserved near Pasargadæ and Persepolis, and in the altars of uncertain date at the rock of Naksh-i-Rustam and elsewhere.

Columns. The Persian columns were slender, and crowned with a peculiar capital in which the heads and forequarters of two bulls are united back to back in the direction of the architrave. Beneath these in some examples were placed multiplied pairs of volutes on end, and then bells, upright and inverted, in incoherent sequence. Thus the capital became long out of all usual proportion to the shaft below.

In its problems of the column and lintel Persian architecture was related to the classic architecture of Greece, which was roughly contemporary with it, and which carried its solutions much further in technical facility and refinement.

THE ÆGEAN

The direct forerunners of the classic races of Greece, in civilization and in architecture, were the early inhabitants of the islands and coasts of the Ægean, whom the later tribes with their iron swords deprived of their birthright. Contrary to earlier belief, it now seems clear that civilization developed almost simultaneously all about the eastern Mediterranean, and remains have been found in Crete and Asia Minor contemporary with the earliest monuments of Egypt, though less advanced in artistic character.

Development. Two principal periods may be recognized which show considerable differences in their types of architecture. The earlier, during which Crete, in close touch with Egypt and Syria, was the leader, has been called the Minoan period, from the legendary sea king, Minos. The later period, the so-called Mycenæan, was that in which the inhabitants of the mainland cities, Mycenæ, Tiryns, Argos, and others—perhaps the Achæans of the Homeric poems—continued the culture of Crete after overthrowing its political supremacy. The long development of Minoan art, following the introduction of bronze about 3000 B.C., was cut off with the destruction of Knossos about 1400. Costumes sewed and fitted, plumbing scarcely rivaled again till the last half of the nineteenth century, are evidences of a surprisingly luxurious civilization. Its continuation on the mainland, somewhat less refined in life and art, lasted till the dark ages following the Dorian invasion, about 1100.

Types. In the patriarchal monarchies of the time the palaces were naturally the chief buildings. In Crete, where dominion rested on sea power, these were quite unfortified; at Mycenæ, Tiryns, and Troy they were walled strongly and ingeniously against land attacks. Religious ceremonies do not seem to have required any highly specialized constructions. Interment was the ordinary funeral custom, but certain tombs excavated in the hillsides were given a monumental character. Building materials and climate placed little restriction on the choice of forms; the column and lintel and the corbeled arch were employed exclusively.

Oriental and European elements. Besides many peculiar native elements, among which the entrance-portico opening **on** two adjacent sides is one of the most striking, Cretan architecture shows a number of features of Oriental character.

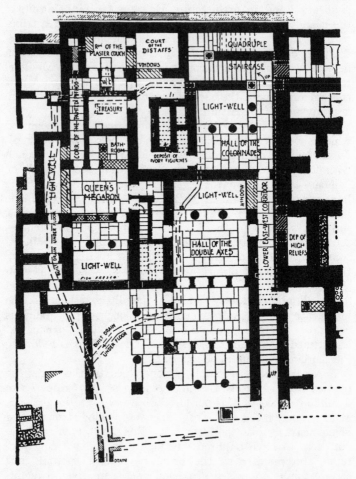

FIG. 12—KNOSSOS.   PLAN OF A PART OF THE PALACE.   (EVANS)

These include the flat roof, with the complex juxtaposition of rooms which it permits, and the court surrounded by a continuous peristyle. The architectural dispositions of the mainland, on the other hand, show signs of a European origin: they can be traced without a break from the primitive hut common to northern races. The isolated position of the principal rooms, with entrances only on one end, suggests that they were covered with gable roofs. The court, instead of forming a homogeneous ensemble, was a resultant of the surrounding units, with walls or porticos independent of one another. Although the dispositions in the two regions thus differ markedly, the decorative forms are largely the same, borrowed by the mainland, with the minor arts, from Crete.

Crete. The palace at Knossos, the greatest of the Cretan centers (a portion of which is shown in Fig. 12), is in very truth a "labyrinth" which might well have given rise to the classic legend. About a long rectangular paved court are grouped rooms and tortuous passages in the greatest confusion. On the eastern side they were superposed in two stories, at least, the lower ones taking what light they have from narrow light-wells. The functions of many of the parts are still uncertain, but they seem never to have been logically grouped. The more important rooms were preceded by the characteristic corner-wise porticos already mentioned. The great staircase running through three stories, with its ramping colonnade, is a notable feature. Another is the "theatral area," a paved space with banks of steps on two adjoining sides, evidently intended for spectators. One of these is also found at the similar palace of Phaistos, which has its own features of special interest, among them the monumental flight of sixteen broad steps before the main entrance. At Gournia a whole city was unearthed, with simple houses of stone and baked brick, narrow, winding streets, and a small central palace and altar.

The mainland. The citadel-palaces at Mycenæ, Tiryns (Fig. 13), and other cities of later importance are irregular in plan, like the fortified summits which they crown, but they show certain recurring elements of similar form. Chief of these was the *megaron*, or men's hall, a square room with a hearth in the center and a vestibule and colonnaded portico in front, opening on the main court. Access to this court, as to the forecourt which might precede it, was obtained through

3

monumental gateways or propylæa. Each of these had a door
which was protected, inside and out, by small porticos between
flanking walls, or antæ.

Walls, openings, and vaults. The walls were sometimes of
the finest cut stone, sometimes of sun-dried brick. Stone was

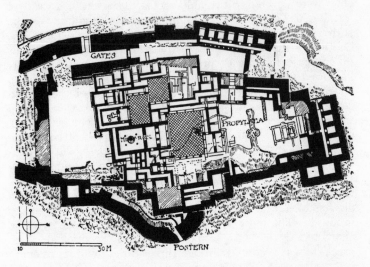

FIG. 13—TIRYNS. PLAN OF THE ACROPOLIS. (RODENWALDT)

used for fortress and retaining-walls, and for the base, at least,
of the walls of dwellings. In the palace at Tiryns sun-dried
brick bonded with wooden beams seems to have been used
for the superstructure. The fortress walls were sometimes
built of irregular blocks, the huge size of which gained them the
name of Cyclopean. Sometimes they were of dressed stone, with
either polygonal or rectangular blocks, as the natural cleavage
of the stone suggested. Though they often used them, the
Mycenæan builders were evidently doubtful of the strength
of large stone lintels, and, not knowing the true arch, they
were led to give an unparalleled development to the corbeled
arch and vault, built of flat stones projecting over one another
till they finally met. The lintel of the "Gate of Lions" at
Mycenæ, for instance, is relieved of any considerable weight by

a corbeled arch (Fig. 14).   Corbeled vaults were used over the
narrow galleries in the walls of Tiryns and they were the
favorite means of covering the chambers of important tombs.
At Isopata in Crete the chambers are rectangular, and the

FIG. 14—MYCENÆ.   GATE OF LIONS

two long sides curve together above to form the vault.   The
superior strength of a circular form was realized, and in some
of the later tombs of Mycenæ and Orchomenos there are
"beehive" vaults nearly fifty feet in diameter.

Column and lintel.   The columns and architraves, both in
Crete and elsewhere, were of wood, and have for the most
part disappeared.   The columns of the "Treasury of Atreus"
show that stone was sometimes employed as well as wood;
and that, in addition to cylindrical columns and columns of
the usual type, larger at the base than at the top, there were

also columns larger at the top than at the base. These contradict the structural tendency, yet the enlargement is so slight that they do not lack grace and piquancy. The stone capitals preserved have a square abacus supported by a circular cushion or torus, sometimes with a quarter-hollow beneath. The stone entablatures are evidently imitative of wooden construction, for the ends of round beams are represented above the architrave. With mud-brick walls, wood was apparently used for facing the openings, as well as the ends of walls, or antæ.

Decoration. The fundamental elements of decoration were the spiral, the chevron, and the rosette, employed in bands or friezes. Another characteristic type of frieze was one consisting of pairs of palmetto ornaments back to back with a rectangular space between. In the triangular space above the lintel of the "Gate of Lions" was a sculptured relief representing a column, or altar, flanked by two lions (Fig. 14). Similar reliefs are thought to have occupied the corresponding spaces in other gateways and doorways, such as that of the "Treasury of Atreus" (Fig. 15).

Relation to Doric architecture. Many of the Mycenæan forms recur in the architecture of historic Greece, especially in the buildings of the Doric style, which was developed by the conquerors of the Peloponnesus. The plan of the propylæa is the same; the plan of the temple preserves the form of the Mycenæan megaron, with its arrangement of columns *in antis*. The Doric capital, the antæ, the high wall base of upright stones, all show reminiscences of the earlier forms which indicate close imitation, if not actual continuity. As in so many instances, the arts of the conquered took captive the conquerors, though new vigor and new needs modified existing types and produced new ones. The prehistoric architecture of the Ægean is not, however, to be considered merely as a barbarous stage in the development of Greek classic architecture. It was itself complete, adapted to the needs of contemporary civilization, with its structural and decorative systems thoroughly established. If it was surpassed in expressiveness and organization by architecture of the classic period, it was not the less superior to the clumsy experiments of the dark ages which intervened.

FIG. 15—MYCENÆ. PORTAL OF THE "TREASURY OF ATREUS."
(RESTORED BY SPIERS)

The preclassical styles which had their seats in the Levant and western Asia developed in three main currents largely native and independent of one another. In their continuous life of two or three thousand years and more, it is a few brief periods to which we owe the vast proportion of enduring monuments. The Fourth and Eighteenth Dynasties in Egypt, the Assyrian culmination and the Babylonian renaissance, the palace-building periods of Knossos and Mycenæ, are some of the moments for which long centuries of political upheaval and artistic groping had prepared. In the first millennium before Christ their influence focussed on Greece, where was evolved a style destined to stamp indelibly the later architecture of Europe.

PERIODS OF EGYPTIAN ARCHITECTURE

		Centers
I.	Prehistoric period, to 3400 B.C.[1]	
II.	Thinite period, 3400–2980. Dynasties I.–II.	This
III.	Old Kingdom, about 2980–2475. Dynasties III.–VI.	Memphis
	The pyramids—Khufu, Khafre, Menkure.	
	First transitional period—decline of the kingdom. Dynasties VII.–X.	
IV.	Middle Kingdom, about 2160–1788. Dynasties XI.–XII.	Thebes Fayum
	Early halls at Karnak. Tombs at Beni Hasan. Pyramids at Lisht.	
	Second transitional period—Hyksos invasion.	
V.	Empire, about 1580–1090. Dynasties XVIII.–XX.	Thebes
	Formative period, to Thothmes III. and Hatshepsut (1501–1447).	
	Mortuary temple at Der-el-Bahri. "Processional Hall" at Karnak.	
	Central period, culminating under Amenhotep III. (1411–1375).	
	Court and Hypostyle Hall at Luxor. Temple at Elephantine.	

[1] In the earlier periods, where there is still some uncertainty, the dating follows the "Berlin" system, the one most widely accepted.

PERIODS OF EGYPTIAN ARCHITECTURE—*Continued*

Centers

Revolution under Ikhnaton (Amenhotep IV.) (1375–1358). } El Amarna

Restoration under Dynasty XIX. Seti I., Ramses II. (1313–1225).
Great Hall at Karnak. Temple at Abu-Simbel.
Ramessid period. Dynasty XX. Ramses III. (about 1198–1167).
Mortuary temple at Medinet-Habu. } Thebes

Third transitional period. Decadence under Libyan and Nubian emperors. Assyrian conquest and supremcy, about 670–660.

VI. Renaissance, about 663–525. Dynasty XXVI.
Psamthik. Fourth transitional period.
Persian conquest. } Sais

VII. Græco-Roman period, after 332 B.C.
Ptolemaic period, to 30 B.C.
Temples at Denderah, Edfou, and Philæ.
Roman imperial domination, to 395 A.D.
Later buildings at Phiiæ. } Alexandria

PERIODS OF MESOPOTAMIAN AND PERSIAN ARCHITECTURE

I. Prehistoric period, to about 3000 B.C.   Lagash (Tello)

II. Primitive period—development and struggle of city states in Babylonia, about 3000–1900.
Palace of Gudea at Lagash, about 2450.
Ziggurats at Nippur. } Sumerian: Lagash
Semitic: Agade, Nippur

III. Old Babylonian Kingdom, about 2100–1750.
Khammurabi.
Main lines of Mesopotamian architecture established.
Kassite domination in Babylonia, about 1750–1100. } Babylon

PERIODS OF MESOPOTAMIAN AND PERSIAN
ARCHITECTURE—*Continued*

Centers

IV. Rise of Assyria, about 1650–1100, culminat- ⎫
       ing in first conquest of Babylonia. ⎬ Ashur
      Assyria overrun by Aramean nomads, about ⎪
       1050–900. ⎭

V. Assyrian Empire, about 885–607. ⎫
      Conquest of western Asia completed by ⎪
        700. ⎪
      Palace of Sargon at Dur-Sharrukin, ⎪
        722–7' ;. ⎪
      Destruction and rebuilding of Babylon. ⎪
      Conquest of Lower Egypt. Sennacherib, ⎬ Nineveh
        Esarhaddon. ⎪
      Palaces at Nineveh. ⎪
      Culmination under Ashurbanipal, 668– ⎪
        626. ⎪
      Palaces at Nineveh. ⎪
      Destruction of Nineveh by Medes and ⎪
       Babylonians, 612. ⎭

VI. New Babylonian Kingdom, 612–538. ⎫
      Nebuchadnezzar II, 604–561. ⎬ Babylon
    Conquest of Babylon by Cyrus, King of Per- ⎪
     sia, 538. ⎭

VII. Persian Empire, about 550–330. Achæme- ⎫
      nian Dynasty. ⎪
      Period of Ionian and Mesopotamian in- ⎪
       fluence. Cyrus. ⎪
       Tomb of Cyrus at Pasargadæ. ⎬ Persepolis
      Period of Mesopotamian and Egyptian ⎪
       influence. Darius, Xerxes. ⎪
      Palaces and tombs at Persepolis. ⎪
      Conquest of Persia by Alexander. ⎭

PERIODS OF ÆGEAN ARCHITECTURE

I. Prehistoric period, Stone Age, to about
    3000 B.C.

II. Early Minoan, about 3000–2200. Beginnings ⎫
     of Bronze. ⎬ Crete
    Second or burnt city on site of Troy. ⎭

PERIODS OF ÆGEAN ARCHITECTURE—*Continued*

Centers

Middle Minoan I., about 2200–2000.
    Earlier palaces at Knossos and Phaistos.
Middle Minoan II., about 2000–1850.
    First culmination, ending with first destruction of Knossos.
Middle Minoan III., about 1850–1600.
    Later palace at Knossos built.
Late Minoan I. and II., about 1600–1400.
    Later palace at Phaistos built, palace at Knossos remodeled. Rise of Mycenæ, Tiryns, and other mainland cities. Fall of Knossos, about 1400.

Crete

III. Mycenæan period, about 1500–1100.
    Megaron-palaces at Mycenæ, Tiryns, Troy (sixth, or Homeric, city), etc.
Dorian invasion of Peloponnesus. Ionian settlement of Asia Minor. Transition to iron.

Greek mainland

BIBLIOGRAPHICAL NOTE

Of G. Perrot and C. Chipiez's monumental *Histoire de l'art dans l'antiquité*, the first six volumes, 1882–1894, deal with preclassical architecture (English translation by W. Armstrong, 1883–1894). Though superseded in many particulars, these volumes are still valuable, especially for their graphic restorations in perspective. The history of excavations is summarized in H. V. Hilprecht's *Excavations in Bible Lands*, 1903, which covers Egypt as well as Mesopotamia and Palestine. A special study of the columnar building, based on the latest researches, is G. Leroux's *Les origines de l'édifice hypostyle en Grèce, en Orient et chez les Romains*, 1913.

Egypt. The only general work in English wholly devoted to Egyptian architecture is E. Bell's *The Architecture of Ancient Egypt: a "historical outline,"* 1915. Another authoritative account appears in G. Maspero's *Art in Egypt*, 1912, arranged chronologically, and including concise bibliographies of the individual periods and monuments. The same author's *Manual of Egyptian Archæology*, translated by A. B. Edwards, 6th ed., 1913, treats architecture systematically, by types of monuments. J. Capart's *Egyptian Art*,

2 vols., 1909–1911, is an excellent collection of illustrations, accompanied by bibliographical references. For the monuments in their historical setting see J. H. Breasted's *A History of Egypt*, 2d ed., 1909; for a topographical treatment see the guides of Baedeker, 1914, or Cook, 1911, as well as A. E. P. Weigall's *A Guide to the Antiquities of Upper Egypt*, 1910. A special study of constructive methods is A. Choisy's *L'art de bâtir chez les égyptien:*, 1904.

Mesopotamia. The most recent general treatment is in P. S. P. Handcock's *Mesopotamian Archæology*, 1912, which also gives a brief history of the excavations. An earlier handbook, including also neighboring countries, is E. Babelon's *Manual of Oriental Antiquities*, translated by B. T. A. Evetts, new ed., 1906. The section of Hilprecht's work already cited which deals with Mesopotamia, especially with the monuments of Nippur, has been reprinted as *The Excavations in Assyria and Babylonia*, 1904. For the complementary work at Babylon see R. Koldewey's *The Excavations at Bcbylon*, 1914, translated by A. S. Johns, 1915. For the cultural background see M. Jastrow's *The Civilization of Babylonia and Assyria*, 1915.

Persia. Babelon's *Manual* is supplanted by A. V. W. Jackson's *Persia Past and Present*, 1906, and F. Sarre's *Die Kunst des Alten Persiens*, 1922.

The Ægean. H. R. Hall's *Ægean Archæology*, 1915, gives a comprehensive view. Among the many special studies devoted to Cretan monuments, R. M. Burrows' *The Discoveries in Crete*, 1907 (reprinted with addenda, 1908), may be named as a scholarly summary, to its date; J. Baikie's *The Sea Kings of Crete*, 1910, as a good popular exposition. C. Tsountas and J. I. Manatt's *The Mycenæan Age*, 2nd ed., 1916, is the standard work on its period. For a summary of the excavations aside from Crete see C. Schuchhardt's *Schliemann's Excavations*, translated by E. Sellers, 1891, and H. Ce Tolman and G. C. Scoggin's *Mycenæan Troy*, 1903. A. Evans' *Th. Palace of Minos*, vol. 1 (1921) is the authoritative presentation by the discoverer of Knossos.

CHAPTER IV

GREEK ARCHITECTURE

The Greek architects devoted themselves above all to the problems of the column and lintel, creating forms which no later Western people has ever wholly forgotten. The open-air life which the climate invited, the simplicity of Greek ideals, made no demands for the covering of large spaces which the lintel could not meet, and the arch remained confined to minor uses. Respect for tradition kept the essential form of certain types relatively constant, and gave opportunity for study of the more delicate problems of expression. Two separate systems of columnar forms, the Doric and the Ionic, were perfected in long development by the two principal branches of the Greek race. When these forms came to be common property, their details were rarely mingled, but kept distinct, as recognized "orders." A third order, the Corinthian, was a relatively late artistic creation.

Natural conditions and materials. In Greece there was less external compulsion in the formation of the architectural style than there was in Egypt or Babylonia, where climatic conditions were extreme and the choice of building materials was restricted. Neither drought nor floods were customary; wood and stone were both available. Natural conditions still made themselves felt, of course, but in a more subtle way. The proportions of the structural members were influenced by the strength and fineness of the stone available. In the West, and on the Greek mainland in early days, it was a coarse, porous limestone. In Ionia it was marble, relatively fine-grained and strong. At Athens marble came into general use in the fifth century. Even in early days, however, the materials everywhere left a wide freedom in the choice of forms.

Personality and ideals of Greek architects. It is in Greece that the personality of individual architects first becomes clear, in spite of the limitations laid on them by tradition. They knew and discussed what they were about, as the titles of a long series of technical writings attest. Their underlying theory was a formal one, which hoped to have exhausted the significance of beauty in the phrase "unity in variety." The favorite instance of beauty was musical harmony with its physical laws. This found its closest analogy, among all the arts, in architecture. It is not surprising, therefore, that the quality sought among all others was symmetry, in a broad sense. The Roman writer, Vitruvius, who drew his material from Greek sources, defines symmetry as "the proper agreement of the same members of a work, and the proportional correspondence of the several parts to the form of the whole object." The Greeks kept units for different purposes distinct, and could impress on each a homogeneous form, symmetrical also in the modern restricted sense of having corresponding halves. They studied proportions to secure not only a general harmony in the relative massiveness or slenderness of all the parts, but also a mathematical relation between their dimensions—an equality of ratios, or a common dividing module. The application of these unifying principles however, was not mechanical. Subtle modifications were introduced for the purpose of securing a still higher degree of organization, and sometimes for the sheer avoidance of too monotonous uniformity.

Development. The development of the architecture of Greece was from uncertainty to extreme refinement, and then to a less restrained magnificence. The elements of the early monuments were gradually co-ordinated and harmonized, until the central moment was reached in Periclean Athens in the fifth century B.C. Then ensued a diffusion of energy in elaboration and variation of the accepted themes, a search for novel motives, accompanied by the solution of the new problems created by wealth and luxury.

Periods. The chief races of historic Greece first appear about 1100 B.C., on the ruins of the older Ægean civilization. The archaic or formative period of their characteristic styles began roughly with the beginning of the Olympic games, in

776, the first expression of national unity. It closed with the final repulse of the Persian and Carthaginian attacks in 480–479, which left the Greeks conscious of their powers and stimulated the production of their maturer works of art. The period of native development extended roughly till the Macedonian conquest of Greece and Asia, 338–323. The splendid expansion known as Hellenistic art, in which the Greek inheritance was modified by Asiatic influences, continued until the Roman conquest, in the second century B.C., and indeed long afterwards.

Relation of Doric and Ionic architecture. Doric architecture and Ionic were at first distinct styles, and their subsequent use side by side should not obscure their separate origin and different fortunes. At the opening of the historic period the Dorians occupied the Peloponnesus and central Greece, having repressed certain of the earlier tribes and forced others to an eastward migration. The Ionians occupied Attica, the central islands of the Ægean, and the coast of Asia Minor opposite, called specifically Ionia; the Æolians the Asiatic coast to the north. It was in Ionia and the Æolian towns, under the influence of Asiatic models, that the style called Ionic had its rise, and to this territory and the neighboring islands it remained confned—with a few exceptions, chiefly Athenian—until late in the fifth century. The rest of Hellas, including Attica, meanwhile, was engaged in developing another style, the Doric, which had its roots in the national inheritance from native civilization. The Ionic might have been called provincial had not Ionia then stood in the lead in civilization, wealth, and art. She held firmly to her own style, so that but a few Doric temples are to be found on Asiatic soil. It was not until after the Athenian naval confederacy brought the two shores into more intimate relations that Ionic forms began to penetrate continental Greece to any considerable extent or to be influenced by those of Doric architecture.

Archaic period, 776–479. The leaders in artistic productiveness during the formative period in Greece were the Ionian cities of Asia Minor and the newly founded colonies, mostly Dorian, of southern Italy and Sicily. Their lands were more fertile, their inhabitants more enterprising, than those of Greece itself, so that they early attained a wealth and culture quite beyond the general simplicity of the mainland cities. Among the more important centers in Ionia may be mentioned Ephesus and Samos, with their gigantic early temples; in the west, Selinus, Akragas, Syracuse, Tarentum, and Pæstum. On the mainland Athens alone, under the wise rule of Pisistratus, gave brief promise of taking rank with these. Aside from buildings of practical utility such as fortifications and fountain houses, almost the only public monuments were the temples. Singly, or impressively grouped on the acropolis or in a sacred inclosure, they dominated the modest houses of the city. In harmony with the materials available, the Ionic forms were delicate, slender, and graceful, the Doric generally heavy—both with full and sweeping curves in the capital. The adjustment of various details was still subject to great uncertainty, especially in the Doric order, with its unconquered difficulties and its local varieties in colonies under Achæan or Æolian influence. Only in the last years of the sixth century was a final solution approached.

Central period: fifth century. The awakening of national consciousness after the Persian wars, and the fifty years of comparative peace that followed, inaugurated what has usually been considered the great period of Greek art. The rebuilding of the ruined monuments of northern and central Greece stimulated a rapid development to maturity during the fifth century. Ionia, to be sure, was slow in recovering, and built little; but elsewhere throughout Hellas there was the greatest activity. Though the western colonies retained their prosperity, the mainland now rapidly took the lead in art and culture. The spoils of victory contributed to the development of the great national sanctuaries, such as Delphi, Olympia, and Delos, with their temples, their propylæa, and their treasuries (Fig. 35). The evolution of the drama now first added the theater to the architectural problems. The forms of the Doric order assumed their normal relations, which imposed themselves wherever the style was used.

Athens under Pericles, 461–430. At Athens, where the destruction had been most complete and the subsequent victory most fruitful, a happy combination of circumstances produced buildings of unique refinement. At precisely the moment when naval supremacy and Asiatic conquests were

FIG. 16—ATHENS. THE PARTHENON, FROM THE NORTHWEST

FIG. 17—ATHENS. THE PARTHENON. (RESTORED TO ITS CONDITION IN
ROMAN TIMES. MODEL IN METROPOLITAN MUSEUM)

placing Athens in close touch with the rich art of her Ionian
kinsmen, all of her sanctuaries were to be rebuilt. The
marble of Mount Pentelicus, now first appreciated, furnished
a worthy medium, permitting more slender forms. Ionic
fervor infused the stately forms of Doric architecture with a
new spirit of grace. The Ionic forms themselves were also
employed, although radically modified by Doric traditions.
The full advantage of the moment would not have been seized

FIG. 18—ATHENS. THE ERECHTHEUM, FROM THE WEST

had not the Athenian democracy been dominated by a man
of the insight of Pericles. His diversion of the Delian treasure
to the adornment of Athens won for him the denunciation of
contemporaries, but made his city the admiration of the world.
The Parthenon (Figs. 16 and 17), the Propylæa of the Acropolis, the temple of Athena Niké, and the Erechtheum (Fig 18),
show the extreme refinement which Greek art maintained for
a few years before seeking other less subtle expressions.
The collaboration of Phidias and his school gave a noble and
appropriate sculptured decoration. At the Piræus, where
Pericles had almost a free hand, he brought the whole city

into architectural composition, according to a rectangular street plan made by Hippodamus of Miletus.

Central period: fourth century. The fourth century found the mainland exhausted by civil war, which continued with brief intervals till the Macedonian conquest, and gave little encouragement to building. At defeated Athens, especially, means were lacking for anything but immediate practical needs. It was from Athens, however, with her daring innovations, her wonderful monuments of the preceding period, that the other cities took their inspiration. Sparta and Thebes, which the turn of events successively brought to power, gave signs of carrying on the patronage of art, although time did not permit them to accomplish much. The new cities of the Peloponnesus, Mantinea, Megalopolis, and Messene, are typical of the period. In the west, the Carthaginian destruction of Greek cities in Sicily in 409–406 was followed by a long paralysis, during which the palace of the tyrant Dionysius at Syracuse was almost the only important production. With the civic revival there toward the end of the fourth century some temple-building once more began. It was in the cities of Asia Minor, though they were still partly under Persian rule, that the greatest and most characteristic monuments of the time were erected. The rebuilding of the temples, many of which had lain in ruins for more than a hundred years, was commenced on a scale that overshadowed everything in the mother country. The Ionic temples at Ephesus and Priene were completed by the time of Alexander's invasion, 334; the temple at Didyma, near Miletus, the greatest of all, was begun immediately after. For the half-independent rulers of Caria, Greek artists laid out the city of Halicarnassus, and built there the colossal tomb of Mausolus which has given its name permanently to funerary architecture.

Types of buildings in the central period. The temple still retained first place in importance, though not in the same degree as formerly. In Greece as well as in Asia, at the national religious centers, notably Olympia and Delos, important monuments were added, and Epidaurus took rank with these through a group of new buildings designed by the sculptor Polyclitus the younger. In Asia the early native

forms of the Ionic order were matured and developed. In
Greece, the Doric, Athenian in proportion, remained most
usual on the exterior. The atticized Ionic and the Corinthian
were now used also, in interiors, and, above all, in the beautiful
circular temples which became popular. In the west the
traditional Doric was still used exclusively, with but little
modification. Greater independence appears in the new
types, responding to new requirements. Every city and every
great sanctuary now aspired to have its theater in stone, a
new monumental problem typical of rising standards of
luxury and convenience. By the time of Alexander the
stadion also was lined with stone. At Megalopolis a great
covered assembly-hall was built by the Arcadians, with
terraced seats for six thousand men. On the other hand,
architecture entered the service of individuals, wealthy
citizens vying with the princes of the monarchical states in
the erection of elaborate houses and tombs.

Hellenistic period. The years 334 to 323 witnessed Alexander's brilliant conquests, which opened the east to Greek influence, not without a strong reaction on the art of Greece
itself. Outer circumstances were never more favorable to
art than in the new empires of his successors, where all was
to be created, yet where every means was at hand. The new
capitals, Alexandria, Antioch, and, later, Pergamon, became
the centers of artistic activity, though Rhodes and the Ionian
cities pressed them closely. In Greece itself the great heritage
of earlier monuments and the prevailing financial exhaustion
were unfavorable to building. The aspect of Athens, Delphi,
and Olympia, for instance, remained but little changed.
Only in regions now first raised to importance, such as Ætolia
and Epirus, were many considerable monuments erected.
In Sicily official art had its last after-glow under the later
tyrants of Syracuse.

Changes in problems. Everywhere architecture had to con-
cern itself with problems in the design of whole cities. It followed the precedents earlier set by Hippodamus in the widespread adoption of a rectangular plan. Traffic and hygiene
were considered, as well as appearance. At Alexandria the
two chief streets had a breadth of over a hundred feet, with
sewers and water-mains beneath. The city took on some of

the many aspects of a modern metropolis, with its museum and library, its great park, its vast harbor with the mole, and the great lighthouse called the Pharos. The embellishment of these cities gave opportunities which the architects employed in striving to outdo all previous works in splendor and magnificence. The execution of the great temples at Miletus and Magnesia, the gigantic altars of Pergamon and of Syracuse, the Serapeion at Alexandria within its vast colonnaded court, all fell in this period. Still more characteristic were the sumptuous palaces of the rulers and even of private citizens, the public buildings of every kind, council-houses, and gymnasia. Philanthropy sometimes gave architecture a new direction, as when parks and gymnasia were established to keep some benefactor of the city in grateful remembrance, the tomb or a commemorative monument being a central but subordinate feature. The market-places were surrounded by porticos and the chief streets even were lined with colonnades.

Changes in detail. Amid all this lavishness something was inevitably lost. The extreme refinements of form, the subtle curves, were succeeded by a richer ornament and a bolder membering. The result was technically more facile, more easily appreciated, and by these very qualities it was fitted to the needs of a sophisticated and complex civilization. The Ionic order, changed by return influences from Athens into its final shape, was now the favorite; the Corinthian order became more and more common. As the interchange of ideas increased, the form of the column was no longer dependent on racial tradition. Instead there grew up a principle by which the traditional forms, though kept distinct, were objects of free choice according to appropriateness of character. The arch and the barrel vault were used oftener and with greater boldness, but never without irreproachable abutment by solid masses of masonry or earth. It was at this time, above all, that theoretical writings multiplied, and mathematical formulation made the Greek system imitable in the barbarian world. Beyond the borders even of Hellenistic Greece, Parthia imitated her clumsily and Rome became her most faithful pupil.

Græco-Roman period. Under the domination of the Roman Empire, the architecture of old Greek lands never wholly lost its individuality, although Roman emperors and connoisseurs delighted to adorn Athens with new monuments. The transformations which continued to take place in Greece and Asia Minor were rather native developments, copied and domesticated at Rome, than importations from the capital. A thousand years after the age of Pericles we shall see that Greek genius, rejuvenated by fresh influences from the Orient, had still vitality to produce a new architecture on the shores of the Bosphorus, after Rome itself had fallen in decay.

Forms of detail. In Greek architecture great attention was directed to the form of individual details, to those of the columnar systems, above all, and knowledge of these and their relations is correspondingly necessary for intelligent study of buildings.

Doric forms. The Doric forms show a fixity in their main lines that is not less surprising than the incredibly painful experimentation by which the precise canonical relations were finally evolved (Fig. 19). The constant elements which distinguish the style are the capital, with its cushion or *echinus*, its heavy, square projecting abacus; the frieze, interposed between cornice and architrave, with its alternation of recessed *metopes* and fluted *triglyphs;* and the *mutules* or hanging plates on the under side of the cornice. The shaft of the column tapered from bottom to top, diminishing a fifth to a third of its lower diameter, usually with a slight curve or swelling, called the *entasis.* The line of the shaft was emphasized by vertical flutings, normally twenty in number during the central period, meeting on a sharp edge or arris. Until Hellenistic times the column remained comparatively stout, ranging in height between four and six times its lower diameter. Such a massive support could rest directly on a platform without seeming to need a transition, and a separate molded base was, in fact, added only in a very few exceptional cases. A common base, or stylobate, was always furnished, however, by raising any Doric portico at least one step above its surroundings.

Formal relationships in the Doric order. Critics have been unanimous in recognizing in the mature Doric system an

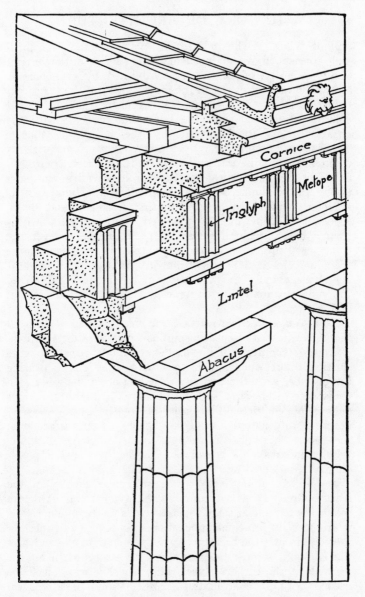

FIG. 19—THE GREEK DORIC·ORDER

organic whole of the most expressive character. Its principle consists, above all, in the masterly balance of the vertical and the horizontal tendencies established by the columns and the entablature, and in the management of the transition between them. The vertical "movement" of the fluted column is arrested, and the horizontal movement of the entablature is foreshadowed, by the horizontal abacus. This is itself prepared for by the spreading echinus with its encircling bands at the base, and by the incision creating a neck below. The vertical lines of the columns are again taken up by the triglyphs, less strongly emphasized, but twice as numerous; once more arrested by their little cap, and finally echoed in the low mutules, doubled to form almost a continuous line, in which the transition is completed. Even the *guttæ* or "drops" beneath the triglyphs and mutules— thought to be descendants of pins in primitive wooden framing—have equally their function in the stone entablature. They are ultimate mediating elements between horizontal and vertical.

Structural expressions in the Doric order. Coupled with all these purely spatial relationships are equally subtle expressions of structural functions. The echinus seems to give elastic support; the triglyphs to act as a series of posts bearing the cornice, with the metopes as filling-plates between. In many cases, to be sure, such members fulfilled these functions only in appearance. The projection of the capital was relieved of any actual load by a slightly raised surface over the shaft. Triglyphs and metopes, instead of being articulate, were often cut on a single block. It was the visual emphasis on structure which was valued.

The problem of the angle. The inherent difficulty of the mature Greek Doric system appeared when it was used in a colonnade turning at right angles, such as the temple peristyle which was its principal application. Since the thickness of the column and the architrave was greater than the width of the triglyph, some adjustment was necessary to bring the triglyph at the corner of the frieze, where it was felt to be needed both as a structural expression and as a musical cadence. The problem was variously solved: by widening the metopes near the corner; by spacing the triglyphs equally

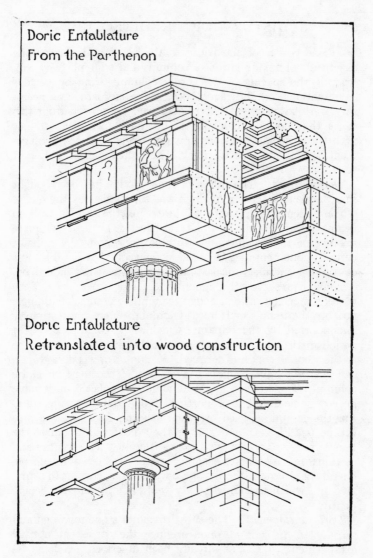

Doric Entablature
From the Parthenon

Doric Entablature
Retranslated into wood construction

FIG. 20—THE GREEK DORIC ORDER, WITH A RETRANSLATION INTO WOOD. (AFTER DURM)

from one corner of the frieze to the other and abandoning exactitude of axial relation of columns and triglyphs; by contracting the spacing of the corner columns; and by various combinations of these methods. The adjustments necessary were so complex that it may well have been from this cause that noted architects of the fourth century, familiar with the Athenian solutions, but preferring a simpler arrangement, stigmatized the Doric style as unfit for the building of temples.

Doric origins. The origin of many forms has been sought in a wooden construction which was superseded by the one of stone. Elements apparently imitative of the ends of wooden beams occur in the entablature (Fig. 20). The complete absence of any fragments of entablature among the ruins of certain monuments leads to the conclusion that entablatures of wood, sometimes incased in terra-cotta, were indeed occasionally preserved throughout the classical period. Classic writers mention also wooden columns in some buildings, notably the temple of Hera at Olympia. Here the testimony is supported by the remains, which show columns of every period in the same building, presumably inserted one by one as the wooden columns decayed. Columns of wood, however, can scarcely have suggested the form of the massive Doric column. The wooden supports which it replaced must have been of some different proportions and detail, now uncertain. For the capital, at least, Mycenæan forms furnished the prototype (*cf.* Figs. 15 and 21), as they did for the plan of the temple and its early mode of construction. The column and certain minor motives of ornament may have been derived from outside of Greece, although these were forms, current in primitive art, which the Greeks may well have invented independently.

Doric development. The substitution of stone for wood and terra-cotta did not at once produce the consistent normal arrangement which has already been described. A long development preceded the central moment, and continued after this moment was past. This development proceeded steadily toward higher organization in such technical matters as the jointing of the stones, such problems as those presented by the corner triglyph, the profiling of the capital, the membering

of the entablature, and the carrying through of a module or
common divisor of the dimensions; but it left great local
freedom in the choice of proportions. Such matters as the
ratio of diameter to height in the column, of diameter to inter-
columination, of lower diameter to upper diameter, which
were formerly thought to have evolved uniformly in the
direction of increasing slenderness, openness, and verticality,
are now seen to vary far more according to local traditions
which remained relatively stable, influenced in part by the
building material available. The idea of a universal trend
in matters of proportion was one arising from the greater
number of early monuments preserved from regions and cities
where heavy proportions prevailed, and from the number and
prominence of later monuments from regions like Attica, with
their slender columns of marble. The later temples of the
west, however, kept the massiveness of their columns along
with their coarser material; those of the east likewise show
no positive tendency.

Archaic period. During the archaic period the capital
retained the wide and bulging echinus of its Mycenæan
ancestor, as well as the hollow beneath (Fig. 21). The
architrave was narrow, flush with the upper face of the

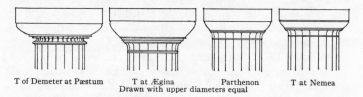

T of Demeter at Pæstum   T at Ægina   Parthenon   T at Nemea
Drawn with upper diameters equal

FIG. 21—PROFILES OF GREEK DORIC CAPITALS, ARRANGED IN CHRONO-
LOGICAL ORDER

column or even set back from it; the triglyphs were broad,
with the result that corner triglyphs could still be nearly on
the axes of the columns. The resulting metopes, however,
were scanty, so that the mutules over them had often to be
less broad than those over the triglyphs. Little attention
was paid to the ordering of the stone joints, which were,
to be sure, covered by the coating of stucco always used with

the porous limestone which was then employed.

Central period. With the central period the hollow of the capital disappeared and the echinus took on a steeper, hyperbolic profile of the utmost subtlety. The architrave lost the narrowness reminiscent of wooden origins, but, in widening, made the problem of a corner triglyph a serious one. In the solution adopted, a contraction in the spacing of the columns at corners became universal. The entablature took on its normal form, and the stone-jointing, exposed when marble was used, became regular, bearing an organic relation to the architectural forms. Great harmony was attained in the proportions between the various elements. Treatises by later writers of antiquity which suggest the use of a "module" or common divisor of the dimensions have led modern students to seek such a module for the Greek temples of the central period, but it appears doubtful whether any unit of measure was employed other than the ordinary scale of feet.

Late period. The forms thus fully established in the fifth century suffered but little subsequent change. Except in the west, to be sure, the Doric style was almost abandoned by the middle of the fourth century. It is perhaps due to influence from Ionic forms that a late Doric example on the mainland, in the temple at Nemea, shows such slender proportions— the height of the column six and one-half times its lower diameter. Late capitals generally lack the subtlety of line of the mature form; their echinus is either almost straight or rounded into a quadrant.

Ionic forms. The characteristic features of the Ionic columnar system, the enduring elements of contrast with the Doric, are especially the volute capital, the molded base, and the cornice, with its blocks or dentils. Unlike the Doric capital, the Ionic projects on two sides only, in the direction of the architrave. A pair of spiral scrolls or volutes forms a seemingly resilient intermediate between shaft and load. In the more customary form which became universal, these volutes were united across the top by a band, resting on a circle of leaves which later took the form of an echinus decorated with "egg and dart." The abacus consisted only of a narrow molded band. The slender shaft of the Ionic column always received an individual base. Among many forms, the most widely adopted in later times was the Attic base—two convex moldings or toruses, with a hollow or scotia between. The shaft itself ranged from seven and one-half to ten lower diameters in height, with a slight entasis, and with twenty-four flutes, normally separated by small, flat fillets. The architrave was divided into three faces, each projecting slightly over the one below. The typical cornice was distinguished by a row of small projecting blocks, which took the name of dentils from their suggestion of teeth. When a frieze was introduced between architrave and cornice it had no subdivision into isolated panels like the metopes, and was usually decorated with a continuous band of sculpture.

Formal relationships in the Ionic order. The Ionic system, especially in the examples without a frieze, presents a harmonization of horizontals and verticals analogous to that of the Doric order, though not carried into such fine detail. The dentils correspond both to triglyphs and mutules, and serve the artistic functions of both. The capital is in some respects even better fitted than the Doric for the task of carrying a transverse lintel, for its projections are limited to the sides where support appears to be needed. The difference between its faces creates a difficulty, however, when a corner is to be turned—a difficulty no less real than that created in the Doric order by the triglyphs. The usual solution adopted was to place pairs of scrolls on the two adjacent exterior faces, making the corner on which they met project diagonally, and letting the rear faces intersect in the interior angle.

Ionic origins. The Ionic structural forms seem to have followed wooden prototypes still more closely than the Doric, even in the column and the capital (Fig. 22). The columns are relatively very slender; their capitals suggest the saddle-piece still found in heavy wooden framing. Indeed the oldest capitals show a simple block, rounded at the lower corners, with scrolls merely painted on the faces. The beam-ends in the entablature are unmistakable. The decorative forms, among which the scrolls of the capital are the most noteworthy, can be traced to origins in Asia and Egypt.

Ionic development. The Ionic development, like the Doric, was less a change of proportions in a definite direction than a change of character. The exuberance of the early examples was transformed into sleekness, coherence, and elegance, simultaneously with the taking up of Doric elements. The volutes of the early capital were widely projecting, leaving the echinus below exposed for its full circumference; later they were drawn in and reduced in relative importance. The frieze was first introduced into the entablature by the Athenian architects of Pisistratus and Pericles, as a result partly of their desire for richer sculptured decoration, partly of their

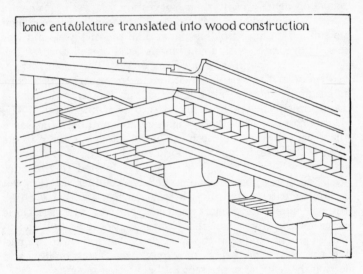

Ionic entablature translated into wood construction

FIG. 22—IONIC ENTABLATURE, RETRANSLATED INTO WOOD. (AFTER DURM)

Doric training. With a fine appreciation of structural expressions as well as of artistic suitability they suppressed the dentils when they used the frieze, since these would have no longer come opposite the ceiling beams, and would have seemed to crush the delicate figure sculpture employed. Later architects were not so scrupulous, and Hermogenes, who transplanted the Athenian innovations to Asia in the third century, used heavy dentils over a frieze of small figures (Fig. 23). The final harmonization was reached in the great temple at Didyma, where the frieze was brought into scale with the dentils by a repeating decoration of large Medusa-heads with garlands festooned between.

Corinthian forms. The Corinthian forms did not compose in Greece a system completely distinct. They were essentially independent inventions, by which one or another of the traditional Doric or Ionic forms could be replaced, and which their common tendency to richness fitted for use in combination. Earliest and most characteristic was the capital, consisting essentially of an inverted bell, surrounded by rows of acanthus leaves, with pairs of scrolls or volutes supporting the corners of the abacus. The example from Epidaurus (Fig. 24) shows the type which later became normal, with two rows of eight leaves each, placed alternately, executed with a sharp-

FIG. 23—MAGNESIA. TEMPLE OF ARTEMIS. DETAILS. (HUMANN)

ness and delicacy in which Greek carving is seen at its best. Further elements which, through association, contributed to the development of a new order, were the curved frieze, and the cornice with supporting brackets—consoles, or modillions, as they are called. The ripened product of this development had a harmonious luxuriance and an adaptability to varied uses which gave it the advantage over the Doric and Ionic forms. Here there was neither the problem of a corner triglyph nor that of an angle capital.

Formal relationships in the Corinthian order. As in the Ionic examples in which a plain frieze reinforced the tendency of the architrave, vertical and horizontal lines were strongly opposed rather than blended, but the capital, by its bell and

FIG. 24—EPIDAURUS.   CORINTHIAN CAPITAL OF THE THOLOS

silhouette, carried the line of the shaft over into the entablature in a way which was none the less adequate.

Corinthian development. The name Corinthian comes from Vitruvius, who relates the famous myth of the invention of the capital by Callimachus at Corinth, on a suggestion from acanthus leaves growing about a basket, with tendrils curling beneath a tile laid over it. The earliest example, however, is probably a single capital employed by Iktinos at Bassæ, about 420, inspired very possibly by the later lotiform capital of the Egyptians, with whom the Athenians were in close touch in the middle of the fifth century. At Bassæ the Corinthian column is simply a variant employed side by side with the Ionic, under the same entablature of Attic-Ionic form. At Epidaurus and elsewhere, in the fourth century, it was often employed independently for an interior colonnade, and in 334 it was used on an exterior for the first time we know, in the delicate Monument of Lysicrates in Athens (Fig. 25). The earliest building still preserved in which Corinthian ordonnance was employed throughout on large scale is again at Athens, the gigantic temple of Zeus, carried up in the second century B.C. on the foundations laid long before by Pisistratus. As the work was done at the charge of the Seleucid emperor, Antiochus IV., it may well be questioned whether the lost monuments of Antioch may not have afforded still earlier examples of a monumental use of Corinthian forms. These

FIG. 25—ATHENS. MONUMENT OF LYSICRATES

reached their greatest vogue and highest development under such Hellenistic sovereigns and their successors the Romans.

Figure supports. In exceptional cases figures of men or of women were used as supports—Atlantes or caryatids, as they are called—with rich and graceful results. This was notably so in the "Porch of the Maidens" of the Erechtheum at Athens (Fig. 18).

Size and proportion of members of the columnar orders. The size of members in all the orders varied greatly without much affecting their form. Examples of all three occur in which the columns are over fifty feet in height, as well as others in which they are less than fifteen.   The distance from axis to axis of the columns ranged from five feet two inches in the temple of Athena Niké to twenty-one feet nine inches in the temple of Apollo at Selinus.   The relation between height and spacing was for the most part an arbitrary and

FIG. 26—AKRAGAS. TEMPLE OF OLYMPIAN ZEUS. (CONJECTURAL RESTORATION BY E. H. TRYSELL, AFTER KOLDEWEY)

formal one, rather than a variable one determined by the ultimate bearing power of the materials.   In temples, the spacing of Doric columns was in general about one-half their height, that of Ionic columns about one-third their height. If structural considerations had been dominant the length of the lintels would have remained more nearly fixed, and the ratios would have tended to vary inversely as the height of the columns.   The proportions of architraves are likewise not strictly dependent on any statical law, though marble architraves, and late architraves generally, are relatively somewhat thinner than the early ones of coarse limestone.   Doric architraves of the mature period, whether of stone or marble, have a height of about one-third of their length; Ionic archi-

traves of the Hellenistic period, about one-quarter. Among
the other factors involved there would seem thus to have been
an increasing structural boldness. The variety in the proportions of constructive forms of different orders, the identity
of proportions in the same order at different scales, are indications, however, of a wide margin of safety, a habitual
generosity of strength.

Walls. Aside from the employment of the column with its
rich apparatus, Greek buildings were simple almost to bareness.
The Greeks ordinarily applied no relief ornament to walls,
but gained their effect by the regular jointing of finely coursed
masonry. Smooth-faced blocks were used for the best work;
but in heavy walls blocks dressed only at the edges, or with
the joints emphasized by marginal draftings, were employed,
a practice increasing as time went on. In cases where a wall
and a colonnade were fused, with the columns attached or
engaged to the wall, as in the west façade of the Erechtheum
(Fig. 18) or the "Temple of the Giants" at Akragas (Fig. 26),
this was usually due to exceptional causes, which over-
balanced the Greek tendency toward simplicity of structural
expression. Where the end of a wall had to support an
architrave it was treated as a special member, the anta, with
its own capital and base, differing from those of the column.

Moldings. The base and the crown of the wall, the transition between horizontal and vertical, were emphasized and
rendered less abrupt by special members, ranging from a
simple vertical plinth or fascia to an elaborate suite of carved
moldings. These moldings (Fig. 27), of which we have
already seen examples in the Doric echinus and the Ionic base,
are among the most enduring of Greek creations. Based
on the simple and universal forms of the convex, concave,
and reverse curves, they attained distinction by subtle variety
of contour, never following an obvious circular arc, and by
judicious selection for the different functions of crowning,
support, and footing. A characteristic instance is the employment of the reverse curve, or cyma. The cyma recta,
in which the thin concave portion projects, was ordinarily
used only as a free crowning feature; whereas the curve in
its other position, the cyma reversa, was used when strength
was required. For the base of the wall in Doric buildings, a

high course of stones standing vertically, with a projecting plinth below, was used; in Ionic buildings, molded bases analogous to those of the antæ, having as their most frequent constituents a torus or a reversed cyma, and a plinth. For the support of projecting beams or cornices the Doric builders used a characteristic hooked beak-molding, the Ionic builders the ovolo — like the echinus in profile — or the cyma reversa. Richer combinations show a studied flow and contrast of line, punctuated by narrow flat fillets or half-round beads.

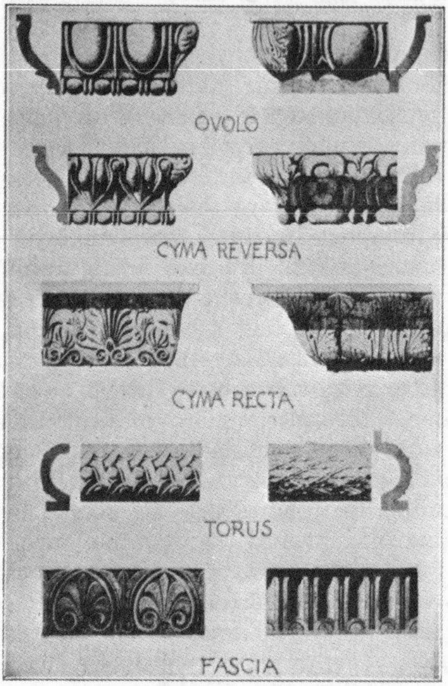

Ornament. Emphasis on the structural anatomy was also gained by carving and painting. These were usually confined to restricted fields, as in the Doric and Ionic friezes, contrasting with the simplicity of the wall surfaces. Moldings themselves were thus enriched by painting in the Doric order, by carving, reinforced by color, in the Ionic marble. The greatest judgment was exercised in the selection of motives of orna-mentation to accentuate rather than disguise the form of surface to which they were applied. Thus the fret, with its severe rectangularity, was reserved for flat bands. Curved moldings were decorated with motives having lines which were parallel or perpendicular to elements of the surface, or which repeated its profile — the egg and dart for the ovolo, a

FIG. 27—GREEK AND ROMAN MOLDINGS.
(REYNAUD)

heart-shaped leaf for the cyma reversa—thus harmonizing from every point of view.

Doors. Doors and windows were always square-headed when used monumentally in mature Greek times. They had their jambs sometimes vertical, but frequently inclined somewhat inward, a device recognized by Hellenistic architects as increasing the apparent height. Important openings were emphasized by a casing of bronze, or by projecting moldings similar to those of an Ionic architrave. These were carried not merely across the top, but down the sides as well, or even, in the case of windows, completely around. The ear, produced by making the lintel project beyond the jambs, was a characteristic instance of Greek structural emphasis.

Arches and vaults. In less highly finished constructions, such as town walls and substructures, corbeled arches and, later, true arches were often used. The oldest arched gateways preserved, in Acarnania, do not date before the fifth century. In the fourth century the barrel vault was used for certain subterranean tomb chambers. In the second century, among a number of vaults at Pergamon, occurs an arched bridge of the bold span of twenty-seven feet. Thus the arch, which was scarcely an element of Greek architecture in its first prime, was handled in Hellenistic times with steadily increasing technical mastery.

Ceilings, roofs, gables, acroteria. The roofs of Greek buildings were of tile, supported by wooden beams, which usually rested on intermediate walls or columns. A knowledge of the truss is not proved. In most cases the beams may have remained visible from below, though in some examples wooden ceilings with panels or coffers are possible. Where marble was at command its strength made stone ceilings over the temple porticos technically possible. In the north porch of the Erechtheum there are marble beams twenty feet in length. The gable roof, traditional from Mycenæan days, was usual; hip-roofs, with four slopes, were rare. The gables formed triangular pediments, with the cornice carried up the slope, and its members, except the crowning cyma, or gutter, running across horizontally also. The pediments were often filled with sculpture in relief or in the round, and the corners of the gable were accentuated by sculptured ornaments called acroteria.

Larger elements of composition. In the larger elements of composition Greek architecture showed the same conservatism as in the details. At the basis of the chief national forms lay the megaron, which remained the essential element of the Greek house after the Dorian invasion, as it had been in Mycenæan times. The long, narrow hall, either with a single nave or divided by longitudinal ranges of columns into two or three aisles, remained the most characteristic element of Greek plans, capable of varied applications. It was employed for the temple, for the stoa, the most typical of Greek secular buildings, and commonly for any buildings which might be required for extraordinary purposes, such as the Athenian arsenal at the Piræus. During the periods of native development the model was scarcely abandoned except under compulsion, in cases when it would have had disadvantages too serious to be overlooked. Such cases occurred when a large company were to assist at a spectacle, as in certain halls of mysteries, the theater, and the odeion, the forms of which were suggested directly by the practical requirements. The exterior peristyle, a continuous enveloping colonnade first adopted in the temples (Fig. 28), was the most striking element of exterior effect, finding later applications in tombs and monuments. The peristylar court and the square hall with an interior peristyle—essentially Oriental motives—became acclimated in Greece in Hellenistic times.

Types of buildings. As the first people of democratic institutions, intellectual freedom, and athletic life, the Greeks first met and solved the architectural problems which these involve, creating the council-house, the theater, the stadium, and other persistent European types. Private life was relatively subordinate and domestic architecture was simple. Sepulchral monuments, in the best Greek time, were modest works of sculpture. All the resources of the state during its prime were lavished on the public buildings, above all, on the temples, the centers of civic life. Rising perhaps on the very site of a Mycenæan palace, the temple, open to every citizen, symbolized the new social order with its rich consequences for art.

Religious buildings. The forms of the religious buildings were in part conditioned by the nature of the Greek cults, in part by traditions of primitive origin. In the worship of the chief gods, such as Zeus, Apollo, Athena, and Artemis, the principal ceremony was a sacrifice performed, not in a closed room, but on a great altar in the open air. A sanctuary of relatively small size sufficed for the house of the god, giving shelter to an image and to the more perishable or

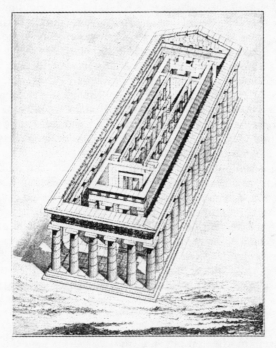

FIG. 28—PÆSTUM. THE GREAT TEMPLE, SO-CALLED "TEMPLE OF NEPTUNE." (CHIPIEZ)

more valuable offerings. Though almost always open to the people, it was not intended for the assemblage of devotees. In the worship of certain infernal gods the ceremonies were performed behind closed doors, but in most of these mystery-cults the number of the initiated was small.

The temple: essential elements. Under these circumstances there was usually no difficulty in adopting the form of the house, the deep and narrow rectangular megaron, as the fundamental element of the temple—namely, the cella or *naos* (Fig. 29 [1]). This was normally either undivided or divided into a central nave and narrow side aisles. Usually the cella was preceded by a vestibule or *pronaos*, with columns *in antis* (Fig. 29 [3], [6], etc.); less often it had a closed vestibule (Fig. 29 [1], [2], [5]) or none at all.

The temple: normal form. Though this simple form alone sufficed for temples of minor importance, the type which became normal (Fig. 28) was elaborated by the addition of two other elements. The *opisthodomos* (Fig. 29 [6], [8]) —an addition at the rear corresponding to the pronaos, but ordinarily not communicating with the cella—was obviously introduced in the interest of formal balance. The peristyle, a colonnade completely surrounding the ensemble so far described (Fig. 29 [5]–[8]), had no practical function sufficiently important to account for its origin. The origin should perhaps be sought in an open canopy supported by columns, like that over the early Christian altar. This may well have sufficed at first to shelter the image, and then have been magnified to cover an inclosing cell. Certain it is that in the temples of Doric style, in which the arrangement seems to have originated, the peristyle had an almost accidental connection with the cella. Although in front it had generally one column to correspond to each of the supports behind, these columns stood in no exact relationship of position either to the walls or to the columns of the pronaos.

The temple: other features. Other elements occasionally appeared in the temple, not limited to any special region or period. There might be an inner room of special sanctity, the *adyton*, housing the image and opening toward the cella (Fig. 29 [1], [2], [5]). A room similarly placed, but opening to the rear, was introduced in several temples, notably the Parthenon, to serve as a treasury under the protection of the god. Intermediate between the simple cella and the peristylar temple were the prostyle temple, with columns running across the front, and the amphiprostyle form, where they were repeated at the rear as well. These were sometimes used as the best substitute for the peristylar

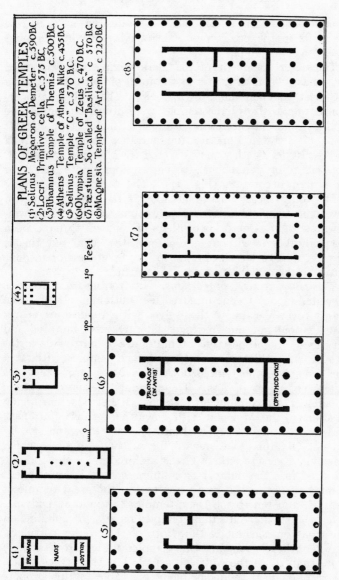

PLANS OF GREEK TEMPLES
(1) Selinus Megaron of Demeter c. 590 B.C.
(2) Locri Primitive cella c. 575 B.C.
(3) Rhamnus Temple of Themis c. 500 B.C.
(4) Athens Temple of Athena Nike c. 435 B.C.
(5) Selinus Temple "C" c. 570 B.C.
(6) Olympia Temple of Zeus c. 470 B.C.
(7) Paestum So called "Basilica" c. 570 B.C.
(8) Magnesia Temple of Artemis c. 220 B.C.

Feet

(1) PRONAOS NAOS ADYTON

(2) (3) (4)

(5) (6) PRONAOS (IN ANTIS) OPISTHODOMOS (7) (8)

FIG. 29—VARIETIES OF THE GREEK TEMPLE PLAN

arrangement when a rich effect was desired in a narrow space, as in the precinct of Athena Nike on the Acropolis at Athens (Fig. 29 [4]).

The outer colonnade of the Doric temple was supported on a massive substructure, in the form of steps, three being the most common number (Fig. 28). These steps, proportioned to the size of the temple, were often too high to be climbed, and this necessitated a special flight of practicable steps or a ramp opposite the entrance (Fig. 26). Cella and peristyle together were covered by a simple gable roof, the gables or pediments serving as appropriate fields for sculptured decoration (Fig. 17). The temple was usually lighted only through its great door at the east, although a few Ionic temples, like the Erechtheum, certainly had windows as well. One or two others are known to have been "hypæthral," or without a roof over the cella, but this is now thought to have been due to incompleteness or to diffi culties in the construction on a wide span.

The temple: size, proportions. In frontage few temples exceeded eighty to one hundred feet, although a half-dozen giants form a class by themselves with dimensions nearly equal, about one hundred and sixty by three hundred and fifty feet. Some peristylar temples are as narrow as forty-five or even thirty-five feet, while the temples without a peristyle, like the temple of Athena Niké, are sometimes but twenty feet or less. The normal "hexastyle" Doric façade, of six columns, itself showed the most surprising elasticity; the Metroön with a width of thirty-four feet, and the temple of Zeus, with ninety-one feet, stand side by side at Olympia—a disregard for relations of scale which was very characteristic of Greek architecture. Beyond one hundred feet the number of columns had to be multiplied, reaching eight in the Parthenon and in the great temple of Selinus, and ten in the Ionic temple of Apollo at Didyma. Even the smaller late Ionic temples have eight columns on the front on account of the width of their outer corridors. The length of the peristylar temples varied from a little more than twice the width to a little less than three times, no chronological tendency being traceable in this proportion. The ratio between the number of columns on the

flank and on the front also varied according to no general
law, though such high ratios as 6 : 17 and 6 : 16 occur only
in the oldest Doric temples, and the low ratio of 6 : 11
only in the most recent.   The height of the temple façade
usually ranged about half its width—more for the temples
with six columns, and less for those with more than six—
more in any case for the Ionic than for the Doric.

Development of the temple: archaic period.   In the early
stages of the development of the temple there was much
local variety, not only in the columnar system, but in the
general arrangement.   In Greece proper the oldest temples
of which the plans can be studied—the Heraion at Olympia
from the seventh century or the beginning of the sixth—already
shows the opisthodomos and the triple division of the interior,
as well as the contraction of the corners of the Doric peristyle.   In other parts of Hellas, however, many less sophisticated forms occur even at a much later time, which may
well represent a more primitive stage of development adhered
to through provincial conservatism.   Early temples in Ionic
regions frequently lacked the peristyle, which seems to have
been developed in the mother country after the separation
of the Ionians, and to have been carried over afterward
into Asia.   Such great monuments as the archaic Artemision at Ephesus and the temple of Hera at Samos, both
built in the sixth century, show the elaboration which the
peristyle soon received on Ionic soil.   In the colonies of
the West, though they were founded later, the single-
ended cella prevailed till the fifth century, and the problems of the peristyle were solved somewhat clumsily.   A
sharp difference in the diameter and in the spacing of the
columns of the front and of the flank, sometimes found in the
mother country, was here the rule during the archaic period;
and the normal solution with sides and front spaced alike,
and a contraction at the corners due to the triglyphs, does
not come in until its close.   In several outlying regions
temples occur with the cella divided into two aisles by a
single line of columns (Fig. 29 [2], [7])—obviously a more
primitive device to support the ridge over a wide span than
the division by two lines (Fig. 29 [6], [8]) which commended
itself to more expert constructors as leaving an axial place

for the image.   This latter arrangement appears very rarely in the West, most of the cellas there being undivided.

Local traditions in temple design.   An extreme instance of adherence to local traditions can be seen at Selinus, the outpost of Greece in western Sicily.   Here were two primitive closed megarons, each with its adyton; and no less than seven peristylar temples in which the adyton is preserved, in three of them even after they had otherwise become completely assimilated to the normal type.   Two of the seven retained the closed vestibule as well, and all of the four archaic ones had an elaboration of the entrance front, either by a second transverse line of columns or by a prostyle development of the cella, which has few examples elsewhere.   Partly as a result of this multiplication of features, the temples were all beyond the average proportion in length.   Excepting one of the megaron-cellas which had a single division, only the gigantic temple of Apollo had interior colonnades.

Temples of the central period.   The fifth century saw the victory of the normal Doric arrangement for all peristylar temples.   A pronaos and an opisthodomos in antis, a cella undivided or with three aisles, were everywhere adopted. The plans of the temple of Zeus at Olympia, the great temple at Pæstum in southern Italy, and the little temple at Ægina off the coast of Attica, all three-aisled, are distinguishable only by minor details.   The same holds even more strongly for the temples with a single nave, such as the later temples at Akragas and the so-called Theseum at Athens. . The great temple at Pæstum is well enough preserved to permit a reconstruction of substantially all its parts (Fig. 28).   The interior colonnades, as in other contemporary temples, were made by superposing two ranges of small columns.   The lower range was united merely with an architrave, and the columns of the upper range continued the taper of those below.

Athens.   The Athenian architects of the second half of the century began a series of unexampled innovations which, while raising the Doric temple to its greatest richness, ultimately set the Ionic in its place.   With Pericles as the leader of the democracy, and the great sculptor Phidias in

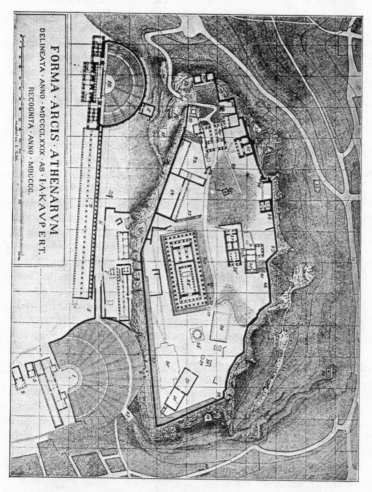

FIG. 30—ATHENS.   PLAN OF THE ACROPOLIS.   (KAUPERT)

(1) Theater of Dionysus   (19) Temple of Athena Niké   (39) Old Temple of Athena
(9) Stoa of Eumenes   (20) Propylæa   (40) Erechtheum
(10) Odeion of Herodes Atticus (28) Parthenon

the rôle of a minister of public works, the most cosmopolitan city in Greece infused new life into the temple form just as it was stiffening into a formula. The elements introduced were not from Ionia only. They include features directly reminiscent of Egypt—the fruit perhaps of the Athenian expedition to Egypt in 454—as well as others essentially new.

The Parthenon. The Parthenon (Figs. 16 and 17), which superseded a more conventional temple projected before the Persian wars, was designed by Iktinos and Kallikrates, and erected between 447 and 432. It had an exceptionally wide cella (Fig. 30 [28]) to give space for the colossal statue of Athena by Phidias. The interior colonnades of the cella were turned across behind the image, making the first peristylar hall in Greece. In the rear chamber the superposed Doric ranges were replaced by Ionic columns, the greater relative height of which enabled a single support to reach the roof without too great diameter. On the exterior the Doric order was retained, with prostyle porticoes of six columns for pronaos and opisthodomos, and a peristyle of eight by seventeen columns. The use of marble made possible a ceiling of coffered stone, instead of wood, over the vestibules and outer corridors, and a richness of sculptured decoration hitherto unknown.

Architectural refinements. A subtle upward curvature of the stylobate, early employed in the Heraion at Olympia and the temple at Corinth, was used in the Parthenon and in the smaller temple known as the Theseum, as part of an elaborate series of modifications in the horizontal and vertical members. The lines of the entablature were also curved upward in the center, as well as inward in plan. The columns were inclined backward toward the walls of the cella, those at the corner sloping diagonally. The walls themselves inclined, in sympathy with the pyramidal effect of the whole. The corner columns were, moreover, slightly thicker than the others, giving a definite end to the colonnade. All these variations—although very slight, like the entasis—sufficed to recognize in the most delicate way every possibility of finer organization, and to give the work of art something of the character of a living thing.

Temple of Athena Niké. In the later temples of the Acropolis the Doric order was abandoned completely for the Ionic, which had newly become familiar. The first of these was the little temple of Athena Niké, the so-called "Temple of the Wingless Victory," built about 435 by Kallikrates on the southwest bastion. It has a shallow cella with prostyle porticoes of four columns at each end (Fig. 30 [19]). Although it is the smallest of all Greek temples, its magnificent situation, its harmony of proportion with the substructure, its perfection of detail, enable it to hold its own worthily with its great neighbors.

The Erechtheum. Another Ionic temple, dedicated to Athena and Erechtheus (Fig. 18), was built at intervals from 435 to 408 to take the place of the old temple north of the Parthenon. It was irregular in plan, corresponding to the variety of cults which it sheltered and the unevenness of the ground on which it stood (Fig. 30 [40]). It had a cella with a prostyle portico of six columns on the east, minor porches to north and south, and columns with a screen wall on the west. In the famous Porch of the Maidens to the south, the sculptured supports show a masterly adaptation to their architectural functions. The six figures, four in front, stand all with their backs to the building. They rest easily on one foot, with the supporting leg, always the one on the outside, enveloped in vertical folds of drapery which serve the same artistic function as the flutes of a column. In the North Porch is the richest of all Ionic capitals, having a double spiral, and a carved necking of honeysuckle, or anthemion. The superb north doorway with its molded architrave enriched by carved rosettes is another striking feature. The columns of the north and west rise from levels different from the features of the east and south. The north portico, moreover, projects beyond the corner of the cella, and includes a door to the sacred inclosure west of the building. Although the junctions show some lack of facility, the very attempt to combine a variety of forms in a building for complex uses was a novelty. The features evolved in the course of the attempt, such as the portico or porch used independently of the main façade, became favorite devices in the subsequent development of architecture.

The temple at Bassæ. Beyond the borders of Attica, Iktinos was employed about 430 to design the temple of Apollo at Bassæ in the Arcadian mountains. It surpassed even the buildings of his native city in the novelty of its arrangements. Not only were both the Doric and the Ionic orders used, but for the first time that we know the rich Corinthian appeared as a third. The Ionic order was used for the interior of the cella, with columns the full height of the room, as it had been used in the treasury of the Parthenon. A change from free-standing columns to engaged columns in the interior was also begun, by attaching the columns to the wall by short cross walls. The Ionic capitals themselves are unlike any previously seen in Greece. They have volutes on all three exposed faces, permitting the colonnade to be turned across the cella without requiring a special corner capital. The nearest prototypes for the form of their volutes are in certain Egyptian scrolls. Egyptian models may also have suggested the single Corinthian capital, which crowned a column at the end of the cella under the same entablature with the Ionic columns.

Sculptured decoration in Athenian temple design. The fifth-century Athenian temples also set new precedents in richness of sculptural features and in modes of introducing them. Elsewhere decoration by figure sculpture had scarcely been employed, in Doric temples, except in the triangular fields of the two pediments, and in the series of metopes on the ends. The characteristic mode of decoration for Ionic buildings had been by continuous bands or friezes of figures, running around the external wall of the cella or its substructure. In the design of the Parthenon, all the metopes of the external Doric order were filled with sculpture. As in older buildings on the site a continuous Ionic frieze was added around the cella. In the Ionic temple of Athena Nike with its prostyle arrangement, whereby cella and portico were united by a single cornice, the sculptured frieze was not confined to the cella, but carried along above the architraves of the two porticoes. This example of a sculptured frieze in the entablature of the Ionic order, immediately followed by a similar use in the Erechtheum and in the interior of the temple at Bassæ, soon influenced current practice.

Fourth-century temples. The revolutionary designs of the Athenian architects did not produce an instant or complete reformation in the temple elsewhere. The temples of the West remained little affected by them. At Segesta, and in the great temple at Pæstum, built soon after 430, curvatures and inclinations analogous to those of the Parthenon occur, but the Ionic order found no favor, even for interiors. In continental Greece the universal adoption of marble resulted in the use of stone ceilings for the peristyle, and of general proportions similar to those of the Attic buildings. The sculptor Skopas, in the temple of Athena Alea at Tegea, followed the lead of Iktinos by employing both the Ionic and the Corinthian columns as well as the Doric. The principal use of these, however, was in the new circular temples, or tholoi—at Epidaurus, Olympia, and Delphi.

Late temples in Ionia. The great temples of the Ionian renaissance naturally reverted to the early national types represented by the temple of Hera at Samos and the Artemision at Ephesus. With eight and sometimes ten columns on the front, they had two rows along the sides or else a width of corridor which would have sufficed for two (Fig. 29 [8]). The columns were aligned with the antæ both on front and sides, making possible a regularity in the ceiling beams which had never been attained in Doric temples. The curvature of the stylobate was taken over from Doric buildings in the Ionic temples of Priene and Pergamon; the use of half columns of Corinthian order for the interior of the cella was adopted in the temple of Apollo at Didyma. An element increasingly used was the podium or pedestal for the whole structure, with base and crowning moldings, which tended to take the place of the stylobate.

Mystery temples. The hall-temples of cults which included initiation into certain mysteries were multiplied chiefly during the late period, though a few examples have come down from a much earlier time. For some of these, the conventional megaron-cella sufficed, either undivided or with longitudinal colonnades as at Samothrace. The peristyle could also be appropriated to mystic uses by the building of screen walls between the columns for a part of the height, as in one of the temples at Selinus. From this it was but a step to the arrangement of the Olympieum at Akragas, in which these screens were carried the full height, and the cella thus extended to the outer engaged colonnade (Fig. 26). The huge size of this temple and the consequent desire for an intermediate support, furnished by colossal male figures between the columns, may have been responsible for this complete closing of the peristyle. For the great hall of mysteries at Eleusis, the traditional temple scheme was already abandoned in the time of Pisistratus for one which gave a greater capacity and a view of the ceremonies from all sides. A square room divided by seven rows of columns in each direction, with tiers of seats about the walls, served to house a large number of spectators, though the forest of columns left most of them but scant glimpses of the central space.

Altars. The sacrificial altars before the great temples, at first of relatively small size, became, in Hellenistic times, monumental constructions, surpassing the temples themselves in area and magnificence. In essence they comprised a platform for the sacrificants and a raised hearth above this for the burning of the offering. Especially noteworthy were the altars at Parion, over six hundred feet on a side, at Syracuse, almost the same distance in length, and at Pergamon, with a sculptured podium and a U-shaped Ionic colonnade surrounding the platform of sacrifice.

Treasuries. In the pan-Hellenic religious centers the temple cellas could not hold a tithe of the offerings showered upon the gods, and the practice early grew up of erecting individual treasuries in which the gifts of each city might be deposited. These took the form of small temples, usually with two columns in antis, although occasionally prostyle. Each bore the stylistic impress of its city and of its time of origin. Ranged on their terrace at Olympia, or picturesquely disposed along the winding sacred way at Delphi (Fig. 35), they were among the most interesting features of the national sanctuaries.

Temple inclosures, propylæa. Monumental gateways, or

propylæa, with porticoes inside and out, gave access to the temple inclosures, and stoas for the shelter of pilgrims ran along the inner face of the walls. A fusion of these elements, unprecedented in its unified complexity, was attempted by Mnesicles in the propylæa of the Athenian acropolis (437–432). Though religious conservatism prevented the complete realization of his design, the part still standing shows its monumental qualities (Fig. 30 [20]). The greater temple precincts, often with many temples and altars, with groves of olive and ilex, with a forest of statues and ex-votos, formed ensembles of grandiose effect (Fig. 35).

Civil buildings. Special buildings for civil purposes were evolved relatively late in Greece, where assemblage in the open air was feasible, and where the temples served many civic functions. The most universal of the forms employed was the stoa, a long narrow hall like the megaron or the temple cella, but, unlike the cella, having an open colonnade in place of one of the side walls. In the varied uses of the stoa as shelter, market, and exchange, subdivision by a single range of columns did not present the same artistic and practical disadvantages as in the temple, and it remained the most usual interior arrangement. Stoas with a triple division, as in the temples, however, were not uncommon. Doric columns carrying stone architraves usually formed the outer colonnade; Ionic columns taller and less closely spaced supported the wooden beams of the roof. In two-storied stoas, first built in the Hellenistic period, the Ionic order was placed above the Doric, each having its full entablature.

Agoræ. The agora, or market-place, originally serving political functions also, was an open place of no fixed form, bordered on one or more sides by stoas. It was frequently placed in the angle of two principal streets, which passed through it along the sides. The several stoas were thus at first independent. Only in later days, in Ionia, was a closed area of regular plan with continuous surrounding colonnades adopted, following the Oriental type of a peristylar court. The agoras at Megalopolis, at Priene (Fig. 36), and at Magnesia (Fig. 31) show successive steps in this process of higher organization. Frequent adjuncts to the agora were shops at the back of the porticoes, and a temple or fountain in the central space;

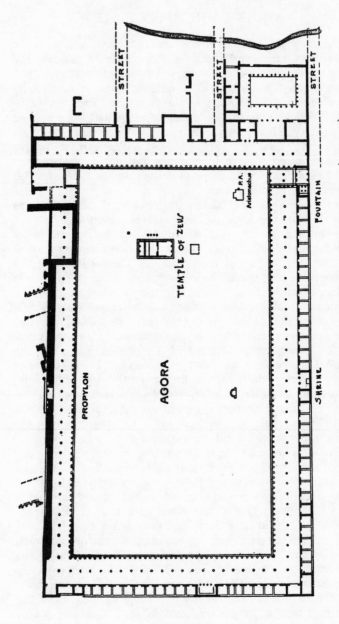

FIG. 31—MAGNESIA. THE AGORA AND SURROUNDING BUILDINGS. (HUMANN)

near it were the *bouleuterion* or council-house and the other civic buildings. Often subsidiary markets for the sale of special classes of goods supplemented the principal agora.

Council-houses. The bouleuterion, like so many other Greek buildings, was in origin a megaron. In the one at Olympia the older portion even conserved the primitive form of house, with an apsidal end and a single longitudinal colonnade. Later examples, such as the Phokikon at Daulis, were like the mature cella in having two rows of columns. Banks of seats were added between them and the lateral walls. The problem was essentially similar to that of the mystery temples and led ultimately, as in them, to abandonment of a longitudinal scheme and adoption of a concentric arrangement of seats facing a speaker's platform. At Priene, in the second or third century B.C., the seats paralleled three walls and the roof was carried by an interior peristyle—a solution unified and technically satisfactory. At Miletus the seats were made semicircular, on the model of a theater, though the building itself was rectangular and the interior supports bore no relation to the seating plan. A monumental court and propylæa were added. None of these buildings accommodated more than a few hundred at most. A special problem was presented by the hall of the Arcadians at Megalopolis where several thousand were to be housed. The architect adopted a series of concentric colonnades and seats about three sides, but avoided obstructing the view as badly as in the hall of mysteries at Eleusis by placing the columns in lines radiating from the central point. The roof was of course of wood, and the solution, though practically satisfactory, was neither permanent nor monumental.

Theaters. The Greek theater was a natural growth, corresponding to the growth of the drama from the primitive cult of Dionysus. The choral songs and dances from which the drama took its departure preserved their place in the later development, and were responsible for the importance of the original element of the theater—the orchestra, or circle of the dance, in the center of which stood the altar. The other ultimate elements were the seats rising in concave tiers, the *skene*, opposite them, containing the dressing-rooms for the participants, and the *proskenion*, a platform before the skene, on which certain of the actors, or all of them, made their appearance. An early stage of development may be surmised in which a convenient hillside served for the auditorium, at first without any architectural features, later with seats of wood. In the fifth century, coincident with the dramatic reforms of Æschylus, the skene was introduced. In the time of Sophocles it still remained of wood with walls of painted canvas. Before long, however, monumental materials were substituted, and the elements were elaborated into the theater of the fourth century, which remained much the same

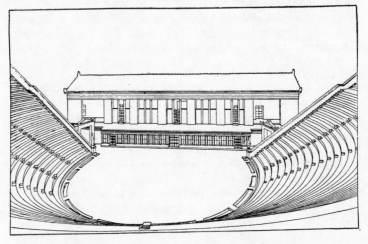

FIG. 32—EPHESUS. THEATER DURING THE HELLENISTIC PERIOD.
(RESTORED BY FIECHTER)

in Hellenistic days. Even then the components were but loosely juxtaposed, not welded into a single unit. Greek modes of design were too naïve to seek the union of parts having forms and functions so distinct.

A typical Hellenistic theater. The theater at Ephesus (Fig. 32) shows the form which became customary in the later Hellenistic period. The orchestra was still laid out so as to include a complete circle, although the circle itself was no longer marked with a curbing, as in earlier examples. Around it were the stone seats, occupying somewhat more than a semicircle, and resting directly on the hillside. They were divided concentrically at half their height by a passage, as well as radially by flights of steps, and were stopped at the sides by oblique walls. Between these and the buildings of the stage were passages for the entrance of the spectators and for the chorus when it was supposed to come from a distance. Tangent to the orchestra, opposite the auditorium, was the proskenion, about ten feet high, with small engaged columns, three doors for the entrance and exit of the chorus, and the remaining openings closed by wooden panels. The skene itself was a long narrow building, two stories high, with a series of large openings in the side toward the proskenion, three of them containing doors. The large openings, which in earlier days had framed somewhat naturalistic stage settings, were now given a more conventional filling of slender columns, the ancestors of the grouped decorative columns of the Roman stage backgrounds (cf. Fig. 47).

Variety in theater designs. In other examples there was abundant variety. The site available did not always permit the auditorium to be regularly geometrical as at Ephesus; it was frequently irregular in its outer boundary and sometimes in the lines of the seats themselves. The conformation of the ground often permitted subordinate entrances to the intermediate circular passage. Seats of honor might be provided about the orchestra, like the beautiful marble thrones of the theater of Dionysus at Athens. A stoa in which people could seek shelter, or promenade, might also be added somewhere in the neighborhood of the skene.

Size of theaters. In accommodation these open-air theaters far exceeded the theaters of modern times. At Athens there was room for 17,000 spectators, at Megalopolis for 25,000. Those in the rear rows were also much farther from the actors, but, in compensation, saw them from a lower angle than those in our upper galleries. The diameter of the auditorium ranged from two hundred to five hundred feet.

Odeions. Related to the theater both in purpose and in the step-like arrangement of the auditorium was the odeion, a covered building for musical and oratorical contests. The first of the sort was the one built by Pericles in Athens. It seems to have had a conical roof, with interior supports. In

Græco-Roman times buildings for such purposes became customary in cities of any considerable size. The smaller ones were rectangular, with curving stepped seats like a modern lecture or recital hall; the larger ones were essentially covered Roman theaters, the most famous being the odeion built by Herodes Atticus against the Acropolis at Athens in the second century after Christ (Fig. 30 [10]).

Stadions. The athleticism of the Greeks did not fail to create its share of their monumental architecture. For foot-races the stadion was evolved, taking its name from the Greek furlong. It was laid out where the topography favored, with seats sometimes in a single bank, but preferably in two long parallel banks close together, connected by a semicircle. Where necessary the seats were built up artificially, either by walls or by mounds of earth, as at Olympia. Seats of stone or marble were a late addition, at Athens not until Roman times. The capacity varied from twelve thousand to fifty thousand. Hippodromes were also laid out on a similar plan but with a wider turn. Means scarcely sufficed for executing these in monumental materials during Greek times. The division in the center of the course remained a simple bank of earth, the starting barriers of wood.

Other athletic buildings. The gymnasium and the *palæstra* served for general exercise and preparation for the great games. Originally, and in strictness, the palæstra was the place for boxing and wrestling, but the two terms are often used interchangeably. In primitive days a simple inclosure sufficed; later a stoa was added along one side; then others, backed by rooms. The arrangement was simplified in Hellenistic times by the substitution of a homogeneous colonnaded court, as at Olympia and Epidaurus. The side of the court facing the south was usually doubled in depth. The surrounding rooms furnished places for instruction, or for the assemblage of friends for readings or conversation. In one of them was the bath, with a simple tank or trough. Separate bathing establishments were not frequent or extensive until late Hellenistic times, when a luxurious elaboration ensued which furnished the prototypes for the great Roman thermæ.

Domestic architecture; the megaron house. The private house **remained** of secondary importance until well into the central period, as a result of the almost exclusively political and public life of the men. It seems normally to have included a modest hall, the descendant of the megaron, and a court closed toward the street, besides minor rooms. The houses of Priene in the fourth century still show an ever-recurring type of megaron-house, with a portico in antis before the hall, dominating the court as in Mycenæan times (Fig. 33). The entrance

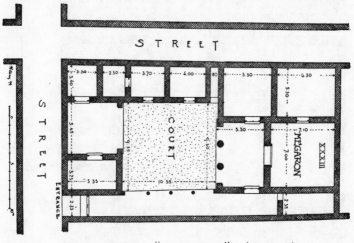

FIG. 33—PRIENE. "HOUSE XXXII". (WIEGAND)

from the street was at one side, opening into a narrow corridor continued along the side of the court by a colonnade. Most of the rooms, however, could only be reached by passing through the open court.

The house with a peristylar court. In the third century this type began to be superseded by one in which the court had a continuous peristyle, the Oriental arrangement. The megaron-hall was given up for a broad hall lying along one side, as is seen especially at Delos (Fig. 34). The peristyle was the characteristic central feature of the kingly residences of the Hellenistic period like those of the Acropolis at Pergamon. All these dwellings alike turned a simple wall to the exterior, with few windows or none, and rarely a portico over the door. A second story over some portions was not uncommon. Wall painting is first mentioned in the time of Alcibiades, who is said to have confined a painter in his house until he decorated the walls.   Later it became usual for the decoration of the interior, as at Pompeii in the Græco-Roman period.

Funerary architecture.   Interment of the dead was the usual custom in Greece, although incineration was not unknown. The burial was for the most part in cemeteries on the plain outside the city gates.   Democratic feeling demanded simplicity in the marking of the grave, so that, except for those

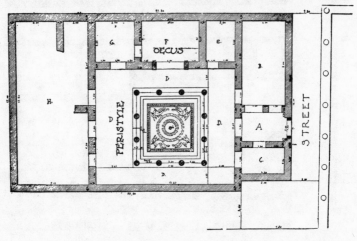

FIG. 34—DELOS.   HOUSE OF THE TRIDENT.   (P. PARIS)

of a few traditional heroes, the most elaborate monuments are to be found outside of Greece proper, in the late period when foreigners appreciated and employed Greek architects.   At Athens an unpretentious slab, or stele, was the favorite type, carved with honeysuckle or acanthus ornament, and often decorated with symbolic sculptured reliefs.   Toward the end of the fourth century the stone sarcophagus, already used in the Orient, appeared in Greece.   The most famous examples are those of the group for the Hellenized rulers of Sidon, in which the details of the house or temple are imitated, as a setting for relief sculpture.   The temple form was also employed at a larger scale for actual sepulchral chambers or chapels to the memory of a hero.   These multiplied, from the end of the fifth century, in Asia Minor, culminating about 350 in the gigantic monument of the Carian King Mausolus. This had a peristylar cella supported on a lofty podium, or basement, and crowned by a pyramid of twenty-four steps bearing a quadriga, or four-horse chariot. Pliny gives the total height as one hundred and forty feet and the perimeter as four hundred and forty. Specially famous was the richness of its sculptured decoration, with no less than three friezes in relief, besides many free standing figures. The arrangement of a peristyle on a podium, made notable by this building, became a typical form for later monuments.

Commemorative monuments. Similar forms were used in commemorative monuments, as in the monument of Lysicrates at Athens, erected in 335-334(Fig. 25). Here a circular super-structure was placed for the first time over a square base. The larger votive offerings at the national sanctuaries embraced monuments of a variety of forms. A column was often used as the support for a figure, and monumental settings were created for groups of statues in hemicycles or *exedræ*. All these are seen in rich array at Delphi (Fig. 35).

Ensembles. The pan-Hellenic centers such as Delphi (Fig. 35), Olympia, and Delos included not merely religious buildings. Like the cities, they show Greek architecture in its ensemble. At Delphi the theater and the stadion were adjuncts of the sacred inclosure of Apollo; at Olympia a vast complex of athletic buildings grew up, with a council-house for the officials, lodgings for distinguished guests, fountains, stoas, and later even private residences. Delos was a port as well as a sanctuary, and had, besides its temples, its warehouses, commercial clubs, and exchanges. On such ancient and sanctified ground—above all at a site like Delphi, which owed its choice to a mountain fissure—no great formality of arrangement could be expected. Great skill was shown, however, in adapting new buildings to the irregular disposition of the old, and there was a responsiveness to the topography which resulted in great picturesqueness.

The cities. The same qualities distinguish the older cities, where the sites were chosen for military strength, and changes were made difficult by inherited restrictions. These cities were the work of time; their plans were the image of their

FIG. 35.—DELPHI. TEMPLE AND PRECINCT OF APOLLO. (RESTORED BY R. H. SMYTHE)

histo.y. Although their domestic quarters remained poorly
and closely built, the centers of civic life were enriched until
they rivaled or surpassed the national places of pilgrimage.
This was true above all at Athens, where the Acropolis gave
an unrivaled setting to a group of superb works, rich in

Citadel   Theater
Temple of Athena   Upper Gymnasium

Agora   Bouleuterion
Lower Gymnasium   Stadium

FIG. 36—PRIENE. BIRD'S-EYE VIEW. (RESTORED BY ZIPPELIUS)

material, unique in perfection of workmanship and subtlety
of form. The approach was from the west, the rock rising
steeply on the other sides, with the theaters clinging to its
southern flank (Fig. 30). In classic times a winding road led
up, past the bastion of Athena Nike, to the Propylæa. Passing
its porticoes and its central wall with the five huge gates, one
came out on the summit of the rock, before the colossal statue
of Athena Promachos. To the right was the Parthenon; to
the left, differently turned to the light, the Erechtheum—
their simplicity and richness serving as mutual foils. Winding

between them was the processional roadway, decked with hundreds of statues and offerings of the highest artistic merit.

Town planning. The later cities show the influence of the Greek tendency to rationalize all things, to reduce them to universal and geometrical types. After the success of Hippodamus with the regular plan of the Piræus, he was employed at Thurii and Rhodes. Rectangular plans, at least for the principal streets, were adopted in most Hellenistic cities. Sometimes there were two main intersecting arteries, sometimes several in each direction. No general rectangular outline of the whole city seems to have been sought. Though Aristotle notes that Hippodamus made provision for the proper grouping of dwelling-houses, it seems that this consideration remained subordinate, in Greek cities, to the spectacular grouping of public buildings. In the application of the newly discovered formulæ the architects were not always scrupulous in regarding topographical conditions. At Priene (Fig. 36) the rectangular street plan was forcibly imposed on a steep hillside site, where the transverse streets became veritable stairways. Well preserved and conscientiously excavated, however, it gives us our best evidence of the aspect of a late Greek city, distantly suggesting the lost magnificence of Antioch and Alexandria.

PERIODS OF GREEK ARCHITECTURE

Magna Græcia and Sicily	*Greece proper*	*Ionia and Asia*
I. PRIMITIVE PERIOD, about 1100–776 B.C.		
II. ARCHAIC PERIOD, about 776–479 B.C.		
	Temple of Hera at Olympia, eighth century.	*Predominance of Ionia, to c. 550.* Temple of Hera at Samos, c. 500.
Earliest peristylar temple at Selinus, c. 575.	*Athens under Pisistratus.*	Older temple of Artemis at Ephesus, c. 560.

Magna Græcia and Sicily	*Greece proper*	*Ionia and Asia*

II. ARCHAIC PERIOD, 776–479 B.C.—Continued

"Basilica" at Pæstum, c. 560.	Temple of Olympian Zeus begun, c. 530.	*Persian conquest of Ionia, 546.*
Predominance of western colonies, c. 550–480.	Earlier Hall of Mysteries at Eleusis.	
Great temple of Apollo at Selinus, begun after 540.	Earlier temple of Apollo at Delphi, c. 530–514.	
Canonical temples at Selinus, c. 500–480.	*Persian wars, awakening of continental Greece, 490–479.*	
Carthaginian war, 480.	Older Parthenon at Athens, c. 490–480.	
	Temple of Aphaia at Ægina, c. 490-480.	

III. CENTRAL PERIOD, about 479–330 B.C.

Prosperity in Sicily, 480–465.	*National Unity, c. 479–460.*	
Temple of Olympian Zeus at Akragas, after 480.	*Embellishment of Olympia, Delphi, and Delos.*	
Temple of Apollo at Selinus completed.	Temple of Zeus at Olympia, c. 468–56.	
Civil war and war with Sicels, 465–444.	Trophy of Platæa at Delphi.	
	Athenian supremacy, age of Pericles, c. 461–430.	
	The Parthenon, 447–432.	
Renewed prosperity in Sicily, c. 444–409.	The Propylæa, 437–432.	
Great temple at Pæstum, c. 430.	Temple of Athena Nike, c. 435.	
Temple at Segesta, c. 430–420.	"Theseum," c. 430.	
Temple of Concord at Akragas.	Later Hall of Mysteries at Eleusis.	
	Laying out of the Piræus.	

Magna Græcia and Sicily	Greece proper	Ionia and Asia
	III. CENTRAL PERIOD, about 479–330 B.C.—*Continued*	
	Peloponnesian war; political downfall of Athens, 431–404. The Erechtheum, 435–408. *Spread of Athenian influence.* Temple of Apollo at Bassæ, c. 430. Temple of Athena Alea of Tegea, after 395.	
Fall of western Sicily before Carthage, 409–406.		*Ionian renaissance, from c. 350.* Mausoleum at Halicarnassus, after 353.
	Temple, tholos, and theater at Epidaurus, c. 350. Rebuilding of Mantinea; building of Megalopolis and Messene, 370 ff.	Later temple of Artemis at Ephesus, 356–334. Temple of Athena at Priene, dedicated 334.
Temple of Castor and Pollux at Akragas, after 338.	*Macedonian conquest of Greece, 357–338.* Philippeion at Olympia, c. 336.	*Conquest of the Persian Empire by Alexander, 334–330.*
	IV. HELLENISTIC PERIOD, about 330–146 B.C.	
	Administration of Lycurgus at Athens, 338–322. Theater lined with stone. Stadion built, c. 330. Arsenal of Philon, c. 330.	*Spread of Greek influence.* Alexandria founded, 332.
Altar of Hieron at Syracuse, 276–215.	Portico of Philon, Eleusis, 311. *Adornment of Athens by Asiatic rulers.*	Antioch founded, 301. Ephesus refounded, 290. Pergamon, flourished esp. 241–138.
Roman conquest of Magna Græcia by 272, of Sicily by 241. Temple of Asklepios at Akragas, before 210. Temple "B" at Selinus.	Temple of Olympian Zeus rebegun, 174. Stoa of Attalos, between 159 and 138. *Destruction of Corinth by the Romans, 146.*	Palace of Eumenes, 197-159. Altar of Zeus, c. 180. Council-house at Priene, c. 200. Bouleuterion at Miletus, between 175 and 164.

Magna Græcia and Sicily	Greece proper	Ionia and Asia
V. GRÆCO-ROMAN PERIOD, after about 146 B.C.		
Corinthian-Doric temple at Pæstum, second century B.C.		Roman province of Asia organized, 133 B.C.
	"Tower of the Winds" at Athens, first century B.C. *Adornment of Athens by Roman emperors and citizens.* Arch of Hadrian, c. 135 A.D. Buildings of Herodes Atticus: Seats of Stadion, c. 140 A.D., Odeion, c. 160. Exedra of Herodes at Olympia, 156 A.D.	

BIBLIOGRAPHICAL NOTE

W. J. Anderson and R. P. Spiers's *The Architecture of Greece and Rome*, 2d ed., 1907, gives a consecutive historical account; A. Marquand's *Greek Architecture*, 1909, a technical analysis. More detailed and authoritative, with full bibliographical references, is J. Durm's *Baukunst der Griechen*, 3d ed., 1910 (*Handbuch der Architectur*, pt. II, vol. 1). Perrot and Chipiez's *Histoire de l'art dans l'antiquité*, vol. 7, 1898, includes the archaic architecture of Greece, with illuminating restorations. R. Koldewey and O. Puchstein's *Die griechischen Tempel in Unteritalien und Sicilien*, 2 vols., 1899, remains the final authority for the temples of the West. H. d'Espouy's *Monuments antiques*, vol. 1, 1910, and *Fragments d'architecture antiques*, vol. 1, 1896, pls. 1–25, vol. 2, 1905, pls. 1–30, contain a choice of the superbly presented restorations of Greek architecture made by pensioners of the French Academy at Rome, ensembles and details, respectively. Many of these drawings, however, involve a large measure of conjecture and embody architectural theories now abandoned. F. Noack's *Die Baukunst des Altertums*, 1910, includes very fine photographs of the Greek monuments, with brief text embodying the results of the latest researches. A topographical treatment is *Pausanias's Description of Greece*, translated with a commentary by J. G. Frazer, 6 vols., 1898, reprinted 1913. Detailed lists of works covering individual sites and regions are given in K. Sittl's *Archäologie der Kunst*, 1895 (*Handbuch der klassischen Altertums-Wissenschaft*, vol. 6). Among studies of special topics may be noted W. H. Goodyear's *Greek Refinements*, 1912; G. Leroux's *Les origines de l'édifice hypostyle en Grèce, etc.*, 1913; B. C. Rider's *The Greek House: Its History and Development*, 1916; and E. R. Fiechter's *Die baugeschichtliche Entwicklung des antiken Theaters*, 1914. On the planning of cities, see F. Haverfield's *Ancient Town Planning*, 1913, chapters 3 and 4; A. von Gerkan's *Griechishe Städteanlagen*, 1924.

CHAPTER V

ROMAN ARCHITECTURE

Between Greek architecture and Roman architecture there is no such sharp distinction as between the various preclassical styles, which developed for the most part independently in regions relatively little in contact with one another. From the very beginning of Greek civilization Italy fell within the sphere of its influence, which was too potent to permit another independent beginning. The character of the Italian peoples, moreover, especially that of the Romans, who became dominant, was not such as to promise much initiative in the field of the arts. It was primarily political, war-like, common-sense, practical—better adapted to receive than to create in matters æsthetic, though capable of remarkable developments in the science of planning and construction. At first Spartanly ascetic, the Romans became, as conquerors of the world, rich and luxurious, superposing on the admirable organization of their material life a culture derived from Greece and from the Orient.

Relation to Greek forms. As they came in direct contact with the Greeks, by the conquest first of Southern Italy and Sicily, then of Greece and western Asia, the Romans realized the superior advancement of Greek architecture, as of Greek literature and sculpture, and sought to adapt its forms to their own monuments. In this adaptation the original structural significance tended to be lost, as in the later and more sophisticated days of Greece itself. Columns and entablatures were used as decorative adjuncts to a wall or to an arch, where they had no structural functions, but where they served both to give visible expression to the classical cultivation of their builders and to make a majestic and rhythmical subdivision of surface. First accepting the forms of the columnar orders as they found them in Hellenistic Greece, the Romans proceeded to enrich them still further in ornamentation and in scale. The arch received a formal accentuation with moldings, to harmonize with the other members of the system.

Importance of types of buildings. Among the Romans, however, it was not so much the individual forms of detail which were significant as the many functional types developed in response to the varied needs of their more complex civilization, and in accordance with a logical analysis of its problems. First came an extraordinary expansion of engineering works, civil and military—roads, bridges, drains, aqueducts, harborworks, fortifications—frankly adapted to their utilitarian functions, yet artistically satisfactory in expression of structure, in broad handling of materials, in proportion. In the train of an active political and commercial life came more extended and magnificent solutions of the problems of the assembly-place and the market—the forum and the basilica. For military and monarchical glorification the monumental types already employed by the Greeks were seized on and magnified, and a new type, the commemorative arch, was added to them. To provide an architectural setting for favorite amusements—comedy, gladiatorial combats, races— the Greek form of auditorium received diverse applications in theaters, amphitheaters, circuses, often built regardless of expense, whether the topography favored or no. To minister to increasing wealth, domestic architecture abandoned its early republican austerity for an Oriental luxury and splendor, culminating in the palaces and villas of the emperors. Their counterpart for the masses lay in the public bathing-establishments or thermæ, in which every form of refreshment and recreation was made accessible to thousands.

Construction. In construction the Romans adapted their methods with great ingenuity and skill to operations on a large scale and to the problem of placing great numbers under cover from the weather. Taking up the arch and vault in a condition still rudimentary and cumbersome, they followed out its form through the elementary geometric possibilities and combinations, at the same time freeing themselves from bondage to the difficulties of cut-stone work. Building in concrete enabled them to extend their undertakings and to deploy upon the surfaces of walls rich materials which could never have been obtained in sufficient quantity for constructive uses. It also permitted them to vault great spans without interior supports, securing a new range of interior spatial effects, specifically Roman.

Planning. In disposing the numerous units which manifold requirements called into being, the Romans progressed from a naïve irregularity, like that of the early Greeks, through progressively higher degrees of organization. Ultimately they far surpassed in this respect the Hellenistic Greeks who were their teachers. The functions of different rooms were specialized, their sequence carefully considered both from the practical standpoint and from the standpoint of spatial diversity and climax. Not content with establishing formal symmetry on a single axis, the architects introduced transverse axes and a variety of minor axial lines parallel to both the major ones, producing a highly complex unity of subordinated parts, with the greatest variety of effect. They accomplished this not merely on level ground, but also on the most irregular sites, making a merit of difficult topographic conditions or artfully concealing the irregularities which resulted from them.

Universality. Roman architecture became, like the Roman Empire, something universal. Race and climate were not greatly determining, for these were diverse, yet the official art, in spite of minor differences conditioned by local traditions and building materials, was surprisingly uniform. Itself largely adopted from the Greeks, it was imposed on other subject peoples, and practised by artists of many racial stocks, who themselves contributed to its general development. Forms much the same were repeated, without sense of incongruity, in the sands of Africa, the foothills of the Alps, the forests of Germany. In this, as in so many other points, Roman architecture was like modern architecture—material and urbane, frequently lacking in delicacy and imagination in detail, while preoccupied with larger questions of planning, construction, and mass.

Periods of development. In the development of Roman architecture three periods may be distinguished, in which, side by side with native developments, Greek influence made itself felt in three different ways.   Until about 300 B.C. the Romans shared with the Etruscans a diluted Hellenism mingled with Italic elements.   From then till near the end of the republic, about two hundred and fifty years, they were absorbing from the western Greek colonies and from Greece itself the grammar

FIG. 37—AN ETRUSCAN TEMPLE.   (RESTORED BY HULSEN)

of the orders, and struggling with the new problem of the arch.   From the establishment of the empire to its fall they drew more and more on the Orientalized Hellenism of Asia, while making their own most important contributions.

Earliest monuments to 300 B.C.   The character of the earliest monuments of Rome must be deduced principally from contemporary Etruscan works, which are known traditionally to have furnished their prototypes.   The principal types are fortification walls with polygonal or ashlar masonry, according to the material available; gates, drains, and bridges, with simple arches between generous abutments, as in contemporary Greece; temples with columnar porticoes and lintels of wood (Fig. 37); houses and tombs of a variety of native forms.

The house.   The most individual and most influential of these types was the dwelling, the ancestor of the Roman house of classic times.   After the seventh century there are but few vestiges of houses of a northern character, similar to the primitive forerunners of the megaron in Greece.   The characteristic form was one distinct from these, seemingly of Oriental origin—the house with an *atrium*, having a central opening in the roof (*cf.* Fig. 54 [A]).   The temple, on the other hand, was strongly influenced from Greece in at least two of its three forms.   The first of these, the circular temple, has evident traditional relations with the circular hut, although it later received a peristyle in the manner of Greek examples. The second form, with a single rectangular cella, reproduced the typical Greek arrangement with few changes: the portico in front was made deeper and the colonnade was frequently omitted from the sides and always from the rear.   The third form, with three parallel cellas (Fig. 37), may be looked on less as a new creation than an adaptation of the Greek scheme to the exigencies of a new cult.   To constitute it, it sufficed to place prostyle cellas side by side, and to give their porticoes somewhat more depth.

Arched construction.   The arches and vaulted drains, such as the gateways at Perugia (Fig. 38), and the Cloaca Maxima in Rome—formerly thought to descend from the legendary Roman kings and to antedate Greek examples of the arch— are now placed in the fourth century at earliest.   They represent no constructive advance on the Greek arches, but show an effort to give architectural expression to the functions of the parts by a decorative emphasis on the keystone   and springing stones, or by projecting members below the springing and around the voussoirs—the impost and label molding.

Columnar system.   The architectural forms of the columnar system reflected those of Greece, all three orders finding crude counterparts.   Most important was the derivative of the Doric, which had always remained dominant in western Greece.   It recurs in both of its later Greek forms: with the profile of the echinus reduced to a straight line and with it rounded into a quadrant; without a base and with a molded base simplified from the Ionic order. It was the latter of these two forms, with rounded echinus and bases, which came to be regarded as specifically Tuscan, though Vitruvius, writing in the time of Augustus, recognized that it was but a variety of the Doric. The triglyph frieze was sometimes cop-

FIG. 38—PERUGIA. "ARCH OF AUGUSTUS"

ied, though more usually the order had no frieze. Instead there were widely projecting eaves formed by the wooden beams and rafters, which, like the architraves themselves, were often cased in richly decorated terra-cotta plates (Fig. 37). A steep gable imitated the Greek pediment, sometimes with figure sculpture.

Republican developments, to about 50 B.C. Greek influence. In the later and more powerful days of the republic, constructive and formal developments went on simultaneously. In the first aqueduct, built by Appius Claudius in 312 B.C., in the bridge of Æmilius across the Tiber, 179-142 B.C., a series of arches was built side by side, their thrusts balancing on the supporting piers. The revival of this principle, applied long before in the store-chambers of the Ramesseum at Thebes and in the great substructure at Babylon, was to prove of uncommon fruitfulness in later Roman architecture. Meanwhile Greek monuments were becoming directly accessible to the Romans. Magna Græcia was conquered by 272 B.C., Sicily by 241; Greece was taken under Roman protectorate in 196; Asia Minor became a province in 133. The spoils of Syracuse in 212, of Tarentum in 209, of continental Greece in 196 and 167, and above all in 146, after the destruction of Corinth, opened the eyes of the Romans to the riches of Hellenic art and awakened a desire for imitation. Greek captives, and other Greek artists attracted by wealth and opportunity, furnished the requisite knowledge and skill. By the middle of the second century B.C. most of the architects active in Rome were Greeks.

Forms of detail. Their influence soon made itself visible in more authentic forms of detail and in a more sophisticated application of the orders generally. As early as 250 B.C. Greek details, individually correct, and effective in spite of their uncanonical combinations, appear in the sarcophagus of Scipio Barbatus. By the first century B.C. the use of conventional detail was universal, the forms of the orders were naturalized, so that conformity with Greek standards need no longer be taken as their criterion. The membering, as exemplified in the Tabularium in Rome, in the so-called temple of Fortuna Virilis, the circular temples of Rome and of Tivoli (Fig. 39), all from the first century B.C., may be examined for characteristics specifically Roman. The peculiarities lie first in the freedom of combination of parts, the original significance of which was now long forgotten. There is, to be sure, always the canonical subdivision of the entablature into architrave, frieze, and cornice, even the Ionic order having uniformly a frieze. In general, the triglyphs are confined to the Doric order and its derivatives, though in certain cases they occur with the Ionic capital and even the Corinthian. Less striking forms, such as dentils, however, were transposed at will. If arbitrary canons were violated, reasonable distinctions were not ignored, and the wealth of detailed forms liberated from inherited prescriptions was applied with unfailing respect for appropriateness to position and expressive functions.

Applications of the orders. A more characteristic feature lay in the freedom with which the columnar system as a whole was combined with the wall. The forms of the free-standing columns of the temple portico were repeated along the walls

FIG. 39—TIVOLI. "TEMPLE OF VESTA"

of the cella, to give the effect of a full peristyle (see Fig. 41). A similar unstructural use of the columnar forms had not been unknown even in the Greece of the fifth century and had since become frequent. Its adoption as the normal treatment of the temple, the outcome of a wish to secure a columnar effect in spite of the breadth of the Roman cella, was a wide extension of its use.

The "Roman arch order." A still further extension lay in the use of columns on a wall with arches, or rather on the piers of a continuous arcade, usually in several stories, a scheme which became so common as to receive a special name, the Roman arch order. The Tabularium, the archive building of the Capitol (78 B.C.), furnishes the first dated example. This scheme, which was later to find its most noted exemplification in the Colosseum (Figs. 40, 59) consisted of the application, to the piers of the arcade and to the horizontal bands opposite the floors, of the columns and entablatures of a Greek stoa with superposed orders. The mere superposition of ranges of

FIG. 40—ROME. THE COLOSSEUM

arches was itself almost if not quite as novel as the use of orders with them. It is really better justified to look on the arrangement as the strengthening of a Greek stoa to support vaulting, thickening the supports and building up arches between the columns—a process similar to that by which the first engaged columns in Greece were produced. The necessity for greater strength lay in the desire to span the passage behind the façade by a more permanent means than the wooden ceilings and roofs of the Greeks, usually by a barrel vault, which sprang from above the crowns of the external arches across to the inner wall. This was indeed a notable step

in construction, for the outward thrust had no such unimpeachable abutment as had the subterranean vaults of the
Orient or the ends of the arcades in aqueducts and bridges.
The experiment succeeded, nevertheless; the resistance of the
heavy outer wall proved more than sufficient. From the
purely formal standpoint the arch order was equally successful, in spite of certain difficulties. The longitudinal vaults,
being semicircular, rose perforce even higher than the top of
the entablature in front of them, but this was overcome by
the insertion of an attic with pedestals between the stories.
The calm and dignified repetition of horizontals and verticals,
mastering and co-ordinating the freer lines of the arches, the
consistent molded treatment of entablature, impost, and
pedestal, combine to form a system of powerful effect, independent of the character of the individual details or of the
contradiction of the structural expressions of lintel and arch.

Domestic architecture. The private houses, which from the
fourth century were built wall to wall in close blocks, followed
the Etruscan model in having a central atrium with surrounding rooms. At the rear was a small garden. Later a more
elaborate inner portion, built about a court with a colonnade,
the so-called *peristylium*, was added under Greek influence
(Fig. 54 [C]). By the second century B.C. this composite type
was the model for the ordinary dwellings of the well-to-do;
from early in the first century the wealthy began to elaborate
them into veritable palaces, with marble columns and pavements. On the other hand, the pressure of metropolitan life
now forced the erection of tenements for the poor, in three
or four stories.

Other types. Throughout this period the principal monumental type remained the temple. Civil buildings, in Italy
as in Greece, were late in developing. Political assembly and
commercial intercourse alike took place at first in the open
air. The senate, to be sure, which in the beginning met out
of doors or in some temple, was housed at an early date in a
special building, the Curia, which seems to have followed the
scheme of the temple cella. By about 200 B.C. began the
construction of basilicas, exchanges for the merchants, which
became the seat of tribunals and gradually accumulated other
uses. The first of which we know was built by Cato the Cen-

sor, in 184 B.C., and others quickly followed.   Regarding the
original form of these and, indeed, of all the basilicas of Rome
prior to the days of Cæsar, we have no certain knowledge.

Grouping: town planning. The grouping of public buildings,
such as the temples and basilicas which fronted the forum,
the principal open space of the city, was an irregular and
accidental one, like that of the great sanctuaries of early
Greece.   Only in a town essentially Hellenistic, like Pompeii,
was there a more uniform treatment such as that of the Ionian
agoras, resulting from the inclosing of the forum, shortly before 100 B.C., by columnar porticoes forming a long rectangle.
Although the city of Rome, with its unexpected growth, conformed to no regular plan, many towns showed in their general
layout common characteristics derived from a principle consecrated in Italy from the earliest times, division by two axes
which crossed at right angles.   Parallel to the principal
streets which marked these axes were minor streets delimiting
the house blocks; in one of the angles was frequently the
forum, as at Pompeii.

Imperial architecture, c. 50 B.C. to 350 A.D.   Development.
The transformation of Roman architecture to its imperial
scale and splendor began with the buildings of Pompey and of
Julius Cæsar, in the middle of the first century B.C.   Pompey
erected in 55 the earliest stone theater, built up from the plain
on an arched substructure; Cæsar did not content himself with
adding a new basilica to the forum, and providing better
quarters for the senate and other assemblies, but initiated
the custom of adding an entirely new forum, beyond the time-
honored buildings which prevented any enlargement of the old
Forum Romanum.   The buildings and rebuildings of Augustus were so numerous as to justify his boast that he found
Rome of brick and left it of marble.   Most noteworthy, perhaps, was the forum which bears his name (Fig. 44 [C]), with
its octastyle Corinthian temple of Mars.   Agrippa, his ablest
minister, gave great attention to the aqueducts, and built the
first of the great thermæ.   In Augustus's reign also the
architect Vitruvius compiled, largely from Greek sources, his
compendium of rules and maxims, designed to assist in the diffusion of correct principles.   Under Nero the destruction of
crowded quarters by fire gave opportunity for rebuilding them

on a regular plan, with better materials, lower houses, and wider streets. With the Flavian emperors, 69–96 A.D., the tendencies toward regal luxury of accommodations and toward elaboration of detail reached their height. Their palace on the Palatine hill with its magnificent vaulted halls, their temples and fora, in the entablatures of which there was scarcely a member left undecorated, the "Composite" capital, in which elements of the Ionic and Corinthian were combined, attest their striving for enrichment of form. Under Trajan, Hadrian, and the Antonines, while the magnitude of constructive undertakings increased still further, there was a reaction in favor of Hellenic forms. In the gigantic Forum of Trajan (Fig. 44 [F])—itself composed on Oriental principles— the great basilica dispenses with the vaulted arcades of earlier works, and employs a purely Greek system of column and lintel. The temples of the time bear entablatures in which the multiplicity of ornament is much reduced—in some cases even to the point of austerity.

Constructive advances. At the same time, however, Roman constructive science was proceeding with rapid stride, conquering successively the difficulties of vaulting semicircular apses, circular rooms, and rectangular rooms requiring lateral openings. In the Pantheon of Hadrian, the halls of the imperial thermæ of Trajan, Caracalla, and Diocletian, these elements attained vast size and monumental effects hitherto unattainable. In the thermæ also Roman architecture achieved some of its greatest triumphs of logical planning at a great scale. The laying out of new towns gave opportunity to extend its principles, as in Hellenistic Asia, to the whole city.

Prevalent types. The temples no longer appeared as the sole or even as the chief monuments. In spite of vast size and costly materials they had become secondary in importance, as an expression of the national life, which was administrative, commercial, pleasure-loving, and egoistic. Besides luxurious palaces and temples for self-deification, the emperors erected triumphal columns and arches, mausolea surpassing the original at Halicarnassus in size and magnificence, and indulged the populace with buildings for their favorite amusements.

Late imperial architecture. In the later monuments a new

logic gradually shows itself in the relations of arch and column, coincident with a fresh wave of Oriental influences sweeping over construction and detail alike. In the Pantheon and the thermæ the arches are not framed in by entablatures and columns, but rest frankly on them; in the second century monuments of Syria and the palace of Diocletian on the Adriatic, at the beginning of the fourth century, further steps are taken in the elimination of the entablature and the bringing down of the arch directly on the head of the column (Fig. 58). Thus at the very end of its development Roman architecture attained, by the abandonment of its formal canons, the solution of the difficulties of expression which confronted it, laying the foundation for the development of the Middle Ages.

Artistic centers. Throughout this long history the center of artistic activity had remained the city of Rome, which focussed the influences of Greece and the Orient. In the last days of the empire the balance of power inclined more and more to the east, and under Constantine, 306–337, the seat of administration was removed thither, to Byzantium or Constantinople, on the shores of the Bosphorus. The wealth and population of Rome rapidly fell away. The adoption of Christianity as the state religion in 330 caused the temples to fall gradually into disuse, and temples and public buildings alike were plundered for materials to build the great Christian basilicas, the only important fresh undertakings of the time. With the sack of Rome by the Goths in 410 and the Vandals in 455 the last vestiges of its imperial power were broken, and the abdication of Romulus Augustulus on demand of the barbarian chieftain Odoacer in 476 marked the end even of the nominal existence of the Roman Empire in the west.

Character of important types. Whereas in Greece it is the development of the forms of detail, to which the Greeks gave the most scrupulous attention, which is of primary importance, in Rome it is rather the development of the great functional types which demands an intensive study.

Temples. In Rome the temple was no more intended than in Greece for congregational worship, and the great size to which it ultimately grew was rather the result of a desire for imposing effect. The ritual, influenced by that of the Greeks.

left considerable liberty in form and orientation, though the image was preferably at the east. In matters of disposition the development was toward a steadily closer approximation to the Greek scheme with a continuous exterior peristyle. The Etruscan temples had never a colonnade at the rear, the Roman cellas, as early as republican times, were provided with a decorative disguise of engaged columns on the rear as well as on the sides, and this was retained in early imperial

FIG. 41—NIMES. "THE MAISON CARREE"

times. The best preserved and most famous example is the so-called Maison Carrée at Nîmes in southern France (Fig. 41), a hexastyle temple of rich Corinthian order, which shows that the Romans were not behind the Greeks in mastery of proportions and subtlety of form. The delicate curvatures of line and surface which relieved the regularity and varied the play of light and shade in Greek monuments recur in its plan. Other temples, like that of Mars in the Forum of Augustus, perpetuate a type already found in Etruscan times, and approaching the peristylar arrangement more nearly—having a free-standing colonnade along the sides as well as the front, but not across the rear. The tendency was more and more toward a complete peristyle, still in use in half-Greek Pompeii

FIG. 42—ROME. INTERIOR OF THE PANTHEON (RESTORED BY ISABELLE),
SHOWING THE CONDITION AFTER THE RESTORATION OF SEVERUS

in the second century B.C. before the establishment of the Roman colony there, and appearing in Rome with the temple completed by Augustus in the Forum of Cæsar. One of the most notable examples was the double temple of Venus and Rome built by Hadrian near the Forum. It had fronts of ten columns, and a cella with two chambers back to back, which were for the first time vaulted with barrel vaults. A magnificent decoration of half columns and statued niches along the interior walls is the lineal descendant of the interior colonnades of the early Greek cellas, through the temple at Bassæ and the temple of Apollo at Didyma. A few temples, though rectangular, varied from the traditional arrangement in having the portico built against the long side, but this was only from special exigencies. Both stylobate and podium were used as substructures; the roof remained steadily a gabled one, fronted by a pediment. In a few instances only were temples left roofless.

Circular temples. A class of considerable importance was that of the round temples. The two well-known republican examples, in Rome and Tivoli (Fig. 39), do not differ greatly from similar buildings in Greece. Both are of the Corinthian order, with unvaulted cellas. The first Pantheon in Rome, built by Agrippa, must have been similar in principle, though on a far larger scale. The Pantheon which stands to-day, rebuilt by Hadrian (120-124 A.D.) and restored under Severus (202 A.D.), shows. on the contrary, an application of the new Roman constructive methods (Fig. 42). A single hemispherical dome spans the circular interior of over one hundred and forty feet diameter, its crown at just an equal height above the pavement. Light comes through a single eye at the top, through which rain may fall without causing any inconvenience, thanks to the area and volume of the interior. The massive walls are pierced by eight niches, alternately square and semicircular, originally arched across, with screens of Corinthian columns; the vault is deeply recessed with coffers diminishing as they ascend, and once decorated with bronze rosettes. A rich veneer of marble slabs over the constructive brickwork of the walls complements the unrivaled abstract unity of the general form.

Temple inclosures Although many early temples in Rome,

FIG. 43—THE FORUM ROMANUM

and their successors on the same sites, stood directly on the borders of the Forum, it was preferred in later days to follow the practice of Hellenistic Greece and place the temple in a colonnaded inclosure, serving both to give shelter to the worshippers who watched the sacrifice and to heighten the architectural effect. At Pompeii, in the precinct of Apollo, this arrangement was a legacy from the Greek days of the town; in Rome it came in, with the peripteral temple, in the Forum of Cæsar, which was at the same time a temple inclosure (Fig. 44 [B]). Later architects were not contented with the simple rectangular plan. In the Forum of Augustus they introduced great segmental exedræ to right and left; in the temple of Jupiter at Baalbek in Syria they added a second, hexagonal court in front of the principal one.

Size of temples. In size the temples varied as much as those of Greece, and within much the same limits. No Greek temple, however, rivaled the one at Baalbek in the complexity and extent of its accessories, with which it covered in all a space a thousand by four hundred feet.

Fora. The forum served at first for all forms of trade as well as for political assembly, and this remained true in the smaller towns. In the cities, and especially in Rome, the volume of trade forced the institution of subordinate fora for various classes of goods, leaving the *forum civile* for the bankers and for general business intercourse. About it were grouped the principal public buildings (Fig. 43). Thamugadi (Timgad), a colony planted by Trajan in Africa, shows the form which might be selected for the forum in imperial times, in a case where all was planned from the beginning—a square court surrounded by an unbroken peristyle. In Rome, the supplementary *fora civilia* built by the emperors culminated in that of Trajan, designed by Apollodorus of Damascus, which included a vast complex of buildings for varied uses (Fig. 44 [F]). It followed in disposition, as has been recognized, the Egyptian temple scheme. First came a broad court, the forum proper, surrounded on three sides by a colonnade, on the flanks of which were enormous exedræ bordered with shops. Across the further side of the court, like the hypostyle hall of the Egyptian temple, lay a basilica of unequaled extent; beyond it, like the Egyptian sanctuary, was the temple

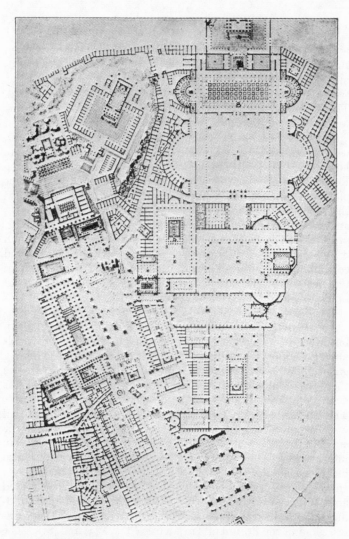

FIG. 44—ROME. THE FORUM ROMANUM AND THE FORA OF THE
EMPERORS. PLAN. (RESTORED BY GROMORT)

(A) Forum Romanum
(B) Forum of Julius Cæsar
(C) Forum of Augustus
(D) Forum of Vespasian
(E) Forum Transitorium
(F) Forum of Trajan

(G) Area Capitolina
(H) Comitium
(1) Tabularium
(2) Curia
(3) Basilica Julia
(4) Basilica Æmilia

(5) Basilica of Maxentius
    (Constantine)
(6) Temple of Venus Genetrix
(7) Temple of Mars the
    Avenger
(8) Basilica Ulpia

of Trajan, surrounded by a second, oblong inclosure. Even
the pylon and the obelisk had their counterparts in the monumental arch which gave access to the first court and the
triumphal column which stood at the entrance to the second.
There was a variety and technical dexterity of planning
which the Egyptian prototypes had lacked.

Adjuncts of the forum. As adjuncts to the Forum Romanum,
which remained the political center, were the Curia or senate
house, the Comitium for the meeting of the assembly, and the
Rostrum from which orators addressed the populace. This
platform, which stood at the end of the principal space toward
the Capitol, was richly decorated with sculptured parapets
and small commemorative columns, as well as with the ships'
prows which gave it its name. On the pavement of the forum
itself was a forest of statues, and such triumphal arches and
columns as could find place, making, with the façades of
temples and basilicas, an effect as rich as those of the national
sanctuaries of Greece.

Basilicas. The basilicas, which served the varied necessities of intercourse under cover, were not uniform in plan,
but were in general buildings of spacious interior, with columnar supports, not narrow and open on one side like a
gallery or stoa, but broad and inclosed, like a hall. In Greece
there were already a few buildings which fall under this
definition, though they were not designated by the same name.
They belonged both to the Greek type of plan, a deep hall
with longitudinal colonnades, and an apse opposite the
entrance, and to the Oriental type, a broad hall with an
interior peristyle. In Rome the existing monuments also
include examples of both types, to neither of which can a
chronological priority be assigned. The Oriental type counted
among its representatives two of the most conspicuous buildings, the Basilica Julia in the Forum Romanum and the Basilica Ulpia in the Forum of Trajan (see Fig. 44 [3] and [8]). The
Basilica Julia turned its long, principal façade to the Forum
and was lined on the rear by a range of shops. Between was
an oblong hall surrounded by two concentric vaulted corridors in two stories, of an ordonnance similar to that of the
Tabularium. The impossibility of securing sufficient light in
the central hall through the lateral openings gives rise to the

assumption that its ceiling was raised on a clerestory with windows above the flat roofs of the aisles, as in the Egyptian temples and in certain late Greek buildings which show Egyptian influence. The building was exceptional in having such an open treatment of the exterior, arising partly, doubtless, from a desire for a rich effect suitable to its conspicuous position. Similar in its general plan to the Basilica Julia was the Basilica Ulpia, in spite of its having columns and lintels instead of piers and an arch order. The central space, although over eighty feet in span, was doubtless covered by a wooden

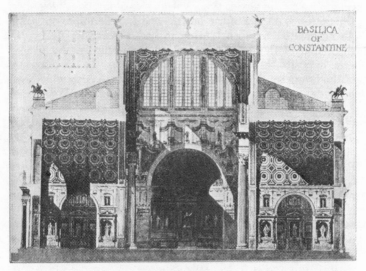

FIG. 45—ROME.   BASILICA OF MAXENTIUS, OR CONSTANTINE. (RESTORED BY D'ESPOUY)

roof. A unique addition was that of the great apses at either end. The Basilica Æmilia, which forms a pendant to the Basilica Julia by its position in the Forum, and owes its existing form to much the same time, seems to show the contrary plan of a narrow and deep hall, turning its flank to the Forum, and having its galleries along two sides only. The same variety could be traced through the provincial examples.

The basilica of Maxentius. Unique in its structure among the basilicas was one in the Sacred Way begun by Maxentius and completed by Constantine (Figs. 44 [5] and 45). A vault was substituted for the wooden roof over the nave, the vaulting system being taken over almost intact from its earliest representatives, the great halls of the baths in which we shall study it. There are but three bays in a length of nearly two hundred feet, and the clear span of the nave is over seventy-five feet. In spite of the considerable modifications necessary in the form of the points of support and of the clerestory, the essential scheme of the basilica is recognizable. It belonged originally to the Greek type, with aisles along two sides only, the entrance on one of the narrow ends, and an apse opposite. As completed by Constantine it had a second entrance in the center of the broad side toward the Forum, and a second apse opposite this, producing a hybrid plan. In the adoption of the fire-proof and permanent methods of covering which had been developed in other classes of buildings the Basilica of Maxentius marks a notable progress, prophetic in many ways of the development of the Christian basilica into the mediæval vaulted church.

Theaters. The preconditions of the development of the Roman theater, in its differences from the Greek theater, are to be found in the native Italic drama and the method of its presentation in early Rome. As the audience at first stood on level ground during the performance, the stage had to be of a moderate height. As there was no chorus there was no necessity for an open space or orchestra before the stage. The first inclosed theaters were of wood, doubtless rectangular, with seats parallel to the stage and soon arranged in ascending tiers (Fig. 46). Stage and auditorium were easily brought into architectural unity and under a single roof. No great change in principle was involved in the substitution, within the rectangular building, of segmental or circular seats, as seen in the small theater at Pompeii, built soon after 80 B.C., under the influence of the existing Hellenistic theater close by. As the dimensions increased, an awning or velarium had to be substituted for a wooden roof, but the walls of the building remained of equal height, and the one at the rear of the stage, the *scænæ frons*, decorated with columns in imitation of the background of the Greek stage, had to be treated in two or three stories. This was the state of the Roman theater when, just before the end of the republic, a single building established the final form.

Stone theaters in Rome. The theater of Pompey, the first stone theater in Rome, built in 55 B.C., is stated to have followed the model of the theater at Mitylene. The features derived from this prototype, however, can have been merely

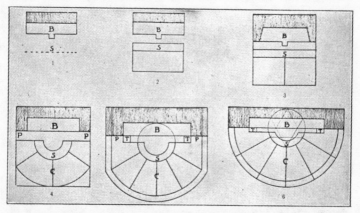

FIG. 46—SCHEMATIC REPRESENTATION OF THE DEVELOPMENT OF THE ROMAN THEATER. (FIECHTER)

(B) Stage   (S) Senatorial seats   (C) Cavea   (P) Passages   (T) Tribunalia

the general idea of the building, with a vast colonnaded court for promenading, and, especially, the dominating circular form of the auditorium. With this came the orchestra, which, however, was reduced as much as possible, to a semicircle. The Roman element retained was the close structural union of the auditorium with the stage, the walls of which doubtless rose to the full height of the seats. A necessary prerequisite for the execution of the auditorium in stone, on a plain, was the development of the Roman technique of vaulting, by which the seats were supported far above the ground, and by which radial openings were left for passages and stairs to the upper ranges. For the façade the scheme of the Tabularium, with arches and columnar decoration, was adopted, as later in the Colosseum (Fig. 40). Thus whereas in Greece orchestra and circle of seats were the primitive elements and the stage with its accessory buildings was a later development, in Rome the stage was the original component, and the orchestra and circular auditorium were additions taken over from Greece. The product of the synthesis, as exemplified in the three great theaters of the city of Rome—those of Pompey, Marcellus, and Balbus—or in the theater at Ostia (Fig. 47), was a creation which had its own merits, not only in adaptation

FIG. 47—OSTIA. THE THEATER. (RESTORED BY ANDRE)

to the requirements of the Roman drama, but in unity of design and splendor of external and internal effect.

Theaters in the provinces. In the provinces the same scheme was repeated, although less ample means usually resulted in the use of convenient hillsides to support at least a part of the auditorium, as at Verona, and at Orange in France. In most of the eastern examples the looseness of connection in plan persisted in spite of the adoption of a high stage background. At Aspendos in Asia Minor, however, the interior shows the full Roman type, with one of the richest developments of the *scænæ frons.* In contrast to most Augustan and later western stage backgrounds, which show an ever greater elaboration of three great niches enframing the doors, this shows the tendency of the east to multiply openings and columnar subdivisions while retaining the flat wall surface.   In both cases the *scænæ frons* was no longer a resultant, a means, but an end in itself, resulting only remotely from suggestions from the drama, treated rather in accordance with the general decorative conceptions of imperial architecture.

Amphitheaters.. Among the Romans the drama was secondary to the more exciting amusement of gladiatorial combats, introduced from Campania in the third century and held at first in the forum or the circus.   In the provision of special architectural arrangements for such contests Rome was also behind Campania, for in Pompeii an elliptical arena with stepped seats was begun soon after 80 B.C., whereas in Rome it was not until 58 B.C. that two theater auditoria of wood, facing each other, were built to form the first amphitheater of the city.   The games of Cæsar were still celebrated within wooden stands, and it was not until the time of Augustus, 29 B.C., that Rome had its amphitheater in stone.   Although in Pompeii, however, the arena was largely excavated in the earth, and the rear seats were supported on solid masonry, in Rome the amphitheater was built up from the plain like the theaters, with a richly arcaded exterior.

The Colosseum.   The Flavian amphitheater, known as the Colosseum, which succeeded that of Augustus in the years 70–82 A.D., shows this arrangement in its final and most splendid form (Fig. 40).   About the elliptical arena rose three successive tiers of seats separated by high parapets, and crowned, very probably, by an encircling colonnade.   On the exterior were, first, three stories of open arcades decorated with the arch order, Doric, Ionic, and Corinthian.   A fourth-story wall, perhaps originally of wood, was treated with Corinthian pilasters.   Corbels near the top carried wooden masts which probably supported the immense velarium, and formed the necessary visual crown for the uniformly repeated orders below.   The regular spacing of the tiers, diminishing rhythmically in perspective, and the unbroken sweep of the cornices about such a vast surface, gave an unequaled majesty and dignity, which justified the identification of the Colosseum with the power of Rome itself.   Structurally the triumph was no less remarkable.   The elliptical plan required every one of the radial passages and every foot of the concentric vaults to differ from its neighbors, yet much was executed in stone, accurately cut to the most difficult geometrical shapes.   In the third arcade, where practical necessities prevented the carrying of a concentric barrel vault above the arches of the façade, as had been done in the previous stories, the vault was dropped to the same level as the arches and penetrated by continuations of them.   The resulting form. the groined vault, here appearing for the first time in Italy, had general advantages which were soon manifest, in that it required for its support, not a continuous massive abutment, but isolated piers on which the thrusts were concentrated.   After the form of the amphitheater in the capital, others were erected in the Italian and provincial cities, notable remains existing at Verona, Nîmes, Arles, and many other places.   These had seats for twenty to twenty-five thousand spectators, while the greatest, in Rome and Campania, had a capacity of twice that number.

Circuses.   Mightier still were the circuses for chariot-racing, the oldest of Roman amusements, first held in the valley between the Palatine and the Aventine hills, where in the course of years was built the Circus Maximus, with seats ultimately for two hundred thousand spectators.   The course was long and narrow, with a sharp turn like that of the Greek stadion, to the seating arrangements of which those of the circus also conformed.   Down the center of the course was the barrier, or *spina*, separating the stretches, adorned with obelisks and monuments; at the end opposite the turn were the starting arrangements, with individual cells for each chariot, in a segment focussing on the first corner.   The exterior was on a system like that of the theaters and amphitheaters.

Baths and thermæ.   The Roman bathing establishments progressed from the simplest utilitarian structures to luxurious institutions, offering facilities not only for bathing and physical exercise, but for the social intercourse of a modern café or club.   Examples from the later days of the republic at Pompeii show, at a small scale, the typical complement of rooms and their arrangement.   A court, or palæstra, for exercise was accompanied by a series of rooms in which different temperatures were maintained: the *frigidarium*, the *tepidarium*, the *caldarium*. The frigidarium contained the cold plunge bath, the caldarium the hot baths, the tepidarium served to lessen the shock in passing from one to the other and

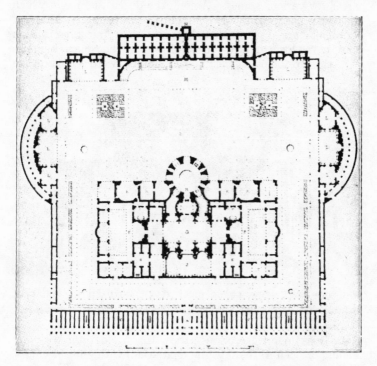

FIG. 48—ROME. THERMÆ OF CARACALLA. PLAN. (RESTORED BY BLOUET)

(A) Entrance
(B, B) Porticoes
(C, C) Private baths?
(D, D) Vestibules
(E, E) Apodyteria
(F, F) Peristyles
(G) Tepidarium
(H) Caldarium
(J) Frigidarium
(L, L) Halls for exercise
(M) Stadium
(N) Reservoirs and aqueduct

also might contain basins for those who found the cold bath too severe. A dressing-room—the *apodyterium*—and a steam bath—the *laconicum*—were further desirable features. In baths intended for both men and women two suites of these rooms were provided, their caldaria abutting near the furnace, with the other rooms successively more distant from it.

The thermæ of Caracalla, 217 A.D. In the thermæ of imperial times, initiated by Agrippa, all these features were magnified to enormous scale and combined with those of the Greek gymnasium.   The bathing establishments proper were surrounded by vast inclosures with shaded walks, exedræ, and areas for various games.   Among the dozen thermæ in which successive emperors tried to outdo one another, those of Caracalla are distinguished both by their fair preservation and by the logic and the formal interest of their plan (Fig. 48). The three principal elements, each unique, were placed on the

FIG. 49—ROME.   THERMÆ OF DIOCLETIAN.   TEPIDARIUM.   (RESTORED BY PAULIN)

main axis in an ascending series, the frigidarium with flat ceiling or open to the sky, the tepidarium with groined vaults, the caldarium with a dome and niches like those of the Pantheon.   To left and right were vestibules and dressing-rooms, with two great peristylar palæstras surrounded by minor rooms, still of large size.   The tepidarium, as the room of medium temperature, was seized on as the key to the circulation of people, and its axis was taken as the principal transverse line of the plan, prolonged through the peristyles and their exedræ.   Separate access to the courts was provided from both front and side, and the rooms of the rear were opened freely to the gardens by means of colonnades.   The gardens themselves had their axes emphasized by the stands opposite

the projecting caldarium, and by subordinate exedræ. The
variety of form of the units and the rich interplay of the axes
have been an inspiration for the complex and elaborate plans
of modern t:mes.

The tepidarium. Most fruitful for later developments was
the typical form of the tepidarium, repeated in the baths of
Diocletian (Fig. 49) for the caldarium as well.   Its length was
divided into three bays marked by enormous columns, each
with a fragment of entablature which served as impost for
the groined vaults.   These had the form of a longitudinal
cylinder intersected by three transverse cylinders, spaced a
short distance apart and projecting slightly beyond the intersections.   The square mass of masonry between the diagonally descending groins rested on the entablatures of the columns.   The entire outward thrust of the vaults, concentrated
on these points, was sustained by the deep transverse walls
behind them, which were carried up as visible buttresses high
above the roofs of the neighboring rooms.   These struck in
at the height of the spring of the vaults, leaving the semicircular spaces beneath the crown free for great clerestory
windows in each bay and at the ends.   The spaces between the
buttress walls were filled with barrel-vaulted niches, across
which were carried screens of relatively smaller columns which
emphasized the great scale of the main order.   As in the
Pantheon the vaults were richly coffered, the walls incrusted
with marble.

Aqueducts. Bridges. The aqueducts which furnished the
water supply necessary for the baths and for the general use
of a Roman city were for the most part not on a pressure system, but were carried into the city at a high level after being
brought with a gradual fall from elevated sources.   For a city
in the midst of a plain, like the metropolis, this necessitated
the support of a great length of the water channel at a considerable height above the ground.   The uniform ranges of
arches on tall piers, by which this necessity was met, show
construction in stone or concrete devoid of every extraneous
ornament, yet impressive by the ruggedness of the material
and the straightforwardness with which constructive methods
are confessed.   Where the aqueduct had to be carried across
a deep valley there was an added interest due to the varied size

of the arches which frankly took advantage of the best footing. The most famous instance is the Pont du Gard at Nîmes (Fig. 50), where there are three ranges of arches one above another, the whole a sixth of a mile long and over a hundred and fifty feet above the stream in the valley. Of the heavy voussoired arches of stone in the two lower ranges, the pair over the river are distinguished by a visibly greater width than the others, those next the slopes by a corresponding reduction.

FIG. 50—NIMES.   THE "PONT DU GARD"

The imposts are placed freely at whatever heights the spans demanded. The upper range of uniform smaller arches leads up to the quiet cadence of the sky-line, like Doric triglyphs intermediate between columns and cornice. Much the same problems as in the aqueducts recur in the highway bridges, and the same division of types recurs. The bridges over wide rivers with low banks have a uniform series of arches, sometimes with the piers lightened by minor arches supporting the roadway, as in the Pons Mulvius at Rome; those over deep ravines have a single arch or several of sharply graded size, as at Narni. The ends of the principal pier might be decorated with a monumental arch or a small shrine.

Monuments: the column; the trophy. The desire of the Romans for military glorification early caused them to appropriate the Greek votive column for monumental use. To commemorate a naval victory, Duilius, in 260 B.C., erected a column decorated with the prows of captured ships, a rostral column, as it was called. The greatest of the columnar monuments were those of Trajan and of Marcus Aurelius and Faustina, each consisting of a marble Doric shaft on a square sculptured pedestal. They carried, at a height of over one hundred feet, gilded statues of their founders, and were decorated with continuous spiral reliefs celebrating their campaigns. From the Greeks also came the custom of erecting on the battlefield a trophy of victory, composed of armor and weapons, or imitated from them in stone. The possibility of a further monumental development of the trophy lay in its pedestal, which was elaborated to an even greater extent than in the Hellenistic examples. In the trophy of Augustus, near Monaco, a circular peristyle in two stories on a tall square basement, and with a steep conical roof, supports the trophy proper at a great height.

The arch. A more characteristically native monumental type was the commemorative or "triumphal" arch, originally of temporary character and perishable materials, erected to welcome a returning victor as he passed through Rome in triumphal procession. In the imperial period such arches, made permanent in stone, were used for various commemorative purposes, in all parts of the empire. The earliest examples, from the time of Augustus, show the arch framed, as in the Tabularium and the theaters, by two columns and an entablature, perhaps with a pediment. In any case there was a pedestal or attic above, serving as a support for statues. Soon a second column was added on either side of the original pair, inclosing a rectangular field—the classic instance being the Arch of Titus in Rome (Fig. 51). The columnar apparatus, here frankly decorative, is handled with the greatest mastery of form. Emphasis is given the central opening by the projecting architrave, uniting the inner columns and casting a deep shadow over the relief sculpture in the triangular spandrels below. The silhouette is enriched by the breaking of the entablature about the corner columns, while they are united with their neighbors by the simple pedestal which quiets the variety above and rests firmly on the earth. As the necessary completion above, one must imagine the quadriga, a bronze chariot with four horses and sculptured figures. A further development of the monumental arch was the widening of the side bays and the insertion of subordinate arches in them, as in the Arch of Domitian, near the Colosseum, later appropriated by Constantine. Here pedestal and entablature

FIG. 51—THE ARCH OF TITUS

break about all four columns, and the unity depends on the rhythmical symmetry of the arches. Later, and in the provinces, the designers of arches sought to exhaust the possibilities of combination of the arch and column.

Gates. The motives of the triumphal arch were also carried over to the city gates, which had often in the days of the Roman peace rather a symbolical than a military significance. Even a gate which retained its fortified character, like the Porta Nigra in Trier on the German frontier, was given a monumental expression by columnar adornment (Fig. 52).

The main openings and the windows of towers and galleries are enframed as in the Colosseum, but with greater sternness and sobriety.

Grave monuments. The same instinct that created the commemorative columns and arches shows itself in the grave

FIG. 52—TRIER. PORTA NIGRA

monuments, which in imperial times took on a magnificence even greater than in Hellenistic Greece. Both burial and incineration were practised, and richly decorated urns and sarcophagi were employed. These were but secondary in many cases, however, to large constructions containing the tomb chamber, and taking the most varied forms. Patrons and artists drew their suggestions from the tombs of every people with whom the Romans had come in contact—the Asiatic and Etruscan tumulus, the Egyptian pyramid, the Greek peristylar monument and exedra, the temple, both

rectangular and circular.   All these appeared in 1ich array
lining the streets which led across the Campagna from
the gates of the city.   Only in special cases, such as
those of the emperors, was interment within the walls
permitted.

The tumulus type.   It was the tumulus, the primitive mound
of earth, girt at the base by a circular wall of stone, which

FIG. 53—ROME.   MAUSOLEUM OF HADRIAN.   (RESTORED BY VAUDREMER)

was selected by Augustus for his mausoleum, erected on the
Campus Martius in 28-26 B.C.   In this and other Roman
examples, however, the cylindrical substructure is developed
into the principal member, and itself raised on a massive square
pedestal after the manner of the Hellenistic circular monuments.   The mausoleum of Augustus had a marble drum of
three hundred feet diameter, bearing a cone of earth planted
with cypress trees and crowned with a colossal statue of the
emperor.   Even more splendid was the mausoleum of Hadrian
(Fig. 53), which still subsists in the Castle of Sant' Angelo.

Its wall was decorated with an order, its cone was of marble steps surmounted by a quadriga.

The temple type. In the erection of tombs of temple form the rectangular type was less employed than the circular. The most elaborate was the mausoleum of Diocletian in his palace at Spalato, about 300 A.D., the domed interior richly membered with superposed columns, the octagonal exterior with a peristyle and a projecting portico. As in other tombs of this class, the cella was used for memorial services, the sarcophagus was deposited in a second chamber below. A notable step was taken in the tomb of Constantia, the daughter of Constantine the Great, who died in 354. The wall on which the dome rests is broken through, and instead of the arched niches there are deep arches supported on pairs of columns united in the thickness of the wall by an entablature. The central space is surrounded by a continuous aisle, the clerestory of the basilica is carried over into a circular building, creating new spatial effects of which Christian architecture was to make great use (Fig. 71).

Domestic architecture. The Roman town house may best be studied at Pompeii, where the débris of the eruption of Vesuvius, 79 A.D., has preserved almost intact a great number of dwellings of every class, ranging over a period of three hundred years. The type of plan was already essentially fixed in the second century B.C., and varied less with time than with the means of the owner and the exigencies of the site. The poorer folk, many of whom in Rome were crowded in high tenements, here lived over their shops along the street, or had a small atrium and a couple of rooms of their own. The middle class had still to content themselves with the arrangements which served for the best in the earlier days of the republic—an atrium and surrounding rooms with a small walled garden at the rear. The entrance was by a narrow passage between rented shops. The atrium was a large oblong room with a roof sloping inward to a central opening, generally of the Tuscan type, supported on beams from wall to wall. Primitively this had been the principal living-room, containing the hearth, the smoke of which escaped through a small opening in the roof. With the transition to urban conditions the size of the opening was increased to light the surrounding rooms, with the result that more sheltered living-rooms had to be provided. To left and right of the atrium were small sleeping-rooms, *cubiculæ*, opening from it. Behind these, forming lateral extensions of the atrium, were two alcoves or *alæ*, put to various uses, survivals perhaps of the day when the house stood isolated, and light could be introduced from the sides. At the rear was the *tablinum*, the reception-room, used also in smaller houses as a family living-room. A second story, with minor rooms, was sometimes added.

Larger houses. In the houses of a wealthier class not only was the atrium enlarged, but the entire apparatus of a Hellenistic house on the Delian model, with peristyle, exedræ, and *triclinium*, or dining-room with three couches, was added to the rear. Four columns were often added at the corners of the atrium opening, creating the tetrastyle type of which Vitruvius speaks, or even more than four, making the room like a Greek court, as appears in the name, Corinthian atrium, then applied to it. The family came more to leave the original atrium to clients and visitors, and to withdraw to the rooms surrounding the peristyle, which were supplemented perhaps by a second atrium, beside the first, about which the domestic apartments were grouped. The most elaborate houses filled an entire block, with a more extensive garden behind the

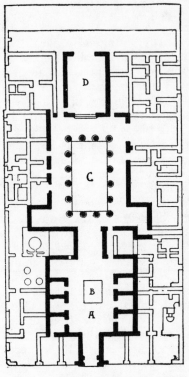

FIG. 54—POMPEII. HOUSE OF PANSA.
PLAN

(A) Atrium   (C) Peristyle
(B) Impluvium   (D) Œcus

peristyle. Such a one, showing a high development of the Pompeian house in differentiation of functions and guarding of privacy, is the so-called House of Pansa (Fig. 54).

Decoration of houses. To the exterior the houses turned a blank, plastered wall, with few small windows, perhaps a richer door frame. The interior walls, on the other hand, where they could not be of costly marbles, were richly painted, at first in imitation of these, later with mythological scenes, in a setting of attenuated architectural forms which were suggested in the first instance by the architectural decorations of the stage.

Villas. In more intimate relation to the landscape were the villas on the outskirts of the city, with terraced courtyards, gardens, and orchards. Others, less formal, served as retreats in the country or by the seaside. The larger villas went far beyond the satisfaction of practical needs, with luxurious provision for dining, bathing, exercise, and amusement. Especially was this true of the imperial villas, of which the villa of Hadrian at Tivoli gives the best idea (Fig. 55). It included, besides the living quarters and festal suites; reproductions of the most famous buildings of Greece and of the Orient, capriciously strewn over a picturesque topography. There were two theaters, libraries, a stadium, thermæ, a so-called academy, and a long canal, bordered by porticoes and terminated by a great niche, in imitation of Canopus, a suburb of Alexandria. The imitations seem to have been less literal than suggestive, however, as all was executed in Roman technique of brick and concrete and designed with a facility in the combination of vaults and the composition of plans which is purely Roman.

The palaces of the Cæsars. The palaces of the emperors in Rome, established on the Palatine Hill (Fig. 56), owe less to the Roman house than to the palaces of eastern capitals such as Alexandria, Antioch, and Pergamon. Begun by Augustus, they were extended by Tiberius and many later emperors, especially Domitian, who built the great series of state apartments in the center. Caligula sought to connect the Palatine with the Capitol by a bridge, to secure easier access to the temple of Jupiter Capitolinus; Nero united the imperial gardens on the Esquiline with the Palatine by building in the

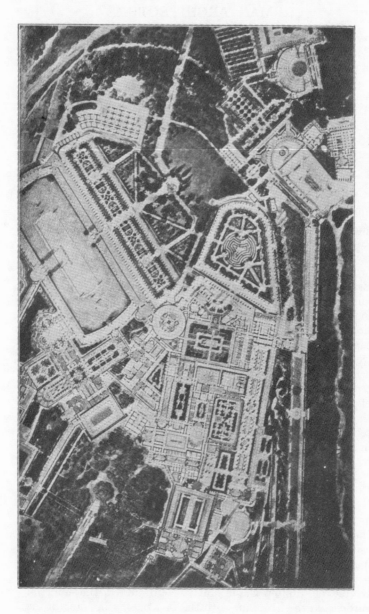

FIG. 55—TIVOLI. VILLA OF HADRIAN. (RESTORED BY G. S. KOYL)

intervening valley, where the Colosseum later stood, his Golden House with its luxurious park. Though these extensions were not permanent, the Palatine itself was covered with magnificent buildings, including several temples. The state

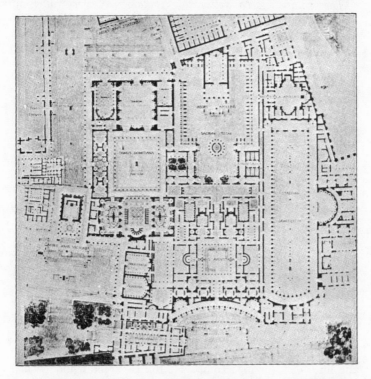

FIG. 56—ROME. PALACES OF THE CÆSARS. PLAN. (RESTORED BY DEGLANE)

apartments formed an oblong block fronted with a long colonnade toward the central area. In the center of the façade was the audience-room, having a barrel vault a hundred feet in span, the walls richly adorned with columns and niches. To right and left were the basilica or imperial tribunal, the lararium or private chapel. Behind this suite lay a square peristyle, at the rear a triclinium, opening into supplementary rooms. The private apartments of the emperor occupied another block centering on a court; beyond them was the so-called Stadium, an inclosed garden surrounded by porticoes and dominated by a great vaulted exedra.

The palace of Diocletian at Spalato. A very different arrangement is that of the Palace of Diocletian (Fig. 57) at Spalato in Dalmatia, on the shores of the Adriatic, to which the emperor retired in 305 on laying down his authority. The

FIG. 57—SPALATO. PALACE OF DIOCLETIAN. (RESTORED BY HEBRARD)

security of the empire was no longer certain, the palace followed the lines of a fortified camp. It forms a rectangular walled inclosure quartered by two colonnaded streets at right angles, with gates and towers at the middle points of the landward sides. Along the seaward face runs a long colonnade behind which are the imperial apartments, also reached from a monumental vestibule at the head of the longitudinal street. Next them, fronting each other in balancing inclosures which filled the remainder of this half of the palace, are a temple, serving as the imperial chapel, and the mausoleum for the emperor. Beyond the transverse streets are quarters for service and for the guards; around the outer walls are store-chambers, reached from a passage which makes the circuit. In the forms of detail eastern influence is seen, and the developments of late Roman architecture in new relations of arch and column appear most clearly (Fig. 59).

Ensembles, town planning. The Romans of imperial times were not satisfied even with the extended and complex symmetry which they had given to individual units such as the palaces, thermæ, and fora, but sought to organize their relations to one another and to give the whole city a coherent plan. Rome as a whole was too vast and too consecrated for this, but in certain portions a unification was effected. Thus a splendid façade, ingeniously planned, was built before the irregular buildings of the Palatine, to give them a symmetrical aspect from the Circus Maximus. More fundamental was the consistent treatment of the island in the Tiber, to suggest a vast galley, with prow and stern. Its buildings were disposed about a series of connected courts, artfully devised to mask the actual irregularity of the plan. On a far greater scale were the harbor works and warehouses of Ostia, at the mouth of the Tiber, of which the hexagonal Port of Trajan surrounded by uniform buildings was the most systematic. Newly founded towns, especially those of a semi-military character like Augusta Prætoria (Aosta), in the foothills of the Alps, and Thamugadi (Timgad) in Africa were laid out in rectangular form bisected by the principal streets with others parallel to them. They marked a formal progress over Hellenistic towns in the regularity of their outline as well as of their minor subdivisions.

Individual forms. Although the individual forms of Roman architecture fall behind their combinations in interest, as behind the forms of the Greeks in originality, they were by no means slavish imitations. In many instances a further formal development took place, in others, new structural functions produced new or modified expressions. For purely utilitarian purposes, post, lintel, and arch were used without ornament in a manner as simple and as effective as the primitive system of the waiting-hall of the pyramid of Khafre in Egypt. In Roman Africa and Syria are many instances of square monolithic piers with square lintels, repeated perhaps in several stories, which, like the arches of the aqueducts, have no other treatment than the constructive membering.

Walls, doors, windows. The problems of a richer expression for the wall and for the post and lintel had already been solved in an exemplary way by the Greeks, whose solutions were too accessible and too authoritative to be ignored. In these features the innovations of the Romans were relatively minor. They made more frequent employment of grooved or rusticated joints, of cap and base moldings, following the Hellenistic tendencies. The profiles of their moldings were less studied and subtle, conforming more closely to arcs of circles than to elliptical arcs and other conic sections. Doors and windows followed late Greek examples in having a molded architrave of stone. A frieze and cornice were often added, sometimes elaborated by the addition of curved brackets or consoles, or of a pediment. For windows and niches an even richer treatment was devised, the tabernacle of two free standing columns with an entablature and pediment—triangular or segmental— best seen in the interior of the Pantheon (Fig. 42).

The Doric order. The Doric order, whether in its Greek or its Tuscan form, was little used in imperial times, except in the lower stories of buildings with superposed orders, where its relative massiveness still gave it the preference. An occasional example shows the echinus of the capital ornamented with egg and dart and the other members multiplied and enriched. The difficulties created by the corner triglyph were overcome in imperial times by placing it on the axis of the column in spite of its leaving a fragment of metope beyond, thus sacrificing functional expression to formal regularity. In the amphitheaters, with their continuous unbroken sweep, this problem did not arise.

The Ionic order. The Ionic order followed the precedents of Hermogenes in having always a frieze, and a capital with relatively small volutes and a low connecting band, which in Roman examples finally lost all its curvature. The Attic base was preferred. The angular capital originated by Iktinos, with volutes on all four sides projecting diagonally, was frequently employed where the colonnade had corners to turn.

The Corinthian order. The Corinthian order was the one

which comported best with the love of magnificence which the imperial Romans shared with the Hellenistic monarchs, and was used almost exclusively in the later monuments. The scheme of capital generally preferred was that of the example from Epidaurus, with two alternating rows of eight leaves each, but the spirit of the execution was bolder, the leafage more luxuriant. Each building still furnished a problem for itself and showed its own design of capital. Among the many superb examples, that of the temple of Castor and Pollux in the Forum Romanum may be given as representative (Fig. 58). A second common type was that of the Temple of Vesta at Tivoli, with the upper leaves close down on the lower, and with a crinkled, parsley-like serration. A variant of the Corinthian was the so-called Composite capital in which the echinus and diagonal scrolls of an angular

FIG. 58—ROME. CORINTHIAN CAPITAL AND ENTABLATURE FROM THE TEMPLE OF CASTOR AND POLLUX. (RESTORED CAST IN THE METROPOLITAN MUSEUM)

Ionic capital were placed above the rows of leaves, as in the Arch of Titus. This attempt to secure still greater richness involved a sacrifice of the organic connection of scrolls and leafage in the original. In the Corinthian entablature the dentils became secondary to great brackets or modillions, sometimes treated as molded blocks, sometimes as scrolls decorated with leafage, as in the Temple of Castor and Pollux. In the temples at Baalbek there are consoles in the frieze as well. Entablature and capital alike took part in the stylistic developments of the imperial period—the passion for decoration of the Flavians, the puristic reaction under Hadrian and the Antonines. The temple of Antoninus and Faustina, 141 A.D., has neither modillions nor dentils.

Pilasters. The Roman counterpart of the anta was the pilaster, which, instead of being studiously distinguished from the column in width of side and profile of capital, was imitated directly from it. Late Hellenistic and republican buildings show the pilaster used not only to respond to the columns of a temple portico but to form a similar termination at the rear corners of the cella, and to continue the rhythm of the spacing between in the same manner that engaged columns were used. Pilasters were used also, instead of engaged columns, in various buildings of the empire where lack of means or a desire for less accentuation suggested the substitution.

The arch. In the formal elaboration of the arch and its combination with the column the Romans had new problems, the solution of which, as we have seen, occupied the whole course of their history. After the simple treatment of republican times in which a projecting molded course of stone was added at the outside of the voussoirs, the voussoirs themselves were molded to form an archivolt, a ring having a section like that of the columnar architrave. In a similar way the impost was given a form like a capital or bed molding, with members suited to the function of support, and the keystone was often treated as a console. The enframement of the arch by column and lintel, although characteristic of the central period of Roman art, was not the final scheme. In the Pantheon the entablature itself was used as the impost of an arch; at Palmyra it was bent into an archivolt spanning the wide central opening of a portico. In the thermæ a fragment of entablature served to lengthen the column and give a larger bearing for the springing of a vault; in Syria and at Spalato this fragment was reduced to a mere molded stilt-block, and finally omitted altogether, so that the arches came down directly on the heads of the columns (Fig. 59). The column thus gradually attained a relation with the arch as structural as its original relation with the lintel.

Wall membering. The relation of the columnar form to wall membering proceeded in the opposite direction from the common starting-point; the contradiction of expressions was reconciled by removing every structural suggestion and leaving the decoration undisguised. In the arch of Domitian (Constantine) and in the Forum Transitorium, begun by

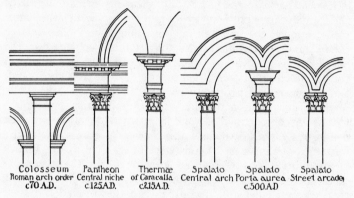

Colosseum   Pantheon   Thermæ   Spalato   Spalato   Spalato
Roman arch order Central niche of Caracalla Central arch Porta aurea Street arcade
c.70 A.D.   c.125 A.D.   c.215 A.D.   c.300 A.D.

FIG. 59—DEVELOPMENT IN THE RELATIONS OF ARCH AND COLUMN IN ROMAN ARCHITECTURE

Domitian, the columns, instead of being engaged against the wall, stand free in front of it, supporting merely an end of entablature and an attic or a statue over it. In the free composition of the stage backgrounds this tendency went still further; the whole apparatus of colonnettes and tabernacles was obviously a mere decorative application. Tabernacle work of this sort came more and more to supersede, for the enrichment of façades, the treatment with engaged columns of the full height of the wall. In the north gate at Spalato, finally, the niches and colonnettes are no longer carried down to the ground, but are supported merely on projecting brackets or corbels. Meanwhile other forces had been at work. The fondness for Greek art in the second century led to the omission of any columnar subdivision of the wall in certain cases. The temple of Antoninus and Faustina, although prostyle, has pilasters only at the corners of the cella. The use of brick and concrete, plastered over with stucco, in vast constructions such as the thermæ and the Villa of Hadrian, encouraged the limitation of membering to the openings, where columns and pilasters fulfilled their original functions.   The tendency was thus, by various paths, toward frankness of constructive expression, in spite of conditions far more complex than those in which the Greeks had achieved their early structural purism.

Elements of plan and space.   For elements of plan and space the Romans drew both on Greece and on the Orient; they later made important contributions of their own.   The temple cella and the basilica with longitudinal colonnades, the exterior peristyle, were of Greek origin; the peristylar hall and court, the clerestory, of Oriental origin.   On the other hand, the forms suggested by vault construction, the apse, the circle, or polygon, with abutting niches, the groin-vaulted rectangle with side compartments, were Roman in development.   In one or two cases a dome was placed over a square room, in the form of a circumscribed hemisphere intersected by the planes of the four walls in the manner later familiar in the Byzantine domical vaults.   The forms of vaults were ordinarily kept rigidlv geometrical, and, in consequence, they often determined the precise proportions of the rooms below.   Thus with groined vaults, in which cylindrical surfaces were employed, the line of intersection fell in a plane only when the two cylinders were of equal diameter.   As a result the Romans employed them by preference only over square bays.   The vaults first made possible a plastic handling of interior space, in which wall and ceiling blend in coherent unity, and adjacent elements open freely into one another.   It was characteristic of the Romans to emphasize strongly the predominance of the central element of a group, the surrounding units being rather shallow bays than long arms, having themselves but minor subdivisions.   A favorite treatment was with niches alternately square and semicircular in plan.

Architectural treatment of vaults.   The vaulted interior involved new problems in detail and exterior treatment as well as in construction.   The vault, like the arch, usually received an impost which was either a full entablature, supported by an order which enriched the wall below, or else a string course composed somewhat on the lines of a cornice. The vaulting surfaces themselves were generally unbroken by any projecting ribs, having merely a recessed pattern of coffers (Fig. 42). Externally, barrel vaults were generally covered by gable roofs. Groined vaults at large scale, as in the tepidaria, had lateral gables over each bay, intersecting the main longitudinal roof and producing valleys by which the rain was discharged over each pier. The tendency was increasingly to rest the tiles of the roofs directly on the massive shell of the vaults, fashioned in inclined planes to receive them. In the case of large domes, like that of the Pantheon, the curved form was retained on the exterior, the upper portion being a saucer-like zone girded by several monumental steps, which carried the visual support to the high exterior wall.

Construction in brick and concrete. For the vast undertakings at the capital, and in other parts of the empire where stone was not rendered by natural conditions the inevitable building material, methods of construction were developed which lent themselves admirably to the scale of operations and to the character of the labor supply. A building of the extent of the thermæ of Caracalla could not be erected wholly by skilled craftsmen as, relatively, the Parthenon had been, nor could it be built wholly of marble. The methods used in the mass of the construction had to be adapted to large forces of slaves and unskilled men, directed by trained superintendents. These conditions were happily fulfilled by the employment of brick, with mortar often so thick as to produce practically a concrete, or of concrete in which the cement itself was the essential element, binding an aggregate of loose and small materials into a monolith. The volcanic pozzolana furnished a cement which left nothing to be desired in strength and quickness of setting.

Wall construction. The Roman bricks were very large, usually square, about a foot on a side, but often triangular, to secure a better bond between face and backing. In some walls the bricks were left to form the final exterior surface, but more usually they were covered with a coating of stucco or a veneer of marble slabs. Walls of concrete were constructed by depositing or pouring the mixture, in a semi-liquid state, into temporary forms built of wood, which were devised so that as much as possible of the lumber could be used repeatedly. They were usually faced with brick or stone fragments in some form, and then generally coated or veneered in the same manner as brick walls.   The kinds of facing received special names according to the pattern produced on the surface— *opus reticulatum* for small squares of stone standing on their corners in diagonal lines, *opus spicatum* for kernel-shaped fragments in herringbone pattern—while the general name of *opus incertum* was reserved for a treatment with fragments of no regular form.   Bonding courses of brick were often laid at intervals to tie the facings firmly to the body of the wall, and angles were sometimes reinforced with brick or stone in the form of quoins. or blocks of alternating length toothed into the mass.

Vault construction.   In the construction of vaults the use of small materials in thick mortar presents constructive advantages greater even than in the construction of walls, for it obviates greater difficulties in the individual shaping of the elements.   A vault of concrete alone, however, lacks any arching action until it has set, and bears with its full weight on the temporary wooden form or centering, which has to be correspondingly cumbersome and wasteful.   The Romans worked to avoid this by constructing first, over light centering, a framework of brick arches, with projections or cells to secure a good bond with the concrete, a great part of the weight of which was thus removed from the wooden supports (Fig. 60). In groined vaults of this sort ribs of brick reinforced the chief constructive lines; in domes they followed principally the elements of the surface.   Once the concrete had thoroughly hardened, of course, such ribs of brick had fulfilled their purpose and no longer served any special structural function, being merged in the mass of the vault.   Coffers were even cut through them without affecting stability.   A second principle was sometimes followed which did not demand even an unbroken surface in the centering, but required merely a light form of slats spaced openly.   Over these was laid a layer of flat tiles, touching each other only at their edges yet strongly cemented; over these another and perhaps another, forming a skin of no great thickness but of surprising strength (Fig. 61). This supported the concrete placed upon it until it had hardened, and formed a permanent interior facing to the vault.

Ornament. In their enrichment of moldings and surfaces the Romans followed, as in so many other matters, the tendencies initiated by the Asiatic Greeks. The moldings, like those of the Greek Ionic order, were carved in marble with decorative forms suggested by their profiles. The egg and dart and other familiar forms recur, made fuller and rounder in harmony with the moldings themselves, and more luxuriant

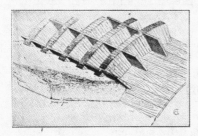 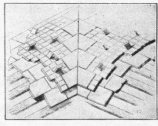

FIG. 60—ROMAN CELLULAR VAULT. FIG. 61—ROMAN LAMINATED
(CHOISY)   VAULT. (CHOISY)

in accordance with Roman taste. In place of the painted polychromy of the Greeks came a polychromy of richly colored marbles, especially in interiors, which was more sumptuous and had the advantage of permanence. Shafts of columns, pavements and walls, exhibited variegated and precious materials employed not only with mastery of pattern and color, but with discriminating avoidance of structural pretense. Dark and richly veined shafts were left unfluted to exhibit the beauty of their material. For the veneering of brick or concrete walls marble blocks were sawn thin to make the most of limited material, and large slabs were applied with a freedom of jointing and an absence of bond that gave no false suggestion of ashlar masonry.

Local variety. Although the official art of the capital was diffused through the empire in much the same way as the official Latin tongue, this did not preclude the existence of provincial varieties or dialects, or the maintenance in the more civilized East of a Greek tradition which held its own with Roman developments.

The West. Provence. Germany. In the West it was less

any survival of pre-existing styles than the influence of the available materials which resulted in special characteristics in certain localities, and these were naturally rather in matters of construction than in matters of form.   Thus in Provence, the Rhone valley region in the south of France, an abundance of fine limestone and an absence of clay gave rise to many technical expedients.   In the lower arcade of the amphitheater at Arles a flat ceiling of long slabs is substituted for the usual concentric barrel vault; in the upper arcade radial barrel vaults are supported on stone beams spanning the corridor. The barrel vaults, in this and other instances, do not have their stones bonded together lengthwise, but are made up of independent rings of voussoirs side by side, which could be erected one by one on a movable centering used over and over. In the so-called Baths of Diana at Nîmes the rings are not kept in a single cylindrical surface, but the alternate ones rest on those between, and could thus be laid on them afterward without any centering of their own.   In Germany the more severe climate led to a greater degree of inclosure and the adoption of devices for artificial heating.   The thermæ and the palace of Constantine at Trier are lacking in colonnaded openings to the exterior, and have double outer walls with exceptional facilities for circulating warm air in the cavities. Although late constructive developments in general were tending to require massive outer walls as a support for vaults, it is not fanciful to suppose in these instances an influence from climate also.

The East. Syria.   The East had itself furnished the originals for many Roman forms and types, and continued to contribute to them during the imperial period.   On the other hand certain arrangements of Roman origin, like the closed theater with its union of seats and stage, found their way eastward.   Besides buildings purely Greek, like many of the temples, and purely Roman, like the Odeion of Herodes Atticus in Athens, every degree of mixture appears, as in the Greek theaters to which Roman stages were added.   In Egypt the ancient native art still persisted for religious buildings, as in Hellenistic days.   A hotbed of eastern developments was Syria, in touch with the interior of Asia where a new artistic fermentation was beginning.   Of the cities which

FIG. 62—MOUSMIEH. PRÆTORIUM. (DE VOGUE)

reflected Hellenistic architecture, Palmyra, the flourishing caravan station of the oasis in the Syrian desert, still gives a vivid picture. The principal streets are lined from end to end with tall Corinthian columns, forming porticoes on either side with richly profiled arches at the intersections and termini. The details of the temples there and at Baalbek show the new spirit that, coming from the Orient and spreading westward, broke through the classical canons. At Palmyra the entablature springs as an arch over the wide central opening of the portico; at Baalbek the carving loses the projection and play of surface always characteristic of Greek and Græco-Roman ornament and tends to be incised below the plane of the surrounding surface—the background plane disappears. In other Syrian buildings, especially in the woodless Hauran district, the departures from the style of the capital are still more marked. The prætorium or guard-house at Mousmieh (Fig. 62) has vaults resting on columns with only a block, instead of a classic entablature, above them; the basilica at Chaqqua is roofed entirely with stone slabs resting on arches as devoid of extraneous adornment and as freely adapted to their constructive functions as those of the bridges and aqueducts.

Influence of Roman architecture. The wide diffusion of Roman architecture, its magnificent associations, and its flexibility in meeting new and complex problems makes it easy to understand the wide influence which it exercised, both on the peoples who immediately succeeded to the Roman possessions and on those who sought, many centuries later, to revive Roman culture. Under the Byzantine rulers of the East the empire still lived on, and its architecture had a direct continuance, though its forms were rapidly modified by forces already at work there. In the West the Christian monuments of the last emperors furnished the point of departure for the architecture of the Teutonic invaders, the indebtedness of which to Rome is well suggested by the name Romanesque.

PERIODS OF ROMAN ARCHITECTURE

All buildings are in the city of Rome unless otherwise stated.

I. Early republican period, to about 300 B.C.   Etruscan influence.
   First temple of Jupiter Capitolinus, dedication ascribed to
      510 B.C.
   Sack of Rome by the Gauls, 390 B.C.
   "Wall of Servius," c. 350.
   Cloaca Maxima, first built in fourth century B.C.
   "Arch of Augustus" at Perugia, fourth century.
   Aqueduct of Appius Claudius, 312 B.C.

II. Later republican period, about 300 B.C. to 50 B.C.   Greek
      influence.
   Conquest of Magna Græcia by 272, Sicily by 241; destruction
      of Corinth, 146; Province of Asia organized, 133 B.C.
   Rostral column of Duilius, 260 B.C.
   Basilica of Cato the Censor, 184 B.C.
   Basilica Aemilia
   Bridge of Æmilius, 179–142 B.C.
   Pons Mulvius, rebuilt 109 B.C., later restored.
   Porticoes of Forum at Pompeii, before 100 B.C.
   Temple of Hercules at Cori, soon after 100 B.C.
   Basilica at Pompeii, before 80 B.C.
   Small theater at Pompeii, 80 B.C.
   Amphitheater at Pompeii, after 80 B.C.
   Tabularium, 80–78 B.C.
   Temple of "Fortune Virilis." ⎫ Toward middle of the first
   Circular temple at Tivoli.   ⎭   century B.C.
   First amphitheater in Rome (of wood), 58 B.C.
   Theater of Pompey, 55 B.C.

III. Imperial period, about 50 B.C. to 350 A.D.   Oriental influence.
   Basilica Julia and Forum of Julius, dedicated (unfinished)
      46 B.C.; Temple of Julius, 42–29 B.C.
   Amphitheater of Statilius Taurus, 30–29 B.C.
   Augustus, 27 B.C.–14 A.D.
      Mausoleum of Augustus, 28–26 B.C.
      "Baths of Diana," Nîmes, 25 B.C.
      Theater of Marcellus, dedicated 11 B.C.
      Forum of Augustus and Temple of Mars the Avenger,
         20–2 B.C.
      "Maison Carrée," Nîmes, 4 A.D.
      Thermæ of Agrippa.
      Pont du Gard, Nîmes.

Nero, 54–68 A.D.
  Burning of Rome, 64 A.D.
  "Golden House" of Nero, 64 *ff*.
Flavian emperors (Vespasian, Titus, Domitian), 69–96 A.D.
    Greatest richness of detail.
  Colosseum, 70–82 A.D.
  Destruction of Pompeii and Herculaneum, 79 A.D.
  Temple of Vespasian, 80 A.D.
  Arch of Titus, dedicated 81 A.D.
  Palace of the Flavians on the Palatine.
  Arch of Domitian.
  Forum Transitorium, completed by Nerva, 98 A.D.
"Good emperors."
  Nerva, 96–98 A.D.
  Trajan, 98–117 A.D.
    Thamugadi (Timgad) founded 100 A.D.
    Forum of Trajan and Basilica Ulpia, dedicated 113 A.D.
    Column of Trajan, 113–117 A.D.
    Thermæ of Trajan.
    Port of Trajan at Ostia.
  Hadrian, 117–138 A.D.   Return to Hellenism in details.
    Pantheon, 120–124 A.D., modified 202 A.D.
    Mausoleum of Hadrian.
    Villa of Hadrian at Tivoli.
    Temple of Venus and Rome.
    Temple of Castor and Pollux.
  Antoninus Pius, 138–61 A.D.
    Temple of Antoninus and Faustina, 141 A.D.
    Buildings of Herodes Atticus in Greece, c. 140–160 A.D.
    Principal group at Baalbek.
  Marcus Aurelius, 161–80 A.D.
    Column of Marcus Aurelius.
Septimius Severus, 193–211 A.D.
  Arch of Severus.
Caracalla, 211–17 A.D.
  Thermæ of Caracalla.
Gallienus, 260–68 A.D.
  Porta Nigra, Trier, c. 260.
Aurelian, 270–75 A.D.
  Wall of Aurelian.
Diocletian, 284–305 A.D.
  Thermæ of Diocletian.
  Palace of Diocletian at Spalato.

Maxentius, 306–312 A.D.
  Basilica of Maxentius (Constantine).
Constantine, 306–337 A.D.
  Arch of Domitian rebuilt, 312 A.D.
  Christianity made the state religion, 330 A.D.
  Capital removed to Constantinople (Byzantium).
  Tomb of Constantia (died 354 A.D.).

BIBLIOGRAPHICAL NOTE

The most authoritative general account of Roman architecture is J. Durm's *Baukunst der Etrusker und Römer*, 2d ed., 1905 (*Handbuch der Architektur*, pt. II, vol. 1), which also supplies references to discussions of individual questions and monuments. Anderson and Spiers's *Architecture of Greece and Rome*, 2d ed., 1907, and F. Noack's *Baukunst des Altertums*, 1910, are richly illustrated, both arranged primarily by classes of buildings, as is R. Cagnat and V. Chapot's *Manuel d'archéologie romaine*, vol. 1, 1917. General works containing measured drawings of Roman buildings are A. Desgodetz's *Les édifices antiques de Rome*, first published 1682 and several times reissued; G. L. Taylor and E. Cresy's *The Architectural Antiquities of Rome*, 2 vols., 1821–22; *Restaurations des monuments antiques*, 8 vols., 1877–90; H. d'Espouy's *Fragments d'architecture antique*, 2 vols., 1896–1905; *Monuments antiques*, vols. 2 and 3, 1910–12.

Among studies of special types or problems may be mentioned G. Leroux's *Les origines de l'édifice hypostyle*, 1913 (for the basilicas); E. R. Fiechter's *Die baugeschichtliche Entwicklung des antiken Theaters*, 1914; A. Choisy's *L'art de bâtir chez les Romains*, 1873 (for constructive methods); P. Gusman's *L'art décoratif de Rome*, 1908; F. Haverfield's *Ancient Town Planning*, 1913. A. Mau's *Pompeii*, translated by F. W. Kelsey, 2d ed., 1902, is especially important for Roman domestic architecture and interior decoration.

The unique importance of the city of Rome and the wide geographical distribution of Roman architecture makes topographical works of special importance. Detailed lists of those published down to its date are contained in K. Sittl's *Archäologie der Kunst*, 1895 (*Handbuch der klassischen Altertums-Wissenschaft*, vol. 6). Recent works covering the city of Rome are H. Jordan and Chr. Hülsen's *Topographie der Stadt Rom*, 2 vols. in 4, 1871–1907 (the most authoritative work for the sections covered by the latest volume); and S. B. Platner's *Topography and Monuments of Ancient Rome*, 2d ed., 1911. T. Frank: *Roman Buildings of The Republic*, 1922, is the latest authority on the dates of these. The panorama published by J. Bühlmann and H. Wagner, *Das alte Rom*, 1892, gives a graphic idea of the city in the time of Constantine. For the other principal regions see A. L. Frothingham's *Roman Cities in Italy and Dalmatia*, 1910; T. A. Cook's *Old Provence*, 2 vols., 1905; Lancoronski's *Städte Pamphyliens und Pisidiens*, 2 vols., 1890–92; H. C. Butler's *Architecture in Northern Central Syria and the Djebel-Hauran*, 1903; A. Graham's *Roman Africa*, 1902; and S. Gsell's *Les monuments antiques de l'Algérie*, 2 vols., 1901.

Of the Roman treatises on architecture preserved from antiquity the most useful editions in English are Vitruvius's *Ten Books on Architecture*, translated by M. H. Morgan, 1914; and Frontinus's *Two Books on the Water Supply of the City of Rome*, translated, with explanatory chapters, by C. Herschel, 1899.

CHAPTER VI

EARLY CHRISTIAN ARCHITECTURE

The medieval point of view. As we approach the study of early Christian architecture, and indeed of all medieval architecture, we must note at the outset a change in the point of view of the designer and builder which strongly impresses the finished work. Medieval architecture, compared with earlier and later styles, represents the spontaneous expression of the artistic ideals of a community rather than the genius of an individual or a number of architects. This does not mean that the individual lost all importance, but that his importance varied more, and was never so great as in earlier and later periods. Moreover ecclesiastical architecture is of strongly predominant importance. Again, this does not mean that medieval secular architecture may be neglected, for at certain times and in certain places it rivals contemporary ecclesiastical architecture in interest, but on the whole the main interest of medieval architecture is in the ecclesiastical work, and the student is justified in devoting the major part of his time to the study of the churchly rather than the secular buildings of the Middle Ages.

Classification. Early Christian and Byzantine architecture. The earliest of what are generally classed as the medieval styles are the early Christian and the Byzantine, the former perhaps slightly antedating the latter. Historians have tended to make a sharp division between the two, and to treat them as distinct and independent movements. The early Christian, frequently also called the Christian-Roman, is regarded as the typical style of the early Christian Church; the Byzantine is considered a very different organic style, forming a link between classic architecture and the flexible vaulted styles of the Romanesque period. This classification,

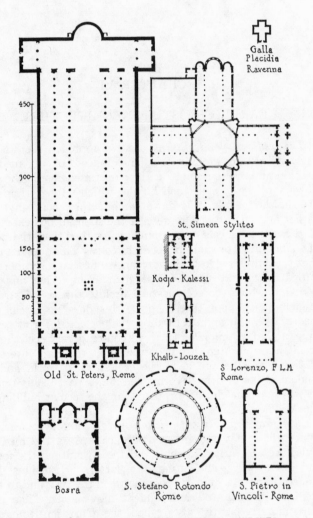

Galla
Placidia
Ravenna

St. Simeon Stylites

Kodja - Kalessi

Khalb - Louzeh

Old St. Peters, Rome

S Lorenzo, F L.M
Rome

Bosra

S. Stefano Rotondo
Rome

S. Pietro in
Vincoli - Rome

FIG. 63—PLANS OF EARLY CHRISTIAN CHURCHES

to obtain a superficial clearness, often engenders a profounder confusion. On account of it one is apt to forget that early Byzantine is *ipso facto* early Christian architecture, that its roots go back as far as those of the architecture of Christian Rome and indeed coincide with them, in short that the two styles are roughly contemporary, frequently interacting, and really somewhat variegated manifestations of the same artistic movement. These facts understood, however, the separate classification of the two styles will be found useful. Taken together the two might be called the medieval architecture of Rome and the East.

Lack of self-consciousness in the early Christian style. The absence of self-consciousness in medieval architecture was never more marked than in the early Christian style. No art was ever a more direct result of environment and need. During the period of gestation, so to speak, of Christian art the Roman Empire was hastening toward disintegration. In other words, classical authority was weakening. At the same time the old Latin stock was being transformed by fresh blood from the East and West into a race barbaric, perhaps, but susceptible to new ideas and ideals. From the West came energy; from the East thought. By far the most significant importation from the East was Christianity itself. At home in the East, at Rome it was at first only one of the weaker Eastern sects. The beginnings of its art, therefore, like the beginnings of its ritual, are wrapped in a baffling obscurity. To conquer, it had to struggle fiercely, and it learned to be not only ruthless but infinitely adaptable. These characteristics, impressed upon the early religion, became marked in the architecture, and never more so than after 330 when the Christian religion emerged triumphant. In the East, however, as one might expect, the struggle was less violent, and the architecture was therefore at once more spontaneous and more suited for subsequent development.

Weakening of classical authority. From the very beginning, both in East and West, the weakening of classical authority was of the highest importance. The Romans, in combining the trabeated architecture of Greece with the arch, had used both elements according to consciously formulated, if varying, canons. With the decline of the empire these canons became

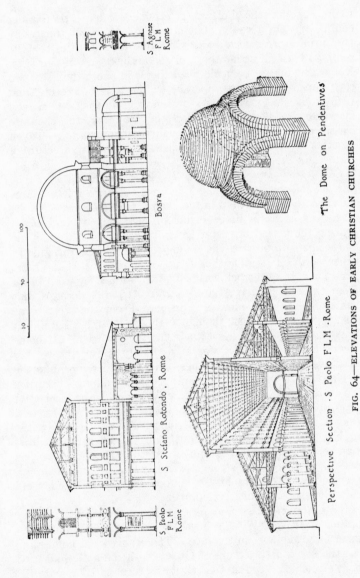

S Agnese F L M Rome

Bosra

The Dome on Pendentives

S Stefano Rotondo, Rome

S Paolo F L M Rome

Perspective Section · S Paolo F L M · Rome

FIG. 64—ELEVATIONS OF EARLY CHRISTIAN CHURCHES

first ignored, then forgotten. The result was decadence from the Roman point of view, but possibility of infinite development from the Christian. One of the first results was the free combination of the column and the arch, anticipated in late Roman imperial work. Set rules once removed, these elements could not only be subjected to many combinations, for example the springing of an arch direct from a capital without the intervening entablature, but could also be varied in scale, shape, and manner of use. From this the invention of new forms was a logical step, and flexibility, the keynote of medieval architecture, was obtained. The inevitability of this tendency in Christian architecture is proved by the same tendency in late classical work.

Basilican and central types. The way being paved by classical building of this sort, Christianity soon evolved a new architecture adapted to its needs and incidentally expressive of its ideals. In general the buildings thus produced may be divided into two classes, according to whether they were designed with reference to a longitudinal or a central vertical axis. The former we may call the basilican, the latter the central type. The basilica, with its long lines centering attention on the apsidal end of the church, the altar, the pulpits, the bishop's chair, and the chancel reserved for the clergy, is perfectly adapted for the ordinary ritual of the Christian church. Every detail of such a building, invented or borrowed, is a direct result of the needs of the service. Receiving its first development in Rome, the basilican ideal persisted in the West, and it is significant that from the liturgical point of view the finished Gothic cathedral is but a vastly complicated and organized ramification of the basilican type. The central type received its greatest development in the East. In plan it might be circular, polygonal, or in the form of a cross with equal arms. Buildings of such character concentrated attention on the central vertical axis and were best adapted for tombs, baptistries, and inclosures of sacred spots. Although not so well suited for the needs of the Christian liturgy as the basilican, this type was frequently designed with only a liturgical purpose in view, and at times, especially in the East, the two types were combined in a manner which makes classification difficult. Thus the domed basilicas of Anatolia partake of elements of both schemes, and Hagia Sophia at Constantinople itself might be classified under both heads.

Material and construction. In material and construction the Western buildings were the lighter. Brick was the usual material in Rome, and vaulting was confined to the apse. Nave and aisles were wooden-roofed. In the East vaulting was the rule, and the use of heavy cut stone, brick, and terra cotta was common, though the timber roof often appears as well. The Eastern buildings were more pretentious on the exterior than the Roman. The drab brick and the plain walls of the latter made the exteriors unobtrusive if not actually unsightly. The interiors, on the other hand, were lavishly decorated.

Conservatism and possibilities of development. The Roman type of building crystallized early, and gives the impression of a finished product. The Eastern type, perpetually changing,

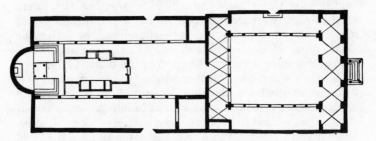

FIG. 65—ROME.   SAN CLEMENTE.   PLAN SHOWING THE ATRIUM

on the whole represents a step in the development to something new. From the Eastern style the Byzantine could develop. The Western, though offering suggestions of unlimited value to the Romanesque and Gothic styles, remained for centuries self-sufficient.

The Christian-Roman basilica. Turning to concrete examples, let us examine first the buildings in Rome. The ideal Christian-Roman basilica is easy to describe. In plan it was an oblong rectangle, divided into three or five aisles, and provided at the end with a semicircular apse. In the finished examples, such as old Saint Peter's and Saint Paul's

Outside-the-Walls, a rudimentary transept, or *bema*, slightly salient at the sides, was introduced between the rectangular building and the apse, giving the plan a form approximating that of the Latin cross. In front of the building was a covered vestibule, or "narthex," and before that a peristylar "atrium," open to the sky, with a font in the center. The atrium, an example of which may be seen at San Clemente (Fig. 65), was for penitents and the unbaptized, and it gave at the same time a dignified seclusion to the church. Penitents might also enter the narthex. The rear of the nave was reserved for the cate-chumens, or neophytes, while the faithful generally took their places in the side aisles. The apse, bema, and often the upper nave were reserved for the officiating clergy. This space was inclosed by a railing, the "chancel," which frequently ran far down into the nave. At the very back of the apse, facing the congregation and on the longitudinal axis, was the bishop's chair, or *cathedra*. Before it, usually at the intersection of the apse and the bema, was the altar of marble, covered with a simple marble canopy, the *ciborium*. Flanking the chancel were two pulpits, or *ambones*, from which the gospels were read and the sermons preached. The common material for all this church furniture was marble, inlaid with mosaic, which has been given the suggestive name of *opus Alexandrinum*. Occasionally two rooms, the *diaconicon* and the *prothesis*, were placed on either side of the apse.

Elevation. In elevation the nave of the basilica was much higher than the side aisles, permitting a broad clerestory through which light was admitted by windows, fitted with wooden grilles, thin, perforated, marble screens, or even oiled cloth. The aisles were covered with slanting roofs, usually hidden from the floor by flat ceilings. The triangular space thus obtained between the aisle ceiling and roof constituted the "triforium." At times the triforia were sufficiently roomy to permit the superimposition of galleries on the aisles, and these were reserved for the catechumens or for the segregation of women (*gynacæa*). The clerestory walls were carried on columns, generally antique, which separated the nave from the aisles. Sometimes the system was trabeated; sometimes, as in old Saint Peter's, the columns bore archivolts on which the walls were set. Nave and bema were covered with gable roofs, reinforced with trusses, and generally, though sometimes at a period later than the original building, hidden from the floor by richly coffered and gilded ceilings. The semicircular apse alone was vaulted.

Decoration. Ample compensation for the dull exterior of the basilica was made by the gorgeous polychromatic decoration of the interior. The pavement consisted of marble flags and tesseræ, in divers brilliant colors and ingeniously complicated geometric designs. The columns were of precious marbles, fluted or unfluted, varying even in scale according to whether or not the builders could steal, for the greater glory of God, a homogeneous set from some pagan building. In like manner the capitals varied, frequently not even fitting the columns that bore them, and the entablature above was often composed of unrelated pilfered classical fragments. That such an apparently accidental hodge-podge should form an extremely harmonious and decorative whole testifies strongly to the underlying good taste of the Christian builder. Finally the wall spaces, and especially the concave surfaces of the apsidal semi-domes, were covered with glass mosaic, gold-backed and flashing with brilliant color. Sacred personages, especially the Saviour, were thus portrayed, and eventually whole cycles of biblical history were taught by means of pictured mosaic. This mosaic, like the opus Alexandrinum, was in origin essentially Eastern.

Origin of the Christian-Roman basilica. The origin of the Christian basilica is somewhat obscure. Superficially the type seems to have sprung into completed being with the reign of Constantine, but this merely proves that the preliminary steps in its development have been lost. The most obvious theory of the creation, dating back to Leon Battista Alberti, is that the Christian architects merely took over and copied the ancient Roman classical basilica. The ancient civil basilicas, however, were of two sorts, one Eastern in origin and the other Western, or Hellenic. The plan of the latter strongly suggests the Christian basilica, and it is reasonable to suppose that the later building was derived from the Greek civil basilica of the classic times. The Christian building seems to have been modified in detail, however, by the imitation of some of the forms of the Roman house, wherein the early Christians were

FIG. 66—ROME. SAINT PAUL'S OUTSIDE-THE-WALLS. INTERIOR SEEN
FROM THE ENTRANCE

FIG. 67—ROME. SAN LORENZO FUORI-LE-MURA. EXTERIOR

wont to worship, and by the invention of new forms for better fulfilment of liturgical needs.

Variations. Within the fixed limits of the type thus set there was room for considerable individual deviation. Indeed no two of the many basilicas in Rome are precisely the same. Some, like old Saint Peter's (Fig. 63), had five aisles; others, like Santa Maria Maggiore, had but three. At times, as in Santa Maria Maggiore, the architrave appears; at times the archivolt takes its place, as in Saint Paul's Outside-the-Walls (Figs. 64 and 66). In general as time went on the archivolt more and more took the place of the architrave. In many of the smaller buildings, like the eighth century church of Santa Maria in Cosmedin, the bema was omitted. Another remarkable deviation appears in the same building, where the colonnade is broken and piers are inserted at regular intervals. Occasionally the side aisles were finished with smaller salient apses suggesting Syriac or Egyptian influence. Such an arrangement appears in San Pietro in Vincoli (Fig. 63). Galleries above the aisles, more typical of the Orient than the Occident, are to be found in Sant'Agnese fuori-le-mura (Fig. 64).

Orientation of the Christian church. An interesting, if freakish, variation occurs in San Lorenzo fuori-le-mura (Figs. 63, 67, and 68). Here two churches, an early one and a later, oriented in opposite directions and juxtaposed apse to apse, have been joined into a single building. In early times, especially in buildings constructed under the influence of Constantine (Saint Peter's, Saint Paul's, the Lateran, San Lorenzo), the façade and not the apse was placed to face the east. Soon, however, the orientation was fixed with the apse to face the east, and this scheme was followed whenever possible throughout the Middle Ages.

The Christian-Roman basilica in Italy outside of Rome. The Christian-Roman basilica is best studied at Rome, but is found throughout the empire frequently alongside of, and contemporaneous with, buildings of a different style. Only in Rome, however, did it show so completely the conservatism which is one of its most marked characteristics. In Ravenna, for example, we find the sixth century church of Sant' Apollinare Nuovo (Fig. 69) essentially basilican in form, yet so

FIG. 68—ROME. SAN LORENZO FUORI-LE-MURA. INTERIOR

FIG. 69—RAVENNA. SANT' APOLLINARE NUOVO. INTERIOR

Byzantine in detail that the work might be classified under either head.   Indeed, even in later periods and in different styles, many buildings, such as the Basse-Oeuvre at Beauvais or the Cathedral of Pisa (Figs. 105 and 106) are so essentially basilican in plan and elevation that they might be so classified.

The Roman building of the central type.   In Rome buildings of the central type, though they are to be found, never attained

FIG. 70—ROME.   SAN STEFANO ROTONDO.   INTERIOR

anything like the importance of the basilicas.   The most characteristic example of the type in Rome is the church of Santo Stefano Rotondo (Figs. 63, 64, and 70).   This structure, consecrated in 468, had originally the form of two concentric aisles inclosing a cylinder raised above them to form a clerestory.   That buildings of the central type, vaulted throughout, were constructed in Rome is proved by the church of Santa Costanza (Fig. 71).   Outside of Rome the buildings of the central type are generally so obviously

Oriental in inspiration that they are best discussed under the diffusion of Eastern influence.

The East. Geographical divisions. The study of Eastern architecture offers a very different problem. In the nearer Orient one finds no conservative, well-developed style awaiting definition. Generally speaking, the early Christian architecture of Rome was static, that of the East dynamic. In the East architecture was in a state of flux, or rather progression, a style changing almost as one seeks to fix its type. Moreover,

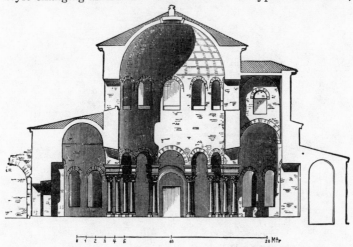

FIG. 71—ROME. SANTA COSTANZA. SECTION SHOWING THE CONSTRUCTION

local variations were striking, and the first step toward clearness involves a subdivision of the East into three distinct regions; Anatolia, Syria, and Egypt. The first, in the north, corresponds to Asia Minor, and its artistic center was Ephesus. The second, farther south and including Palestine, was guided artistically by Antioch. Alexandria controlled the third. A fourth broad division might be made of northern Africa, not so important historically, yet affording many examples of early Christian art.

The Syrian basilica. Beginning with Syria, let us first consider the basilica. Here, besides examples very like the Roman buildings, other structures appear, absolutely new in

the history of art.   Only within comparatively recent times
has attention been directed to Antioch and the so-called
"dead cities" of Syria, where receding civilization has left
ruins as impressive as any to be found in Pompeii.   In the
typical Syrian basilica the atrium was abandoned and a covered
porch, flanked by two monumental towers, was substituted
for the narthex.   A unique façade, very suggestive of later
medieval architecture and quite probably influencing it,

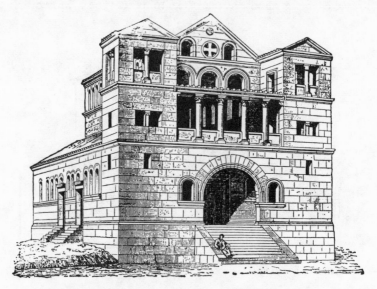

FIG. 72—TOURMANIN.   THE BASILICA RESTORED

was thus obtained.   In the interior, generally three-aisled, the
Greek colonnade gave way to great piers, bearing an arcade,
sometimes double and wide of span, giving an impression of
great space.   Between the clerestory windows corbels often
bore colonnettes which ran up to receive the transverse beams
of the timber roof and gave the structure something of the
feeling of logical articulation so commonly associated with the
organic Romanesque and Gothic styles.   There were generally
three apses at the east end, usually round, though occasionally
square, in plan, and at times horseshoe-shaped.

Examples. Good examples of Syrian basilicas may be seen at Ruweiha, at Mchabbak, and at Tourmanin (Fig. 72). Perhaps the finest example of the Syrian façade is that of Tourmanin, and the most complete, and probably the best single example of Syrian architecture, is the church of Khalb-Louzeh (Fig. 63). In the Hauran, on account of the scarcity of wood, an even more remarkable development took place,

FIG. 73—KALAT-SEMAN. THE BASILICA OF SAINT SIMEON STYLITES

and one finds buildings constructed entirely of monumental cut stone. Transverse arches were thrown across the naves, and these supported roofs of stone flags laid parallel to the main axis of the building. The timber roof then entirely disappeared. The originality of these buildings really indicates a reversion of the Orient to its native genius.

Buildings of the central type in Syria. The buildings of the central type in Syria were equally important. Constantine himself set the style with the famous church of the Holy Sepulchre, crowned with a dome supported on an interior

colonnade, and surrounded by a circular aisle carrying a
gallery above it. Two buildings of capital importance in the
history of architecture are the churches of Ezra and Bosra
(Figs. 63 and 64) in Syria. The former is in plan an octagon
inscribed in a square. The octagonal drum is covered by an
egg-shaped dome, the transition from the drum to the dome
being made by squinches. A salient apse, semicircular within
and three-sided without, appears at the east end. The system
of Bosra is even more ingenious. The plan is that of a circle
inscribed within a square. The great central dome was
carried on eight pillars, and, to neutralize its thrust, was surrounded by an annular barrel vault, fortified by four semicircular exedræ at the angles of the square. Three apses were
placed at the east end. Perhaps the most perfect of the
Syrian buildings of the central type was the monastery of
Saint Simeon Stylites (Fig. 73). Round an octagonal court,
in the center of which was the column of the famous ascetic,
four great three-aisled basilicas were placed to form a gigantic
Greek cross. The eastern arm, finished with three apses, was
the church proper; the others were reserved for pilgrims.
The extraordinary fertility of invention in these buildings
shows the beginning of an attempt to produce a satisfactory
ecclesiastical building of the central type. The architects of
Byzantium were to be preoccupied largely with this problem.

Syrian decoration. The Mschatta frieze. Not less significant
was the decoration of the Syrian building. We have seen at
Spalato, imported from Syria, the modification and free use
of classic detail to embellish the exterior of an edifice. The
same procedure was maintained with infinite variations in
Syria proper. Moreover, the Syrians evolved a new scheme
of sculptured decoration, superbly shown in the frieze from
Mschatta (Fig. 74) now in the Berlin museum, wherein classic
and Oriental motives are combined in the richest of patterns
and crisply cut in low relief. Polychromatic decoration, too,
was common in Syria. In short, the region showed, at an
early date, new developments in architecture which unquestionably aided in paving the way for the Byzantine style, and
perhaps even for the remote Romanesque of Europe.

Early Christian architecture of Egypt. In plan and construction the buildings of Egypt show far less ingenuity than

FIG. 74—BERLIN MUSEUM.   THE FRIEZE FROM MSCHATTA.   (STRZY-
GOWSKI)

those of Syria.   An interesting class of Egyptian monuments is marked by the use of an immense trefoil-shaped sanctuary, divided from the three-aisled nave by a wide transept.   The trefoil sanctuary, however, may well be an importation from Syria.   One Alexandrian invention, the cistern with its cover supported on columns, was caused by local needs and destined to exert a strong influence in Constantinople.   The special importance of Egypt lay in the decorative schemes evolved there.   For centuries Alexandria had been the center of a school of lively pictorial decoration.   To this was added in the early Christian centuries brilliant work in glass mosaic and inlaid marble.   Thus equipped, Egypt was able to dower both Byzantium and Italy with the rich polychromatic interior decoration which became the vogue practically throughout Christendom.

The basilica in Anatolia.   In Anatolia the architects proved themselves structurally the most inventive of all.   The controlling city was Ephesus, but the sites where the architecture may be studied are very numerous, the best perhaps being Bin-bir-Kilissé (the thousand and one churches), in the plain of Konieh in southeastern Anatolia.   Here the majority of the basilicas recall the buildings of Syria.   They are generally three-aisled with a single strongly salient apse, either circular or polygonal.   At the entrance to the nave is a porch flanked by two towers.   All this might be Syrian, but the Anatolian strikes his special note by vaulting his structure, and numbers of these buildings have heavy barrel vaults over nave and aisles.   An excellent example of this type of building may be seen at Daouleh.   Side by side with these vaulted structures, however, may be seen the Græco-Roman type, with atrium, brick walls, and timber roof.

The central type in Anatolia.   Anatolia, too, abounded in buildings of the central type.   We have an interesting description of a Martyrium, written in the fourth century by Gregory of Nysa.   The monument was to be cruciform, the arms of the cross bound at their intersection by semicircular niches, and a conical dome was to cover the crossing.   The use of the conical dome suggests the influence of Persia, and indeed the most significant element in Anatolian architecture is the Persian.   The Syrian conical-domed buildings, like the churches of Ezra and Bosra, may have been copied from Anatolia or themselves inspired direct from Persia. Many variations of Gregory's scheme may be seen to-day, especially at Bin-bir-Kilissé.

The Anatolian domed basilica. Historically the most interesting of the types evolved in Anatolia, however, is what has been called the domed basilica. The first step in its development was made by placing a square bay before the apse to enlarge the *presbyterium*, and adding galleries above the aisles for the faithful. To give a lighter effect to buildings of such large dimensions, without weakening the barrel vaults by piercing them with windows, the architects hit on the scheme of breaking the barrel vault with a dome, and thus the domed basilica, destined to exercise an enormous influence on later architecture, came into being. A perfect example of the type may be seen at Kodja-Kalessi (Fig. 63), where the dome occupies two bays of the nave. The same type, constructed in brick, occurs in Saint Clement's at Ancyra. In both the dome is carried on squinches. On the other hand, at Saint Nicholas of Myra, and at Dehr-Ahsy in Syria, we find domed basilicas with the domes carried on pendentives.

The problem of the dome. Many and ingenious were the solutions of the problem of the dome in Anatolia. Materials were varied, and bricks and terra-cotta, adopted from neighboring Persia, were used to reduce the thrusts of heavy domes. To make the transition from the square or polygon below to the round dome above, the architects adopted many methods. Squinches were commonest, sometimes merely of flat stones laid across the angles of the square, reducing it to a polygon, and then other stones laid across the angles of the polygon, making them still more obtuse, until in successive courses the mass was coaxed into the roughly circular form necessary to receive the base of the dome. Sometimes arches were thrown across the angles of the square or polygon, and again, when the dimensions were sufficiently small, single blocks at the angles were hollowed out in pendentive form.

The pendentive. By far the most important solution of the problem, however, was the true pendentive. In mathematical terms a pendentive is a segment of a hollow hemisphere, the diameter of which is equal to the diagonal of the square to be covered.   In non-technical language, however, the member is not so easy to describe.   Imagine a square to be covered by a dome of such dimensions that its edge would touch the square only at the four corners.   Obviously the dome would project beyond the four sides of the square.   Imagine all portions of the dome projecting beyond the sides of the square to be shaved off vertically, and the result would be a pendentive dome, or, technically, a continuous dome on pendentives.

FIG. 75—RAVENNA.   THE MAUSOLEUM OF GALLA PLACIDIA.   DRAWING OF THE EXTERIOR

Imagine then the top of the pendentive dome to be sliced off horizontally at a point just above the crowns of the lateral arches caused by the vertical cuts.   The result would be four spherical triangles or pendentives, segments of a sphere, the diameter of which would equal the diameter of the square below.   On these a true dome could be placed, producing a dome on pendentives (Fig. 64).

The origin of the pendentive.   The pendentive was destined to become one of the most marked characteristics of Byzantine architecture. Though its origin is open to dispute, it must have been the logical outgrowth of the Persian vaults of light material without centering. The strong probability is that the architects of Anatolia, in close contact with the Orient, independently created this most important member.

Diffusion of Oriental influence in the West. Buildings at Ravenna. Through the influence of commerce and monasticism the fourth, fifth, and sixth centuries were marked by a widespread diffusion of Oriental influence in the West. Although it appears, as we have noted, in the fourth century palace of Diocletian in Spalato, and again later in Rome in the decorations of the basilicas, and especially in the buildings of the central type, its full force in Italy is best judged in the architecture of Ravenna. Here two buildings of the mid-fifth century, the Mausoleum of Galla Placidia (Figs. 63 and 75) and the so-called Baptistry of the Orthodox, attest the almost complete domination of Oriental inspiration in this Western city. The former, now the church of Santi Nazzaro e Celso, is Greek cruciform in plan, the crossing being covered with a continuous dome on pendentives, ingeniously constructed of hollow terra-cotta amphoræ inserted one within another. The material alone establishes the influence of the Orient, especially of Persia. The exterior is plain, the brick walls being lightened somewhat by blind arcades. Externally the dome appears as a square. The interior shows a complete incrustation of precious glass mosaic in the Alexandrian manner. The Baptistry of the Orthodox (San Giovanni in Fonte) is a polygonal structure, with a dome constructed like that of the tomb of Galla Placidia.

Mingling of early Christian and Byzantine elements. Although in point of time such works fall within the early Christian period, to classify them merely as early Christian would produce a deep misconception of their architectural significance. Already they anticipate so many elements of the Byzantine style that they might as justly be called Byzantine. This does not mean that they were importations from Constantinople. On the contrary, they were Italian products of the same Eastern influences that were already at work in Constantinople to produce the Byzantine style.

Conclusion. Early Christian architecture may, therefore,

be regarded from two points of view. From one it is a self-sufficient style, amply providing the early Church with buildings beautiful in themselves and even finer in their complete fulfilment of the needs for which they were designed. Regarded from this point of view, the Christian-Roman basilica is the supreme product of early Christian architecture. From the other and broader point of view, the early Christian style is a link in the great architectural chain, connecting the weakening classic art with the vigorous new style of Byzantium. Especially the buildings of Eastern Christianity, experimental, lawless in their disregard of classic tradition, at times even crude though always full of promise, herald in no uncertain tone the advent of the art so soon to appear in Constantinople.

CHRONOLOGICAL LIST OF EARLY CHRISTIAN MONUMENTS

It must be noted that it is often impossible to date medieval monuments exactly, and we must frequently be satisfied with the half century or century in which a building was erected. A single date, without qualification, refers to the beginning of the portion of a building referred to in the text. In general it is always well to remember that an error in dating a medieval monument is apt to give the monument greater antiquity than it deserves.

ITALY

Rome, Old Saint Peter's.—Consecrated 326.
Rome, Santa Costanza.—Built 323–337; rebuilt 1256.
Rome, Saint Paul's Outside-the-Walls.—Founded 386, but rebuilt 1823.
Rome, Santa Maria Maggiore.—Rebuilt 432–440.
Rome, San Pietro in Vincoli.—Founded ca. 450.
Ravenna, Mausoleum of Galla Placidia.—Ca. 450.
Ravenna, Baptistry of the Orthodox.—Mid-fifth century.
Rome, Santo Stefano Rotondo. 468–483.
Ravenna, Sant' Apollinare Nuovo.—Soon after 500.
Rome, San Lorenzo Fuori-le-Mura.—Rebuilt 578; remodeled 1216–27.
Rome, Sant' Agnese, Fuori-le-Mura.—Rebuilt 625–638.
Rome, San Clemente.—Rebuilt 1108.

THE EAST

Jerusalem Church of the Holy Sepulchre.—312–337.
Ruweiha.—Fourth century.
Kodja-Kalessi.—Fourth or possibly fifth century.
Mschatta Frieze.—Possibly fourth, possibly sixth century.
Mchabbak.—Fifth century.
Daouleh.—Fifth century (?).
Saint Simeon Stylites.—End of fifth century.
Ancyra, Saint Clement.—Fifth century (?).
Myra, Saint Nicholas.—Fifth century (?).
Bosra.—512.
Ezra.—515.
Tourmanin.—Sixth century.
Khalb-Louzeh.—Sixth century.

BIBLIOGRAPHICAL NOTE

A. Michel's *Histoire de l'art*, vol. 1, pt. 1, 1905, contains valuable articles by André Pératé and Camille Enlart summarizing early Christian art, including architecture. H. Marucchi's *Basiliques et églises de Rome*, 1902, is an authoritative work, forming vol. 3 of the author's series, *Eléments d'archéologie chrétienne*. A. Venturi's *Storia dell'arte italiana*, vols. 1 and 2, 1901 and 1902, contain an account of early Christian architecture in Italy. G. T. Rivoira's *Le origini della archittetura lombarda*, vol. 1, 1901, is an exhaustive study of the origins of Italian medieval architecture by an eminent scholar, who believes that these origins, whether they involve early Christian or Byzantine architecture, are Occidental rather than Oriental. G. Leroux's *Les origines de l'édifice hypostyle en Grèce, en Orient, et chez les Romains*, 1913, is a scholarly work, important for the light it throws on the origin of the Christian-Roman basilica. W. Lowrie's *Monuments of the Early Church*, 1906, is a skilfully arranged hand-book of early Christian art, with architecture soundly treated. A. L. Frothingham's *Monuments of Christian Rome*, 1908, is another hand-book with good summaries of the histories of the monuments. M. de Vogüé's *Syrie centrale*, 1865–77, a monumental and ground-breaking piece of scholarship, now somewhat out of date, is the most important of the author's many publications dealing with early Christian architecture and other arts in Syria. By H. C. Butler are two works—*Architecture and Other Arts*, 1903, and *Ancient Architecture in Syria*, 1907. The former is the publication of an American expedition to Syria in 1899; the latter is the second division of the "Publications of the Princeton Expedition to Syria, in 1904–1905." Both works present masses of new material in the most elaborate way, and are worthy successors of the publications of de Vogüé. J. Stryzgowski's *Orient oder Rom, 1901, Kleinasien, 1903,* and *Byzantinische Denkmäler* are publications, the last a series of publications, by an original scholar of encyclopedic information. Though the works deal more with Byzantine than early Christian monuments, they are important for both, especially on account of the author's thesis, successfully defended, that the creative impulse in early Christian and Byzantine art came from the Orient. C. Diehl's *Manuel d'art byzantin,* 1910, is a highly authoritative synthesis of the history of Byzantine art, with a valuable discussion of the early Christian architecture of the East as an introduction. O. Wulff's *Altchristliche Kunst,* 1914 (*Handbuch der Kuntwissenschaft*), ch. 4, *Die altchristliche Baukunst,* is the most recent summary of all, with exhaustive references to the latest discussions of individual points.

CHAPTER VII

BYZANTINE ARCHITECTURE

Origins. Byzantine architecture came, like the Wise Men, out of the East, the rôles of the Magi being played by the three great cities: Alexandria, Antioch, Ephesus. From the first of the three came the polychromy which remained a characteristic of the style from beginning to end. The second supplied the Byzantine ideal of sculptured decoration, flat, crisply cut relief and an all-over covering of the surface. The third, most important of all, gave the structural elements which the Byzantine architects fused, systematized, and developed for ten centuries.

Centralization. Although the style was diffused over a vast area, from Armenia to France and from Russia to Africa, the nerve center remained practically always at Constantinople. To this centralization are due the main characteristics and general homogeneity of the style. Byzantium took the ideas of the Orient, handled them with the lavish means and broad conceptions of Rome, and welded them with a refinement literally neo-Attic. The result was a new art, but, like the Roman, a distinctly imperial one. Architecturally as well as politically, Constantine supplanted imperial Rome by imperial Constantinople.

Ecclesiastical and secular work. Byzantine architecture was primarily ecclesiastical, but this generalization must often be qualified. During the reigns of important emperors, such as Constantine (323-337), Justinian (527-565), and Basil I. (867-887), civil architecture played an extremely important part. The churches exercised a greater influence on other styles than civil buildings, and were often preserved when the civil buildings were destroyed, but this fact should not blind us to the importance of the non-ecclesiastical work.

Lack of self-consciousness of the style. Whether lay or ecclesiastical, however, Byzantine architecture was on the whole unselfconscious. Lavish as the decoration might be in church or palace, the important consideration was always a satisfactory solving of structural needs, and this became the real, if unconscious, canon of Byzantine esthetic theory. Moreover, the style tended to be corporate rather than individual, though not to nearly so complete an extent as the medieval styles of western Europe. Especially in the earlier period individuals were apt to dominate the works, but later craftsmen and obscure architects were given very free rein, and even in the earliest times the individual appears as the voice of the civilization rather than its teacher.

Conservatism and development. Byzantine art has generally been considered rigidly conservative. It was, in truth, conservative, yet only in so far as conservatism was not inconsistent with development. Nothing could be more mistaken than the too common conception of the Byzantine style as one which crystallized in the sixth century and continued as a chain of monotonous repetitions until the fifteenth. The art was always conscious of and taught by its past, but it never slavishly copied its past, and development was none the less steady for being slow.

Materials. The materials used in Byzantine architecture were very varied. Brick and mortar were commonest and most expressive of the ideals of the style. By means of light, porous material the architect got his most striking effects, and mortar joints were frequently increased to the width of the bricks bonded. Concrete was used for cores, but the rigid concrete vaults of the Romans disappeared. Cut stone was used freely, but nearly always as an adjunct to other material. A homogeneous use of ashlar was practically unknown in Byzantine architecture outside of certain restricted regions, notably Greece and Armenia. For purposes of decoration the Byzantine architects used mosaic and marble, the latter sometimes carved in flat, tapestry-like relief, sometimes applied as a veneer. In the later style decoration in brick became common, and wall surfaces were enriched with an infinity of patterns in brick, or brick alternating with cut stone. The absence of formulated esthetic criteria gave full play to the invention and good taste of the designers.

Structure. The originality and fertility of the Byzantine architect never shows more happily than in the solving of problems of structure. The style was essentially a vaulted one, and the most important form of vault was the dome. Wood being scarce, the problem of centering was serious, and the architects, taking their cues from Anatolia and Persia, soon learned to construct important vaults without centering.

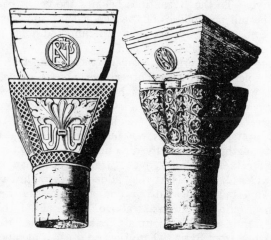

FIG. 76—RAVENNA. SAN VITALE. EXAMPLES OF BYZANTINE CAPITALS

To that end they developed the lightest and most durable materials, bound by thick, adhesive mortar joints. Then by completing the vaults in successive, concentric, self-sustaining rings, by slanting brick courses so as to require little or no support from below, and by the invention of ingenious devices for the definition of vault surfaces during the process of construction, the architects succeeded almost entirely in eliminating the necessity for centering. Moreover, the stability of the finished structure was further insured by an equilibrium of thrusts. Domes and vaults were grouped compactly and logically, their thrusts opposing one another, and the thrusts of a great central dome were neutralized and carried off by a number of subordinate domes grouped round it. The style thus had, especially in the later period, a large measure of that structural logic which one associates with Gothic architecture.

Supports. The same logic was shown admirably in the use of supports. The use of squinches for the support of domes was inherited from the East and continued with variations throughout the entire development of the style. Far more important in the history of architecture was the use of the pendentive. To the Byzantines belongs the credit of recognizing the full possibilities of the pendentive, and the use of these members as a support for a superimposed dome was inaugurated in Byzantium (Fig. 64).

Capitals. Moreover, the logic of the architects was not confined solely to the immediate supports of the dome. The capitals, which carried the weight of the vault, were of an entirely new and logical design. Unlike the Roman entablature with its merely crushing weight, the mass which the Byzantine capital had to carry was heterogeneous and exercised a variety of thrusts in many directions. To meet this mass the architects first designed a sturdier Corinthian capital, with a wider abacus. Next they added a heavy thrust block, like an inverted, truncated pyramid, to make the transition from the capital to the mass above. Capitals of this sort may be seen in the Eski-djouma in Salonica. The idea of the impost came from Syria, where the use of such members was current in the fifth century, the Syrians in turn having probably received it from Persia. A further step was taken in San Vitale at Ravenna (Fig. 76), when the Corinthian character of the capital was almost abandoned, and it was shaped like a richly ornamented impost block. Finally, at Hagia Sophia at Salonica, the form appears on which all Byzantine capitals were based, an impost block, carried on a broad, thin abacus, whence the load is transmitted to a high, convex bell, broad at the top and slender at the base where it meets the slender shaft. The form thus invented combines elements of the three Greek classic forms, and is both apt and beautiful. It was, moreover, flexible, and capable of infinite variety, from the stern simplicity of the rudimentary capitals in the cistern of Bin-bir-direk to the rich profusion of the melon, bird and basket, and wind-blown acanthus capitals of the fully developed style.

Types of ecclesiastical buildings. Since the Byzantine ecclesiastical buildings surpass all other sorts in importance, we must devote most of our study to them. The types created were diverse. In the earlier period the type developed from the domed basilica of Anatolia was the favorite, the most famous example being Hagia Sophia at Constantinople. In the so - called second golden age, in the ninth, tenth, and eleventh centuries, the Greek-cross plan became the fashion, although both types existed in both periods. Sometimes the plan was that of a Greek cross inscribed within a square, the cross marked in the actual building only by the clerestory. At other times a true Greek cross was designed on plan. In the beginning the so-called triconch or "three-shell" plan, with a trefoil division of the apsidal end, was popular, and this

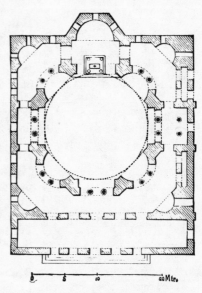

FIG. 77 — CONSTANTINOPLE.   S A I N T S
SERGIUS AND BACCHUS.   PLAN

type persisted, with modifications, throughout the history of the style. The true basilican plan, though not wholly forgotten, was never popular. Circular and polygonal buildings were also designed, but by far the most popular form of building of the central type was the Greek cross.

Churches earlier than Hagia Sophia of Constantinople. Although Hagia Sophia may be regarded almost as the proclamation of Byzantine architecture, it was preceded by a number of buildings outside of as well as within Constantinople that heralded the approaching style. We have already noted

Ravennate buildings which might well be called Byzantine. Similarly the Stoudion basilica, built in Constantinople in 463, although it conforms to the Hellenistic type and retains the post and lintel system, is Byzantine in spirit, and the purely Byzantine church of Saints Sergius and Bacchus in Constantinople (Fig. 77) slightly antedates Hagia Sophia.

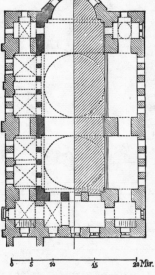

FIG. 78—CONSTANTINOPLE. SAINT IRENE. PLAN

This building recalls the churches of Ezra and Bosra (Figs. 63 and 64) in Asia Minor, but is more skilfully planned and executed.

Saint Irene, Constantinople. In 532 Justinian caused the building of another church, Saint Irene, in Constantinople (Fig. 78), which brings us still nearer the full-fledged Byzantine style. The architect of Saint Irene was probably inspired by the church of Hagia Sophia at Salonica, a building which probably antedates somewhat its great namesake in Constantinople. Both Saint Irene and Hagia Sophia at Salonica are variants of the Anatolian-domed basilica. In Saint Irene the domes are abutted by barrel vaults grouped about them in the shape of a cross, and it seems possible that we have here the germ of the Greek-cross form.

Hagia Sophia. All these buildings appear insignificant, however, beside the "Great Church," the church of the Divine Wisdom, Hagia Sophia at Constantinople. This building embodies more fully than any other the full-fledged Byzantine style of the first golden age. Justinian began it in 532, to replace a Constantinian church of the same name which had been destroyed in the Nika sedition. Anthemius of Tralles and Isidorus of Miletus were the architects, both of Anatolian origin. The church was completed in five years and dedicated with the most impressive ceremonies and amid

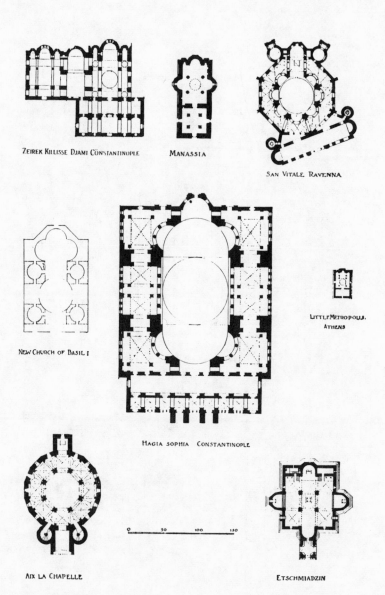

ZEIREK KILLISSE DJAMI CONSTANTINOPLE   MANASSIA

SAN VITALE RAVENNA

NEW CHURCH OF BASIL I

HAGIA SOPHIA CONSTANTINOPLE

LITTLE METROPOLIS. ATHENS

0   50   100   150

AIX LA CHAPELLE

ETSCHMIADZIN

FIG. 79—PLANS OF BYZANTINE CHURCHES

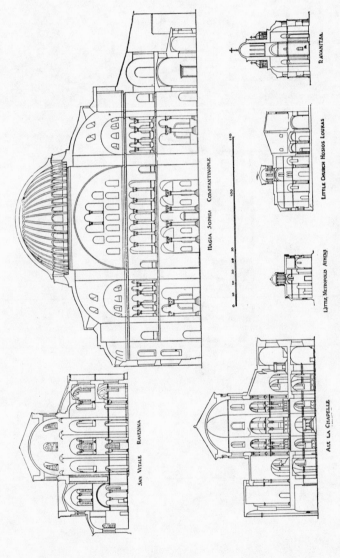

SAN VITALE   RAVENNA

HAGIA SOPHIA CONSTANTINOPLE

LITTLE METROPOLIS ATHENS

LITTLE CHURCH HOSIOS LOUKAS

KAVANITSA

AIX LA CHAPELLE

FIG. 80—SECTIONS OF BYZANTINE CHURCHES

general thanksgiving December 27, 537, by Justinian. In 558 the central dome fell, but a nephew of Isidorus rebuilt it according to a somewhat less ambitious design, and the church was reconsecrated by the Emperor in 562.

Plan and construction. In plan (Fig. 79) Hagia Sophia occupies a great square which, excluding the apse and the narthex, measures about 250 by 240 feet. A narthex, later doubled, galleries, and an atrium precede the nave. In the

FIG. 81—CONSTANTINOPLE. HAGIA SOPHIA. EXTERIOR

center is a great dome on pendentives, 107 feet in diameter, carried on four huge piers, 25 feet square, and abutted east and west by two half-domes of the same diameter as the central dome (Fig. 80). These mark the longitudinal axis of the building. Abutment to the north and south is supplied by four tremendous buttresses of marble-faced rubble. The half-domes are in turn abutted at the springing by paired smaller half-domes, and thus, partly by opposing thrust to thrust and partly by carrying off the thrust of the great dome in descending stages to the outer wall and the ground, the whole structure is admirably stabilized. At the east end a salient apse.

polygonal on the exterior, opens into the eastern half-dome. Right and left of the central dome and its half-domes are aisles, groin-vaulted, and surmounted by galleries which are covered with domical vaults.   At present four minarets of an incongruous Turkish design stand free at the four corners of the building.

Exterior.   Although the apex of the dome is 180 feet above the pavement, the external appearance of the building is

FIG. 82—CONSTANTINOPLE.   HAGIA SOPHIA.   INTERIOR LOOKING
TOWARD THE APSE

squat (Fig. 81).   The Byzantine architect of the first golden age fully appreciated the difficulty of properly abutting a lofty dome, and seldom sought to make the dome a striking feature externally.   The dome of Hagia Sophia, less than a semicircle in cross-section, is in height from springing to crown but 47 feet.   The external effect, however, is none the less fine, combining monumentality with compactness and a strong feeling for the esthetic value of sturdy, frankly safe construction.

Interior. The interior, on the other hand, gives a strong impression of height (Fig. 82). The ring of small openings piercing the base of the dome lightens the whole structure, so that the dome appears almost miraculously suspended over the great central void. Moreover, the columns of various proportions in ground story and galleries give a much-needed scale, which permits the eye easily to grasp the monumental proportions of the building.

A domed basilica. Although Hagia Sophia is roughly square, it is not properly of the central type, but is planned with reference to a longitudinal axis, and therefore fulfils the liturgical ideal of the early Christian basilica. It may be regarded as the supreme Byzantine development of the Anatolian domed basilica.

Decoration. The decoration of Hagia Sophia, true to the ideals of the first golden age, is drab on the exterior, but brilliant on the interior. The exterior is now painted in horizontal reddish bands, but in the original design there was no attempt at enlivening the wall surfaces with colors or even patterns in the material used. The interior, on the other hand, was gorgeously decorated with veneered marbles and glass mosaic. The marble, sawn thin, was highly polished and skilfully placed so that reversed patterns from the veining of a single block were juxtaposed. Above the ground story the interior was crusted with gold-backed, glass mosaic, now unfortunately whitewashed by the Turks. The capitals and some of the surfaces were decorated with crisp carving in flat relief, suggesting the art of Syria. Occasionally the interstices of the carving were filled with black marble, further accenting the already sharp impression of light and shade.

The Holy Apostles, Constantinople. Although Hagia Sophia was the greatest and most typical building of the first golden age, many other buildings were constructed during this period, some of them of the greatest importance historically. The most significant building after Hagia Sophia was another work of Anthemius and Isidorus, the church of the Holy Apostles in Constantinople (Figs. 83 and 84), destroyed by the Turks to make way for the mosque of Mohammed II. This building, known to us by descriptions and a manuscript illumination (Fig. 83), was in the form of a Greek cross obtained by the intersection of two basilican naves, vaulted and aisled (Fig. 84). Over the crossing was a dome pierced with windows, and over each arm another dome. The type thus suggested was never received with much favor in the first golden age, but it unquestionably formed the basis for numerous churches which were erected in later Byzantine architecture. Saint Mark's in Venice is but a development of the lost church of the Holy Apostles.

FIG. 83—ROME. THE VATICAN. MANUSCRIPT ILLUMINATION SHOWING THE CHURCH OF THE HOLY APOSTLES AT CONSTANTINOPLE. (DIEHL)

Building of Justinian's age outside of Constantinople. The important architecture of Justinian's time was not, however, confined to Constantinople or even to the East. At Parenzo in Istria Bishop Euphrasius raised an important church in the beginning of the sixth century, basilican in form, but Byzantine in spirit and decoration. Italy played a still more important rôle in this period, and the buildings at Ravenna scarcely yield in beauty and creative genius to those of Constantinople.

Buildings at Ravenna. Two buildings in Ravenna, the churches of Sant' Apollinare in Classe and Sant' Apollinare Nuovo (Fig. 69), are of basilican plan and Byzantine detail and decoration. The latter was commenced under Theodoric

(493-526), but was decorated by Byzantine workmen. The former was consecrated in 549. By far the most important Ravennate church of the period, however, was San Vitale (Figs. 79 and 80), begun between 526 and 534 and finished in 547, a building showing great originality and destined to exercise strong influence on subsequent architecture. It is in the form of an octagon crowned with a dome on a drum, carried by eight stout pillars.

These pillars are bound one to another by an ingenious system of exedræ similar to those of Saints Sergius and Bacchus. To diminish the thrust, the dome is constructed as in the tomb of Galla Placidia, of long terra cotta amphoræ, fitted one into another. Each pier is bound to the external wall by an arch, and each salient angle is strengthened with a pier buttress.

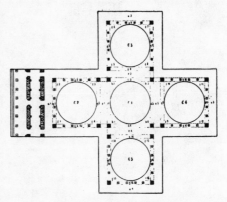

FIG. 84—CONSTANTINOPLE. THE HOLY APOSTLES. PLAN, RESTORED

Later architecture of the first golden age. The death of Justinian did not interrupt the architectural activity which his reign initiated. The art continued to show both vitality and originality. At Constantinople the mosque of Kalender-hane-djami, probably once the Diaconessa, built by the Emperor Maurice, dates at the latest from the seventh century, and shows a reversion to the domed basilican type. From the same period comes the ancient church of Saint Andrew—now the mosque of Hodja-Moustapha-pasha—with a great central dome, abutted like Hagia Sophia's by half domes.

Development in Armenia. Outside of Constantinople the art flourished in this period, and especially showed originality in Armenia. The cathedral of Etschmiadzin (Fig. 79), with its Greek cross inscribed in a square and the four arms terminated by salient apses, certainly influenced the tenth century churches of Mount Athos, and appears to be imitated in the ninth century French church of Germigny-les-Prés.   In its present form Etschmiadzin dates from the seventh century. The seventh century architecture of Armenia showed so much vitality that there is little doubt that it strongly influenced

FIG. 85—AIX-LA-CHAPELLE.   CHARLEMAGNE'S CHAPEL.   INTERIOR

Constantinople itself, as well as Byzantine architecture outside of the central city.

The Iconoclastic controversy.   Diffusion of the Byzantine style in Europe.   In 726 the development of Byzantine art was impeded, though not arrested, by the beginning of the Iconoclastic controversy.   Though Leo the Isaurian's decree was directed against images, all the arts were affected, and architecture in Constantinople went through a period of semi-stagnation which was not relieved until Theodora's restoration of image worship in 842, and not really removed until the accession of the Macedonian dynasty in 867. Nothing better illustrates the vitality of Byzantine architecture than its diffusion in this dark period. The very throttling of the art at home tended to spread it abroad, and what Constantinople lost the Occident of the Carolingian Renaissance gained. From the very beginning of the ninth century dates Charlemagne's fine chapel at Aix-la-Chapelle (Figs. 79, 80, and 85), a direct imitation of San Vitale. Somewhat later Germigny-les-Prés was planned on lines suggested, as we have seen, by the Armenian architecture of the seventh century. Byzantine architecture was, therefore, not arrested, but merely temporarily ceased to center in Constantinople.

The second golden age. With the accession of the Macedonian dynasty Constantinople resumed her sway, and there began what is generally known as the second golden age of Byzantine art. Prosperity came once more to the empire, power to the ruling house. Fresh Oriental influence vivified the art, and architects sought inspiration in the monuments of the past. Inspiration was, however, far removed from imitation. The architecture of the second golden age differs widely from that of the first, and ably demonstrates the dynamic power of the art.

Changes in plan. In the second golden age the basilican plan entirely disappeared. The octagon went with it, and the triconch type occurred only in a radically modified form. Even the domed basilican type became very rare, although the ninth century church of Saint Theodosia (now the Guldjami) at Constantinople shows it.

The Greek cross plan of the second golden age. By far the favorite plan was the Greek cross, but this differed essentially from the earlier Greek cross as seen in the mausoleum of Galla Placidia and the church of the Holy Apostles. In the older form the arms of the cross appear in the contours of the plan, and subordinate domes are placed on each arm of the cross. In the latter, the re-entrant angles are filled on plan, the ground story plan being square and the cross appearing only in the

upper stories.   The arms of the cross are covered with barrel
vaults, and the subordinate domes are placed in the angles
between the arms.   The plan is thus a Greek cross inscribed
within a square, with a central dome and four domes, usually
placed so low as to be hidden, at the angles.   The thrusts of the
subordinate domes and barrel vaults tend to neutralize one
another, and all oppose the thrusts of the central dome.   Thus
the whole system is so logical and organic that one is reminded
of the organic systems of Romanesque architecture.   The germ
of the typical Greek cross building of the second golden age is to
be found, therefore, not in the classic example of the Greek
cross of the first golden age, the church of the Holy Apostles,
but in the domed basilica, and especially in such a building as
Saint Irene at Constantinople (Fig. 78).

Changes in expression.   Along with this change in plan there
came a change in architectural expression.   The vertical line
was accented.   The height of the building became greater in
proportion to its breadth.   Domes were constantly raised upon
drums, and became striking features externally.   The logical
spirit of the construction was reflected in the lines of the
exterior.   Thus a curved vault in the interior was represented
on the exterior not by a gable, but by a curved line.   As the
construction became more daring the scale decreased, and the
buildings of the second golden age were, in general, much
smaller than those of the first.   Finally, the whole exterior
was regarded as suitable for decoration, polychromy was
applied to it, and the texture of the wall received especial care.
Bricks of various shapes and colors were used and ingenious
patterns devised, so that the exterior of a twelfth century
Byzantine church bears but slight resemblance to that of one
of the sixth.

La Nea.   La Nea (Fig. 79), the "new church" of Basil I.
(d. 886), was to the second golden age what Hagia Sophia was
to the first.   Unfortunately it has been destroyed, but we
know its plan from descriptions.   It was in the form of a
Greek cross, with a central dome and four smaller domes generally hidden placed in the angles between the arms of the
cross.   Unquestionably this building set the type for the
majority of the churches that followed.

Evolution of the type.   The evolution of the type can be

traced in extant monuments. It appears in a rudimentary form in a church at Skripou in Bœotia, dated 874, which lacks subordinate domes, and is heavy in construction, but which shows the Greek cross plan with barrel-vaulted arms. It may be seen fully developed in the Kilissé-djami (formerly Saint

FIG. 86—CONSTANTINOPLE. THE KILISSEDJAMI. VIEW FROM THE EAST. (EBERSOLT)

Theodore Trio) in Constantinople (Figs. 79 and 86), dating from the first half of the tenth century. Here appear both barrel-vaulted arms and angle domes. The exterior lines are harmoniously curved, and the surfaces finely treated in alternate bands of brick and ashlar.

Examples. The Greek cross within a square continued as the favorite church plan throughout the Macedonian and Comnenian dynasties. One sees it in the small church of Saint Luke at Stiris in Phocis (Figs. 84 and 87), dating from the second half of the eleventh century, and later, in the epoch of the Comnenes, it appears finely developed in the triple church of the Pantocrator, built about 1124 in Constantinople

by Irene, empress of John Comnenus. Of the three buildings
which form this work two, those on the north and south, are
perfect examples of the classic plan of the second golden age.
The central church has but two domes.

Variations. It must not be supposed, however, that the
favorite type was slavishly copied everywhere in the later
period. The commonest variation was the omission of the

FIG. 87—HOSIOS LOUKAS (PHOCIS). MONASTERY OF SAINT LUKE OF
STIRIS. VIEW FROM THE EAST SHOWING THE TWO CHURCHES. (SCHULTZ
AND BARNSLEY)

four subordinate domes, and some of the most beautiful
Byzantine churches are of this form. The finely composed
Nea Moni at Nauplia is of this type, as well as the better
known churches of Saint Theodore and the Little Metropolis
(Figs. 79 and 80) at Athens. All of these date from the
twelfth century.

The squinch group. Another variation in the churches of
this period might be called the squinch group. In these the
dome is broader in diameter and is carried on a sixteen-sided
drum, and the proportions are squatter than in the other
churches of the period. To this genre belong the monastery

of Saint Luke of Stiris (Fig. 87), the Nea Moni of Chios, and
the fine church at Daphni, near Athens.

Churches at Athos. The churches of Athos and the vicinity,
with their semicircular apses terminating the lateral arms of
the cross, form another group. One, the catholicon of Lavra,
deserves special mention. It is a three-aisled building, the

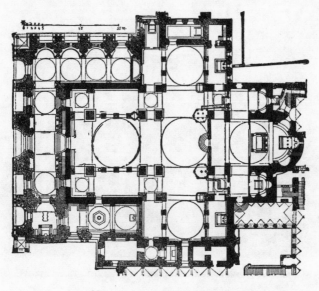

FIG. 88—VENICE. SAINT MARK. PLAN

three-fold division being indicated on the exterior by arcades,
and it thus appears to combine the types of the Greek cross
and the domed basilican churches.

Saint Mark's, Venice. By far the most important example
of a variation from the favorite plan of the second golden age
occurs in the famous church of Saint Mark in Venice (Fig.
88), begun in 1063. This building is a frank reversion to the
plan of Anthemius' church of the Holy Apostles at Constantinople. The plan is that of a Greek cross defined on the ground
story, with a dome on pendentives in the center and a
smaller dome on pendentives over each arm of the cross. A

galleried narthex embraces three sides of the western arm of the cross. The great piers which carry the dome are pierced to give greater space in the ground story, and are connected by galleries, the width of the piers, carried on marble columns. Light is admitted through rings of openings round the bases

FIG. 89—VENICE. SAINT MARK. VIEW FROM THE PIAZZA

of the domes, which are less than semicircular. On the exterior (Fig. 89) the domes are masked by false domes of wood, lead covered, which form a striking feature of the church as seen from the Piazza. Within (Fig. 90), the decoration is extremely rich, veneered marbles and precious mosaics being used as freely as in Hagia Sophia at Constantinople. The exterior, with its clustered marble columns, polychrome marble veneer, and flashing mosaic, is as lavishly decorated as the interior. The building as it stands is by no means homogeneous. There are many Gothic details in the façade, and some of the mosaics date from the Renaissance and even from modern times.

Byzantine influence in Aquitaine. The same prototypes

which influenced Saint Mark's had an effect on other Occidental architecture.   In France the twelfth century church of Saint Front at Périgueux (Fig. 99) repeats almost verbatim the plan

FIG. 90—VENICE.   SAINT MARK.   INTERIOR LOOKING TOWARD THE APSE

of Saint Mark's, though the narthex and all the polychrome decoration within and without are omitted.   Many other buildings of Aquitaine were similarly constructed, so that the architecture of that region might be classified alike under the headings of Byzantine and French Romanesque.

Georgia and Armenia.   Among the most original buildings

of the second golden age are those of Georgia and Armenia. Some are very early in date, for example the church of Pitzounda on the Black Sea, probably of the tenth century, and that of Akthamar on Lake Van (Fig. 91), surely of the

tenth. In these buildings the Greek cross form was used most freely, though older forms such as the domed basilica and the three shell type survived. In other respects, however, these buildings showed striking originality. The central dome, raised on a lofty, ashlar-built, many-sided drum, became almost a tower. On the exterior it often appeared, as at Akthamar, as a sharply pointed cone. The apse often ceased to be salient, and became but a tri-

angular cut in the thickness of the wall. Brick at times disappeared entirely, and the buildings were constructed or faced with cut stone, even the roof tiles being of this material. The exteriors, in a manner hitherto unknown in Byzantine architecture, were decorated with crisp cut relief, suggesting the earlier art of Syria. So great was the originality of this Georgian and Armenian architecture that of late a theory has been advanced, not without plausibility, that from this region came the creative genius which controlled all the Byzantine architecture of the second golden age and also influenced the architecture of western Europe.

The "Byzantine Renaissance." Byzantium's brilliant prosperity under the Macedonian and Comnene dynasties and the second golden age came to an end in 1204, when the disgraceful fourth crusade was diverted to Constantinople and the city sank into ruins. Culture rose again on the ashes and in the later thirteenth, the fourteenth, and the early fifteenth centuries came the period known as the "Byzantine Renaissance." Constantinople, however, was weak. Her scientists and men of letters were eminent, but she lacked money for architectural enterprises. Thus we find the more important buildings of the last Byzantine period outside of Constantinople, in Greece, in the Balkan states, in Asia Minor. Divergences occur in these buildings, caused by local taste and material, but the style still has strong unity. Moreover, the art continued to develop and never sank to mere repetition of earlier works.

Plans. The Greek cross plan continued to be, on the whole, the favorite. At the same time there was a frequent reversion to the old domed basilican type. Especially at Trebizond, in such churches as Hagia Sophia and the Chrysokephalos, the western arm of the cross was lengthened, aisles were added, and the longitudinal axis of the building emphasized. At Athos a development suggesting the ancient Syrian three-shell plan occurred.

Elevations. In elevation the churches of this last period showed striking changes. The vertical line was unsparingly accented. Frequently, as at Manassia in Serbia (Figs. 79 and 92), the ground story was made very high, and subdivided by thin vertical engaged columns suggesting narrow pilaster strips. The drum became startlingly elongated, and the dome, for safety's sake, made smaller. The Angle domes were now often striking features on the exterior. In some Serbian buildings, for example Ravanitsa (Fig. 80), Manassia (Fig. 92), and the church of the Archangel near Uskub, the dome is almost invisible and the drum has the appearance of a slender tower. In other cases the drum is lowered, the diameter of the dome widened, the whole surmounted with a cone. The massy appearance of this form, as at Hagia Sophia at Trebizond, makes it still a striking—almost donjon-like—feature of the exterior.

Decoration. Decoration as well underwent a change. Mosaic, being very costly, was less freely used, and the cheaper

FIG. 92—MANASSIA (SERBIA).   (POKRYCHKIN)

medium of fresco came into great vogue. Some of the frescoes, for example those at Mistra (the Peribleptos), bear comparison with those of contemporary Italy. On the exterior polychrome marble was almost completely abandoned, to give place to the richest decoration in multicolored and patterned brick that the style ever invented. At times even glazed tiles were intermingled with the brick, and the exterior of such a church as Saint Basil's at Arta is a brilliant example of the beautiful effects which the later Byzantine artist could get by the refined color and texture of his surfaces.

Inspiration. Of late years several theories have been advanced to explain the source of this extraordinary last burst of activity in Byzantine art. By far the most plausible is that western Europe at last paid off a part of its heavy debt, and returned to Byzantium something in the way of inspiration. The prevalence of the three-aisled building in Byzantium, the almost Gothic emphasis on the vertical line, the resort to fresco such as was common in Italy, all support a theory suggested by the close political and cultural ties which bound fourteenth and fifteenth century Constantinople to western Europe. On the other hand it is as reasonable to suppose that the creative genius and vitality which Byzantine art showed in its first two great periods also produced the third, and remained at work down to the fateful year of 1453, when the weakened city, abandoned by Christian Europe, surrendered to the Turk.

Secular building. The early palace. Albeit the historical importance of Byzantine architecture lies primarily in the ecclesiastical buildings, the style also showed great originality and activity in its secular works. The building of great palaces accompanied the building of great churches. Constantine set the example by raising a magnificent palace in the new city, of which now there is no trace, but which must have followed the general lines laid down by Diocletian at Spalato. We know the appearance of an early Byzantine palace from the mosaic in Sant' Apollinare Nuovo at Ravenna, representing the palace of Theodoric, now destroyed. This mosaic shows us a long, arcaded structure composed of a central porch with a gable and two wings. The wings are two-storied, with square windows in the second story arcade. Apparently exigencies of space suppressed the Syrian court, and the colonnade opened directly on the street.

Secular building in Justinian's time. Shortly afterward, the reign of Justinian produced a great burst of secular building in Constantinople. At this time the Senate was built, all in white marble, the baths of Zeuxippus were splendidly decorated in marble polychrome, the baths of Arcadius were restored, and aqueducts were raised which rivaled those of the Roman Campagna.

The cistern. The need for storing water produced a unique type of civil building in Constantinople: the cistern. The earliest was apparently the Cisterna Maxima, constructed under the forum in 407. As the size of these cisterns increased they became really important monuments of architecture, daring in plan and delicate in detail. The cistern called

Pulcheria, built in 421, had a surface of over 1000 square metres and the vault was carried on thirty granite columns. In less than a century, however, the ambitions of the architects produced such tremendous works as the cistern of Bin-bir-direk (the thousand and one columns) with a surface of over 3500 square metres. The idea of these colossal works came from Alexandria, but their development in Constantinople was absolutely unprecedented. They prove the engineering genius of the Byzantines to have been no whit inferior to that of the Romans.

Palaces of the second golden age. In the second golden age the activity in secular building was as great as in the first. Basil I. ushered in the age by building a new palace, the Cenourgion, to the splendor of which many writers have testified. To this he added many buildings, the Pentacou-bouclon, the so-called Pavilion of the Eagle, the treasury, and others. Later Nicephorus Phocas raised the Boucoleon on the shore of the Sea of Marmora. Starting with a small building already on the site, this Emperor produced a palace at once lavish in its appointments and donjon-like in its strength. Each generation added something to the Sacred Palace or other imperial residences. In the twelfth century the Sacred Palace was somewhat neglected, and the Comnenes built the Blachernæ, a palace at the end of the Golden Horn. Enthusiastic accounts of crusaders attest the beauty of this building, and in the graceful architectural fragment which the Turks call the Tekfour-Serai we probably have an extant part of the original. This ruin shows a refined pattern and surface texture in brick and ashlar similar to that of the churches of this period.

The Sacred Palace. Much has been written about the appearance of the Sacred Palace (Fig. 93), yet archeologists are still disputing as to its plan. Indeed the term "Sacred Palace," indicating as it does a single building, is confusing. The work was a conglomeration of buildings, lay and ecclesi-astical, heterogeneous in plan, dimensions, and date, covering a total area, roughly triangular in shape, of over 400,000 square yards. One side was bounded by the Sea of Marmora, and one by the Hippodrome, a gigantic structure 1400 feet in length, easily capable of holding 80,000 persons. The third side faced the city, but was protected from the poorer quarters by terraces and gardens. Within were churches, fora, schools, council chambers, gardens, and even a private

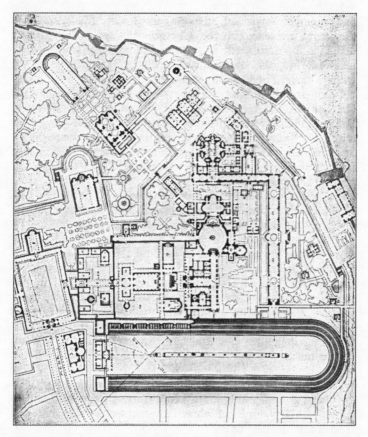

FIG. 93—CONSTANTINOPLE. PLAN OF THE SACRED PALACE, RESTORED. (EBERSOLT)

hippodrome. The general effect must, therefore, have been bewilderingly complicated, and not wholly unlike that of the Kremlin to-day. Both to the complication of the plan and the unbelievable richness of the decoration numerous descriptions of visitors testify. The complexity of the plan served to exaggerate the tremendousness of the site. Recognizing this the emperors were wont to have visiting ambassadors led through hall and court, where luxury succeeded luxury and richness surpassed richness, until they finally reached the royal presence in the Chrysotriclinium, an octagonal domed hall, decorated, if accounts of eye-witnesses can be believed, in gold, enamel, and precious stones beyond the wildest dreams of the Thousand and One Nights.

Later palace building. After the sack of the city in 1204 the Sacred Palace never recovered its pristine splendor. Palace building received a fatal set-back. At the same time numerous Frankish châteaux sprang up in Byzantine territory and influenced Byzantine civil architecture. The latest Byzantine palaces partake, therefore, more of the fortification than of the palace proper.

Fortifications. It must not be supposed, however, that warlike architecture had been neglected in the earlier periods of the Byzantine style. The willingness of the Byzantine architect to suppress, for reasons of defense, the graceful in favor of the strong is well proved by the great enceinte of Constantinople, much of which dates back to the reign of Theodosius II. (408-450). Africa especially retains monuments of early Byzantine military architecture which were, in their day, absolutely impregnable. Of such a type are the citadels of Lemsa in Tunisia, and of Haïdra (Fig. 94). In the second golden age the still extant works of Manuel Comnenus at Constantinople show the same power of military design at home.

The ensemble. In the period of Constantine and Justinian the general appearance of Constantinople must have been, aside from topographical variations, not unlike that of Rome. The Roman constructive sense and broad grasp of the essentials of city planning were inherited by the Byzantines. In the later period, however, the city must have assumed an appearance of inchoate complexity. Within the inclosure of the Sacred Palace, building after building was added, until all semblance of a synthetic plan was lost. Without, the same lack of a logical scheme prevailed and, except for differences in architectural detail and material, the Constantinople of Basil I. must have looked much like the Stamboul of to-day. Streets had become narrow and irregular, houses crowded, and the broad planning of classical antiquity had given way to the apparently thoughtless and illogical grouping of houses characteristic of so much of the building of the Middle Ages.

The dwellings of the rich. No examples of the less palatial Byzantine habitations remain, but illuminated manuscripts

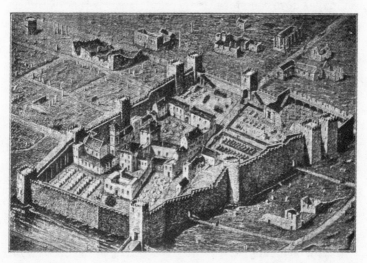

FIG. 94—HAIDRA. THE FORTIFICATIONS, RESTORED. (DIEHL)

give us some idea of the appearance of the houses of the wealthy. They were apparently not unlike those still to be found in the "dead cities" of Syria. The houses were of two or three stories, the façades ornamented with porticoes. From the ninth to the twelfth century open loggias decorated the upper stories and towers or lateral pavilions often flanked the main building. Balconies projected over the street, and the roofs were sometimes steep, sometimes terraced, and sometimes ornamented with small domes. Windows were square, with small squares of glass set in grilles. The prevailing materials were brick and marble. The façades were generally of combined brick and marble, and the floors of one or the other material. The outer doors were of nail-studded iron:

the inner of wood, carved, paneled and inset with plaques. The better dwellings were, therefore, both luxurious and graceful.

The poorer quarters. If, however, the public buildings and habitations of the rich were splendid, the dwellings of the poor were of the meanest, and the parts of the city used by the common citizens ill built, vilely planned, and worse kept. If we may believe contemporary accounts, such as that of Eudes de Deuil, who visited the city in 1147, in the common quarters the housetops often met above the streets, and the streets themselves were indescribably filthy, at times even barred by pools of mud in which men and beasts were drowned. The odors were noisome, and the streets unlighted at night, so that from sundown to sunup they were wholly given over to thieves, cutthroats, and yammering scavenger dogs like those which until recently infested Constantinople. If the reader could, by some strained flight of fancy, imagine a combination of present day Stamboul, the Campo Marzo region in Rome, and the Tatar city in Pekin, he would probably have a not inaccurate idea of the ensemble of twelfth century Constantinople.

The influence of Byzantine architecture. No discussion of the Byzantine style would be complete without a word about the powerful influence which the art exerted on contemporaneous and subsequent architecture. At times, as in Aix-la-Chapelle (Figs. 79, 80 and 85) and Germigny-les-Prés, as in Saint Front de Périgueux (Fig. 99) and many of the churches of Norman Sicily, this influence showed itself in terms of a partial imitation. A subtler influence is recorded in the acceptance by the West of the unformulated principles which underlay both the forms of detail and the constructive scheme of the Byzantine building. The Byzantine architect, rejecting all single forms of the classic capital, evolved by a gradual combination of all the elements of the classic capital a new form suited to new needs. The Gothic capital is but a refinement of the Byzantine, or rather a further development along the lines laid down by the Byzantine. The Romanesque and Gothic development of the vault, too, was made possible by the flexible treatment of the vault inaugurated by the Byzantines. Even the basic Gothic principle, the stabilizing of a complex vaulted system by means of an equilibrium of opposing thrusts, finds its antecedent, as we have seen, in the Byzantine architecture of the second golden age.

Influence on later styles. Moreover, Byzantine influence on other styles was not confined to the contemporary Middle Ages. We shall see that Renaissance and modern architecture are largely indebted to Byzantium. In the Balkans, in southern Russia, and in Greece, where the style was native, the recurrence to it has been constant, and such a building as the New Metropolis at Athens, though a debased imitation of older work, has the merit of being a wholly natural reversion to a native art. Finally, Saracenic architecture may be regarded as an outgrowth of Byzantine.

Significance of Byzantine architecture. The importance of Byzantine architecture is, therefore, threefold. It may be regarded as an important link between the Roman and Romanesque styles, as a source of inspiration in contemporary and subsequent architecture, and finally as a powerful and self-sufficient art in itself. On the whole, writers have tended to emphasize the first two points of view at the expense of the third. The result has been a stressing of the architecture of the first golden age before the development of the great medieval styles of western Europe, and a neglect of the equally important Byzantine architecture which postdates the Iconoclastic controversy. The dynamic quality of the art has largely been overlooked, and the style invested with a false conservatism which recent writers on Byzantine architecture are only beginning to dispel. It is well, therefore, especially in a general history of architecture, to emphasize the fact that the Byzantine style was not only an architecture of transition, but especially an independent, self-sufficient art which showed ever new vitality from the age of the first Constantine in the fourth century to that of the last in the fifteenth, and, in a sense, shows it even to-day.

CHRONOLOGICAL LIST OF MONUMENTS

Early Period, to the Accession of Justinian in 527

Constantinople, Palace of Constantine.—323–337.
Constantinople, Senate.—323–337.
Constantinople, Cisterna Maxima.—40°.

Constantinople, Cisterna Pulcheria.—421.
Constantinople, Walls of Theodosius.—First half of fifth century.
Constantinople, Eski-djouma.—First half of fifth century.
Constantinople, Stoudion basilica.—463.
Ravenna, Sant' Apollinare in Classe.—Begun before 526.
Ravenna, Palace of Theodoric.—Begun before 526.

First Golden Age, Inaugurated by Justinian, 527–726

Constantinople, Bin-bir-direk cistern.—528.
Ravenna, San Vitale.—526 or 534–547.
Salonica, Hagia Sophia.—C. 530.
Constantinople, Saint Irene.—532.
Constantinople, Hagia Sophia—532–562.
Cathedral of Parenzo (Dalmatia).—540.
Constantinople, Holy Apostles.—536–546.
Ravenna, Sant' Apollinare Nuovo.—549.
Constantinople, Saints Sergius and Bacchus.—First half of sixth century.
Constantinople, Baths of Zeuxippus.—First half of sixth century.
Lemsa (Africa), Fortifications.—Sixth century.
Haïdra (Africa), Fortifications.—Sixth century.
Saint Gregory, near Etschmiadzin (Armenia).—640–666.
Constantinople, Kalender-hane-djami (the Diaconessa of Emperor Maurice?).—Seventh century.
Constantinople, Hodja-moustapha-pasha (Saint Andrew's).—Seventh century.
Cathedral of Etschmiadzin (Armenia). — Begun in fifth, restored in seventh century.

Age of Iconoclasm, 726–842

Aix-la-Chapelle, Charlemagne's Chapel.—796–804.
Germigny-les-Prés (France).—Ninth century.

Second Golden Age, Inaugurated by Basil I., 867–1204

Constantinople, "La Nea" (Basil I.).—Before 886.
Constantinople, Cenourgion (Basil I.).—Before 886.
Constantinople, Pentacoubouclon (Basil I.).—Before 886.
Constantinople, Gul-djami (Saint Theodosia).—Second half of ninth century.
Skripou (Bœotia).—874.
Constantinople, Boucoleon (Nicephorus Phocas, Emperor).—963–969.
Akthamar, Lake Van (Armenia).—915–921.
Pitzounda (Armenia).—Tenth century.?

Lavra, Catholicon.—End of tenth or beginning of eleventh century.
Hosios Loukas (Phocis), Saint Luke of Stiris.—Beginning of eleventh century.
Chios, Nea Moni.—Mid-eleventh century.
Venice, Saint Mark's.—Begun 1063.
Hosios Loukas (Phocis), Theotokos (Small Church of Saint Luke).— Mid-eleventh century.
Constantinople, Kilissé-djami.—Second half of eleventh century.
Daphni.—End of eleventh century.
Périgueux (France), Saint Front.—1120.
Constantinople, Pantocrator.—1124.
Nauplia, Nea Moni.—1144.
Athens, Saint Theodore.—Mid-twelfth century.
Athens, Little Metropolis.—Mid-twelfth century.
Constantinople, Palace of the Blachernæ (Manuel Comnenus).— Soon after 1143.
Constantinople, Walls of Manuel Comnenus.—Soon after 1143.

Byzantine Renaissance, mid-thirteenth century—1453

Arta, Saint Basil.—Thirteenth century.
Trebizond, Hagia Sophia.—Thirteenth century.
Trebizond, Chrysokephalos.—Thirteenth century.
Ravanitsa (Serbia).—1381.
Kucevista, near Uskub (Serbia), Church of the Archangel.—Fourteenth century.
Mistra, Peribleptos.—End of the fourteenth century.
Manassia (Serbia).—1407.

BIBLIOGRAPHICAL NOTE

A. Michel's *Histoire de l'art*, 1905, vol. 1, pt. 1, contains a brilliant summary of the history of Byzantine art, by Gabriel Millet. C. Texier and R. P. Pullan's *Byzantine Architecture*, 1864, is a monumental work, now out of date, with excellent text and superb lithographic plates of a wide range of Byzantine monuments and details. A. Choisy's *L'art de bâtir chez les Byzantins*, 1883, is an old but authoritative work, well illustrated and especially important for Byzantine construction. J. Strzygowski's *Kleinasien*, 1903, and *Byzantinische Denkmäler* are important recent publications of research, already noted, emphasizing the Eastern origin of Byzantine art. C. Diehl's *Manuel d'art byzantin*, 1910, re-edition 1925, an authoritative, scholarly, up-to-date handbook, embodies the results of ancient and modern research in the Byzantine field. T. G. Jackson's *Byzantine and Romanesque Architecture*, 1913, is an up-to-date, scholarly, and readable work, liberally illustrated. Charles Bayet's *L'art byzantin*, 1884, is a handbook of Byzantine art, of great range and catholicity, though out of date. G. T. Rivoira's *Le origini della architettura lombarda*, 1901–07, already noted, is even more important for Byzantine than for early Christian art. A. Venturi's *Storia dell' arte italiana*, vol. 2, 1902, is a scholarly and well-illustrated volume on Italian art from the sixth to the eleventh centuries, publishing much original material and important for Byzantine architecture in Italy. F. de Verneihl's *L'architecture byzantine en France*, 1851, though out of date, discusses in an able way the churches of Byzantine character in central France. G. Millett: *L'ecole grec dans l'architecture byzantinem* 1917, and *L'art ancien serbe. Les Eglises*, 1919, are scholarly and beautifully illustrated books on the buildings of these fields. W. Salzenberg's *Altchristliche Baudenkmäler von Konstantinopel vom. 5. bis 12. Jahrhundert*, 1854, is an out-of-date but authoritative and interesting work. A van Millingen's *Byzantine Churches in Constantinople*, 1912, is a scholarly, readable, and well-illustrated volume on the churches of Constantinople; the same author's *Byzantine Constantinople*, 1899, is an interesting work on the Byzantine monuments of the city of Constantinople. L. de Beylié's *L'habitation byzantine*, 1902, with a *Supplément* in 1903, is a monumental and superbly illustrated work on the Byzantine dwelling. W. R. Lethaby and H. Swanson's *Sancta Sophia*, 1894, an exhaustive monograph on the most important monument of the earlier Byzantine period, is here mentioned on account of the light it throws on Byzantine architecture as a whole. J. Ebersolt's *Le grand palais de Constantinople*, 1910, a modern and ingenious monograph on the Sacred Palace at Constantinople, is important for an attempted historical arrangement of the many buildings in the inclosure. It is the last, but perhaps not the final, word on the subject. E. A. Grosvenor's *Constantinople*, 1900, is a popular and readable book on the city, with fine reproductions and interesting accounts of the monuments. G. Barker's *The Walls of Constantinople*, 1910, is an interesting history and description, well illustrated, of the defenses of the city. J. B. Bury's *A History of the Eastern Roman Empire*, 1912, a history of the empire, will be useful for those who need to acquire the proper historical background for a study of Byzantine art. Another excellent general historical review is W. S. Davis' *A Short History of the Near East*, 1923.

CHAPTER VIII

ROMANESQUE ARCHITECTURE

Definition. A discussion of Romanesque architecture inevitably begins with a definition of the term Romanesque. The name, though an accepted one, and apt when understood, is nevertheless confusing to the beginner. Comprehension comes most quickly when we compare Romanesque architecture to the Romance languages. After the break-up of the Roman Empire there ensued a period of cultural confusion. From this confusion homogeneous nationalities slowly emerged. Based on Latin civilization, quickened by northern energy, modified and differentiated one from another by conditions of race and geography, nations arose. These nations possessed each a speech also based upon Latin yet differing from the speech of other nations similarly based. Thus the Romance languages, reminiscent of Rome, yet individual and national in character, came into being. Precisely the same phenomena appear in architecture, based upon Roman as a point of departure, but differing from it, each school being individual and expressive of the peculiar genius of the race which produced it, yet all bound by a common root and thus included in a common classification: Romanesque.

Date. This much understood, new difficulties begin. From the break-up of Roman civilization in the fifth century to the clearly defined rise of the nations about 1000 there occurred a formative period in which chaos was more frequent than order, yet in this period language was spoken and written, buildings erected. At times, as during the reign of Charlemagne (the Carolingian Renaissance), civilization in this period was even brilliant. Should one call the speech of this period Romance; its architecture Romanesque? In very general classifications all west-European architecture, outside of mere Byzantine imitation, roughly from 500 to 1150, is called Romanesque. The field may then be subdivided, the period of later development from 1000 to 1150 placed by itself, and the earlier architecture classified as Carolingian, Carolingian and Ottonian, or even pre-Romanesque. Once the distinction is comprehended the danger disappears.

Relation of Romanesque to Gothic. The comprehension and appreciation of Romanesque architecture has been more hindered, albeit innocently, by writers on Gothic architecture than by anything else. One of the most brilliant, Quicherat, summed up the style in the clever yet misleading definition that has appeared in every subsequent book on the subject. According to the French archeologist, Romanesque is an architecture that, retaining elements of Roman, has ceased to be Roman, and anticipating elements of Gothic, is not yet Gothic. Every phrase of this definition is true, yet its total is pernicious, as it overlooks the self-sufficiency of the Romanesque style and relegates it to the position of a mere architecture of transition. Nothing more clearly shows its weakness than its over-emphasis of organic Romanesque styles, such as Lombard, which led up to Gothic, and its utter inapplicability to some of the most monumental, if inorganic, styles such as the Tuscan.

Organic and inorganic architecture. The distinction between what is called an organic and an inorganic style of architecture may well be made here. An organic architecture is a vaulted one, the vaults supported by ribs, buttresses, and piers, and the latter deliberately arranged with sole reference to the needs of supporting the vault and opposing its thrusts. Such an architectural system, so often compared to the bony structure of a living organism, deserves the adjective organic. An architectural system may, however, be more or less convincingly organic. The omission of one or more structural ribs in a vault, the maladjustment of one or more supports to the thrusts which they are designed to meet, may mar the organic feeling of the system but not destroy it. On the other hand a very splendid building may be completely inorganic, like the cathedral of Pisa, which is covered with a timber roof carried on a simple wall. Romanesque architecture must, therefore.

be studied for itself alone and not as a result of what has gone before or as an excuse for what is coming after.

National feeling. This point must be insisted upon the more strongly, since so much of the charm of the study of Romanesque comes from the variety of the style. The causes of these variations were, of course, historical and geographical. In the early period, so often called pre-Romanesque, from 500 to 1000, European architecture showed considerable homo- geneity, but naturally with the growth of separate nations came a growth of national styles; and within the nations, often sharply divided into districts which were themselves *regna in regno*, there grew up local styles of great individuality and charm. Thus Romanesque is, outside of France where organic Gothic developed, perhaps the most distinctly national of each country's architectural styles.

Ecclesiastical interest. The study of Romanesque is much simplified by one fact. In no other style, not even Gothic, is the interest so confined to ecclesiastical architecture. So true is this that in a brief discussion of medieval architecture, secular architecture is most profitably studied in its Gothic aspects, leaving the student free in the Romanesque period to concentrate on the vastly more important church and monastic buildings.

Corporate quality. The style was not only a natural and religious expression, it was an expression of the common ideals of the whole people. In other words it was distinctly corporate. A *magister operarius* directed the works, but great freedom was allowed his swarms of assisting craftsmen. The result was variation and inequality of workmanship, but for that very reason a freshness lamentably lacking in many an otherwise impeccable modern work.

Architectural refinement. This freshness, which seems to invest Romanesque, and indeed all medieval buildings, may come partly as well from the asymmetrical quality of the work. Whether the variations in plan, in the heights of columns and of arches and the like, which may be observed in practically all medieval buildings, is the result of inaccurate measurements, settling of members, or as is more likely, of deliberate design after the manner of Greek architectural refinements, the result is a living quality, a sense of movement and picturesqueness that banishes all monotony and keeps the building vitally interesting when more painstaking and elaborate works seem dry as dust.

General characteristics. Though the plans of Romanesque churches are widely diverse (Fig. 99), all are a development of the arrangement with special reference to liturgical needs embodied in the Christian-Roman basilica. In general, buildings of the central type were confined to baptistries and tombs, and when churches of this type occur, they represent Byzantine influence. The round arch, as opposed to the Gothic pointed arch, is a general characteristic of Romanesque, though many examples of pointed arches occur in the style.

Classification. Although many classifications of Romanesque have been offered, the main divisions of the movement at the period of its great development in the eleventh and twelfth centuries are fairly clear. Italy had a style of her own, subdivided roughly into the northern, central, and southern. Germany, too, had an individual style, on the whole semi-organic in the Rhine Valley and inorganic elsewhere. France offers the most complicated problem of classification, with no less than six main subdivisions in her Romanesque art. In the south we find a distinct Provençal style, highly classic in feeling. Farther north we find the Auvergnat, most precocious of the French schools, which may be classified with that of Languedoc, the artistic center of the latter being at Toulouse. In Aquitaine another school grew up, showing marked Byzantine affiliations, although some modern writers have urged an autochthonous growth for the Aquitanian churches. Still another subdivision may be made of Burgundy, with its emphasis on monastic architecture. In the north two highly organic styles developed, the most precocious being the Norman, the most finished that of the district around Paris called the Ile de France. England afforded a very homogeneous type of Romanesque, which may be regarded as an offshoot of Norman, and Spain had an individual style largely imported from Languedoc, though influenced, especially in the south, by Eastern architecture.

Carolingian architecture. A closer examination of the style in its various manifestations must begin of course with the art which we have called Carolingian or pre-Romanesque, or which might perhaps better be called by a more neutral and less descriptive term—the art of the dark ages. This art, though occasionally it takes on something of a national aspect, as in the Saxon architecture of England, was European rather than national. Moreover, some of the most important monuments of the style, like Charlemagne's chapel at Aix-la-Chapelle (Figs. 79 and 85) or the church of Germigny-les-Prés, we may pass over lightly, since they only emphasize how closely at times Byzantine architecture was copied.

New developments. There was, on the other hand, much building in the period which strikes a new note. The basilican plan was not merely used, it was developed. Apses were often added at the west end, free-standing towers or turrets were included, and often the bema was thickened to produce the exaggerated T form of plan so common in German architecture of the Carolingian epoch (Salvatorskapelle, Frankfort). With the accumulation of relics, the need for more altar space led to a multiplication of chapels, in the form of absidioles. Sometimes these radiated from the rounded east end of the church (Saint Martin, Tours), sometimes they were given a place in the bema. With the elaboration of the liturgy, ceremonial demanded an ambulatory for processions round the apsidal end, and this important member was included. The diaconicon and prothesis of the early Christian basilica soon became the sacristy and vestry of the later works.

Saint Gall. By far the most illuminating example of Carolingian architecture is the ninth century monastery of Saint Gall (Switzerland) known to us by a manuscript plan (Fig. 95). This drawing shows the main characteristics of the projected monastic church and the subordinate buildings about it. The church itself is of the modified basilican plan, with three aisles, an eastern and a western apse, two flanking western towers, an exaggerated bema, ambulatory about the eastern apse, and flanking vestry and secretary's room. The complicated plan of Saint Gall is useful, too, in emphasizing the importance of the monastery and, indeed, the strength of the monastic system in this period. The church is but the most prominent building among a host of others. About it are packed separate structures, shops, baths, kitchens, stables, hospitals, servants' and guests' quarters, vegetable and flower gardens, in fact everything which could contribute to make the monastery a self-sufficient, self-sustaining community.

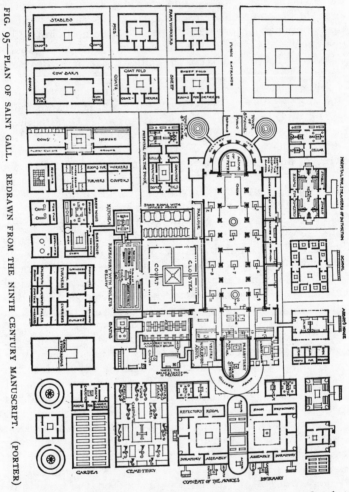

FIG. 95—PLAN OF SAINT GALL. REDRAWN FROM THE NINTH CENTURY MANUSCRIPT. (PORTER)

Existing monuments. We are not, however, confined to plans for our knowledge of the architecture of the dark ages. Many extant monuments, though usually damaged and marred by alteration, remain to show us what the original work was like. In France at Beauvais the so-called Basse-œuvre is one of the best known examples of the architecture of the dark ages, though the building is so severe in design, with its plain walls and timber roof, that it aids little in the study of Carolingian buildings. Perhaps the most highly developed type of Carolingian church is that of Montier-en-Der (Upper Marne), where a large proportion of the tenth century building is preserved for the student. Among the many German examples of this art perhaps the one most worth emphasizing is Lorsch (Rhine Valley, near Worms, Fig. 96). Here the façade of the basilican gate is preserved in its original form.

FIG. 96—LORSCH. ONE BAY OF THE BASILICAN GATE

Carolingian decoration. These fragments show us other innovations and contributions made to architecture by this style, the most striking being the triangular decoration, an easily recognized characteristic of the architecture all over Europe. Windows were framed in triangles, gable-like triangular decoration applied in relief to the walls, and the walls themselves composed of lozenges, sometimes vari-hued, with the emphasis on triangular form. The important billet mold appeared for the first time, and the window design of two lights, separated by a column and embraced by an arch, is reiterated and handed on to Romanesque and Gothic. This form may well have originated in the campanili of Carolingian Italy.

Pre-Romanesque architecture of England. On account of geographical conditions, the pre-Romanesque architecture of

England shows an individualistic tendency. Such monuments as Earl's Barton (Fig. 97) are not to be confused with contemporary continental monuments, though they were founded on Roman traditions, modified by barbarian ideas. Towers were frequent, the angles re-enforced by the very characteristic Saxon long-and-short work, of stone slabs embedded alternately horizontally and vertically. Walls were also decorated with strongly salient strips of stone, some placed vertically and running from the ground to the summit, some banded horizontally round the building. Openings were divided by clumsy wall shafts, strongly suggesting wooden forms. The east ends were usually square. The masonry handling in the Saxon buildings was extremely rude, but the style was sturdy and might well have developed into one of great beauty had its evolution not been arrested by the Norman conquest.

FIG. 97—EARL'S BARTON.   THE TOWER

Pre-Romanesque architecture of Spain. Geography affected the Carolingian architecture of Spain as well. The peninsula, like the island of Sicily, was always a battle-ground between races and civilizations, and a bridge over which Oriental influence entered Europe. The Spanish architecture of the dark ages, like that of the north, developed the basilican plan, but showed decidedly individualistic tendencies in arrangement of detail and especially in decoration. Barbaric elements came with the Visigothic occupation, and to them were soon added a decided Oriental influence, especially in decoration. Sassanian ideas crossed the straits of Gibraltar as easily as Tarik himself. As a result we find horseshoe arches, fluted scallop shells, and other details which give the architecture a semi-exotic character. Extant monuments are abundant. Among the most interesting may be named the church of Santullano (Oviedo), San Miguel de Linio (near Oviedo), and Santa Maria de Naranco (Fig. 98), near San Miguel.

Architectural activity about 1000 A.D. Although undue importance has been given to the effect on building of the safe

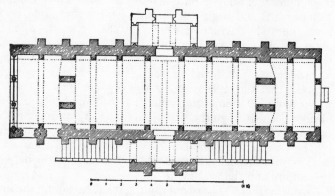

FIG. 98—SANTA MARIA DE NARANCO. PLAN

passage of the year 1000, when so many people, relying on a passage in the Apocalypse, believed the end of the world was at hand, the date is, in round numbers, a good one for the beginning of Romanesque architecture proper. Building received an extraordinary impetus about that time. The fact may be accounted for in many ways, but chiefly by the growth of the individual nations and the economic prosperity which their comparatively orderly governments insured.

Priority. In this later Romanesque, Italy, Germany, and France each claims priority for its own style, and the controversy is complicated by the fact that almost all the monuments have suffered from repair, restoration, addition, and alteration more or less complete. The majority cannot be dated by documents and the minority which can may have suffered from a subsequent, undated alteration. In general Brutail's rule is excellent: a documented building cannot be earlier than the date of its document, but may be, and generally is, later.   The critic must proceed with extreme caution, checking documentary against internal evidence, and vice versa, avoiding as far as possible the mistakes which come from preconceived ideas, and above all steeling himself against the appeals of a patriotic bias.

Lombard Romanesque. On weighing the evidence, the oldest theory seems not only the most convenient but the most plausible, and we may assume the priority of Lombard Romanesque and begin our discussion with that style.   This gives the credit of creative genius to Italy, but insists upon the necessity of Germanic (Lombard) blood to quicken this genius. Opponents of the theory call attention to the fact that Lombard architecture as designed in the eleventh century is highly organic, that the style soon lost this organic quality, that the movement died prematurely, and that Italian architecture has always been distinguished from northern by its fondness for inorganic forms, but all these phenomena may be explained by the weakening of the Lombard stock and the commercial decline of Lombardy coincident with the struggle between the empire and the papacy.

Characteristics.   The ribbed vault.   What then were the main characteristics of this architecture?   Since it was organic it was, of course, vaulted, the favorite form being the domical groin vault.   This form we have seen developed in Byzantine architecture, as in the vaults over the aisles of Hagia Sophia, from the heavy concrete vaults of the Romans.   To the simple groin vault the Lombard architecture added strongly salient ribs, reinforcing the groin angles and binding the vault sides. They thus created a set of six ribs in all: two longitudinal or wall ribs; two transverse which crossed the nave at right angles to the long axis of the building; and two diagonal or groin ribs, which met in the center of the vault and divided it into four cells.   The advantage of these ribs can hardly be exaggerated.   They could be built separately and act as centering for the construction of the web.   They were independent of the latter, which rested largely upon them, and thus the web could be thinned and the vault shell made much lighter.   They concentrated the vault thrusts at, or near, the springing of the ribs, where the architects contrived to meet them with salient pier buttresses, and they divided the whole

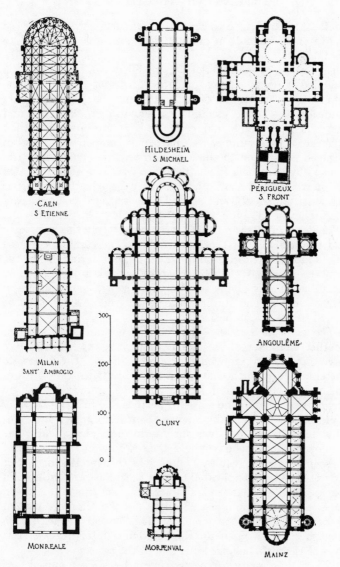

CAEN
S ETIENNE

HILDESHEIM
S MICHAEL

PÉRIGUEUX
S. FRONT

MILAN
SANT' AMBROGIO

ANGOULÊME

300

200

100

0

CLUNY

MONREALE

MORIENVAL

MAINZ

FIG. 99—PLANS OF ROMANESQUE CHURCHES

vault of a building into separate compartments or bays, so that a crack or fault in one bay was not liable to spread to another.

Compound supports. Such a modified vault demanded a modified support. An aggregate of ribs of different sizes, springing in different directions, could be gathered only clumsily on a round column or a square pier. A compound pier was needed and produced. In Sant' Ambrogio at Milan (Fig. 101), for example, we find a pier compounded with an engaged pilaster on the nave side to bear the transverse rib, flanked by two engaged shafts to carry the diagonal ribs. On the northern and southern faces an engaged pilaster carries the longitudinal rib, and against it an engaged column bears the arches of the ground story archivolt. On the aisle side an engaged pilaster and shaft carry respectively the transverse and diagonal ribs of the aisle vaults. The capitals of these shafts face in the direction in which the ribs spring, hence the capitals of the shafts which carry the diagonals are set obliquely to the main axis of the building. In short, logic appears in every member, and structural logic, a term we shall often be forced to use, is emphasized.

The alternate system. The same structural logic inspired another characteristic of Lombard architecture, destined to have far-reaching influence on later styles: the alternate system. On plan the naves were roughly twice the width of the aisles. It occurred logically to the architects that by having two bays in the aisles to balance one in the nave they could make their vaults square (Sant' Ambrogio, Fig. 99). This necessitated, however, an intermediate pier to carry the ribs of the aisle vaults where their springing did not meet those of the nave vaults. Obviously this intermediate pier did not need the complicated form or the robustness of the main piers, hence smaller and simpler piers alternated between larger and more complicated ones, and the alternate system of vaults and piers was created. This system was used with great success in Romanesque and Gothic architecture when two bays of the aisle balanced one bay of the nave.

The pilaster strip. A new structural system required new members, therefore the pilaster strip, whether against a pier to receive a member of the vaulting system, or appearing on

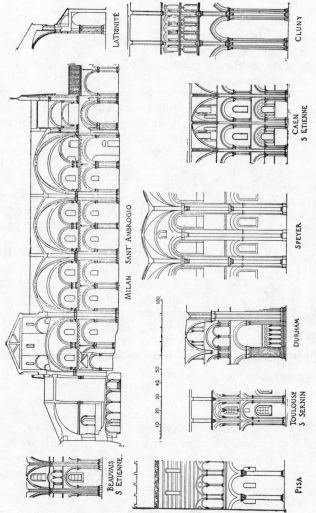

FIG. 100—SECTIONS OF ROMANESQUE CHURCHES

BEAUVAIS S ETIENNE

MILAN SANT' AMBROGIO

LA TRINITÉ

CLUNY

CAEN S ETIENNE

SPEYER

DURHAM

TOULOUSE S SERNIN

PISA

the exterior as a buttress, received unprecedented development.

Decoration. Aside from the fundamentally organic quality of the Lombard building, which is its most important characteristic, the style developed a very original decorative scheme. Corbels were used unsparingly. Arched corbel tables were run under the eaves and following the rake of the pitched gable roofs. Decoration was attained by means of arcades, some-

FIG. 101—MILAN. SANT' AM-
BROGIO. DRAWING OF ONE
BAY SHOWING VAULT RIBS AND
SUPPORTS.   (MOORE)

times open, but more often blind. Doors were enriched with porches, covered with gables supported by columns, which were themselves carried on the backs of sculptured lions. Sculpture, sometimes of a very rude sort, sometimes with Byzantine refinement, played a not unimportant part, but it was chiefly confined to portals, lintels, capitals, and the like. On the exterior color was generally eschewed. For decorative effect on the exterior the builders relied on architectural detail, carving, and differentiation of textures in the arrangement of fairly monochromatic material. Mosaic and marble veneer were excluded from the interiors, but these were enlivened with painting, now almost wholly gone, which must, in the original,

have been garish. Further enlivement of the interior was obtained by rich church furniture, sometimes of carved marble, or backed with ivory, sometimes of exquisitely modeled stucco, and at times even incrusted with silver, gold, and enamel.

Sant' Ambrogio at Milan. Turning to the monuments which exhibit the style, we find the best known and most perfect example in Milan in the church of Sant' Ambrogio (Figs. 99, 100, 101, 102, and 103). This building has of late years figured largely in archeological dispute. It, and the neighboring and equally typical San Michele of Pavia, were long considered to date from the mid-eleventh century, but modern archeology tends to date the vaults of Sant'

FIG. 102—MILAN. SANT' AMBROGIO. INTERIOR LOOKING TOWARD THE APSE

Ambrogio from the second quarter of the twelfth. They would thus be antedated by Romanesque monuments of Normandy. The point is not as important as at first appears, for the form of the vaults would have been determined by the time the first tier of stones in the piers was placed. The piers themselves reveal this. Moreover, such finished monuments could not spring spontaneously into being, but would imply a long development of experimental building before them, and modern research has revealed a number of examples of ribbed vaults of the eleventh century in Lombardy, some of them even constructed in the second quarter of the century.

Plan and elevation. In plan (Fig. 99) Sant' Ambrogio is basilican, with three groin vaulted bays in the nave, a crossing with an octagonal lantern, and a short choir of half a bay. Two bays in the aisles correspond to one in the nave. The eastern termination has a great semicircular apse, flanked by two smaller apses of the same shape, on the axis of the aisles.

FIG. 103—MILAN. SANT' AMBROGIO. EXTERIOR

This form, typically Carolingian, surely belongs to the ninth century building. There is no clerestory, the space being occupied by a large triforium gallery, the vaults of which receive the thrusts of the nave vaults and transmit them to the salient pier buttresses attached to the walls. The nave vaults (Fig. 100), very domical, have a full complement of transverse longitudinal and diagonal ribs. The aisle vaults are groined without diagonal ribs. The façade shows an open narthex, with an open gallery above it. The first story is divided from the second by a horizontal string-course, with an arched corbel table, and a similar corbel table follows the rake of the gable. Pilaster strips to the first story, and engaged shafts to the roof, divide the façade vertically into five sections. The octagonal lantern is decorated with two open galleries, and attached to the church is a square campanile reinforced at the angles by pilaster strips, divided horizontally by string-courses with corbel tables, and vertically by engaged

FIG. 104—VERONA. SAN ZENO. GENERAL VIEW

columns. The church has an atrium with vaulted portico which prevents a distant view of the façade.

Architecture outside of Milan. The farther removed it was from Milan the less organic Lombard architecture tended to become. San Michele of Pavia, to be sure, exhibits an organic feeling fully the equal of Sant' Ambrogio. Perhaps the most original church after these two is Sant' Abondio at Como, which affords one of the most pleasing and monumental designs of the style. This building has a fivefold vertical division of the façade, corresponding to the five aisles of the interior, a well-proportioned clerestory, and fine twin campanili symmetrically arranged. It is, however, unvaulted.

The Maestri Comacini. One might expect monumental architecture at Como and, indeed, throughout Lombardy, on account of the Maestri Comacini, a famous band of workmen first mentioned by the Lombard King Rotari (636–652), the name of which suggests an origin on a little island, "Isola Comacina," in Lake Como. The importance of this mysterious band has probably been exaggerated, but there seems little doubt that it had some influence both in the creation and in the spreading abroad of the Lombard style.

Reversion to inorganic type. Throughout northern Italy the Lombard style held sway, stretching west into Piedmont and east into Emilia and the Veneto. In later monuments, however, as well as in those distant from Milan, there was a reversion to an inorganic type. At the same time the works tended to become more monumental, more showy. Parma cathedral (1117), with its lofty if inept vaults bound with tie-rods, its broad façade, its soaring campanile, has, at least, a superficial impressiveness that is denied the more organic but less obtrusive Sant' Ambrogio. Similarly Modena (consecrated 1184), on account of well-proportioned façade and profuse sculpture, is more monumental in effect than the Milanese building.

San Zeno, Verona. Perhaps the most pleasing and the least organic of all Lombard Romanesque buildings is San Zeno at Verona (consecrated 1138, Fig. 104). This church has probably the most satisfactory proportions of any building of its class. Its portal is ennobled by a gabled porch of the type popular in this style, and quite probably invented in Verona. The exterior is further enhanced by a free-standing campanile, decorated with vertical pilaster strips and horizontal strips of alternating red and white marble. The interior with its great height and raised crypt is impressive, but the inorganic quality of the building is revealed by its timber roof, trussed after the manner of the frame of a ship. The wooden roof, without thrust, permits a generous clerestory.

Tuscan Romanesque. Farther south we next come to the architecture of central Italy which, for convenience, we may

FIG. 105—PISA. THE CATHEDRAL AND LEANING TOWER, SEEN FROM THE SOUTHWEST

call Tuscan, though it overstepped the limits of what is now the Tuscan province. The student will at once be struck with the inorganic quality of the style. The plans are chiefly basilican, and the architects strongly preferred the timber roof to a vaulted structure. At the same time the buildings were often extremely monumental in size and striking in decoration. In lieu of organic originality the Tuscan Romanesque offered a gorgeousness in striking contrast to the comparatively drab appearance of the art of the north.

Decoration, general character. This effect was obtained principally by means of polished marble panels, and a profusion of arcades, blind and open, applied to the exterior. The exterior of such a building as the cathedral of Pisa is covered

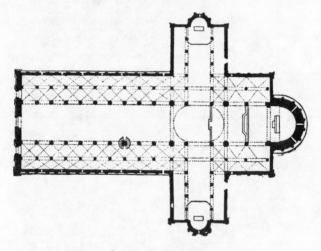

FIG. 106—PISA. CATHEDRAL. PLAN

with arcades, and the material used is colored marble applied in panels, squares, lozenges, and all manner of pure design, so brilliant in color as literally to be dazzling (Fig. 105). Interiors were generally basilican, the walls enlivened with horizontal strips of light and dark. Domes over the crossing were common, but nave vaults rare. At times one feels a certain amount of Lombard influence in central Italy, as at

Toscanella and Montefiascone, but in general the style is very individual.

The group at Pisa.   The cathedral.   The best point of departure for a study of Tuscan Romanesque monuments is, of course, the cathedral group at Pisa (Figs. 100, 105, 106, and

FIG. 107—PISA. CATHEDRAL. VIEW OF THE INTERIOR LOOKING
TOWARD THE APSE

107), where the cathedral, the leaning tower and baptistry offer the most resplendent examples of the style. The cathedral is five aisled basilican (Figs. 100 and 106). Its exterior arcades vary slightly in height and spacing, looking almost as though they were drawn and constructed free-hand. The building is wooden-roofed, but over the crossing is an egg-shaped dome curiously small for so large a nave. The wide transepts afford a striking feature. The effect of the exterior (Fig. 105) is one of rich color and interesting design. The interior (Fig. 107), however, is decorated with the typical bands of light and dark marble, the contrasts being so strong as to shock the eye rather than please it.

The Leaning Tower. The same decorative system, open arcades with colored marble veneer, is applied in concentric rings to the campanile (Fig. 105). Though there is still dispute as to whether the lean of this famous monument is caused by settling of the foundation or was included in the original design, the latter explanation seems the better attested, and there is little doubt that the builders chose to make one of Italy's most beautiful towers into architecture's most famous freak.

The Baptistry. The baptistry is not so important for our study as the other two monuments of the group, since it belongs partly to the Gothic period. The peculiar shape of the roof is caused by a unique system of doming, the building being first covered with a cone of masonry, exerting slight thrust, and then the superficial effect of a dome later attained by springing a segment of an annular vault over the aisle, from the cornice, or upper string-course, to a point about two-thirds the way up the masonry cone.

Buildings at Florence. Florence affords a local variation of the style, the best example being the church of San Miniato al Monte. This building follows the general scheme of decoration of the style, with a variant in the emphasis on the square in pure design. It also emphasizes another element noticeable in Tuscan Romanesque: the imitation of classical form. Some of the columns and pilasters follow the Corinthian order very closely, others are actually taken from Roman remains, and we can understand why the term "proto-Renaissance" has been applied to the age which produced such works. In another Florentine building, in the same style, the baptistry of San Giovanni, this classic feeling is still stronger, and has led some authorities even to consider the reconstruction of about 1200 less important than is generally supposed, and to argue that the present structure dates back to the late classical period. The ingenious doming of the building, with its double shell and stiffening barrel vaults between the ribs, influenced Brunelleschi in his design for the dome of the cathedral of Florence.

South Italian Romanesque. Finally, in the third subdivision of Italian Romanesque, that of southern Italy and Sicily, or

of the Two Sicilies, as the region is generally called, geography
plays an important part.   Since the beginning of Mediterranean history this region has been fought over by conflicting races.   Here barbarian, Greek, Phœnician, Roman,
Goth, Byzantine, Italian, Moslem, and Norman battled,
prevailed, succumbed, and disappeared.   The result was a

FIG. 108—CEFALÙ. CATHEDRAL.   VIEW OF THE WEST END

lawless and confused society, and an art that combined
Oriental and Occidental ideas.   Although a hybrid, it actually
succeeded in blending harmoniously the ideals of a half-
dozen races, and we may find in a single building Lombard
corbel tables, Norman interlacing arches, classic capitals,
Byzantine mosaics, and Saracenic domes.   If one's idea of
Italian Romanesque is confused, it is a correct one.

The style in Sicily.   In general the admixture of styles shows
more clearly in Sicily than in southern Italy.   At Cefalù
(Fig. 108), for example, we find the Norman flanking towers

embracing the façade, the Norman interlacing arches, and the Moslem dome.   One need not, however, leave Palermo, and its suburb, Monreale, to study Sicilian Romanesque in its most typical form.   The cathedral, to be sure, is almost wholly spoiled by baroque alteration, but in the Cappella Palatina in the royal palace south Italian Romanesque appears in its most harmonious blend.   The plan of this chapel is

FIG. 109—MONREALE.   CATHEDRAL.   VIEW OF THE INTERIOR LOOKING
TOWARD THE APSE

basilican, its pavement is of marble inlay, and its walls are covered with precious Byzantine mosaics.   The modified Corinthian columns which divide the nave from the aisles are low, the archivolts which they support are lofty with pointed arches, here surely of Saracenic origin.   The interior, completely incrusted with marble and mosaic, gives an impression of unsparing richness.

Monreale.   Probably the finest example of the style, however, is the cathedral of Monreale (Figs. 99, 109, and 110), some five miles from Palermo, founded in 1176. This church is of Latin cross plan and wooden roofed. The pavement is marble, the dadoes are marble veneered, and the upper walls are incrusted with mosaic. The arches of the main archivolts are much stilted and pointed. The exterior shows Norman

FIG. 110—MONREALE. CATHEDRAL. SYSTEM OF THE NAVE AND THE EXTERIOR OF THE CHOIR

façade towers and interlacing, Saracenic decoration and construction. Adjoining the church is a cloister, with a portico carried on a series of paired columns richly carved in shaft and capital, and adorned with glass and marble mosaic. Such cloisters form specially charming features in many south Italian Romanesque churches, though they are to be found elsewhere in Romanesque work.

German Romanesque. The Romanesque of Germany is, on the whole, much more homogeneous than Italian, and the most distinctly national of the country's styles. The Romanesque style there was exceedingly prolific, and lingered longer

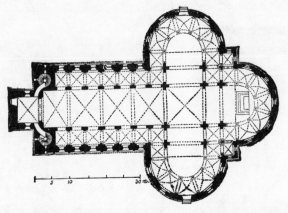

FIG. III—COLOGNE. SAINT MARY OF THE CAPITOL. PLAN

than in any other country. Its unity and strength may be explained by the unity and political power of Germany beginning in 919 with the reign of Henry the Fowler and lasting through the period of the Ottos and the later Henrys.

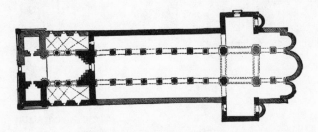

FIG. II2—PAULINZELLE. PLAN

In studying it we must seek to distinguish the Germanic elements from those which represent importation from outside. The former came from a development of the native

Carolingian style; the latter appear in the increasing tendency to use an organic Lombard structural system, and in a certain amount of Byzantine imitation. The last was not nearly so common in the later Romanesque as in the Carolingian epoch, though certain buildings, especially those at Cologne, with

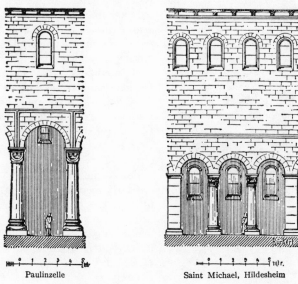

Paulinzelle   Saint Michael, Hildesheim

FIG. 113—SYSTEMS OF GERMAN ROMANESQUE CHURCHES

their apse-like transepts recalling the triconch churches of Syria and Egypt, seem surely to represent Oriental influences.

General characteristics. The most striking and typically German characteristic of the style is its complexity and picturesqueness, acquired by a multiplication of architectural members. Apses were placed at the west as well as the east. Lanterns not only covered the crossing, but were placed at the west end of the building. Towers, and especially turrets, at both ends were common. These elements, as we have seen, are of Carolingian derivation. Even the churches which seem to reflect most clearly Oriental influence develop the complexities of Carolingian prototypes, which were themselves influenced by the East. Thus the Holy Apostles at Cologne is but a development of Saint Mary of the Capitol (Fig. 111), and combines Germanic complexity with the main dispositions of an Oriental plan. The earliest German Romanesque buildings are generally basilican and tended to retain the timber roof; the later are partially or even completely organic. Generally, however, the organism of a church is marred by the omission of one or more structural members. This organic quality, appearing late as it does, may be explained as an imitation of Lombard work. In general the more organic as well as the more monumental churches are to be found in the valley of the Rhine.

FIG. 114—DRÜBECK. DRAWING OF ONE BAY, SHOWING THE SYSTEM

Basilican churches. Turning first to the basilican churches we find them all alike in this lack of organic feeling, but differing widely in the disposition of detail. Thus the Collegiate Church of Paulinzelle (Figs. 112 and 113) shows a blind triforium and a uniform system of massive columns dividing the nave from the aisles. The Collegiate of Gernrode has a triforium gallery, reduced clerestory windows, and an alternation of a column with a square pier in the ground story arcade. Further variety is offered by Saint Michael, Hildesheim (Figs. 99 and 113), which reverts to the blind triforium, but places two columns between the square piers in the main arcade. At Drübeck (Fig. 114) we note the simpler alternation of single column and pier, but the arches from pier to column are embraced by great blind arches of double width and height which spring from pier to pier. Variation is, therefore, almost infinite in these churches, but all are alike in the heaviness of their systems, the massiveness of their walls, and in their simple wooden roofs supported on trussed timbers.

The organic architecture of the Rhine. As a foil to these basilican churches one may turn to the great vaulted churches of the Rhine Valley: Speyer, Worms, and Mainz. These combine most happily the Lombard vaulted system with German picturesqueness. Speyer (Figs. 100, 115, 116, and 117) has an organic vaulted system, complete but for the missing diagonal ribs. It has a lantern over the crossing, two square towers at the east end, two more at the west, a western transept and a western lantern. Despite its complexity the

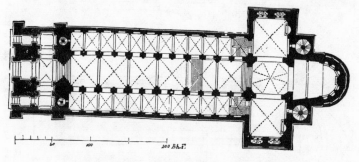

FIG. 115—SPEYER. PLAN

building is compactly arranged and monumental in effect. Worms (Fig. 116) shows as great complexity as Speyer, and moreover has a full complement of ribs. Both exhibit the alternate system, the intermediate piers on the nave side having engaged shafts which support an archivolt embracing the clerestory windows. Later than either of the preceding, and perhaps most imposing of all, is the cathedral of Mainz (Figs. 99, 116, and 118). Here the arches are freely pointed, and complexity is carried to the extreme, the church having its full complement of turrets, western lantern, western apse, and the like. The western apse adds picturesqueness, but mars the design of the façade, as the flanking doors are mere insignificant inlets for worshippers as compared to the welcoming portals of French churches.

Summary of German Romanesque. To understand German Romanesque, therefore, one must above all keep in mind the two divisions of elements: those developed from the Caro-

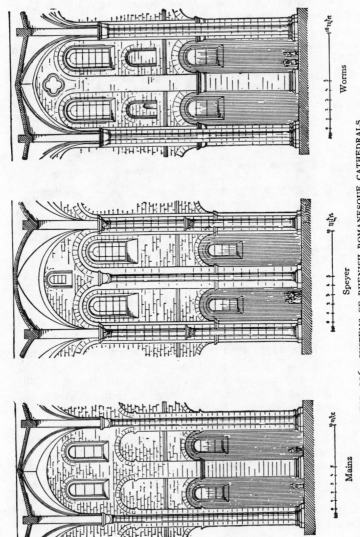

Mainz   Speyer   Worms

FIG. 116—SYSTEMS OF RHENISH ROMANESQUE CATHEDRALS

lingian, and those which are imported; the latter may be sub-divided roughly into Byzantine and Lombard. At times all three may combine in a single building, as in the church of the Holy Apostles at Cologne, where we find a semi-organic system, native picturesqueness, and a three shell east end which suggests Syria, but by keeping the main divisions in mind we may analyze and comprehend the host of Romanesque monuments which Germany offers.

Approach to the study of French Romanesque. As we approach the discussion of French Romanesque, clearness suggests that we begin with the southern styles and work toward the northern. This will, at times, falsify chronology, but the provincial styles of France are so nearly contemporaneous that the fault is not a serious one, and the advantages of examining the southern styles first are great. The southern and central styles have one important common characteristic: predilection for the barrel vault and consequently inorganic feeling.

FIG. 117—SPEYER. CATHEDRAL. VIEW OF THE INTERIOR LOOKING TOWARD THE APSE

Provence. One may characterize Provençal Romanesque as the most classic of all Romanesque styles. It was inevitable in a district which still preserves the Pont-du-Gard, the Baths of Diana at Nîmes, the amphitheater at Arles, the triumphal arch at Orange, and countless other monuments of Roman antiquity, that architects should be influenced strongly by the examples constantly before their eyes. The result was not only a predilection for the barrel vault, especially the barrel vault supported on transverse semicircular arches, as

FIG. 118—MAINZ. CATHEDRAL. VIEW FROM THE NORTH

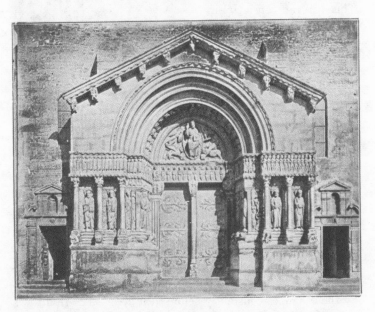

FIG. 119—ARLES. SAINT TROPHÎME. THE MAIN PORTAL

in the Baths of Diana, but also for detail strongly classical in feeling.

Monuments. An examination of the monuments emphasizes this fact. The façade of Saint Trophîme at Arles (Fig. 119) has capitals which are almost true Corinthian and a suggestion of entablature that is modified, not debased, classic Roman. The interior is barrel vaulted, with transverse arches, but the barrel vault is pointed in cross section. Saint Gilles (Gard) boasts a façade similar to Saint Trophîme, but more elaborate. Here even the masonry recalls classic Rome, and the main portal is flanked by channeled pilasters of almost deceptively classic character. Some of the Corinthian columns, too, need only a delicate entasis to appear stolen from a classic edifice. These are well-known examples, and the more obscure reiterate the same effects. The word "Romanesque" in its literal sense applies more aptly to the Provençal style than to any other.

Auvergne. Farther north and west a somewhat different development was taking place. In Auvergne we find the same predilection for barrel vaults, but new dispositions in plan. The Auvergnat churches, as one would expect in the earliest of the French Romanesque styles, have a Carolingian affiliation and something of the picturesqueness of the Romanesque of the Rhine.

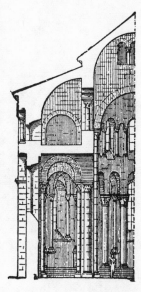

FIG. 120 — CLERMONT - FERRAND. NOTRE DAME DU PORT. TRANSVERSE SECTION, SHOWING HALF - BARREL VAULT OVER THE AISLE

Apses are provided with ambulatories and radiating absidioles, and absidioles are often added to the eastern walls of the transepts. At the same time the barrel vault is treated with more freedom. The nave is usually covered with a barrel vault, but the aisles are often provided with but half - barrel vaults which thrust inward and counteract the thrusts of the vault of the nave (see Fig. 120). An inevitable result of this arrangement was inadequate lighting. Light was admitted through the ground story windows, and through windows in the triforium gallery beneath the half-barrel vaults, but by the time it had filtered into the nave it was much weakened, and most Auvergnat churches give one

the sensation of a black cloud overhanging the nave, an effect which, if not cheerful, is at least impressive. The individual members and general construction of the Auvergnat church, according with its early date, are generally very massive, another fact which again makes the churches impressive, if sometimes ungraceful. The exterior is lightened by the absidioles, stepped lanterns, arcades, and general multiplication of members, which give the building picturesqueness.

FIG. 121—CLERMONT-FERRAND. NOTRE DAME DU PORT. VIEW OF THE EAST END

Monuments. The best known and historically most interesting of Auvergnat churches is Nôtre Dame du Port at Clermont-Ferrand (Figs. 120 and 121). It is a heavy, barrel-vaulted, ill-lighted but impressive church, with a multiplication of absidioles and the general picturesqueness which well typifies the style. Other monuments, as illuminating if less famous, are numerous. Among them we must mention Saint Saturnin, and Orcival (Puy-de-Dôme).

Languedoc. Closely allied to the style of Auvergne is that which we may call, for want of a better name, the school of Languedoc, though the district involved embraces a vast territory from Auvergne to the Pyrenees. The styles of Auvergne and Languedoc have often with reason been classified together, but the latter tends to a more monumental

scale, and greater delicacy in single members and sculptured
detail.   The most prominent example of this style is, of course,
Saint Sernin at Toulouse (Figs. 100 and 122), a five aisled,
barrel-vaulted structure with a lofty and very graceful lantern
over the crossing.   The building is on so elaborate a scale, and
exhibits so great delicacy of material and detail, that one does
not at first identify it as a
close relative of the buildings
of neighboring Auvergne, yet
such it is.   The architectural
sculptures   alone   of   Languedoc   would   differentiate
the buildings of that district
from those of Auvergne.

*Aquitaine.   Byzantine
character of the building.*
North   of   Languedoc   and
west of Auvergne we find a
very   vigorous   and   distinct
school   flourishing   in   Aquitaine.   The Aquitanian
buildings have generally been
characterized   as   the   most
Byzantine   of   French   Romanesque churches.   Saint
Front at Périgueux (Figs. 99
and 123) has repeatedly been

FIG. 122—TOULOUSE. SAINT SERNIN.
THE INTERIOR SEEN FROM THE WEST

called a direct copy of Saint Mark's at Venice, and the numerous other churches of the district, with their domes on pendentives so unique in French Romanesque, have been said to be
inspired by Saint Front.   To this theory a reaction has lately
set in.   Saint Front postdates many of the buildings in the
neighborhood with the same characteristics, and there are great
differences between the so-called Byzantine details of these
buildings and the details of the real Byzantine buildings
whence they are supposed to be derived.   These facts have led
certain scholars to conclude that the domed churches of
Aquitaine owe no more to Byzantium than the Romanesque
of the rest of France, but convincing as these arguments at
first seem, they can be overthrown by the juxtaposition of the

plans of Saint Mark's and Saint Front (Figs. 88 and 99).
We note the salient Greek cross, the barrel vaults, the central
dome on pendentives, and the four subordinate domes on the
arms of the cross. Such similarities are not coincidences.
Certainly Saint Front is not a copy of Saint Mark's; surely,
however, the two are inspired by a Byzantine original, quite

FIG. 123—PERIGUEUX. SAINT FRONT. GENERAL VIEW FROM THE
SOUTHEAST

possibly the church of the Holy Apostles at Constantinople.
It is correct, therefore, to classify the Romanesque of Aquitaine
as most Byzantine in character.

Originality of Aquitanian architecture. Not all the churches
of Aquitaine, however, have the Greek cross plan or even the
domes on pendentives which mark the style as Byzantine in
character. In the cathedral of Angoulême, for example (Fig.
99), the dome vaults are arranged in the form of a Latin cross,
and at Notre Dame la Grande at Poitiers (Fig. 124) the dome
on pendentives is abandoned in favor of the barrel vault.
The churches of the region are, nevertheless, bound into one

style by the system of decoration, curious cone-shaped turrets with scale-like tiles, bossy masonry, and a unique intermingling of architectural and figure sculpture as ornament over portals and windows.

Burgundy. We may conclude our examination of southern and central French Romanesque with a brief review of the Burgundian style. As might be expected from geographical considerations, this style is the most organic of the southern-central group, and therefore makes a good transition to the study of the art of Normandy and the Ile de France. The characteristics most worthy of emphasis are its accent on monastic architecture, its increasingly organic quality involving frequent use of the groin vault, its originality in the hand-

FIG. 124—POITIERS. NOTRE DAME LA GRANDE.
VIEW OF THE WEST END

ling of the barrel vault, and its vigorous, racy sculptured decorations, especially as applied in the vestibule or narthex, a feature which received unprecedented development at the hands of the Burgundian architects.

Cluny. The abbey of Cluny (Figs. 99 and 100) was perhaps, the most typical Burgundian church. It was founded in 1089, destroyed in 1125, and rebuilt in 1130. Unfortunately it was razed during the French Revolution, but we know it by drawings and descriptions. It was five-aisled, the nave covered with a barrel vault and the aisles with groin vaults. Its transepts were double, those to the east smaller than those to the west, giving the plan the archiepiscopal-cross form so common in English Gothic buildings. Round the ambulatory were five absidioles, and others were added on the eastern faces of the transepts. The nave was preceded by an elaborate narthex, almost a separate church, of five bays.

FIG. 125—VEZELAY.   CHURCH OF THE MADELEINE.   THE INTERIOR SEEN FROM THE VESTIBULE

There was a lantern over the crossing, towers over the transepts, and towers were placed at the west end. The impression of the building must have been not unlike that of Rhenish church of the period, and, indeed, a connection between the two has often been urged.

Extant Burgundian monuments. Burgundy possesses, however, many extant monuments in which the style may be judged. The cathedral of Autun, for example, exhibits an elaborately ornamented narthex, and a nave in the form of a pointed barrel vault. An ingenious variant in the treatment of the barrel vault may be seen at Saint Philibert at Tournus. The gravest fault of the longitudinal barrel vault over a nave is its tendency to suppress, usually entirely, the window openings in the clerestory.   In Saint Philibert this difficulty is avoided by roofing the nave with a series of sections of barrel vaults, placed at right angles to the long axis of the building. These sections mutually abut one another, and their wall arches leave ample room for clerestory openings, but the esthetic effect of the series of transverse arches is unhappy, and the experiment was rarely copied in other buildings.

Vézelay.   The best known and the most interesting historically of the Burgundian buildings is the abbey church of

FIG. 126—ROMANESQUE ORNAMENT

Vézelay (Fig. 125).   Here we find the Burgundian narthex, with its richly sculptured decoration, but the barrel vault disappears entirely, even the great bays of the nave being covered with groin vaults.   The groins lack ribs, so that the system is only partially organic, but despite the lack we feel an increase in organic interest which signals the approach of the northern styles.

Northern French Romanesque. Normandy.   As we have seen, northern French Romanesque falls naturally into two divisions, the Norman and that of the Ile de France.   We shall begin with the former.   The most marked characteristics of fully developed Norman Romanesque are its strong sense of structural logic and its inventiveness.   No style which we have examined, except the Lombard, has been marked so strongly by the former, and it seems clear that Lombard architecture exercised a strong influence on the Romanesque of Normandy.   Those who urge an autochthonous growth for the Norman style run counter to what we know of Norman history. Lanfranc, for example, one of the most famous of Lombards, established himself successively at Bec, Caen, and Avranches, and, after the Conquest, became archbishop of Canterbury. He was followed in the same places by Anselm of Aosta, afterward canonized. Unquestionably such men as these carried Lombard influence into Normandy, though this fact should not blind us to the precocity and inventiveness of the Norman style.

FIG. 127—JUMIÈGES. ABBEY CHURCH. THE SYSTEM

Norman originality. Ribbed vaulting, the alternate system, compound piers, are features common both to Lombard and Norman. To the latter, however, belongs the credit of inventing a new vault form, specially adapted to the alternate system. In the nave of the Abbaye-aux-Hommes (Saint Etienne) at Caen (Figs. 99, 128, and 130), it occurred to the builders to throw an intermediate transverse rib from the intermediate pier, dividing the vault surface into six cells instead of four. In this system the crowns of the lateral cells run obliquely, instead of at right angles to the long axis of the building. The vault surfaces are somewhat distorted, but the window space was enlarged, and the aptitude of the form to the alternate system is attested by the number of Gothic buildings in which the two are combined (see plan of Paris cathedral, Fig. 139). Normandy also developed a number of decorative motives. The billet mold was adopted from Carolingian architecture, and new forms such as the dog-tooth, zigzag, and interlacing arcade were invented (Fig. 126). The technique of stone cutting and stone fitting, too, was notably finer in Normandy than in contemporary schools of Romanesque.

Jumièges. The earliest important extant example of Norman Romanesque is the abbey church of Jumièges (Fig. 127). In this building, now a ruin, we find the alternate system. Although the church was designed for a timber roof, a compound engaged shaft runs from the main piers, through the clerestory, to the level of the cross beams of the roof. It is

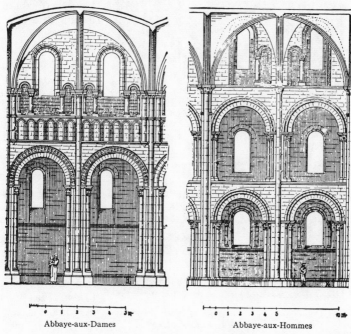

Abbaye-aux-Dames · Abbaye-aux-Hommes

FIG. 128—CAEN. THE ABBEY CHURCHES. SYSTEM OF THE INTERIORS

probable that we have here a reminiscence of the early Lombard wooden-roofed church in which the roof was supported, at least partially, by stone arches thrown across the nave.

The Abbaye-aux-Hommes at Caen. Sexpartite vaults. At Caen the so-called Abbaye-aux-Hommes (Figs. 99, 128, and 129), built and dedicated to Saint Stephen by William the Conqueror, gives us the most complete example of the style. Though the church was founded in the eleventh century, the vaults are a reconstruction of the first half of the twelfth. The original building was wooden-roofed but had the intermediate engaged shaft, which occurs in Lombardy, and there supports only the corbel table of the triforium string. It is reasonable to suppose that the presence of the intermediate

shaft suggested the intermediate rib, and the Norman invention of the sexpartite vault (Figs. 99, 128, and 129) was the result. In the Abbaye - aux - Hommes there are also numerous passageways in the thickness of the walls, which give access to the clerestory windows and other parts of the church, and an open lantern over the crossing. These features are almost surely Norman innovations.

FIG. 129—CAEN. SAINT ETIENNE. VIEW OF THE INTERIOR LOOKING TOWARD THE APSE

The Abbaye-aux-Dames at Caen. Rudimentary flying buttresses. As a pendant to the Abbaye-aux-Hommes, William's wife, Matilda, built the church of the Trinity, called the Abbaye-aux-Dames (Figs. 100 and 128). This church, on a smaller scale than Saint Etienne, is more compactly composed and more profusely and delicately ornamented. The architects of La Trinité invented one feature of the greatest significance. In the Abbaye-aux-Hommes the builders had tried to abut the thrust of the nave vaults by a half-barrel vault over the triforium galleries, a system which we have already noted in Auvergne and Languedoc (Nôtre Dame du Port, Clermont-Ferrand; Saint Sernin, Toulouse). The thrust of such a half-barrel vault, being continuous, well meets the continuous thrust of the barrel vault of the nave, but the thrusts of a groin vault, like that of the Abbaye-aux-Hommes, are not continuous. They are concentrated at the intersection of the ribs, and the half-barrel vault is, therefore, useless, except at and near points coinciding with the intersection of the ribs. Recognizing this fact, the builders of the Abbaye-aux-Dames omitted all portions of the half-barrel vault where it was not needed to abut the thrusts of the nave vault. The result was a series of arches, hidden under the lean-to aisle roof, which carried the thrusts of the nave vaults over to the pier buttresses set against the outer walls of the aisles (Fig. 100). Hidden and rudimentary as these members are, they are nevertheless embryonic flying buttresses, and to Norman Romanesque belongs the credit of inventing this important feature.

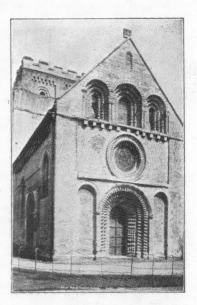

FIG. 130—IFFLEY.   PARISH CHURCH.
VIEW OF THE WEST END

Romanesque architecture of England. English originality.
Before passing on to the architecture of the Ile de France we must pause to note the Romanesque architecture of England. The transition is wholly logical, for, although England and Normandy are now politically divided, during the later Romanesque period they were one. Naturally the architects of William the Conqueror created buildings of the same style in England a few years after the Conquest as they had in Normandy a few years before. It must not be supposed, however, that Norman Romanesque underwent no modifications in

England. England often borrowed, but seldom slavishly copied. Norman Romanesque in England became more massive, as though the heavy Saxon architecture which it superseded had influenced it. Sometimes this massiveness was emphasized by extreme bareness and absence of decoration, as in Saint John's chapel in the Tower of London; sometimes it was disguised by a luxuriant profusion of Norman

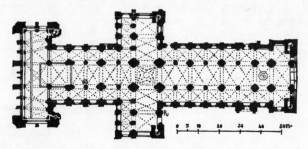

FIG. 131—DURHAM. CATHEDRAL. PLAN

decorative motives, as in the parish church of Iffley (Fig. 130). In general the style tended to abandon the structural logic of Normandy and to revert to wooden roofs. Even in vaulted Durham (Figs. 131 and 132), the finest and most homogeneous of the Anglo-Norman cathedrals, the alternate system was used with an illogical, if ingenious, vault system. No transverse ribs are thrown from the intermediate piers and the latter have no engaged shafts. Extra diagonals, however, spring from corbels above the intermediate piers, and the result is what one might call a septapartite vault. The transverse arches of Durham are pointed and the east end is square (like the Saxon), a phenomenon quite common in Anglo-Norman churches. English Romanesque does, therefore, show originality, despite its close relation to Norman.

Romanesque of the Ile de France. Returning to France, we may now take up the most completely organic of all Romanesque styles: that of the Ile de France. One may think of it as the most, or the least, finished of styles, according to whether one thinks of it as completed Romanesque or rudimentary Gothic. The problem is greatly complicated by the fact that in this region Gothic architecture developed, and the Romanesque buildings from which it sprang were usually either altered during the later Gothic period or modified by the architectural experiments by means of which finished Gothic was reached. Much that might otherwise come under the head of Romanesque architecture of the Ile de France must be discussed in connection with developing Gothic, and may,

FIG. 132—DURHAM. CATHEDRAL. GENERAL VIEW FROM THE SOUTHEAST

therefore, be omitted here. In general the Romanesque monuments of the region are not large in scale or striking in esthetic effect. To an even greater degree than in the buildings of Lombardy their greatest interest is historical, in the light they shed on future organic styles, and this impression is greatly exaggerated by the destruction and alteration of so many of the finest buildings.

Earlier and later buildings. The earlier buildings of the Ile de France were not organic, and inorganic buildings were erected even contemporaneously with those of the budding Gothic style. Such a church as Vignory, for example, is timber-roofed, with massive piers, plain walls, and no organic structure whatever. In the second half of the eleventh century, however, a highly organic style appeared. The idea of organic vaulting, with logical piers, probably came from Normandy, though the Norman alternate system was not taken over and does not appear in the Ile de France till the Gothic period. Ideas of plan, notably in the ambulatories, and decoration were borrowed from the south.

Development of the style. The development of the style was one of increasing delicacy and nicety of adjustment of load to shaft. At times, as at Saint-Loup-de-Naud, the vaults and piers are massive and clumsy in appearance, but always exactingly logical in arrangement. In finished examples, as at Saint Remi, Reims, the shafts are slender, delicately cut, and delicately adjusted to the load they bear.

Full development. Saint Remi, however, like most examples of the style, is not homogeneous. The fine Romanesque shafts and piers carried not Romanesque but Gothic vaults, now destroyed, which really emphasized the structural good taste of the former, so well could the two harmonize. In like manner the church of Saint Etienne, Beauvais, one of the most famous Romanesque monuments of the region, is finished with Gothic vaults.

FIG. 133—BEAUVAIS. SAINT ETIENNE. DRAWING OF ONE OF THE AISLE VAULTS AND ITS SUPPORTS. (FROM MOORE)

The elegance of the Romanesque portions, however, especially the side aisles (Fig. 133), shows the advanced point which the style reached in the district.

Morienval. The beginnings of Gothic. One of the best known examples of the style is the little church of Morienval (Fig. 99). The nave is covered with an early Gothic vault, but the north aisle (Fig. 134) retains its Romanesque vault, lacking diagonal ribs, though the diagonals are supported by a pilaster strip in the pier.   In the same aisle one may note a tendency to stilt the transverse rib in order to raise its crown nearer the level of the crown of the vault, a tendency which we might also have noted in the aisle vaults of Saint Etienne at Beauvais (Fig. 133).   Here we reach a limbo in which organic Romanesque and the most rudimentary Gothic meet.

If we but walked from the north aisle of Morienval to the apsidal ambulatory of that church we might see a transverse arch not only stilted that its crown may approach the crown of the vault, but also for the same reason pointed.   With this observation we should pass, however, from the consideration of Romanesque to that of Gothic architecture.

Spanish Romanesque. Before bringing to a close the discussion of the schools of Romanesque architecture, a word is necessary with regard to Spain.   In general Spanish Romanesque represents an importation of the styles of Auvergne and Languedoc.

FIG. 134—MORIENVAL. PARISH CHURCH. VIEW OF THE NORTH AISLE

The most famous of the Spanish churches, that of Santiago at Compostela (Fig. 135), strikingly resembles Saint Sernin of Toulouse.   Just as the English modified the Norman, so the Spanish modified the southern French, and impressed it with their own nationality.   In a temperate climate roofs became flatter, so that at times the triforium space was practically eliminated and its openings made into windows, as in the Colegiata of San Isidoro at Leon (Fig. 136).   Forms specially characteristic of Spain, such as the so-called Visigothic horseshoe arch, were used, and above all sculptured decoration became profuse.   Undercutting was deepened, edges sharpened, forms crowded, until the decoration attained that sparkling character so typically Spanish. The common phenomenon, therefore, of Spanish naturalization of immigrant forms never appears more strikingly than in the case of Romanesque architecture.

Development of single features. Obviously in an architecture so heterogeneous as Romanesque it is impossible to trace a strictly chronological development of any single feature, or group of features. Nevertheless, at the risk of repetition, it will be well to note the progress made by the style in the development and adaptation of certain details or features of churchly architecture.

Plans. The discussion of the plan may be dismissed summarily with the statement that the style offered material for almost all subsequent types of church plans. The prototype of the finished French Gothic building, with its complicated chevet, ambulatory,

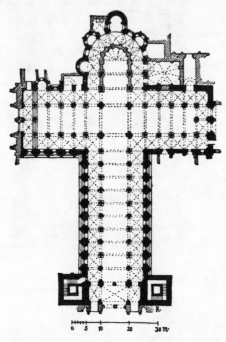

FIG. 135—COMPOSTELA. SANTIAGO. PLAN

and radial chapels, is to be found in southern French Romanesque, just as the favorite English archiepiscopal-cross plan is to be found in Burgundy.

Vaults. The progress in vault forms was as marked. Besides innovations and modifications of barrel vault forms, such as pointed barrel vaults and cross barrel vaults, we find Lombardy and Normandy developing the Byzantine domed vault into the organic, domical groin vault of quadripartite or sexpartite form, and handing on to Gothic the ideas necessary for its future development.   Ingenuity and originality were shown even in the trussed wooden roof, and it was given new and interesting forms, as at San Zeno in Verona.

Supports.   Corresponding to the ribbed vaults, we find the supports developing, with compound members for a compound

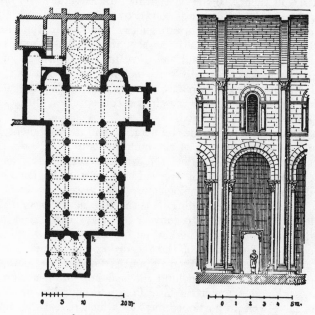

FIG. 136—LEON.   SAN ISIDORO.   PLAN AND SYSTEM

rib system.   We find the Lombard alternate system brought into accord with the sexpartite vault, and the shaft capitals signaling the direction of the springing of the ribs.   Chronologically we may note a steady refining of the proportions of the supports, suggesting approaching Gothic, which culminates in the delicate proportions of the best Romanesque of the Ile de France.

Buttresses.   The progress of the buttress was no less remarkable.   Lombardy supplied the pilaster strip against the outer wall, used as a buttress, which was the germ of all future development. This pilaster or pier buttress was steadily deepened and strengthened. At the same time numerous solutions of the problem of carrying the thrusts of the nave vaults to the aisle walls and the buttresses were made. In Lombardy this was done by omitting the triforium and carrying the thrusts of the nave vaults over to the gallery vaults, and thence to the outer wall. In Auvergne and elsewhere the same problem was solved by barrel vaults and half-barrel vaults over a triforium gallery, binding in the great vault of the nave. Finally, at the Abbaye-aux-Dames, the continuous half-barrel vault, illogical for the abutment of a groin vault, was cut into sections, and these sections, or rudimentary flying buttresses, were placed under the aisle roofs to neutralize and carry off the concentrated thrusts of the groin vaults of the nave.

Construction. With the refinement and development of details went a lightening of the building as a whole. As the parts became more slender, the whole became less massy. This development did not proceed equally in all regions, nor did it even proceed chronologically. There were, as we have seen, massy, inert buildings in the Ile de France. The tendency was, however, to convert the heavy early type into a lighter one presaging the Gothic building.

Façades. The design of the façade progressed notably in this period. In spite of their organic structure, the Lombard buildings were masked behind illogical and often unsightly façades, though some of the later Lombard churches, like San Zeno, have well-proportioned façades which reveal the inner structure of the building. Logical façade composition received its fullest Romanesque development in Normandy where, as in the Abbaye-aux-Hommes, the vertical divisions of the interior are marked on the exterior by pilasters, the horizontal by rows of windows, the pitched roof revealed by a gable, and the whole flanked by two monumental towers. All the germs are here which were developed into the complete Gothic façade. At the same time façades which lacked organic expressiveness and logic, but added other beauties, were being designed in other styles of Romanesque. Thus the Tuscans designed rich polychromatic façades, adorned with arcades, and the Germans picturesque ones with a profusion of turrets, apses, and the like.

Lanterns and towers. Meanwhile lavish invention was devoted to lanterns and especially to bell towers. In Italy the latter were constructed at a very early date round and free-standing. In the north these turret-like members, even in Carolingian times, were incorporated with the building. Eventually the square or angular tower became the favorite, and infinite variations were played on it. At times the tower was merely carried up in a series of stepped squares and topped by a pyramid as at Morienval. Again it was square, but its pointed roof polygonal, the angles being filled with little polygonal members, themselves covered with peaked roofs, as at Beaulieu-les-Loches. A variant of this type appears at Auxerre, where the square tower is surmounted by a polygon, and the tapering roof springs from that. Sometimes the round tower, ornamented with blind and open arcades, is used in France (Uzès); sometimes the round turret above a square and crowned with a cone appears (Saint Front, Périgueux). In the most elaborate examples stepped square is placed on square, stepped polygon on polygon, until as at Jumièges, the towers produce an aspiring effect very suggestive of Gothic.

Openings. In openings we must note a constant elaboration of the splaying characteristic of Carolingian architecture. In the latter a splay to aid in the distribution of light was introduced by means of a simple chamfer. In later Romanesque the splay was deepened, and was obtained frequently in window and door by means of multiple orders. It was thus given architectural dignity as well as utility. Compound openings, too, were evolved, sometimes of two lights, sometimes of two lights embraced by a blind arch, and in variants of this motive. At the same time portals were ennobled by elaborate porches, the finest being those of Lombardy and Burgundy.

Decoration. New decorative schemes also came into being. Figure and foliate sculpture was applied to the exterior, at times haphazardly as in Lombardy, at times with extraordinary subservience to architectural expression, as in Provence and Languedoc. In addition, new motives in pure design, like the Norman zigzag and dog-tooth, were applied to the exterior and the interior. For the interior new sculptured capitals were invented, some of them modified classic or Byzantine, some in original foliate designs, and many more of the "storied capital" type in which the purpose was didactic as well as decorative and the sculptures represented ecclesiastical, mythological, and unidentifiable scenes of the greatest raciness and originality. Polychromy was obtained in the interiors by means of paint. On the exterior its use varied with the style. The Tuscan architects got fine exterior effects by the use of polychromatic marble veneer. Outside of Tuscany polychromy played a less important part on the exterior, though fine effects were obtained by the use of several sorts of stones (Sicily), by patterned brick (Languedoc) and the like.

Secular architecture. The ensemble. For several reasons we may omit almost entirely any consideration of the secular architecture and the ensemble in the Romanesque period. In the first place the extant Romanesque secular monuments are few, and nearly all altered. In the second place they differ slightly, except in the application of detail, from the much more numerous Gothic buildings of the same type. This does not mean that there are no monuments by which we may judge Romanesque secular architecture. One needs but look at the enceinte of Avila (Castile, Fig. 137) to see Romanesque secular building, and get an idea of the appearance of a Romanesque city seen from without. The impression will, however, be very much like that obtained from a similar town, say Carcassonne (Fig. 178), of the Gothic period. Single secular monuments, in whole or in part, notably castles such as the Wartburg at Eisenach, exist for the archeologist, and show distinctive arrangements especially in the court and court façades, but it seems more sensible to discuss the whole question of medieval civil and domestic architecture in connection with the Gothic period.

The influence of Romanesque. Finally, something should be said about the influence of Romanesque architecture on subsequent styles. The influence of organic Romanesque on organic French Gothic has, of course, always been emphasized, but other equally significant examples of the influence of this architecture on later art have been overlooked.   Few people, as they admire the gorgeously polychromatic Gothic cathedrals of Tuscany with their striped interiors, realize that these buildings are comparatively slight modifications of the Tuscan Romanesque style.   In England the massive Norman con-

FIG. 137—AVILA.   GENERAL VIEW OF THE FORTIFICATIONS

struction was handed down to the Gothic style, though it was disguised by what was, after all, but an appliqué of pointed detail.   In German Gothic, where it is not mere imitation of French work, we note the picturesqueness of Rhenish Romanesque.

Self-sufficiency of the style.   Although at the conclusion of our study we are led inevitably to assert the influence of Romanesque on later architecture, we should be at the greatest pains to avoid the common error of thinking of the architecture merely as one of transition.   It was a heterogeneous art, and consequently well able aptly to express the genius of not one but many races.   Nevertheless, whatever its subdivisions, it was primarily a self-sufficient, independent style.   To regard it in any other light is wholly to miss its meaning.

CHRONOLOGICAL LIST OF MONUMENTS

For convenience monuments of a single country are grouped together, with the exception of Saint Gall (Switzerland), which is placed under Germany.   When a date is given exactly and without qualification, it refers to the beginning of the portion of the building referred to in the text.   Often round numbers, half centuries or centuries, are all that are possible or necessary, and at times, when a building has been remodeled in the period under discussion, several dates are given.   In general it will be well to call to mind again that an error in dating a monument usually tends to give it greater antiquity than it deserves.

ITALY

Milan, San Satiro.—Eighth century.
Como, Sant' Abondio.—C. 1035–95.
Toscanella, San Pietro.—1039–93.
Pisa, Cathedral.—Begun 1063.
Milan, Sant' Ambrogio.—c. 1077 to mid-twelfth century.
Modena.—Begun 1099; consecrated 1184.
Florence, San Miniato.—1013 and later.
Parma.—1117.
Pavia, San Michele.—1127 (?).
Palermo, Cappella Palatina.—Before 1132.
Verona, San Zeno.—Begun 1138.
Cefalù.—1145.
Pisa, Baptistry.—1153–78.
Pisa, Campanile.—Begun 1174.
Monreale.—1174–89.
Florence, Baptistry. — Founded seventh or eighth century; remodeled c. 1200.

GERMANY

Lorsch (porch).—774; possibly later rebuilt but in old form.
Aix-la-Chapelle (Charlemagne's chapel).—796–804.
Frankfort, Salvatorskapelle.—852.
Saint Gall (Switzerland).—Ninth century.
Cologne, Saint Mary of the Capitol.—After 1000.   (Founded 700.)
Cologne, the Holy Apostles.—Eleventh to thirteenth century.

Eisenach, Wartburg.—Built 1067; rebuilt 1130–50; remodeled 1190.
Hildesheim, Saint Michael.—Built 1001–33; remodeled 1186.
Speyer.—Founded 1030; remodeled twelfth century.
Drübeck.—Early twelfth century.
Gernrode.—Founded ninth century; rebuilt twelfth century.
Paulinzelle.—Twelfth century.
Worms.—Twelfth century.
Mainz.—Begun 978; largely thirteenth century.

FRANCE

Beauvais, Basse-Œuvre.—Eighth century (?).
Germigny-les-Prés.—801–806.
Beauvais, Basse-Œuvre.—c. 998.
Montier-en-Der.—960–998.
Vignory.—1050–52.
Jumièges.—Begun 1040; consecrated 1067.
Clermont-Ferrand, Nôtre Dame du Port.—Mid-eleventh century.
Toulouse, Saint Sernin.—Begun 1080; worked on in twelfth and
  thirteenth centuries.
Cluny.—1089.
Poitiers, Notre Dame la Grande.—End eleventh century.
Tournus, Saint Philibert.—Eleventh and twelfth centuries.
Beaulieu-les-Loches.—Eleventh and twelfth centuries.
Angoulême.—1105–28.
Périgueux, Saint Front.—C. 1120.
Vézelay.—Rebuilt 1132.
Caen, Saint Etienne.—Begun 1064; vaults c. 1135.
Caen, La Trinité.—Begun 1062; remodeled c. 1140.
Reims, Saint Remi.—Romanesque parts 1110.
Morienval.—Older part c. 1080; later 1122.
Auxerre, Saint Germain.—Tower, early twelfth century.
Autun.—First half of the twelfth century.
Beauvais, Saint Etienne.—Vaults 1180, but building planned earlier.
Saint Gilles.—Late twelfth century.
Saint Saturnin.—Twelfth century.
Uzès.—Tower, twelfth century.
Arles, Saint Trophîme.—Nave, first half of the eleventh century;
  porch second half of the twelfth.

ENGLAND

Earl's Barton.—Early eleventh century (?).
London, The Tower, Saint John's Chapel.—End of the eleventh
  century.

Durham.—C. 1096-1133.
Iffley.—Late twelfth century.

SPAIN

Santullano.—Ninth century.
San Miguel de Linio.—Ninth century.
Santa Maria de Naranco.—Late ninth century.
Avila, the Walls.—1090-99.
Compostela, Santiago.—Begun 1075; finished 1128.
Leon, San Isidoro.—End of the eleventh, beginning of the twelfth century.

BIBLIOGRAPHICAL NOTE

A. Michel's *Histoire de l'Art*, vol. 1, pt. 2, 1905, contains a brilliant and authoritative summary, by Camille Enlart, of Romanesque architecture. F. von Reber's *History of Medieval Art*, 1886, is a general history, now out-of-date, but still useful, and especially good on German medieval architecture. E. E. Viollet-le-Duc's *Dictionnaire raisonné de l'architecture*, 1884–88, although in dictionary form, is a history of architecture in many volumes, profusely illustrated, and representing probably the most monumental piece of research in the field of medieval archeology. G. Dehio and G. von Bezold's *Kirchliche Baukunst des Abendlandes*, 1892-1901, is a scholarly and comprehensive work, with many plates useful for the architect and student. J. A. Brutail's *L'archéologie du moyen âge*, 1900, is a cautious and shrewd study in medieval archeology, tending to correct the mistakes and exaggerations of earlier and more monumental works. A. Marignan's *Les méthodes du passé dans l'archéologie française*, 1911, on the other hand, is an iconoclastic book attacking the so-called orthodox school of medieval archeology in France. It is interesting as representing a healthy reaction against dogmatism, but not convincing. J. Quicherat's *Mélanges d'archéologie*, vol. 2, *Moyen âge*, 1886, is one of the earlier synthetic books on medieval architecture, important at the time of publication and not to be neglected to-day. Anthyme Saint-Paul's *Les écoles romanes* (Annuaire d'archéologie française, 1878) is a similar early work of research, by one of the most brilliant of the French archeologists. L. Courajod's *Origines de l'art romane et gothique*, 1889, a scholarly work, is more important for Gothic than for Romanesque art, but valuable for the study of either. T. G. Jackson's *Byzantine and Romanesque Architecture*, 1913, already cited, devotes more space to Romanesque than to Byzantine architecture. F. M. Simpson's *A*

ROMANESQUE ARCHITECTURE 273

History of Architectural Development, vol. 2, *Medieval*, 1909, presents a summary of medieval architecture, especially clear in the study of the development of details. C. H. Moore's *The Character and Development of Gothic Architecture*, 1906, is a powerful study in Gothic architecture, with some treatment of Romanesque in the early chapters. A. K. Porter's *Medieval Architecture*, 1909, in two large volumes, lavishly illustrated, represents painstaking research in the field. It is important, however, only for organic architecture.

R. Cattaneo's *L'architettura in Italia dal secolo VI. al mille circa*, 1889, is a profound piece of research in the field of Italian medieval architecture, especially important for Lombard Romanesque. F. de Dartein's *L'architecture lombarde*, 1865-82, is an early but profound study of Lombard Romanesque architecture. G. T. Rivoira's *Le origini della architettura Lombarda*, 1901-7, already cited, is of great importance for the study of Lombard Romanesque. A. K. Porter's four-volume work, *Lombard Architecture*, 1917, including an exhaustive portfolio of splendid illustrations, is the most modern work on the subject, and by a scholar of universally recognized authority. A. Venturi's *Storia dell'arte Italiana*, vols. 2 and 3, 1902 and 1904, are subdivisions of an encyclopedic history of Italian art, already cited, important for the publication of new material and profuse illustrations. E. Bertaux's *L'art dans l'Italie méridionale*, 1904, presents an exhaustive publication of research in the field of south Italian medieval architecture. It was followed in 1911 by A. Avena's *Monumenti dell'Italia meridionale*, covering all the monuments of the district, but especially important, both in text and superb illustrations, for Romanesque architecture. C. A. Cummings's *A History of Architecture in Italy*, 1901, is a popular, accurate, and well-illustrated work on Italian medieval architecture. There are two volumes, the first important for Romanesque architecture.

H. Otte's *Geschichte der romanischen Baukunst*, 1874, though old, is an exhaustive and scholarly work on German Romanesque architecture. A. von Haupt's *Die Baukunst der Germanen von der Völkerwanderung bis zu Karl dem Grossen*, 1909, is a modern work by a profound student of the architecture of the dark ages, using the term "German" in the broadest sense, and discussing the architecture throughout Europe. R. Adamy's *Die frankische Thorhalle zu Lorsch*, 1891, an exhaustive work on a single monument, is here mentioned on account of the light it throws on the whole movement of the architecture of the dark ages. B. Ebhardt's *Deutsche Burgen*, 1901, is an illuminating work on the German medieval castle.

C. Enlart's *L'architecture réligieuse en France*, 1902, is an exhaustive study of French medieval church architecture, really carrying on the work of Viollet-le-Duc.   The same author's *L'architecture civile et militaire en France*, 1904, is a similar work on medieval secular architecture.   R. de Lasteyrie's *L'architecture réligieuse à l'époque romane*, 1912, is the most up-to-date and authoritative work on Romanesque architecture, devoted principally to the style in France.   J. Baum's *Romanesque Architecture in France*, 1912, presents a collection of excellent reproductions of French Romanesque buildings, with an introduction (translated) by Dr. Julius Baum. F. de Verneihl's *L'architecture byzantine en France*, 1851, gives the old point of view of Aquitanian architecture in a scholarly way. H. Revoil's *L'architecture romane dans le midi de la France*, 1873, is an old but exhaustive work on the Romanesque architecture of southern France.   V. Mortet's *Recueil de textes relatif à l'architecture en France*, 1911, presents a collection of original documents, relating to the 11th and 12th century architecture of France, in an illuminating way.   V. Ruprich-Robert's *L'architecture normande*, 1884–89, is a monumental book of research on French and English Norman Romanesque architecture, lavishly illustrated.

T. Rickman's *An Attempt to Discriminate the Styles of Architecture in England*, 1881, a work now out of date and more important for Gothic than for Romanesque architecture, is significant as a step in the analysis of English church architecture.   Similarly, E. Sharpe's *The Seven Periods of English Architecture*, 1871, a more elaborate classification of English medieval architecture, is more important for Gothic than for Romanesque.   G. G. Scott's *English Church Architecture*, 1881, is a synthetic work by a learned author, devoted primarily to Gothic architecture, but treating Romanesque.   C. H. Moore's *The Medieval Church Architecture of England*, 1912, is a broad elaboration of the point of view toward English medieval architecture revealed in the author's *Gothic Architecture*.   It is a somewhat biased but up-to-date and scholarly book.   F. Bond's *An Introduction to English Church Architecture*, 1913, is an exhaustive, scholarly, and up-to-date work, lavishly illustrated, on English church architecture from the eleventh to the sixteenth century.   J. D. Mackenzie's *The Castles of England*, 1887, an exhaustive, elaborate, and richly illustrated volume, is excellent for the study of the English medieval castle.

V. Lamperez y Romea's *Historia de la Arquitectura Cristiana Española en la Edad Media*, 1909, is by far the most original and exhaustive work on medieval Spanish architecture.   A. G. B. Schayes's *Histoire de l'architecture en Belgique*, 1850–60, a work of several volumes, now out of date, is still the important authority on the medieval architecture of Flanders.

CHAPTER IX

GOTHIC ARCHITECTURE

Origin of the term. The word "Gothic," applied to art, originated as a term of opprobrium. From the beginning of the Renaissance to the romantic revival in the nineteenth century medieval art was regarded as barbaric. The most striking as well as the most numerous monuments of medieval architecture were those of the pointed style, and these came to be called "Gothic" as a synonym for "barbaric." It is in this sense that Molière speaks of

> . . . Le fade goût des monuments gothiques
> Ces monstres odieux des siècles ignorants
> Que de la barbarie ont vomis les torrents. . . .[1]

Boileau, La Bruyère, Rousseau, attacked Gothic art with a violence at once bitter and illuminating. By the time taste changed the word was fixed. Now the oblivion which generally shrouds the origin of the name is perhaps the best proof of the vindication of the art.

Priority of France. At the period of its development, Gothic architecture was generally called "French work" (*opus francigenum*) and the priority of France in the style is thus attested. For this reason some writers have urged that the style be called not Gothic, but French. Such a change would be, however, not only impractical but misleading. As a variant of this classification, it has been suggested that the word Gothic be retained, but that it be applied only to the

---

[1] The besotted taste of Gothic monuments,
These odious monsters of the ignorant centuries,
Which the torrents of barbarism spewed forth.

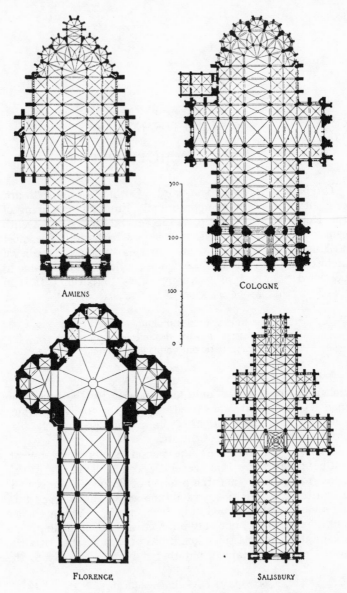

AMIENS

COLOGNE

FLORENCE

SALISBURY

300

200

100

0

FIG. 138—COMPAR.TIVE PLANS OF GOTHIC CATHEDRALS IN FRANCE, GERMANY, ITALY AND ENGLAND

architecture of the Ile de France, and that the contemporary styles outside of France be called merely "pointed architecture." In support of this attitude it has been pointed out that fundamentally organic architecture was developed in the Ile de France, and the so-called Gothic styles of other countries either consisted of imitation of this or of a superficial application of pointed or Gothic detail to buildings which were constructed according to Romanesque principles.

Definition of organic Gothic. There are, however, grave objections to this point of view. Regarded strictly from the point of view of organic structure, Gothic is a system of vaults, supports, and buttresses, the supports being strong enough to bear the crushing weight of the vaults only, and the stability of the structure maintained chiefly by an equilibrium of counterthrusts. Such a system is to be found perfected only in the Ile de France or in imitations of the architecture of that district. Many buildings of the same age, however, though they lack the complete organism of the French, display the same characteristics, especially the consistent use of the pointed arch. In France the systematic use of the pointed arch became general for structural reasons. In other countries that member was used unstructurally, apparently for esthetic reasons, but this does not justify the argument, which so often appears in books, that the use of the pointed arch outside of the Ile de France represents but a superficial application of French detail to Romanesque building by architects who did not understand the structural reasons which underlay the use of this detail in France. As we have seen, the pointed arch was used in the Romanesque period, and its use for esthetic purposes in England developed synchronously with its use for structural reasons in France.

French the great organic Gothic, but not the only Gothic style. Use of the term. We must, therefore, avoid the mistake of calling Gothic architecture solely French, or French Gothic the only Gothic. Aside from the futility of tilting at firmly established terms, a broader application of the term is more convenient. We may consider Gothic architecture that style, specially marked by the general use of the pointed arch, which in all European countries succeeded the Romanesque style, and flourished until it was in turn superseded by the style of

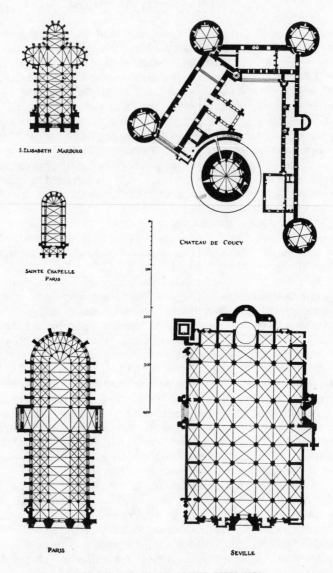

S. ELISABETH MARBURG

SAINTE CHAPELLE
PARIS

CHATEAU DE COUCY

PARIS

SEVILLE

FIG. 139—PLANS OF GOTHIC BUILDINGS

the Renaissance. We may then subdivide the field and examine the characteristics of the art in any one region. In so doing, however, we must inevitably emphasize the structural superiority and priority of the organic architecture of the Ile de France.

Esthetic effect of revealed structure. So true is this of the Gothic of the Ile de France that the chief esthetic effect of the buildings of that district is felt in the logical expression of the structure. Outside of France this is not true, except in works clearly under French influence.

Lack of self-consciousness. Whether governed by structural or esthetic considerations, the Gothic style was developed inarticulately. Its architects did not seek to formulate, at least in writing, the ideas which their buildings expressed. Though the pointed arch almost completely superseded the round one, there was no audible condemnation of the Romanesque art of the past, as the Gothic art was later condemned in the period of the Renaissance.

Socialistic character. This naïveté may well have been caused by the corporate quality of the work, for the Gothic cathedral, like the Romanesque, was the expression not of an architect, or a patron, but of a community. It is significant that, though archeology has often published the names of the architects, or *magistri operarii*, of the great Gothic cathedrals, these names are almost universally unfamiliar and unnoted. The cathedrals of Amiens and Reims are as well known as those of Florence and Rome, yet people who would be ashamed not to know about Brunelleschi or Bramante would look blank at the mention of Robert de Luzarches or Jean-le-Loup. In a sense Gothic art is strongly socialistic.

Ecclesiastical and secular interest. Although the main interest in the Gothic period is in ecclesiastical building, it is not so completely so as in the Romanesque period preceding it. Especially in late Gothic times civil and military buildings attained great importance. The scholar must, therefore, examine not only churches and monasteries, but town and guild halls, castles, manors, farms, city houses, and even well heads and gibbets to gain anything like a complete acquaintance with the style. Moreover it must not be assumed that the craftsmen employed even on the churches in the Gothic

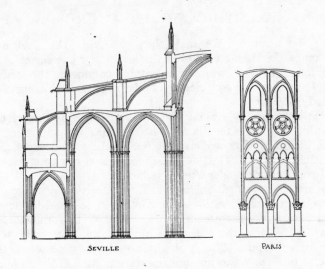

SEVILLE   PARIS

10 20 30 40 50 60 70 80 90 100

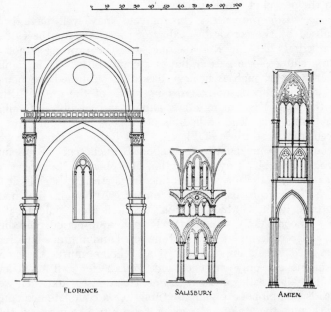

FLORENCE   SALISBURY   AMIEN.

FIG. 140—SECTIONS AND SYSTEMS OF GOTHIC BUILDINGS

period were ecclesiastics. Great bands of lay builders, like the *maestri comacini*, traveled from place to place as they were employed successively on one great building after another. This fact, and the frequent presence of blasphemous and obscene carvings in Gothic churches, has given rise to a theory that Gothic architecture is essentially a style of lay construction, and repre-

sents a revolt against the monkish domination of an earlier age. The facts do not bear out such a theory, nor does the profoundly religious expression of the finished building.

Gradual emphasis on revealed structure. Though in France the most important expression of the developed cathedral lay in the self-revelation of its structure, the realization of the esthetic importance of revealed structure did not come to the builders immediately. In the beginning such essential structural members as flying buttresses, which later came to be one of the most important features externally, were concealed. The evolution of Gothic from Romanesque may be traced by the gradual acceptance of structural character, even sometimes when more apparent than real, as the most important aid to esthetic effect.

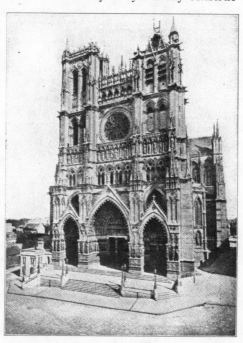

FIG. 141—AMIENS. WEST FRONT OF THE CATHEDRAL

Aspiring quality. The aspiring quality of the art has often been noted.   The emphasis on the vertical line, the soaring expression of the architecture, inevitably suggest all that was finest in the religious ideals of the Middle Ages.   To see, however, in the vertical lines and branching ribs of the Gothic church a reflection of the poetic sylvan setting of primitive pagan ceremonies is to wander in the realms of pure fancy. Aside from the source of inspiration, however, the Gothic architect was very clever at gaining the effects he sought. Desiring height, above all, he narrowed his naves and tapered his piers to exaggerate this effect.   The desired impression of size he got by including and multiplying small members admirably adapted to give scale.

Date.   In date the Gothic period extended roughly from 1150 to 1550.   Certain indications of the approaching style do, of course, antedate the mid-twelfth century, just as certain isolated structures in the Flamboyant Gothic style postdate the mid-sixteenth, but in general the four centuries indicated compass the style.

Homogeneity.   Gothic architecture had a national homogeneity much greater than Romanesque.   Though there are local schools of Gothic in France, they do not differ one from another so markedly as did the Romanesque, nor are they as numerous.   This fact is precisely what history would lead us to expect.   In the later Middle Ages nations themselves had become more homogeneous.   Central authority became stronger, language purer, and individuals more conscious of their own nationality.   In districts where less federal authority was felt and where national consciousness was less awakened, as in southwestern France, it is significant that local schools of architecture differed especially from the national style.   As always, we find architecture recording history, and history impressing architecture.

General development.   Before attempting even a classification, it will be well to say a word about the development of the style as a whole.   Our point of departure must clearly be the transitional architecture of the Ile de France.   Although many English writers have called attention to the early use of the pointed arch in England, the English buildings can, nevertheless, be regarded as Romanesque and not transitional Gothic.   Subsequent variations of the style sometimes neglect-

FIG. 142—AMIENS. THE CATHEDRAL. VIEW OF THE INTERIOR, LOOKING
INTO THE APSE

ed organic structure, but organic structure plays so fundamental a rôle in the art that to the country which developed
it belongs priority in the style.   The late twelfth century and
the early thirteenth saw the transition and development of
the organic Gothic style in the Ile de France.   By 1220 (the
date of the foundation of Amiens cathedral) the style was well
understood, and the thirteenth century is the age of early but
fully developed Gothic.   Building in this style, with refinement and superficial modification, continued in France through
the fourteenth century, but toward the close of the period a
radical change came over the art.   Flamboyant architecture
was developed, having been introduced from England.

*Development in England.   Origin of continental Flamboyant
architecture.*   England, as we have seen, used the pointed
arch at an early period, but the first truly Gothic buildings on
British soil represent French influence.   The early style,
called early English, or Lancet, coincided roughly with the
thirteenth century.   The form of English Gothic, however,
soon changed.   The Englishmen in power in the late Middle
Ages were scarcely more than naturalized Frenchmen and
inevitably borrowed from France.   Quite as inevitably, however, they changed what they borrowed and impressed it with
their own genius.   In the later thirteenth and fourteenth centuries, therefore, the English Gothic style assumed a new expression, and the Decorated style came into being.   Toward the end
of the century Decorated details were copied in France, and the
fifteenth century Flamboyant (or flaming) style was developed
along lines suggested by the late Decorated or Curvilinear style
in England.   This Flamboyant style spread from France all
over the continent, and is characteristic of fifteenth and sixteenth century architecture outside of England.   England, once
more asserting her originality, developed in the later fourteenth
and fifteenth centuries the Perpendicular style which flourished
there until the advent of the Renaissance.

Classification.   France.   With this general development in
mind, we may attempt a fuller classification, and number the
various centers of activity in the Gothic period.   France we
have put at the head, and in France we must give priority
to the Ile de France.   Normandy nearly kept pace with the
Ile de France in creative activity, and Picardy and Artois can

scarce be classified apart from these two. Together these districts formed the home of developing organic Gothic. Other divisions are less important. Burgundy had a style of its own, retaining the porches, often the square ends, and other features reminiscent of Burgundian Romanesque. Another division might be made of Champagne, midway between Burgundy and the Ile de France, though approaching so close to the latter architecturally that the subdivision is hardly necessary. A very original style, the so-called Plantagenet, flourished in southwestern France, and was marked by the use of aisles the height of the nave, by unusual domed vaults, and other peculiar features, showing strong English affinities. Still another style developed in the south, bare in decoration and characterized by a free use of terra cotta. Further divisions might be made of Brittany, architecturally as well as geographically close to Normandy, and central France, where flourished a hybrid partaking of the characteristics of many styles. We must, therefore, note that, though Gothic architecture had more national homogeneity in France than Romanesque, it did vary decidedly according to the district, and the point must be more insisted upon, since we must concentrate attention on the structurally important architecture of the north and are in danger of forgetting the divergences of the style in other parts of the country.

England, Germany, Italy, and Spain. Outside of France the problem is simpler and the style varied with the period rather than the district. In England, for example, though the Perpendicular style differed widely from the Lancet, each is found throughout the country during its period. In Germany we find generally an imitation of French work. At times this imitation is almost slavish, as in the cathedral of Cologne; at times it is very free, as in the so-called Hallenkirchen. One may, therefore, subdivide the German buildings into two groups, the one imitative, the other with a strongly native flavor. In Italy Gothic architecture began as an importation of the French Cistercian style, but was almost immediately modified to suit the esthetic demands of the Italians. Here geography played some part, as in Tuscany, where the Tuscan Romanesque so stamped the Gothic art of the district, but the chief variation was caused by the individual source of inspiration and by date. In Spain the style was generally homogeneous. In the beginning it was an importation from Languedoc and Auvergne, soon modified, especially in the south, however, by Moorish detail and Spanish taste.

Gothic in other countries. In the Low Countries Gothic was imported from France and shows little originality except in secular architecture. The town halls and guild halls of Flanders, however, show an originality which gives the district real importance. Finally, attention must be called to the

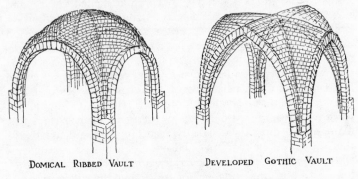

DOMICAL RIBBED VAULT   DEVELOPED GOTHIC VAULT

FIG. 143—EXAMPLES OF MEDIEVAL VAULTS

important architecture which was built, and much of which still remains, in the Holy Land, in Cyprus, Rhodes, Crete, and other islands of the Mediterranean. For these monuments we have, of course, to thank the crusaders.

Importance of the development of details. Unfortunately for the logical student, one cannot select a number of buildings which exhibit in chronological order the steps in the development of organic Gothic architecture. Progress was so rapid and buildings so seldom homogeneously completed that the advance of the style may best be illustrated by selecting one or more details from many buildings. One may then arrange these details to show the steps in the development of organic Gothic, even though the arrangement be not necessarily chronological. Archeologists may dispute as to the locality and date of the first single flying buttress, but for us it will be enough to recognize that the single flying buttress, occurring as it does in many buildings, represents a structural step between the hidden flying buttress and the double one. With a grasp of the development of the important Gothic features, we are then in a position to reconstruct a fully developed organic Gothic building, or, if we prefer concrete examples, to understand why the naves of Amiens (Figs. 138 and 142) and of Reims (Fig. 144) have been considered perfect examples of the fully developed early style.

FIG. 144—REIMS. THE CATHEDRAL. VIEW OF THE VAULTS AFTER THE FIRST BOMBARDMENT IN 1914, SHOWING THE LEVEL CROWNS OF DEVELOPED GOTHIC VAULTS

The vault. The most important single feature of the Gothic building is, of course, the vault. Indeed the whole study of Gothic architecture hinges upon the treatment of the vault and its abutment. In connection with the Romanesque architecture of the Ile de France we have seen that architects came to realize that the vault with level crowns could be made lighter and constructed more flexibly than the domical vault. To make the crowns of the vault level it was necessary obviously to raise the crowns of the transverse and longitudinal arches.

This could be done either by stilting or by pointing these arches or by doing both. When the pointed arch was thus structurally used for the first time transitional Gothic began. Just where or just when this first occurred it is impossible to say. That the process was slow and experimental can be proved by many monuments, like the churches of

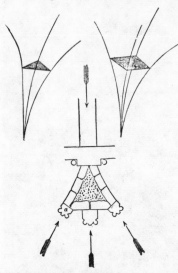

Creil, Langres, and Morienval, where the transverse arches are not sufficiently pointed, and are pieced out by flat walls built above them, which raise the crowns of the arches to a point level, or nearly level, with the point of intersection of the diagonal ribs or, in other words, the crown of the vault. Once this plan was tried and found successful, the advantages of the level-crowned vault were realized and the use of this graceful, essentially Gothic form became the rule (Figs. 140, 143, and 144).

The abutment. With the creation of a lighter, loftier form of vault came a more searching study of its abutment. Even when the hidden flying buttress was used in Norman Romanesque the thrusts of the vault were but partially concentrated on it, and much of the resistance to them was supplied by a sturdy wall. The Gothic architect was slowly feeling his way toward a complete elimination of the wall, the place of which was ultimately to be taken by stained glass, and his greatest problem was the concentration of the vault thrust on the buttress which was to oppose it.

FIG. 145—SECTION OF GOTHIC VAULT-ING CONOID, SHOWING THE DIREC-TIONS OF THE THRUSTS AND THEIR ABUTMENTS

Stilting of the longitudinal rib. The solution of the problem came in the stilting of the longitudinal ribs. In Romanesque architecture all ribs sprang from the same level. A horizontal section of the vault and its infilling some feet above the springing, at a point where the ribs had had a chance to spread, would be square. The whole mass exerted a thrust outward, however, so that a buttress to oppose it had to have a face as broad as one side of the square, or as the distance from one diagonal at the given level to the other at the same level. By the stilting of the longitudinal rib all this was changed. While the diagonal ribs began to spread at the main impost the two longitudinals ran up vertically some distance before springing, thus pinching in the vault on the wall side. A cross-section of the vault and its infilling, or vaulting conoid as we may call it, at a point some distance above the main

FIG. 146—SAINT LEU D'ESSERENT. VIEW OF THE INTERIOR, SHOWING THE VAULTS AND, THROUGH THE WINDOWS, THE FLYING BUTTRESSES

impost, would be not square, but triangular, one angle of the conoid touching the wall (Fig. 145). The oblique thrusts of the diagonal ribs thus met and pushed out at right angles to the long axis of the building in the direction of the thrust of the transverse rib, and all these thrusts were concentrated on a narrow surface against which the narrow face of an opposing buttress could be placed. The stilting of the longitudinal rib thus accomplished what the architect most desired—a perfect concentration of the vault thrusts against a narrow surface. Such a form involved a warping of the vault web, and its surface now took on the peculiar, plowshare form, difficult if not impossible to describe geometrically, but which the builders soon learned to construct with remarkable skill (Figs. 142 and 146).

Flying buttresses. While the vault with its concentrated thrusts was being evolved, architects were no less busy in

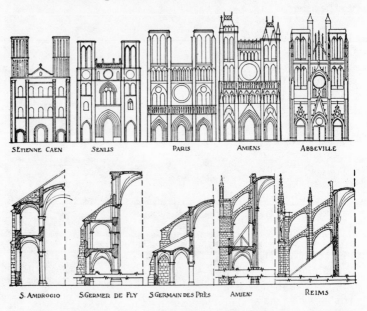

S.Etienne Caen   Senlis   Paris   Amiens   Abbeville

S. Ambrogio   S.Germer de Fly   S.Germain des Près   Amiens   Reims

FIG. 147—ARRANGEMENT OF MONUMENTS AND DETAILS TO ILLUSTRATE THE DEVELOPMENT OF THE BUTTRESS AND THE DEVELOPMENT OF THE FACADE

developing buttress forms to stabilize it. The hidden flying buttress, designed to carry the thrust over the aisle roofs to pier buttresses on the outer wall, was to hand in Norman Romanesque, and though this type was wofully inadequate, it was adopted in a modified and refined form in the transitional church of Saint Germer-de-Fly. Obviously such buttresses touched the wall at a point too low properly to meet the thrusts of the nave vault, and the architects soon raised them above the aisle roof, as at Saint Germain-des-Prés, Paris, where they appear on the exterior as genuine flying buttresses. A virtue was then made of necessity, and the flying buttresses were soon one of the most esthetically expressive as well as structurally important features of the building.

Their development. Structural logic ruled their development. Architects, knowing that the chief points of thrust of an arch or vault were at the springing and at the haunch, soon abandoned the single buttress, with its single arch, and composed a double one, with an arch to oppose the thrust of the vault at the springing and another for that at the haunch. When the buttresses sprang over a single aisle this form was adequate; when the aisles were double the first pair of arches came to an end between the inner and outer aisles, where a pier was placed, and two more arches, repeating the first two, carried the thrusts to the outer wall. The former system may be seen in the nave of Amiens, the latter in the apsidal end of Reims (Fig. 147). When there were no aisles, as in the Sainte Chapelle in Paris, the pier buttress was adequate and was retained (Figs. 139 and 148).

FIG. 148—PARIS. THE SAINTE CHAPELLE. TRANSVERSE CUT

Their form and decoration. At the same time the forms of the buttresses were refined. Their regular pitch was established, and they were made to carry, by means of covered channels, the water which gathered on the nave roofs. At the extremity of the buttresses this water was thrown clear of the face of the wall from the mouths of widely projecting gargoyles, grotesquely carved. The backs of the buttresses were decorated with crockets, and the tops of the great pier-buttresses, to which the arches sprang, were weighted with pinnacles. The outer side of these great piers was given many set-offs, which tended to resist the weather and carry off the vault thrusts more easily to the ground.

The apse. After one has grasped the development of the vault and the abutment, that of other features is easy to understand. A single principle holds for all: the fulfilment

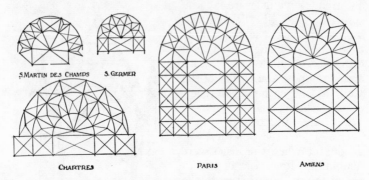

S.MARTIN DES CHAMPS   S. GERMER

CHARTRES   PARIS   AMIENS

FIG. 149—PLANS OF THE EAST ENDS OF FIVE GOTHIC CHURCHES, ILLUS-
TRATING THE DEVELOPMENT OF THE CHEVET

of structural needs and the recognition of the esthetic value of such a fulfilment frankly revealed. Let us examine, for example, the development of the apse. Nothing is more characteristically Gothic than the tremendously complicated *chevet* or east end of the French Gothic building, yet it was attained simply and logically (Fig. 149). The primitive form of apse, as we have seen it in early Christian times, was a semicircular wall covered with a half-dome. At the period of the earliest transitional Gothic, the form of the half-dome was changed and the vault given cells resembling the gores of a melon, which were carried on ribs in harmony with the other vaults. Such a form, though not necessarily the oldest example, appears at Saint Martin-des-Champs, Paris. The process then became one merely of deepening the cells, or raising their crowns, until eventually they reached the level of the intersection of their ribs. An intermediate stage may be seen at Saint Germer-de-Fly, a fully developed example at Amiens.

GOTHIC ARCHITECTURE 293

Arrangement of the apsidal ribs. At first the intersection of
the apsidal ribs came at a point touching the last transverse
rib of the choir, as at Saint Germer. This gave the ribs the
dangerous appearance of all thrusting against the last transverse arch of the choir. The defect was remedied in many
ways, but most successfully at Amiens, where the apse was
made more than semicircular, and two ribs sprang obliquely
from the last choir imposts to meet the apsidal ribs at their
intersection. All the ribs were then radii of a circle (Fig. 149).

The ambulatory and apsidal chapels. Meanwhile the
ambulatory and apsidal chapels developed apace. The vaults
of the former, being not rectangular but trapezoidal, offered
some difficulty, since the diagonal ribs would not meet at the
center of the vault. This was remedied by breaking these

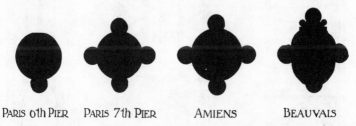

PARIS 6th PIER   PARIS 7th PIER   AMIENS   BEAUVAIS

FIG. 150—PLANS ILLUSTRATING THE DEVELOPMENT OF THE GOTHIC PIER

ribs at the intersection and thus forcing them to meet at the
vault center. A similar arrangement sufficed for the ribs of
the irregularly shaped apsidal chapels (Fig. 149).

The pier. The common sense of the Gothic architect and
his willingness even to compromise never show more clearly
than in the treatment of the piers. The most logical arrangement was to give each member in the vault a place in the
compound pier, and carry all to the ground. Such a cluster
of supports, however, took up much floor space and obstructed
the view of the worshipper. Accordingly the builder first
grouped all his shafts at the ground story impost, and gave
his main pier a semicircular form. Feeling, however, that
more support was needed, he first added (at the sixth pier of
the nave of Paris) a single engaged shaft on the nave side to

carry the weight of the nave ribs to the ground. At the seventh pier of the same building he added three more engaged shafts on the three remaining sides of the round pier, and the fully developed Gothic form was created and needed only refinement (Fig. 150). The old Romanesque system of each rib being represented to the ground in the pier recurred,

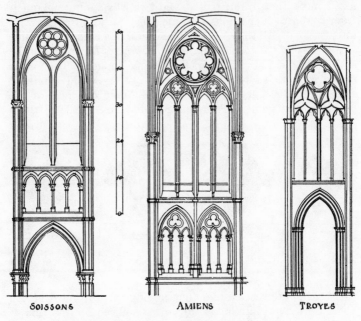

SOISSONS   AMIENS   TROYES

FIG. 151—THE DEVELOPMENT OF THE WINDOW OPENING.   EXAMPLES OF
PLATE AND BAR TRACERY

however, in French Flamboyant Gothic and in English Perpendicular.

The opening. Plate tracery. The Gothic system of construction tended inevitably toward the suppression of the wall. With the perfect concentration of thrust, the function of the wall became one merely of excluding the weather, and this could be done as adequately by glass as by stone. Moreover the northern builder desired glass, as the southern fresco, both for decorative and didactic purposes. The result was an almost complete substitution of stained glass for stone wall, and the building became as it were a vaulted glass cage. The unit for the development of the opening was the window of two lights, separated by a column and embraced by an arch. In Romanesque, and even in Byzantine, architecture the stone tympanum above the lights had been pierced with a third opening. In early Gothic these openings received complicated geometric forms, and plate tracery, a tracery consisting of openings in geometric design pierced in a thin plate of stone, was the result.

Bar tracery. While the architecture was still developing, however, architects gradually discovered that a more complicated and beautiful tracery could be designed if the system of merely piercing a stone tympanum were abandoned, and a new tracery of thin stone bars, ingeniously interlocking on the principle of the arch, were substituted. The substitution of bar for plate tracery became general in the later transitional period, and remained constant in Gothic architecture. The stone bars, or mullions, were cut very thinly and delicately, and were merely an enframement for the glass. The bits of glass, in the thirteenth century scarcely ever more than six inches long, were joined by leads which at once bound them and supplied most of the drawing in the design. The whole was then set in the tracery. The swiftness with which bar tracery was accepted is proved in the cathedral of Paris by the juxtaposition of windows with plate and bar tracery in bays differing only slightly in date. Good examples of plate tracery may be seen at Soissons, and of bar tracery at Amiens and later buildings (Fig. 151).

Wheel and rose windows. Bar tracery also made possible the enormous wheel or rose windows which commonly occurred in the west end of the churches of the Ile de France. At first the designs for these were severely geometric, but later, especially in the Flamboyant period, the lines were freer and bewilderingly complicated. Chartres and Reims afford good examples of the early wheel window; the later rose may be seen at Amiens (Fig. 141) and elsewhere. As the style developed, the passion of the builders for lightness caused them to fill even the triforium with glass. This space, generally blind on account of the lean-to roof over the aisle, was opened by covering the aisle with a gable instead of a lean-to. In fourteenth century buildings, as at Troyes, the triforium is, therefore, lighted like the clerestory.

The façade. The development of the design of the west front kept pace with that of the other elements of the building.

Logic demanded a preservation of the tripartite division of the façade, both horizontally and vertically, to indicate the interior division of the nave and aisles and the three stories. Development was in the direction of refinement and expressiveness. The splaying of the openings was deepened, and porches with a deep splay and covered with canopies were placed in front of portals. Openings were enlarged until they took up practically all the space between the buttresses which marked the vertical division of the building. In time, as at Reims and later buildings, the bases of these buttresses were lost in the splaying of the porches, and the gables in the porch roofs were increased in size and importance until they became striking architectural features. Flanking western towers increased in size, and were bound by a stone gallery, open, which revealed the gable roof of the nave. To understand the development of the west front, one needs but examine the fronts of the Abbaye-aux-Hommes at Caen, of the cathedrals of Senlis, Paris, Amiens, and Reims in that order. Add a later work, like the west front of Abbéville, as an example of the Flamboyant development, and the progression will be self-revealed (Fig. 147).

FIG. 152—VENDOME, THE SPIRE

The spire. The spire developed in like manner. Romanesque architecture had shown many complicated forms of spires. The Gothic development was merely toward the substitution of the pointed arch, with its vertical accent, for the round one, and in general toward a more skilful suppression of all horizontal lines which might hamper the eye from being led upward (Fig. 152). In some of the most perfect examples, as at Senlis (Fig. 153), the transition between the square tower and the octagonal spire is made with great subtlety, the angles being filled with miniature towers and spires, and the vertical lines of these re-echoed and carried up by gables set against the faces of the sloping octagonal spire above. Although the spire changed in detail, and in later works we find extreme delicacy and openwork treatment, the ideal and the general tendency remained the same. In addition to the western towers and spires, tower-like lanterns were often placed over the crossing, though this detail is much more characteristic of Normandy and England than of the Ile de France. In France the crossing was more often marked by a slender *flèche*.

FIG. 153—SENLIS. THE SPIRE

Capitals and their decoration. The development of other details in the building harmonized with that of those which we have studied. New loads demanded new capitals, and forms were developed, based essentially on Byzantine types, but none the less original. The capital was given greater height, greater slenderness below, and greater breadth above. It was decorated with foliate and animal sculpture, more generally the former, carefully studied from nature. In the early work, unfolding, bud-like forms were preferred, and we find the young water-cress or unfolding fern carrying the four angles of the abacus. As the style progressed the sculpture became more naturalistic and less expressive functionally. Still later the forms became brittle, suggestive of the withered leaf, but at all times the carving was crisp and delicate. Esthetically the foliate work gave infinite life and vitality to a style which might otherwise have been but logically satisfactory.

The use of sculpture. The didactic as well as the esthetic value of sculpture was fully recognized and, as a result, carving was profuse all over the building. It is not mere rhetoric to say that the Gothic cathedral summed up all the learning, all the science, of the Middle Ages. The decorative purpose of the sculpture was, however, never lost. With all the freedom and naturalism of single details, the whole, whether on porch, gallery, or roof, was designed with strict reference to esthetic effect. At times all didactic purpose appears to have been lost, and we find sculptures, like the grotesques and gargoyles, which are the result of a free play of the carver's fancy and joy of creation. These works give the impression of a building always peopled. On account of them the Gothic cathedral is never empty, never dead.

Moldings. As one would expect, such a completely new system of architecture exhibited a completely new system of moldings. Since he was not bound by precedent, the architect studied and conventionalized nature, and created moldings which gave the most masterly effects of light and shade. The general system was that of the inclosure of convex curves within concave ones, and the resultant profiles remind one of vegetable forms such as fruits in a pod, or buds in a calix. Sculpture and molding appeared, of course, on the exterior as well as on the interior. Parapets were evolved, to serve the crowning function of the classic cornice, and pinnacles were applied to many parts of the building, especially the buttress piers. The latter were decorated with bud-like forms called crockets, and were topped with ornate finials.

Polychromy and stained glass. Polychromy played a much more important part than is generally recognized in Gothic architecture. Of course, the most gorgeous polychromatic effects were obtained by a complete infilling of window space with rich stained glass. An infinity of subjects was represented, but representation was always subordinated to pure design. Some of the most masterly of the world's designs in color may still be seen in the interior of Chartres. The color, sometimes flaming, sometimes hushed, played vividly upon the religious imagination. How much is lost with the destruction

of stained glass may be gauged by comparing the interior of
Chartres, where the glass is largely preserved, with that of
Amiens. Although the latter is probably the more perfect
building architecturally, its effect, as the cold light streams in
from the white glass of the windows, is vastly less impressive
than that of Chartres. The rich polychromy of the stained
glass was fortified by painting the stone members of the
interior. Almost all traces of the original painting of medieval
interiors is lost, and modern attempts to restore it, as in the
Sainte Chapelle at Paris, have generally been gaudy and
displeasing.

Fourteenth century Gothic in France. By the end of the
thirteenth century, with the raising of such structures as
Amiens and Reims (Figs. 141, 142, and 154), Gothic architecture in France attained a full development. The architecture
of the succeeding century may be sketched summarily. The
fourteenth century in France was a period of refinement rather
than of change. Vaults and ribs became lighter, foliate
sculpture unfolded and further accented the vertical tendency,
and tracery became so frail that long bars were made monolithic for safety's sake. In some churches, as at Chartres
(Fig. 155), the chapel of the Virgin at the end of the
chevet took on especial importance and became almost
a separate little church. In general, however, the plan
of the buildings remained the same, and no decided change
occurred until the fifteenth century. Before we examine
the later art, we must take up the Gothic architecture of
England.

English Gothic. General characteristics. Gothic architecture in England may be subdivided into three styles, corresponding roughly to the thirteenth, fourteenth, and fifteenth
centuries. Before we examine individually any one of these,
however, it will be well to note certain main characteristics of
the art as a whole. These will show how widely divergent,
even at an early period, English Gothic was from French.
First and foremost one must notice a difference in structural
principle. Organic Gothic, in the sense that we have studied
it in France, was not developed in England. There is, for
example, hardly a fully developed flying buttress system on
the island. To the end the Englishmen depended on Roman-

FIG. 154—REIMS. THE CATHEDRAL VIEWED FROM THE NORTH BEFORE THE BOMBARDMENT OF 1914

esque sturdiness for structural safety, and this inevitably gave
a different expression to the building.

The plan. In the plan the English building was long, or
rather appears to be long on account of its narrowness (Fig.
157). Though Salisbury and Amiens are approximately the
same in length, the former appears much longer. The English
building was given boldly projecting transepts, and the
transepts were generally doubled, the shorter east of the
longer, giving the church the archiepiscopal-cross form which

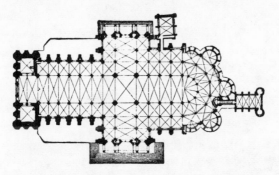

FIG. 155—CHARTRES. CATHEDRAL. PLAN

we have met in Burgundian Romanesque. The east end of
the English church was almost invariably square, and this,
like the archiepiscopal cross, may represent a Cistercian influence, although it was encouraged by the same feature in
Anglo-Saxon work. The same phenomenon we have observed
earlier in English Romanesque, as at Durham. In elevation the
English building was much lower than the French (Fig. 140),
though the same narrowness which increased the impression of
length increased the impression of height. The English works
abounded in towers, and a very striking feature was early
made of a great square stone lantern above the crossing.

The vaulting system. Façades. The English vaulting system,
except in a few early instances, was more complicated, if less organic, than the French. Ribs soon came to be used even more
for decorative than for structural purposes and applied from
the point of view of pure design. Façades became decorative

screens, hiding rather than revealing the arrangement behind them. Though sometimes extremely effective, these façades suffered as entrances, and portals shrank to comparatively tiny openings, mere possibilities of ingress rather than portals. Although occasionally the façades were adorned with sculptures, as at Wells, in general sculpture played a far less

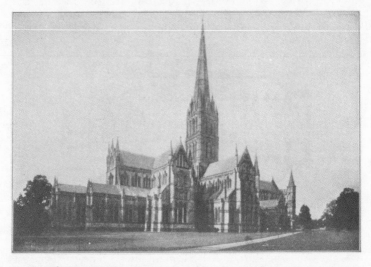

FIG. 156—SALISBURY. THE CATHEDRAL, SEEN FROM THE NORTHEAST

important part in England than in France. Even in the interiors sculpture was scant, and the result was a certain bareness and less vitality than in French work.

The site. To make up for this the English building was, on account of its complicated plan, extremely picturesque, and was almost invariably placed on a fine site, which was cared for at the time the building was erected and has been cared for ever since. Whether or not this may be accounted for by the fact that so many of the English churches were of monastic foundation is unimportant. To any one who has seen the finest buildings of France masked by the unsightly structures which are permitted to crowd about them, the beautiful placing of the English buildings will come as a great relief.

The Early English style. French influence. We may now take up the various styles of English Gothic. As we have seen, in the beginning French importation plays an important part, though at times it is, so to speak, once removed. Thus even the dependence of English Gothic on English Romanesque is ultimately a dependence on Norman Romanesque. In other cases, as at Canterbury, the influence is much more

FIG. 157—SALISBURY.   INTERIOR OF THE CATHEDRAL, LOOKING TOWARD
THE EAST END

concrete. Here William of Sens, a Frenchman as his name reveals, was called to build the church, and on his death an Englishman, taught by him, took up the work. The building of Lincoln was ordered by Bishop Hugh, a Frenchman, and the architect was Geoffrey de Noyers, whose name proves his extraction, even though he may have been born in England. In short we may say that in origin the Early English style is a combination of French and Anglo-Norman influences.

Character of Early English architecture. The most striking characteristic of the style is its simplicity. Sculpture is scant, decoration restrained, and the effect of the building depends on fine proportion and severe dignity. The openings are generally high and narrow, or lancet-shaped, and are so characteristic that the style is frequently called the Lancet style. The construction is very sturdy. Frequently shafts were not brought down even to the main impost. The massiveness of the round piers was frequently disguised, however, by clusters of shafts, engaged or free, about them.

These shafts were often made of the dark Purbeck marble which was the delight of the English builder. The Early English style may be studied in the more important parts of Canterbury, Lincoln, and Wells, and in other monuments. Salisbury, however, which was begun in 1220, the year of the foundation of Amiens, and was practically finished by 1258, is the most homogeneous building in the style (Figs. 138, 140, 156, and 157).

FIG. 158—LINCOLN. THE CATHEDRAL. THE ANGEL CHOIR

The Decorated style. By the end of the thirteenth century the severity of the Early English style was abandoned and the Decorated style, sometimes called the Geometric, and, in its later aspect, the Curvilinear, took its place. It was marked by a profusion of ornament. Ribs were multiplied, and liernes and tiercerons, or intermediate ribs, were run from rib to rib, or from rib to impost. Arches received many orders, and were enriched with complicated moldings. Above all, openings were enlarged and fitted with elaborate tracery design. This tracery, profuse as it was, at first followed severe geometric patterns, but later it grew more riotous, and eccentric curves were introduced. In time the wavy-lined tracery became the rule, and interlaced arcades with ogee curves became common. The general effect was richer and less orderly than that of the Early English style. There are few homogeneous Decorated cathedrals, but large portions of buildings, like the famous angel choir of Lincoln (Fig. 158), the nave of Lincoln, and the west front of York Minster, exhibit the style. Exeter and Lichfield are the most complete.

The Perpendicular style. Despite its richness the Decorated style was destined to be driven out in the fifteenth century by the Perpendicular, the last, and in some respects the most original, of the English styles. In it unsparing emphasis was laid on the vertical line. This is well seen in one of the earliest works of the style, the choir at Gloucester (Fig. 159). Ribs were brought direct to the pavement. Openings were tremendously enlarged, and filled with tracery composed of vertical bars, which ran from top to bottom, joined at intervals by shorter horizontal members. The effect was to emphasize not only the perpendicular but the rectangle.

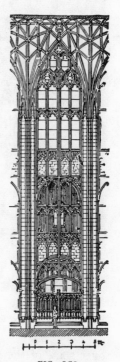

FIG. 159
GLOUCESTER. THE
SYSTEM OF THE CHOIR

Vaults and supports. Vaults received the most complicated treatment in the history of Gothic. Liernes and tiercerons were multiplied until it became almost impossible to distinguish the functional ribs from the decorative. Indeed there scarcely were functional ribs, for the vaults were practically homogeneous, with an appliqué of decorative ribs. At the same time the "fan vault" (Fig. 161) was developed—the most famous vault form of the style. The name is both descriptive and misleading. In a fan vault the ribs radiate fanwise from the main impost. The vaulting conoid is, however, nearly circular, so the ribs branch to follow roughly the lines of an inverted concave cone. The effect from below is very like that of the branching foliage of a tree, and the form is one of the most beautiful in English Gothic. With the complication of the ribs came further ramifications. Keystones, for example, were designed as large pendent stones, safe, since monolithic. Openwork, too, in the members of vault and support, became common.

Arches. Arches were given new forms. They were flattened, struck from several centers and sometimes came to a flattened

point like a depressed ogee. The flattened, so-called "Tudor" arch became a great favorite at a later date. At the same time the square east ends were finished with tremendous windows, filled with Perpendicular tracery.

Examples. Examples of the Perpendicular style are more numerous than those of the Decorated. One of the best is Henry VII.'s chapel, Westminster (Fig. 160), and an equally fine and consistent specimen is Saint George's chapel, Windsor. Perhaps the finest of all is Gloucester, where transept, choir, and cloisters (Fig. 161) are in the Perpendicular style. The last named

FIG. 160—LONDON. WESTMINSTER ABBEY. HENRY VII.'S CHAPEL

offer some of the most perfect specimens of the fan vault in England.

Flamboyant Gothic. The style in France. Turning to France we may now study the Flamboyant style. No new constructive principle is here involved, the style being one merely of a new arbitrary decorative system, the basis of which is an opposition of curve to counter-curve. All the germs of French Flamboyant are to be found in English Curvilinear. French vaults became complicated. Liernes and tiercerons were introduced, although the tendency was to join rib to rib, rather than rib to impost.   Above all, the lines were wavy and the ogee arch common.   The pointed arch, especially in the interlaced arcade, had an alternate concave and convex profile.   Openwork, whether in porch gable, spire, or abutment, became common, and extraordinary lace-like effects were obtained.   The expression was one of delicacy rather than strength, and a certain nervous restlessness is added.   The flattened arch

FIG. 161—GLOUCESTER.   THE CATHEDRAL.   INTERIOR OF THE CLOISTERS

became very common.   Local differences broke down, and the same Flamboyant style was applied in all localities of France.   It was a unified France which saw the elements of the style and accepted them from England.

Examples.   The first clearly Flamboyant building in France is the chapel of Saint John in Amiens cathedral, built from 1337 to 1375.   Thence the style spread abroad, good examples being the cathedrals of Quimper, Nantes, and Chambéry, Saint Ouen at Rouen (Fig. 162), and the church of Saint Vulfram, Abbéville (Fig. 163).   These are all of the fifteenth century, but the style continued vigorous until long into the sixteenth.   Saint Maclou at Rouen (Fig. 164), one of the finest of French Flamboyant buildings, was not completed until

1541, and the Flamboyant south transept of Beauvais dates from 1548. The dates of these later buildings are especially interesting, since they coincide with what is generally considered the Renaissance in France.

German Gothic. Original and imitative qualities. When we approach the subject of German Gothic we find that different conditions produced different results. The Germans accepted Gothic with reluctance. They already had a vigorous, highly original style in their Romanesque, which expressed their national genius. The Gothic movement in Germany was, therefore, a late one, and the period of transition, when Gothic was being accepted, was long. Germany generally owed her Gothic to France, and we are even indebted to a German for the phrase "opus francigenum" as a description of Gothic. This does not mean, however, that the German style does not show originality, and frequently differ widely from the French. For purposes of classification, as already suggested, one may divide the German Gothic buildings into two classes, original and imitative, according to the degree of originality in the work.

Early monuments. As one would expect, the early German Gothic buildings showed a high degree of originality. They represent a reminiscence of German Romanesque with a free application of French Gothic detail. Such a cathedral as Bamberg (Fig. 165), for example, shows a clear compromise between two architectural styles, the Gothic character showing only in the consistently pointed vaults and arches and in the moldings. Nor is Bamberg an isolated example. Many other churches of approximately the same date, among them

FIG. 162—ROUEN. SAINT OUEN. SYSTEM

the cathedrals of Naumburg and Münster (Fig. 166), exhibit the same compromise between French Gothic and German Romanesque, though they differ in detail, as German Romanesque buildings differ one from another. As time went on the tendency to imitate French forms became more marked.

Imitative works. By far the best known of the so-called imitative monuments are copies, more or less free, of the churches of northern France. What has often been called the first purely Gothic church of Germany was built between 1227 and 1243, at Trèves, in fairly faithful imitation of the church of Saint Yved at Braisne. The minsters of Strasburg and

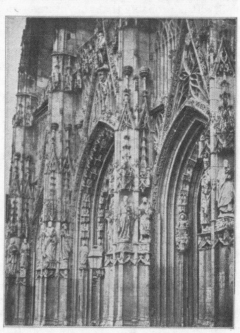

FIG. 163—ABBEVILLE. SAINT VULFRAM. THE WEST PORTALS

Freiburg (Figs. 167 and 168) soon followed it, the latter largely dependent on the former, but both harking back to the abbey of Saint Denis as a prototype, though in neither building do we meet mere copyism. Perhaps the most imitative of all the German cathedrals is Cologne (Fig. 138), reproducing the system of Amiens with great fidelity and possibly even begun by a Frenchman. This cathedral has, however, more homogeneity than Amiens, and diverges from it in many minor details.

The Hallenkirchen. Probably the least imitative and most

native Gothic churches of Germany were the Hallenkirchen, or hall churches. These were three-aisled buildings, with domical vaults, the aisle vaults being as high as those of the nave, and the building thus having the appearance of a great hall. It is probable that they were originally inspired by the churches of much the same sort characteristic of southwestern France. However this may

FIG. 164—ROUEN. SAINT MACLOU. VIEW OF THE WEST FRONT AND SPIRE

be, the Hallenkirchen were developed in Germany and increased in popularity from the early Gothic through the Flamboyant period, and became the most characteristically German of all the Gothic types. The first frankly Gothic example seems to have been the church of Saint Elizabeth at Marburg (Figs. 139, 169, and 170), erected between 1235 and 1283. Here, as though to emphasize the native German quality of the type, the plan is made three shelled, with a polygonal apse the breadth of the aisleless choir, and transepts of the same size with polygonal ends. This type was later extensively followed, as in the Wiesenkirche at Soest, and the church of Saint George at Nördlingen (Fig. 170), and on account of its simplicity it found particular favor in districts where brick was the chief building material.

Fourteenth century Gothic in Germany. In the fourteenth century Gothic art, so reluctantly accepted in Germany, expanded prodigiously. Fourteenth century German Gothic did not, however, show great originality. The period was one of expansion rather than progress. As in France, progress was in the direction of lightness, and forms at times became almost emaciated. Sculpture aped the prevailing French mode, exaggerating the French grimace, and foliate carving flung off all restraint. On the other hand the plans were kept simple and the Hallenkirche was a great favorite. Among the most original monuments of the period may be mentioned the cathedral of Ulm, built in 1377. As types of the fourteenth century Hallenkirchen we may mention the church of the

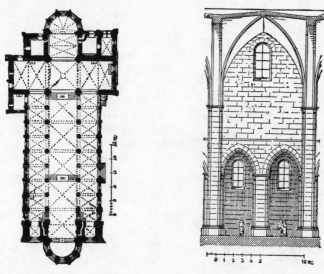

FIG. 165—BAMBERG. CATHEDRAL. PLAN AND SYSTEM

Holy Cross at Gmünd, and that of Saint Lawrence at Nürnberg.

Fifteenth century Gothic in Germany. The fifteenth century Gothic of Germany, except for the importation of some Flamboyant French details, developed from that of the fourteenth. The style was in large measure independent, and was able to influence even Italy and France. In general the art was a culmination of the lightness aimed at in the fourteenth century. Columns were simplified to the point of nudity, forms thinned, but combinations of members became extraordinarily complex. Thus without direct imitation the style approached the character of English Perpendicular Gothic. Vaults, for example, were often merely barrel vaults interpenetrated at right angles by other barrel vaults of less height, and the inner surfaces of both covered with a network of decorative ribs. At the same time a decorative system of lozenge-like paneling was developed which bears the closest analogy to the English Perpendicular paneling. The Hallenkirche, always popular, now received its greatest development. At the same time the technique of the builders and carvers became very skilful, and they were generally regarded in other countries as the equals if not the superiors of the French.

FIG. 166—MÜNSTER. CATHEDRAL. SYSTEM

The fifteenth century Hallenkirche. As examples of the Hallenkirche in the fifteenth century one may cite the five-aisled Liebfrauenkirche of Mülhausen, the cathedral of Munich, and many others. Even where the clerestory is preserved, however, the fifteenth century building appears scarcely less distinctively German, and one would never mistake the vaults of Saints Peter and Paul at Görlitz (1423–97) or those of the church of Saint Mary at Halle (1535–54), with their thinned members and lozenge decoration, for anything but German.

Spanish Gothic. The history of the Gothic in Spain is analogous to that of the style in other countries outside of France. There occurred the same importation of French detail, the same modification of the art according to local needs, climate, and national taste. In the beginning the importation from France and especially from Auvergne and Languedoc was very marked, but soon inspiration came from all over France.

General characteristics. Many special characteristics, however, differentiated the Spanish church from its French model, and gave it originality. Exigencies of climate as well as the abundance of classical monuments suggested a flattening of roofs and an accenting of the horizontal. Large window space was not needed in a sunny climate, and often the clerestory almost disappeared. The triforium was frequently suppressed, as suggested by the almost flat aisle roofs. With the accent on the horizontal line and the contraction of openings, came inevitably broad wall surfaces, which increased the classic feeling of the edifice. There is a diminishing of Gothic restlessness and an increase of classic repose in the Spanish work. Decoration, on the other hand, took on a characteristically Spanish sparkle. Undercutting was deep, edges crisp, contrast strong, and broad contrasts arranged between profusely decorated and wholly bare surfaces. Carving became especially exuberant during the Flamboyant period, and

FIG. 167—FREIBURG. THE MINSTER, SEEN FROM THE SOUTHEAST

a steadily increasing Saracenic influence tended to exaggerate the already exotic quality of the forms.

The interior. The interior of the Spanish church was generally dark and roomy. Piers were widely spaced and massy, vaults lower than in France. Peculiarities of the Spanish buildings were the *capilla mayor* and the *coro*. The former was the apsidal chapel, bounded by the ambulatory, almost completely screened from the rest of the church. The latter was an equally screened choir, arranged west of the crossing. These features tended to break up the interior and render its size more difficult to appreciate (Fig. 171).

Twelfth century Spanish Gothic. As one might expect, the twelfth century Spanish buildings are somewhat chaotic. In Catalonia, for example, the abbeys of Poblet and Santa Creus were founded by monks from near Narbonne, and show the influence of the architecture of Langue-doc. On the other hand, the Cistercian churches of Alcobaza (Portugal) and Las Huelgas, near Burgos, display the strongly domical vaults and nave and aisles of equal height which south-western France gave alike to them and to Germany.

Thirteenth century Spanish Gothic. In the thirteenth century inspiration came from northern France, and Span-ish architecture, without losing its own identity, rivaled French. The best known and finest works of the period are the cathedrals of Burgos, Toledo (Fig. 171), and Leon. The inspiration for the first two came from Bourges; that of the last from buildings farther north in the Ile de France and Cham-pagne. Burgos and Toledo resemble each other closely. The former was founded in 1226, the latter somewhat later, and the same architects may well have worked upon both. Leon cathedral is more eclectic than Burgos or Toledo, though it shows the influ-ence of Chartres more than that of any other single French building. It does not suggest any dry eclecticism, however, but rather has the spon-taneity of its great French prototypes,

FIG. 168—FREIBURG. THE MINSTERS SYSTEM

and seems to spring, as they do, from fine models only slightly earlier in date.

Fourteenth century Spanish Gothic. In the fourteenth century Gothic of Spain there appeared the same tendencies as in France, although refinement never went so far in the

former country as in the latter.   The influence of northern
France weakened somewhat, and we find such works as the
cathedral of Gerona, begun in 1316, inspired once more by the
architecture of southern France.

Fifteenth century Spanish Gothic.   The prosperity of Spain
during the fifteenth century favored architectural development.   As in Ger-
many, we feel
much originality
in the later work.
This is attained by
an emphasis on
the qualities which
we have called
characteristically
Spanish.   Flat
roofs became more
common,   carving
more sparkling,
buildings more
spacious.   The
octagonal lantern
came to be a very
prominent feature,
as at Barcelona
and Valencia.
The openwork
detail of French
Flamboyant was
specially suited to
Spanish taste, and

FIG. 169—MARBURG.   SAINT ELIZABETH.   THE
INTERIOR, LOOKING TOWARD THE APSE

was very characteristic of late Spanish Gothic.   The best
known examples are the openwork spires of Burgos, begun in
1442, imitated not from a French work but a German one, the
cathedral of Cologne.   The most ambitious church of fifteenth
century Spain, the cathedral of Seville (Figs. 139, 140, and 172),
was begun in 1401.   Here the warm climate of Andalusia and
the Moorish influence of a country long under Moslem domination exaggerated the typically Spanish characteristics of the
architecture.   Roofs are never so flat, piers never so widely

spaced, interiors never so gloomy, as at Seville. The detail has a specially Moorish eccentricity. Indeed the Spaniards combined Moorish and Christian detail so skilfully that buildings like the famous Sevillan Giralda (Fig. 172) present

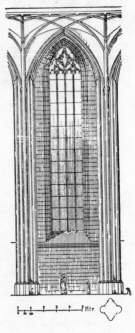

Marburg, Saint Elizabeth   Nördlingen, Saint George

FIG. 170—SYSTEMS OF HALLENKIRCHEN

a harmonious whole when actually constructed in several different and seemingly antagonistic periods.

Origin of the Gothic style in Italy. In no country were the fundamentals of the Gothic structural systems as completely disregarded as in Italy, nevertheless the style attained there a strong position and produced monuments of great charm. It was, however, purely adventitious. Italy was the home of classical Roman architecture. It received Romanesque readily, but gave it so strong a flavor of classic art that the style, as we have seen, has often been called that of the proto-

Renaissance. Italy had always been prone to classic revivals, and in the Romanesque period showed signs of being ready for the greatest of them all—the Renaissance—when the peninsula was overwhelmed by the wave of Gothic fashion, and for two centuries the pointed style was supreme. It was, however, an imported, foreign fashion, just as fashion in dress at the same time was imported from Paris. It arrived in almost complete purity, at the hands principally of the Cistercians, who settled at Fossanova in Latium (1187), and thence spread to Casamari near Rome (1217), San Galgano in Tuscany (soon after 1217), and other sites. These monks built Cistercian Gothic churches of a severe but monumental sort, and roused the Italian taste for the pointed style, but Italian taste promptly modified the style imported.

General character of Italian Gothic. The Italian architects had little sense of logical structure, and thus produced buildings which included meager buttress systems, tied vaults, and

FIG. 171 — TOLEDO. CATHEDRAL. VIEW OF THE INTERIOR, LOOKING TOWARD THE APSE

lacked all that the French considered most important in the Gothic style. Along with this lack of structural sense went a disguised but recognizable classical feeling. Classical detail gave way, but classical arrangements and emphasis were retained. The horizontal line, as in Spain, was emphasized. Intercolumniations were broadened, with a consequent loss of scale. Wall spaces were broad, openings small, and interiors gave an impression of roominess which frequently went over into bareness. Climate, as well as classical reminiscence, played a large rôle in these changes. Since openings were small and wall spaces broad, stained glass was neglected. Its place was taken by mosaic, and especially by fresco, or painting in water color on wet plaster, which began as a cheap substitute for mosaic. The timber roof was

FIG. 172—SEVILLE.   THE CATHEDRAL AND GIRALDA TOWER, SEEN FROM
THE SOUTHWEST

often substituted for the vault. Façades became gorgeous screens, richly decorated in carved marble and glass mosaic, behind which the church often seemed vainly to attempt to conceal itself. The Italian Gothic style varied geographically, being simpler in the north, and emphasizing polychromy in central Italy. It also varied chronologically. We find very simple buildings in the early Cistercian period, and very ramified ones when Flamboyant Gothic came into vogue.

Early Gothic architecture in Italy. Perhaps the best example of the early Cistercian building in Italy is the church of San Martino, near Viterbo, built in the early thirteenth century.

About the same time the church of Saint Francis was built
at Assisi (Fig. 173), and the Italian modification of French
structure began. In proportion and general external effect
this building might be Romanesque. In the second half of
the century many Gothic buildings were raised, the most
interesting of which is the cathedral of Siena. Here one sees

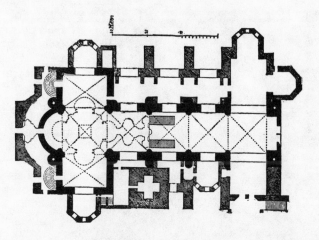

FIG. 173—ASSISI. SAN FRANCESCO. PLAN

a good example of the Italian screen-like façade, decorated in
carved marble and polychromy, and the striped marble interior
characteristic of Tuscan architecture. Many minor churches
were constructed in imitation of the cathedral buildings. In
the north an architecture with more organic feeling was
developed at Bologna, where the church of Saint Francis
(1236–40) shows a real buttress system. In the south
Cistercian ideas were mingling with architectural ideas from
the Latin Orient, and, as always in southern Italy, the result
was an interesting architectural hybrid.

Fourteenth century Italian Gothic. Fourteenth century
Gothic in Italy, as elsewhere, developed chiefly from the local
architecture of the preceding century. In Florence we find
the cathedral (1296–1367) exaggerating the Italian trend
toward wide intercolumniations, bare interiors, and the

Tuscan violent polychromy applied to the façade (Figs. 138, 140, 174, and 189). The triforium was omitted, the clerestory reduced, and the openings greatly diminished in size. The plan was given a trefoil shape which reveals Germanic influence (compare Figs. 111 and 138). The free standing clock tower, Giotto's "Lily Campanile," is one of the most graceful examples of the Italian polychromatic pointed style. In Umbria the cathedral of Orvieto (Fig. 175), dating from the end of the thirteenth and the beginning of the fourteenth century, shows an imitation of Siena. The wooden roof was frankly used here, however, and the contrast of interior stripes is less violent than in Siena. The body of the church is unobtrusive, the façade one of the most gorgeous and

FIG. 174—FLORENCE. THE CATHEDRAL. VIEW OF THE INTERIOR, LOOKING TOWARD THE APSE

least spoiled by modern restoration. The combination of the two is marred by inevitable incongruity. In the north important Gothic work was done in Venice, in the church of Saints John and Paul, and in other towns. At the very end of the century the graceful Carthusian abbey of Pavia was begun, with its triconch ending, lanterns, and exterior galleries, which reveal the influence of Germany once more.

Fifteenth century Italian Gothic. This influence becomes

most important in the fifteenth century. Important secular architecture in Flamboyant Italy is seen in many buildings, but the ecclesiastical architecture of the period is best summed up in the cathedral of Milan (Fig. 176). In this work Italian, French, and German influences mingle. The Italian lofty ground story and wide intercolumniation were retained. The triforium disappeared and the clerestory was reduced. Windows were kept small and tie-rods were used to hold in the vaults. The workman-

ship is German, the Flamboyant detail French, modified by Germans. On the exterior the vertical line was unsparingly emphasized, as in English Perpendicular, though the detail is German in character. Pitched roofs were abandoned in favor of nearly flat ones, but the consequent horizontal lines were disguised by a multitude of pinnacles. The material was fine marble throughout, and the carving was so delicate and profuse in figure work, pinnacle, and detail that a very lace-like effect was obtained.

FIG. 175—ORVIETO. THE CATHEDRAL FRONT, SEEN FROM THE SOUTHWEST

Long before the completion of Milan cathedral the Renaissance was in full sway in Florence, and it is to the credit of the Milanese that they finished a structure so harmoniously at so late a date.

Gothic architecture of the Latin Orient and elsewhere. There are many subdivisions of the Gothic style which we have had time merely to mention in connection with our classification, and the discussion of which we shall have to omit. It will be well, however, at least to call attention to the fact that Gothic architecture of real interest was produced in Austria, Scandinavia, Switzerland, and elsewhere. The regret is especially keen that we have thus summarily to dismiss the

Gothic architecture of the Latin Orient. The crusaders carried their builders with them, set up Western civilization in the nearer East, and the result was a series of imposing Gothic monuments, ecclesiastical and secular, in Palestine and Syria and in the Mediterranean islands. Even when the tide of conquest turned and the Occidental invaders were being

FIG. 176—MILAN. EXTERIOR OF THE CATHEDRAL

driven out, they carried on their building operations, as at Gaza, until the last days of their occupation. The turning of this tide meant, however, that Gothic buildings were to be rare in Palestine and on the mainland, and frequent and more complete on the islands where the Occidentals held longer sway.

Secular architecture. As always in the Middle Ages, ecclesiastical architecture is more important than secular in the Gothic period, but this very fact has caused writers to over-emphasize medieval ecclesiatical art at the expense of secular. At times the secular monuments rival the ecclesiastical in importance. In every period, of course, the character of the detail of the secular buildings corresponded to that of the ecclesiastical buildings. Quite as obviously the progression from early to late date was one from comparative simplicity to greater complication. Different sorts of secular works received greater emphasis according to the period. In the Romanesque and early Gothic periods interest centers almost entirely on buildings, public or private, of a military character. In the later periods, especially in the latest Flamboyant, when civic order was the rule and the individual felt himself secure, lay monuments largely lost their military character, and one finds the greatest development of the medieval town and guild hall, and the slightly fortified palace of the petty noble or merchant prince. The powerful nobles continued to build well-nigh impregnable castles until the centralization of power in the king forbade such monuments. We shall be able to give only the main characteristics of each type of secular monument, with the mention of a few distinctive examples, and point out roughly the periods in which each type attained its greatest importance.

The fortified town. The most imposing secular monuments, and of course among the earliest, are the fortified towns. The fortifications of a town were so composed with a view to defense that the whole became a unit, and it is not fanciful to think of the town as a single monument. The principle was that of surrounding the town with walls, especially strong wherever the town was unprotected by natural defenses such as cliffs or rivers, and of fortifying angles of the walls by salient towers which provided for enfilading fire on besiegers attacking the curtain wall between the towers. We have already noted such a system at Avila, in the Romanesque period, and variations were infinite. Secondary walls of defense were built outside the stronger inner walls. Beyond the outer walls moats were dug, and frequently filled with water. Access to the space between the inner and outer walls was provided by drawbridges, ramps, and triple or quadruple gates, covered with stone galleries, pierced with openings, through which missiles might be dropped on the heads of invaders. Once an entrance had been forced within the outer wall, the invader found himself in a cul-de-sac, exposed to the fire of the inner defenders until such time as he could pierce the vastly stronger inner fortifications. If at last he succeeded in winning the inner works he might take the town, but had yet to besiege the citadel, a strong fortress placed in the strongest position in the town, into which the defending military retreated.

Aigues-Mortes and Carcassonne. Examples of fortified towns are to be found in most European countries, though the

FIG. 177—AIGUES-MORTES. GENERAL VIEW OF THE CITY AND FORTI-FICATIONS

finest and most complete are in France. Here two examples far surpass the others: the towns of Aigues-Mortes and Carcassonne. The former (Fig. 177), founded in 1246 by Saint Louis, presents fortifications in the form of a rectangle roughly 600 by 150 yards, with twenty well-preserved towers, some square and some round. The moat has disappeared, but the machicolations and inner galleries for defensive fire may still be studied, as well as the defenses of the ten gates. The monotonous regularity of the plan shows that the picturesque irregularity of most medieval secular building was the result of the architect's adapting himself to eccentricities in site or warping his building to take military advantage of such eccentricities. Where the site is a plain, architectural irregularities disappear. For an example of the picturesque and irregular town site, the Cité of Carcassonne (Fig. 178) will serve our need. Here the fortifications date in part to the Visigothic period in the fifth century and were frequently reconstructed up to the fourteenth century. They were skilfully restored in the mid-nineteenth century by Viollet-le-Duc. The site was by nature lofty and inaccessible, and man exaggerated this inaccessibility to a picturesque degree. No one part of the fortification repeats any other part. Ramp, curtain-wall, turret, and cul-de-sac all conform so skilfully to the natural advantages of the terrain that human handiwork appears part of bed-rock, or bed-rock part of the human structure. The outer enceinte is more than 1600 yards in circumference, and the inner more than 1200. The walls are fortified by

FIG. 178—CARCASSONNE. LA CITE. VIEW OF THE FORTIFICATIONS

fifty round towers and the whole dominated by the citadel. The major portion of the work dates from the late twelfth and the thirteenth centuries. The whole affords the most imposing, and in some respects the most interesting, secular monument of the Gothic period which has come down to us.

The castle. The chief characteristics of the castle coincide with those of the fortified town. In the fully developed examples one finds the outer and inner walls, the towers fortifying the wall angles, the moats, machicolations, corbelled galleries, and ramps, such as the towns afforded. Even the town citadel is reflected in the donjon. This, however, was placed either at the least accessible part of the site or at the weakest, the idea in the latter case being further to strengthen the weakest part. Not all castles have this completeness. In the Romanesque period castles like the famous Chateau Gaillard of Richard Coeur de Leon, were simpler than in the Gothic, and

FIG. 179—COUCY.   GENERAL VIEW OF THE CASTLE GROUNDS, SHOWING
THE DONJON BEFORE ITS DESTRUCTION IN 1917

even before the Romanesque period there were castle-like defenses, mounds protected by earthworks, ditches, and palisades. These mounds and ditches often became part of the system of defenses of castles subsequently raised upon the sites. Some castles lacked donjons; some retained the square keep in preference to the round. In the earlier castles the systems of defense were single; later they became concentric. Diversity was great, but fundamental characteristics were the same.

Examples of Gothic castles. Coucy. Many countries exhibit important and well-preserved examples of the medieval castle. In England there are many, both of the Norman and of later periods, among which we may emphasize the castle of Harlech, one of the most stupendous fortresses of the Middle Ages. The medieval builders learned much of fortress building in the crusades, and the Latin Orient contains some of the most impressive remains of military architecture. As so frequently in medieval architecture, France offers perhaps the finest mouments of all, especially good examples being the castles of Pierrefonds and Coucy, the latter destroyed by the Germans in April, 1917 (Figs. 139 and 179). Pierrefonds has been restored by Viollet-le-Duc, and, though in a sense a false document, presents a most vivid reconstruction, on the part of a profound medievalist, of a Gothic castle. The more impressive Coucy was blown up by Mazarin but its donjon, 210 feet in height, with walls in some places 34 feet thick, stood until it had to yield to the power of modern high explosives. Such a building, before the days of gunpowder, was literally impregnable, and Coucy was never taken. To understand

FIG. 180—A MEDIEVAL TOWN HOUSE. (VIOLLET-LE-DUC)

the spirit which dominated the medieval castle, and the consequent architectural expression which it attained, one needs but read the motto of the Sieurs de Coucy: "Roi ne suys, ne prince, ne duc, ne comte aussi; je suys le Sire de Coucy."[1].

So superbly insolent a motto was justified by the lordship of such a building.

Later castles. As time went on the nobles lightened the appearance of their dwellings and sacrificed somewhat, though never to a dangerous extent, the defensive character of the

[1] I am not king, nor prince, nor duke, nor even count; I am the Lord of Coucy.

work. For instance the castle of Jean-de-Berry at Méhun-sur-Yèvre, built in 1386 and known to us by an illumination, succeeded in combining late Gothic delicacy with adequate defense. Defense was, however, still the underlying idea.

The town house. The need of defense lay like a shadow athwart all civil architecture. The town house (Fig. 180) was

FIG. 181—THE COUNTRY DWELLING OF A MEDI-EVAL PEASANT. (VIOLLET-LE-DUC)

arranged for defense, not against soldiers but against roisterers and ruffians. The entrance was raised well above the street and the stairs arranged along the flank of the wall. Before reaching the platform on which the door opened, the way was blocked by an open grille, through which a pike could be thrust to repel undesirables. In the town house exigencies of space caused the upper story to expand, and, carried on beams or corbels, to overhang the street in the manner already noted in medieval Constantinople. This scheme was followed whether the house were of stone or of wood.

The peasant's house. The country peasant's house (Fig. 181) commonly had the same raised doorway, flanking stairway, and platform for defense as the city house. There was generally no connection between the upper story and the ground story, the latter being used for the animals. The walls and gable ends were often of monumental cut stone; the roofs usually steeply pitched and thatched. Such peasant houses had all the charm of picturesqueness, honesty, and directness in fulfilling architectural needs.

The fortified manor. Of more ambitious dimensions and defenses were the country fortified manors. These were generally square, with turrets at the corners, reaching to the ground or carried on corbels. The manor was surrounded by a moat, and the approach to the small gate made by means of a draw. Within was an open court. Such a type of dwelling may be seen at Saint Médard-en-Jalle (Fig. 182), near Landes, and at Camarsac (Gironde).

FIG. 182—SAINT MEDARD-EN-JALLE. SKETCH OF THE MANOR. (VIOLLET-LE-DUC)

Municipal and corporation halls. Especially in the later Middle Ages the municipal and corporation halls attained great importance. The Hôtel de Ville of France and Flanders, the Palazzo Pubblico of Italy, the Rathaus of Germany, received monumental treatment. Of the same sort were the guild halls, semi-communistic in character, which were common in free towns all over Europe, but especially in Flanders. The hall survived or fell with the town, and was not intended to resist assault if the town were taken, consequently plans were more regular, esthetic considerations were more emphasized. The buildings lacked the frowning character of fortified works, were more delicate, more profusely ornamented, and better mirrored the contemporary style. This is especially true in the buildings of late date, and the finest belong to the Flamboyant period.

The town and guild halls of Flanders. The town halls were generally of fairly regular plan. The lower story was usually the record office. In Flanders a *beffroi*, or clock tower, with a bell for summoning the citizens, was a common adjunct. The buildings were usually two or more stories in height, with the central portion carried up as a tower which started square and became octagonal. Roofs were very steep, and generally supplied with picturesque dormers. Among the fine Flemish halls we may mention those of Ghent (1481), Brussels (1401–

FIG. 183—YPRES. THE CLOTH HALL AS IT APPEARED BEFORE THE BOMBARDMENT OF 1914

55), and Louvain. The trade and guild halls of Flanders usually differed only in interior arrangement from the town hall, and were frequently taken over at a later date, and used as town halls. The finest of all the Belgian trade halls was the so-called Cloth Hall of Ypres (Fig. 183), dating from the thirteenth century, but wholly destroyed by shell fire in 1914.

Halls and mansions of France. In France we find the same types of monuments, especially important in the Flamboyant period. These buildings were erected as town halls, as trade halls, or often merely as private residences of the very wealthy

bourgeois. The private mansion usually lacked the beffroi
of the town hall, otherwise the buildings were similar. The
main unit was the bay of two or more stories. Tiers of
windows were divided by buttresses with Flamboyant detail,
the Flamboyant arch, with delicate and eccentric curves,
being used throughout. The favorite form of window was the
transom or cross window, the light being divided by an upright mullion in the center, and a cross-bar of stone one-

FIG. 184—BOURGES. MAISON DE JACQUES COEUR

third of the distance from the top. Each window was thus a
rhythmic reproduction of the one below. Roofs were very
steeply pitched, and provided with dormers which repeated
the motifs of the windows perpendicularly below them. In the
courtyard the ground story arcade was usually open. Plan
and skyline were broken by pavilions, and by elaborate
chimneys. The whole effect was delicate, orderly, yet
picturesque. Good examples of this Flamboyant French
secular architecture may be seen at Paris in the Hôtel Cluny,

at Rouen in the Palais de Justice, and at Bourges in the Maison de Jacques Cœur (Fig. 184).

Domestic architecture in England.   In England, as in France, domestic architecture followed civil architecture in detail.   At first the mansions were built around a court, but the entrance side of the square came to be omitted, and irregularities were soon introduced.   The trend was toward picturesqueness, irregu-

FIG. 185—FLORENCE.   THE PALAZZO VECCHIO

larity, and small scale, so that the Tudor houses give a greater impression of intimacy than any works on the continent.   The Middle Ages thus prepared the way for later English domestic work, and such a building as Compton Wynyates, though medieval in detail, is Renaissance in spirit.

Secular architecture in Italy.   Municipal individuality.   In Italy, as in Flanders and France, there was little difference architecturally between the town hall, the ducal palace, and the private residence of the wealthy citizen, and the same building often combined two or more functions.   Differences came from date, and above all from geography. Nothing more clearly shows the independence and self-sufficiency of the Italian medieval civic spirit than the way in which each city arrogated to itself a peculiar type of secular architecture, a fact which held true when towns were near together and in constant communication. In certain general

ways all Italian medieval mansions resembled one another. They were usually regular in plan, built round a court, and provided with a campanile incorporated or free standing. Divergence occurred principally in the arrangements of details in a bay, in the treatment of detail, and in the general expression of the building.

Domestic architecture of Florence and Siena. In Florence, as we may see by the Palazzo Vecchio (Fig. 185) or the Bargello, the appearance of the building was forbidding. There was no division of the exterior into bays, and the stone used

FIG. 186—SIENA. THE PALAZZO PUBBLICO

was dark and roughly rusticated. The characteristic window had two lights, separated by a mullion and embraced by a pointed arch, the intrados and extrados of which were not concentric but wider apart at the crown than at the springing. On the other hand, the Palazzo Pubblico of Siena (Fig. 186) shows that the Sienese architect, like the Sienese painter, sought more graceful and less forbidding forms. The material received a finer finish, and the use of brick was common. The campanile was made more slender and loftier. The window form was a design of three lancet-like lights, with very pointed arches and delicate cusps, embraced by a single highly pointed arch with concentric intrados and extrados. Each town thus sought a native form, especially of window opening, for its own, and originality is always found except where one city was able to force its ideas upon another.

Secular buildings of Venice. The most famous, and in many ways the most charming and original Italian secular buildings of the Middle Ages were those of Venice. These, like so much secular work, attained greatest heights during the Flamboyant period, and the secular buildings were new in general expres-

FIG. 187—VENICE. THE PALAZZO DUCALE

sion as well as detail. Ground story arcades were almost invariably left open, and, as the eye ascended, the building became less broken, so that the effect was to reduplicate by the reflection of the canals the most complicated parts of the architecture. Rich but harmonious polychromy was used to fortify crisp carving. Sometimes exteriors were veneered with polished marble, sometimes terra cotta, or smaller stones in two colors giving the impression of terra cotta, were used. The most sinuous and graceful of ogee curves was used for openings and arches, the curves being counterpoised by delicate cusps, giving the actual opening a pointed trefoil form. Such arches were commonly interlaced, and the consequent quatrefoils between them were cusped and given round or slender pointed form. Roofs, like all Italian palace roofs, were kept flat. In lieu of cornices the roof edges were decorated with conventionalized spiny battlements, of colored stone or even wood, which added to the piquancy of the effect. In a sense all the Venetian medieval palaces were offshoots of the Palazzo Ducale (Fig. 187). This most monumental of secular buildings in Venice set the fashion which was followed with delicate variation and refinement in many other buildings, and from Venice the style spread over the Venetian contado.

Other Gothic monuments. Though we must here bring to a close our discussion of medieval secular architecture, it is necessary to point out the existence of numerous monuments of medieval art, usually wholly forgotten, which aid in a comprehension of the style. Bridges, such as that at Avignon or the Pont Valentré (Fig. 188) at Cahors, are often really great monuments of Gothic architecture, combining the needs of defense with logical construction and fine proportions. Similarly much can be learned from boundary monuments, *lanternes des morts* (monuments to signalize the presence of a cemetery), well heads, dove-cotes, and even latrines. In short the mass of material is enormous, and a little explored field is open to the student of medieval secular architecture.

The medieval ensemble. Picturesqueness and its cause. As one would expect, the ensemble in medieval times is noteworthy for its irregularity and picturesqueness. Buildings as a group were not planned in an orderly way, except in the case of buildings for defense, when everything gave way to a definite scheme. Even here, as we have seen, the result was generally asymmetrical, except where the terrain was absolutely without variety. The picturesqueness of the medieval ensemble was not, however, the result of mere haphazard grouping. It came principally from a logical conformity to the peculiarities of the site, and is allied to the structural logic which produced the Gothic cathedral. For example, if a Gothic architect were designing a bridge he would not design a symmetrical one with an even rise and fall, and force his

workmen to place it across a river of any sort of bottom. He
would consider first the river bottom, discover the position of
the channel, and then design the bridge with the arch of
longest span over the channel. If this were toward one
bank, as it frequently was, the result was asymmetry and
picturesqueness, but picturesqueness created and governed by

FIG. 188—CAHORS. THE PONT VALENTRÉ

structural good sense. The picturesqueness of the ensemble
was similarly governed. Those who regard the medieval town
plan as merely haphazard have as their ideal a construction
which, by means of leveling, grading, and difficult engineering,
oftentimes destroys the local flavor of the site in order to pre-
pare for an artificial grouping. The medieval architect, from
whatever motive, preferred to harmonize buildings to site
rather than vice versa, and as a result the medieval ensemble
more frequently looks as though it belonged properly to the
country than the ensemble at an earlier or a later date.

The influence of Gothic structural principles. The influence of Gothic architecture on later styles was of many sorts. The subtlest, and perhaps the most important, was the influence of Gothic structural principles. These, once learned, could never wholly be forgotten. Even at a period when Gothic itself was despised, Gothic structural designs lived, were freely applied, and, it must be confessed, were often wofully misunderstood. Even the Gothic details, moldings, carving and the like, left their impress on later detail, especially in the early Renaissance.

Influence of Flamboyant Gothic in France. Turning to more concrete examples of Gothic influence, the importance of the Flamboyant style in the history of architecture has never properly been emphasized. Outside of Italy, where the Renaissance was a natural classical revival, Flamboyant Gothic determined the most significant expression of later architecture. In the early Renaissance the system was but one of a superficial application of imported Italian Renaissance detail to a structure fundamentally and in significant motifs Flamboyant Gothic. One need only compare the Hôtel Cluny with the Château de Chenonceau to prove this. Even much later, when the Renaissance in France became more formal, essentials of Flamboyant Gothic remained. If we analyze, say the formal portions of the Louvre, and ask ourselves what gives the building its peculiarly French flavor despite its classic detail, we shall be forced to reply the steep roofs, the dormers, the broken skyline, the pavilions. All of these are of native medieval French origin, and withstood the assaults of Italian classicism.

Influence of fifteenth century Gothic elsewhere. What is true in France is true elsewhere. The Perpendicular Tudor house determined the form of the Early English Renaissance dwelling. The picturesqueness, the irregularity, the small scale which we associate with English domestic architecture, is of medieval origin, and the modern Englishman reverts to it as his national style. In Germany and the Low Countries the stepped gables and picturesqueness of medieval architecture were but overlaid with classical detail. In Spain the Plateresque style was the freest warping of classic detail to make it fit the lines of Flamboyant Spanish Gothic. Flamboyant Gothic was, therefore, one of the most influential of the world's styles, and its power is by no means spent.

CHRONOLOGICAL LIST OF MONUMENTS

FRANCE AND FLANDERS

Morienval.—Earlier parts c. 1080; later c. 1120.
Saint Germer de Fly.—1130–60.
Paris, Saint Martin des Champs.—c. 1136.
Creil.—c. 1140.
Senlis.—c. 1155–91.
Paris, Saint Germain des Prés.—Dedicated 1163; some parts considerably earlier.
Paris, Cathedral.—1163–1235.
Avignon, Pont Saint Bénézet.—1177–85.
Langres.—Twelfth century.
Carcassonne, Fortifications.—Chiefly late twelfth and thirteenth centuries.
Soissons.—Choir finished 1212; rest mid-thirteenth century; spire c. 1160.
Chartres.—Façade c. 1145; rest chiefly 1194–1260; earlier spire c. 1250; later spire 1507–14.
Reims.—1211–90.
Amiens.—1220–88.
Coucy.—Early thirteenth century.
Aigues-Mortes.—Town founded 1246; fortifications begun 1272.
Paris, Sainte Chapelle.—Dedicated 1248.
Saint Médard-en-Jalle.—First half of the thirteenth century.
Ypres, Cloth Hall.—Thirteenth century.
Camarsac.—Late thirteenth or early fourteenth century.
Rouen, Saint Ouen.—1318–39 and later.
Amiens Cathedral, Chapel of Saint John.—1373–75.
Méhun sur Yèvre, Castle of Jean de Berry.—1386.
Pierrefonds.—c. 1390.
Cahors, Pont Valentré.—Fourteenth century.
Brussels, Hôtel de Ville.—1401–55.
Louvain, Hôtel de Ville.—1448–59.
Abbéville, Saint Vulfram.—Begun 1480.
Ghent, Hôtel de Ville.—1481.
Paris, Hôtel Cluny.—1490.
Quimper.—Chiefly fifteenth century.
Nantes.—Chiefly fifteenth century.

Chambéry.—Chiefly fifteenth century.
Bourges, Maison de Jacques Cœur.—End of the fifteenth century.
Rouen, Saint Maclou.—Finished 1541.
Beauvais Cathedral, Flamboyant transept.—1548.
Troyes.—Sixteenth century.

ENGLAND

Canterbury.—Begun 1175.
Lincoln.—Early English Work.—1185-1200.
Salisbury.—1220-58.
Wells.—Dedicated 1239.
Lincoln Cathedral, Angel Choir.—1255-80
York, choir and west front.—1261-1324.
Harlech Castle.—c. 1300.
Gloucester.—transepts and choir 1331-37; cloisters 1351-1412.
Windsor, Saint George's Chapel.—1481-1537.
London, Westminster Abbey, Henry VII.'s Chapel.—1500-12.
Compton Wynyates.—1520.

GERMANY

Bamberg.—1185-1274.
Münster.—1225-61.
Marburg, Saint Elizabeth.—1235-83.
Naumburg.—Nave before 1249; choir 1250-1330.
Cologne.—Begun 1248; choir consecrated 1322; much work modern.
Strasburg.—1250-75; façade 1275-1318.
Freiburg.—Nave 1260; choir 1354.
Trèves.—Remodeled thirteenth century.
Soest, Wiesenkirche.—Founded 1314.
Ulm.—Begun 1377; finished sixteenth century.
Gmünd, The Holy Cross.—Fourteenth century.
Mülhausen, Liebfrauenkirche.—Fourteenth and fifteenth centuries.
Nürnberg, Saint Lawrence.—Begun end of the thirteenth century; nave 1403-45; choir 1445-72.
Görlitz, Saints Peter and Paul.—1423-97.
Nördlingen, Saint George.—1427-1505.
Munich, Frauenkirche.—1468-88.
Halle, Saint Mary.—1535-54.

ITALY

Fossanova.—1187.
Casamari.—1217.
San Galgano.—c. 1220.

Assisi, Saint Francis.—1228–53.
Venice, Santi Giovanni e Paolo.—Begun 1234.
Bologna, Saint Francis.—1236–40.
Siena.—c. 1245–84.
Viterbo, San Martino.—Mid-thirteenth century.
Florence, Bargello.—Begun 1255.
Siena, Palazzo Pubblico.—1289–1309.
Florence, Cathedral.—1296–1367.
Orvieto.—End of the thirteenth and beginning of the fourteenth
centuries.
Florence, Giotto's Campanile.—Designed 1334–36.
Venice, Palazzo Ducale.—Founded 814; outer walls rebuilt 1340;
west façade early fifteenth century.
Milan.—Founded 1386; finished sixteenth century.
Pavia Abbey Church.—Begun 1396; finished in the Renaissance.

SPAIN AND PORTUGAL

Alcobaza (Portugal).—1148–1222.
Santa Creus.—1157.
Seville, Giralda.—1184–96; remodeled 1568.
Las Huelgas en Burgos.—1187–1214.
Poblet.—Second half of the twelfth century.
Burgos.—Founded 1221.
Toledo.—c. 1227.
Barcelona.—1298–1420.
Leon.—c. 1280.
Gerona.—1316.
Seville.—Begun 1401.
Burgos Cathedral, spires.—Begun 1442.

BIBLIOGRAPHICAL NOTE

In A. Michel's *Histoire de l'Art*, vol. 2, pts. 1 and 2, and vol. 3,
pt. 1, 1906–07, are excellent and authoritative accounts of the development of Gothic architecture, and of the character of the art
in the thirteenth and fourteenth centuries and the Flamboyant period.
The bibliographies are especially valuable.   E. E. Viollet-le-Duc's
Dictionnaire raisonné de l'architecture, 1884–88, already quoted, covers much more than Gothic, but, in dictionary form, is one of the most
monumental pieces of research in Gothic.   As an original source
Villard de Honnecourt's *Album*, 1906, and earlier editions (written in
the thirteenth century), is the most interesting and important. K.

Schnaase's *Geschichte der bildenden Kunst*, 1866–76, presents two volumes on medieval architecture, out of date but important. One of the most illuminating and best illustrated general works, G. Dehio and G. von Bezold's *Kirchliche Baukunst des Abendlandes*, 1884–99, has already been quoted. Similarly B. and B. F. Fletcher's *History of Architecture*, 1905, has been quoted, and is specially useful for English Gothic. F. von Reber's *History of Medieval Art*, 1886, covers the whole field but emphasizes German architecture. F. M. Simpson's *History of Architectural Development*, vol. 2, 1909, is useful for the study of details of structure. C. H. Moore's *Gothic Architecture*, 1906, is one of the most important and profound works on the subject, tending, however, to over-emphasize structural logic, and cursory and unsympathetic in the treatment of the art outside of thirteenth-century France. A. K. Porter's *Medieval Architecture*, 1912, already cited, treats the subject frankly from the structural point of view and is a monumental and up-to-date piece of scholarship. J. Quicherat's *Mélanges d'archéologie*, vol. 2, *Moyen-âge*, 1886, is one of the most important early studies of the Romanesque and Gothic styles. It was followed by L. Courajod's *Origines de l'art roman et gothique*, 1889, a shrewd though out-of-date analysis of the origin of the styles. Both works emphasize the art in France. L. Gonse's *L'art gothique*, 1890, is a monumental volume covering all Gothic art, but specially useful for the study of French Gothic. J. A. Brutails' *L'archéologie du moyen-âge*, 1900, has already been quoted as a clever study of the methods of medieval archæology, as well as A. Marignan's *Les méthodes du passé dans l'archéologie française*, 1911, the most extreme though somewhat discredited work on the subject.

E. Corroyer's *Architecture gothique*, 1891, is an out-of-date but compact and interesting little volume on Gothic architecture in France and Flanders. The best modern histories of medieval, and especially Gothic, architecture in France are C. Enlart's *Architecture réligieuse en France*, 1902, and *Architecture civile et militaire en France*, 1904, encyclopedic works of research which are worthy successors to the publications of Viollet-le-Duc. For the thirteenth century E. Mâle's *L'art réligieux en France au XIII. siècle*, 1902, is especially fine. The Abbé Bossebœuf's *L'Architecture Plantagenet*, 1897, affords an interesting study of a specially significant local variety of the style. G. H. West's *Gothic Architecture in England and France*, 1911, is a small but well-arranged and fair-minded study of the architecture in both countries.

Although wofully out of date, J. Britton's *The Cathedral Antiquities of Great Britain*, 1836, is a five-volume work of real value for the study of English Gothic. E. Sharpe's *The Seven Periods of English Architecture*, 1871, and T. Rickman's *An Attempt to Discriminate the*

Styles of Architecture in England, 1881, cited under Romanesque, are immensely more important works of research in the styles of English Gothic. G. G. Scott's *English Church Architecture*, 1881, despite its date, is a valuable work on the English style. E. S. Prior's *A History of Gothic Art in England*, 1900, is a valuable and modern synthetic work. R. and J.A. Brandon's *An Analysis of Gothic Architecture*, 1903, is a profusely illustrated work, especially useful for the study of detail. F. Bond's *Gothic Architecture in England*, 1905, is one of the most scholarly of the modern books on the style, and it was succeeded by the author's *English Church Architecture*, 1913, the most modern and probably the most valuable work to-day on English medieval architecture. C. H. Moore's *Medieval Church Architecture of England*, 1912, is an important book by the great Gothic scholar amplifying and modifying somewhat the author's views on English Gothic expressed in earlier publications. G. H. Polley & Co.'s *English Gothic Architecture and Ornament*, 1897, presents a valuable collection of plates for the study of the style. G. T. Clark's *Medieval Military Architecture in Great Britain*, 1884, though out of date, is a scholarly work in a special field. *Bell's Cathedral Series* will be found useful as presenting a long series of monographs on single buildings.

W. Lübke's *Geschichte der deutschen Kunst*, 1880, is a monumental work, out of date but authoritative in the treatment of German Gothic. H. Otte's *Handbuch der kirchlichen Kunst-Archäologie des deutschen Mittelalters*, 1883, though very general and old-fashioned, is still useful for the student. H. Bergner's *Kirchliche Kunstaltertümer in Deutschland*, 1905, is an encyclopedic and modern work covering the German field of ecclesiastical architecture. *Bürgerliche Kunstaltertümer in Deutschland*, 1906, by the same author, discusses the secular art. C. Schaefer and O. Stiehl's *Die mustergiltigen Kirchbauten des Mittelalters in Deutschland*, 1901, is a superbly illustrated folio. An equally valuable folio is H. Hartung's *Motive der mittelalterlichen Baukunst in Deutschland*, 1904. B. Ebhardt's *Deutsche Burgen*, 1901, already cited, is useful for the study of castellan architecture.

C. E. Street's *Gothic Architecture in Spain*, 1865, is one of the first great works of research in Spanish Gothic. V. Lamperez y Romea's *Arquitectura Cristiana en la Edad Media*, 1909, already cited as the most valuable work on Spanish medieval architecture, is as authoritative on Gothic as on the earlier styles.

C. E. Boito's *Archittetura del medio evo in Italia*, 1880, is an ancient and limited but still useful work on the Italian medieval field. C. C. Cumming's *A History of Architecture in Italy*, 1901, treats the Gothic architecture in as popular and able a way as the earlier styles. C. Enlart's *Origines françaises de l'architecture gothique en Italie*, 1894, is still the most important and illuminating book on the origins of Italian Gothic. G. E. Street's *Brick and Marble in the Middle Ages,* 1874, is an interesting volume on the medieval architecture of Italy, with some discussion of the northern styles. G. R. de Fleury's *La Toscane au moyen âge,* 1873, is a superbly illustrated folio work on medieval Tuscan architecture. C. E. Norton's *Church Building in the Middle Ages,* 1902, itself a work of art on account of the author's style, presents an interesting description of the building of the cathedrals of Venice, Siena, and Florence. E. Bertaux's *L'art dans l'Italie méridionale,* 1904, covers the monuments of southern Italy in an interesting and scholarly way.

A. G. B. Schayes's *Histoire de l'architecture en Belgique,* 1850–60, already quoted, is of great value for the study of Gothic architecture in Flanders. C. Enlart's *L'art gothique en Chypre,* 1899, is a scholarly work illuminating as a study of the Gothic architecture built in the East by the crusaders.

CHAPTER X

RENAISSANCE ARCHITECTURE

The architecture of the period of the Renaissance was, in a greater measure than any other art, veritably a rebirth of the forms of classical antiquity. This involved, however, neither a sharp interruption of the developments of the Middle Ages nor a negation of originality and modernity. Most of the forces which tended to bring about the new era in Europe were already at work in the later Middle Ages and were thus not primarily results of the revival of classical learning. The decay of the medieval church and empire, the decline of the feudal system and the rise of nationalities and languages, were movements which appeared everywhere in the fourteenth and fifteenth centuries, along with a more human and a more naturalistic view of life. The growing tendency nowadays to regard Dante, Giotto, and the sculptors Pisani as true men of the Middle Ages—essentially at one with the poets of Provence, the painters of Burgundy, and the carvers of the portals at Reims—emphasizes the continuity of the Renaissance with medievalism. In many of these men there mingled with the Christian and northern tendencies other tendencies which were pagan and classical, forming a steady undercurrent throughout the Middle Ages. It needed merely a change in the relative strength of these tendencies to bring the classical current to the surface. By the early years of the fifteenth century this change was accomplished in Italy, and art and literature alike were profoundly influenced. The humanists, who tried to reconstitute a free and natural life by the aid of Greek and Roman literature, had their counterparts in Brunelleschi, Donatello, and Masaccio, who enriched the arts not only by observation of nature but by study of the works of ancient Rome.

Retrospective, traditional, and original elements.   In architecture there resulted an imitation of the Roman vocabulary of architectural forms, employed in part for the translation of ideas fundamentally medieval, in part for the expression of ideas essentially novel.   Medieval dispositions clothed in details of the classic orders, medieval craftsmanship exercised in the application and variation of classical motives of ornament, are characteristic of much Renaissance work, especially work that is early or removed from the center of origin.   Even more characteristic, however, are the new conceptions in the composition of space and in the modeling of surface, which are embodied both in some of the earliest productions and in many mature ones.   These conceptions, although likewise realized in forms inspired by antiquity, were themselves quite modern.   Even the forms of detail, supposedly classical, differed inevitably in a hundred respects from those which furnished their ideals.   The uses to which buildings and forms necessarily correspond were likewise different in many respects from those of preceding periods.   The relative importance of the various types of buildings was radically changed, the church, though still of great importance, being rivaled by the luxurious private dwellings of merchant princes, churchmen, and nobles.   Thus, in spite of retrospective and traditional elements, it was the novel elements which predominated in the new architectural synthesis.

Contrasts with medieval architecture.   Compared with the medieval architecture which preceded it, Renaissance architecture was less concerned with problems of structure and more with those of pure form.   As in the case of Roman architecture, the forms of detail were sometimes used as trophies of classical culture, with relative indifference to their original structural functions.   The forms were not merely ends in themselves, however, but means for a rhythmical subdivision of space, more complex and more varied than either ancient or medieval times had known.   A further contrast between the Middle Ages and the Renaissance, though one which has often been exaggerated, lay in the relation of the designer to his work. ˙ The architect, in the ancient and in the modern sense, reappeared.   We now realize that in both the Middle Ages and the Renaissance the general design was controlled by a single mind, and that in both periods there were sculptured details of which the design was left to the initiative of individual sculptors. Unlike the medieval master-builder, however, the Renaissance architect did not himself work on the scaffold, whereas he did dictate, in a greater measure than his predecessors, the form of many uniform details.

Centers and diffusion. The center of the new movement was Italy, where the forces everywhere at work had their effect earlier than in countries less richly endowed with the heritage of antiquity. During the fourteenth and fifteenth centuries Florence was the intellectual capital of the peninsula, as well as one of the greatest commercial powers in Europe. It was in Florence that the Renaissance in architecture had its birth, and it was the Florentine school which dominated the style down to the year 1450. Before the beginning of the sixteenth century papal Rome, now fully recovered from the exile of the popes and the schism of the church, assumed the leadership which it retained to the end of the Renaissance period. By the same time the new architectural forms had been adopted, with characteristic local modifications, throughout Italy, and had begun to penetrate France, Germany, and Spain. In these countries and in England, where the introduction came still later, it was many years before the transition from medieval forms was effected. Thus the phases of Renaissance architecture in different lands do not coincide in time, and, outside of Italy, forms of later origin sometimes mingle with those of truly Renaissance character. Both for these reasons, and because of strongly marked national differences, the several countries may best be considered successively.

Italy. The soil in Italy was particularly favorable for a revival of the forms of classic architecture. The remains of ancient buildings existed on every hand, in far greater completeness than they do to-day. They still served, as they had in the time of Constantine, as sources from which not only stone and lime but also columns, entablatures, and archivolts could be obtained ready made. Partly for these reasons, partly because of racial inheritance, the feeling for classical architecture had never wholly died out in Italy, and Gothic forms had been employed only with radical modifications which brought them nearer to the classic spirit. All this was especially true in Florence, which prided itself on direct descent from Etruria and Rome. The buildings of the eleventh and twelfth centuries—the Baptistry, San Miniato—are so classical in their details as to have been described as "proto-Renaissance." Even during the Gothic period—in the cathedral and the Loggia dei Lanzi—there was a largeness of scale and of interior space which is more classic than medieval. The round arch and other classical details and forms of ornament still persisted.

The early Renaissance. Brunelleschi's dome. It involved no break with

FIG. 189—FLORENCE. CATHEDRAL FROM THE SOUTHEAST

Florentine medieval traditions when Filippo Brunelleschi (1379–1446) made his proposal, in 1406, to vault the central octagon of the cathedral of Florence, which the builders had long feared to attempt. He followed the general form laid down from the beginning by Arnolfo in the thirteenth century, and there was little in his solution which was not medieval in inspiration, except the boldness of span. His direct prototype was the dome of the baptistry of Florence, also octagonal, with intermediate ribs on each face and arches spanning between them. He proposed a dome in two shells with segmental arches in each of the eight faces, and ribs with iron anchors supporting the inner shell. By giving a steep curve to the dome he was enabled to construct it, as Byzantine vaults had been constructed, without centering. The whole was raised on a high drum with circular windows, and surmounted by a lantern—features in themselves not new, but carried out on a larger scale and with somewhat more classical details (Fig. 189).

Brunelleschi's other works. The first true monuments of the Renaissance were the other works which Brunelleschi undertook while the dome was progressing. In these from the beginning, with no period of transition or hesitancy, appeared the classical forms of columns, pilasters, entablatures, all very clearly understood, though used with a freedom like that of late Roman architecture. In front of the Spedale degli Innocenti, the foundling hospital, he constructed in 1421 a portico with circular archivolts descending on the heads of Corinthian columns. The end bays are enframed by pilasters in the

FIG. 190—FLORENCE. INTERIOR OF SAN LORENZO

manner of the Roman arch order, and the windows of the upper
story, in the axis of each bay, have architraves and pediments
of classical form. In the church of San Lorenzo (begun about

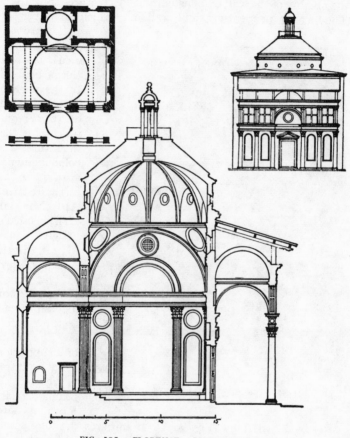

FIG. 191.—FLORENCE. PAZZI CHAPEL

1420) Brunelleschi reverted to the type of the early Christian
basilica, using a wealth of classical detail (Fig. 190). The aisle
walls and chapel openings are treated with an arch order; the
nave arches descend on fragments of entablature which respond to the entablature in the aisle. The aisles are covered

with domical vaults and the crossing with a dome on pendentives. The Pazzi chapel at the church of Santa Croce, like
the sacristy of San Lorenzo (from 1429 and 1419), has a
membering of the wall by pilasters and entablatures (Fig. 191).
They carry pendentives and a dome, which, however, is

FIG. 192—FLORENCE.   PALAZZO MEDICI-RICCARDI

constructed
like the apse
vaults of a
Gothic church.
In the portico
before the
chapel reap-
pears for the
first time the
colonnade with
a horizontal
entablature.
Another of
Brunelleschi's
designs, Santa
Maria degli
Angeli (1434),
is the first
building of
modern archi-
tecture to fol-
low the mode
of composition
about a central
vertical axis, so
common in late
Roman and

early medieval times (Fig. 207). It initiates the long series
of experiments in the combination of different forms of interior space, free from practical or liturgical restrictions.

Palace designs. The models of domestic design were given,
not by Brunelleschi, but by Michelozzo, the favorite architect of the Medici rulers of Florence. The typical palace of
the time is the Palazzo Medici (now Palazzo Riccardi) by
Michelozzo, begun in 1444 (Fig. 192). Its unbroken rusticated

wall with windows of paired arches resting on colonnettes are features of medieval derivation, whereas the emphasis laid on the horizontal divisions and the details of the colonnettes and the cornice are inspired by antiquity.

The later Florentine School. The followers of Brunelleschi in Florence—Simone del Pollaiuolo, called Cronaca, Giuliano da San Gallo and his brother Antonio, with many others—employed the new classical forms expertly, but without contributing many elements which were new. They were occupied rather with making new combinations with the elements already created. Thus in the

FIG. 193—FLORENCE. PALAZZO RUCELLAI

octagonal sacristy of Santo Spirito in Florence, by Giuliano da San Gallo and Cronaca 1488–96), a rhythmical grouping is introduced in a building of the centrally balanced type, by an alternation of niches and shallow recesses. Giuliano designed the first of the monumental country villas, the Villa Poggio a Cajano (1485). On the exterior this came to expression through a pedimented portico imitating the classic temple front, though not projecting before the plane of the wall.

Rome. Rome first experienced an artistic revival during the papacy of the humanist, Nicholas V. (1447–55). He began a rebuilding of the Vatican and proposed to replace the crumbling basilica of Saint Peter by a new edifice.

His architect was Leon Battista Alberti (1404–72), a gifted humanist, who introduced a more strictly classical tendency. In his paganization of the church of San Francesco at Rimini (1447) he adopted, for the flank, a massive range of classic piers and arches, for the facade, the triple motive of a Roman tri-

FIG. 194—ROME. LOGGIA OF THE CHURCH OF
SAN MARCO

umphal arch with engaged columns and a broken entablature. He also projected, as a termination for the building, a circular domed room of the proportions of the Pantheon, a form which he later emphasized in the church of the Annunziata in Florence (1470). For the façade of the Palazzo Rucellai in Florence (1451–55) he imitated for the first time the superposed engaged orders of the Tabularium and the Roman amphitheaters (Fig. 193). Pilasters and entablatures were applied to the typical rusticated wall with

grouped windows. His Palazzo Pitti has a range of vast
rusticated arches reminiscent of the Roman acqueducts.
Another time-honored scheme which Alberti revived was the
Greekcross plan, with four equal arms, in the church of San
Sebastiano at Mantua (1459). In Sant' Andrea at Mantua,
begun in 1470, he again made use of the triumphal arch motive,
not only in the porch, but also on the interior walls of the nave,

FIG. 195—MANTUA. SANT' ANDREA. INTERIOR

where a rhythmic alternation of broad arched chapels and
narrow bays bordered by pilasters was introduced (Fig. 195).
For the first time in a Renaissance church the nave itself was
vaulted in a classical manner, with an unbroken coffered
barrel vault. First in modern times also were Alberti's writings on architecture, which have fundamentally influenced both
theory and practice even to the present day. Other monuments under Alberti's influence, such as the Palazzo Venezia
and the vestibule of the church of San Marco in Rome (Fig. 194),
include also some of the most literal reproductions of the
antique yet attempted. Their great ranges of superposed

porticoes in the Roman arch order successfully imitate Roman examples in their proportions as well as in their breaking of the entablatures and pedestals at each engaged column.

Laurana. Alberti's ideas were further developed by Luciano Laurana, architect of the Ducal Palace at Urbino

FIG. 196—THE CERTOSA NEAR PAVIA.   FACADE

(1465–1482). In a series of imaginary compositions he suggested a circular temple and gave the models for most of the schemes later used in palace design by his two great followers from Urbino: Bramante and Raphael.

In the Palazzo Cancelleria in Rome (1486–95), where the system of the Palazzo Rucellai, with its slighter relief, was followed, one of Laurana's innovations was adopted. A continuous alternation of wide and narrow spaces between the pilasters—the "rhythmical bay" which Alberti had used in an interior—was employed. Terminal masses of slight projection, 'end pavilions," appear for the first time.

Other schools. Lombardy. Elsewhere, except for isolated works of the Florentine and Roman school, the new forms were only adopted gradually after the lapse of some time, and then often for their more superficial decorative qualities. In north Italy, smallness of scale, freedom in modifying the forms and proportions of the orders, and richness of sculptured orna-

FIG. 197—VENICE. PALAZZO VENDRAMINI

mentation are the outstanding features. In Lombardy, where the Florentine details first found a wide application, they remained for the most part, throughout the fifteenth century, a mere clothing for medieval dispositions. In the façade of the Certosa at Pavia, begun probably in 1491, the details are of a lavishness and multiplicity elsewhere unequaled, smothering the architectonic outlines (Fig. 196). About 1490 began a change, under the leadership of Donato Bramante (1444–1514). Inspired by the works of Alberti and Laurana, he took up the main thread of development. In the sacristy

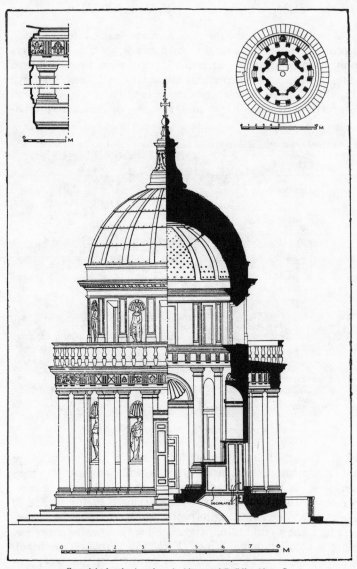

FIG. 198—ROME. "TEMPIETTO" AT SAN PIETRO IN MONTORIO

of Santa Maria in San Satiro in Milan and other churches he made important contributions to the problem of buildings composed about a central axis.   At Abbiate Grasso (1497) he prefixed to the church a great arched porch, recalling an ancient exedra.   It was supported on pilasters which here, almost first time, were coupled or grouped in pairs.

FIG. 199—ROME.   SAINT PETER'S.   INTERIOR

Venice.   Venice scarcely took up the new forms before 1470, when the family of architects called Lombardi began their work there.   In general their work is a translation of the local Byzantine and Gothic motives into pseudo-classic forms, carried out with rich marble incrustation.   The Palazzo Vendramin (1481) is perhaps its best representative (Fig. 197). As in the Palazzo Rucellai the façade is decorated with superposed orders; but here engaged columns, resting on pedestals in the lower stories, are elements of closer similarity to ancient examples. On the other hand the arches are subdivided by tracery, which is essentially medieval in spite of its classic details. As usual in Venice, the retention of a threefold subdivision of the width results in a complicated rhythmical grouping of the supports.

The Sixteenth Century. Bramante. The second, mature period of the Renaissance, the "High Renaissance" as it is

FIG. 200—ROME. PALACE OF RAPHAEL. (RESTORED BY HOFFMANN)

sometimes termed, began at Rome with the papacy of Julius II. (1503–13) and Leo X. (1513–21). Their lavish court and great undertakings attracted to the city the finest talent of all Italy, including Bramante, Raphael, Leonardo da Vinci, and Michelangelo. Bramante was the moving spirit in the new Roman school of architecture. In the shrine at the place of Saint Peter's martyrdom, Bramante outvied all his predecessors in classical ardor, by constructing a Roman circular temple with its peristyle (Fig. 198). This so-called "Tempietto" (1501–02), at the church of San Pietro in Montorio, is surmounted by a dome on a tall drum, and was intended to be surrounded by a circular colonnaded court.

Bramante's later works. Bramante was soon intrusted with the two most ambitious schemes of Julius, the extension of the

Vatican and the rebuilding of Saint Peter's, so long proposed. To unite the Vatican with the Belvedere he designed a court almost a thousand feet in length, surrounded by superposed galleries with the rhythmical triumphal-arch motive, and terminated by a vast semicircular exedra like those of the Roman thermæ (Fig. 222). The rise of the ground within the court was given a novel treatment by high terrace walls and balustraded flights of steps. In the new Saint Peter's Bramante thought less of meeting traditional liturgical requirements than of creating a monument to the glory of God, the founder, and the church. For this purpose he chose his favorite form of the

FIG. 201—ROME. LOGGIA OF THE VILLA MADAMA. INTERIOR

centrally composed building, magnified and elaborated. He proposed, in the words of his own metaphor, to raise the Pantheon above the vaults of the Basilica of Maxentius (Fig. 199). His studies for the building involved new solutions of a great number of current problems, and were a school for the whole younger generation of architects. Toward the end of his life he also gave new suggestions for palace design in the projected building for the papal courts of justice, with its gigantic rusticated blocks in the ground story.

Raphael and Peruzzi.   The principal followers of Bramante, although strongly influenced, likewise made new contributions to the general development.   Raphael (1483–1520), Bramante's nephew and protégé, embodied some of Bramante's

FIG. 202—ROME.   PALAZZO DELL' AQUILA.   (RESTORED BY GEYMULLER)

ideas for Saint Peter's in the little Chigi chapel at the church of Santa Maria del Popolo.   His own palace (Fig. 200), executed with Bramante's aid, had the ground story treated as a heavy rusticated basement, and the principal story—the *piano nobile* —emphasized by coupled engaged columns.   On Bramante's

death in 1514 Raphael succeeded to the architectural dictator-
ship. In executing the loggias of the Court of San Damaso at
the Vatican, he revived the stuccoed decorations of the Roman
interiors, then recently discovered. Thus arose the graceful
compositions of leafage, figures, and small medallions imitated
by his pupils at the Villa Madama (Fig. 201) and elsewhere.
In the Palazzo dell' Aquila similar decorations were applied to
a façade, in which there was also a rich alternation of niches
and pedimented tabernacles (Fig. 202). The large engaged
column, there restricted to the shop fronts of the basement
story, disappears entirely in Raphael's design for the Palazzo
Pandolfini in Florence. With its tabernacles relieved against
a stuccoed wall having angle quoins, this was the model for
many later Roman palaces. The Villa Madama, begun from
Raphael's designs and left unfinished, had like the Belvedere an
intimate architectural connection between house and gardens.
This was achieved not only by elaborate axial relationships,
but by terraces, stairs, and niches recalling the Villa of Hadrian
at Tivoli. Peruzzi, who outlived the youthful Raphael by
sixteen years, continued the development in the direction of
greater freedom in plan and in façade. The Villa Farnesina,
which may be either his or Raphael's, has end pavilions
suggested by those of the Cancelleria, but projecting two bays,
so as to inclose a U-shaped court. His plan for the two
palaces for the Massimi in Rome (1535), on an irregular site,
shows a remarkable facility in the adaptation of classical
elements (Fig. 203). In one the façade is curved to follow the
line of the street, and a multitude of consoles in the enframement of windows and doors begin to relieve the strictly geometrical lines of earlier architectural forms. All these
tendencies find their strongest expression in Michelangelo,
and doubtless depend, in large measure, on his earliest architectural designs, which had been for the façade of San Lorenzo
in Florence (1514) and for the Medici chapel there (1521–29,
Fig. 204). These, however, with his other buildings, form
the point of departure of the following phase of style, the
baroque, and thus must be discussed later.

Other schools. Venetia. The architects of the High Renaissance in the rest of Italy took their inspiration from Rome, as
those of the early Renaissance had from Florence. The

grammar of classical forms was now everywhere understood, and thus local differences are less marked, but characteristic schools nevertheless existed. Most notable of these was that of Venetia, headed by two other disciples of Bramante, Sanmicheli (1484–1559) and Sansovino (1486–1570). These men followed the more robust use of the orders in the work of

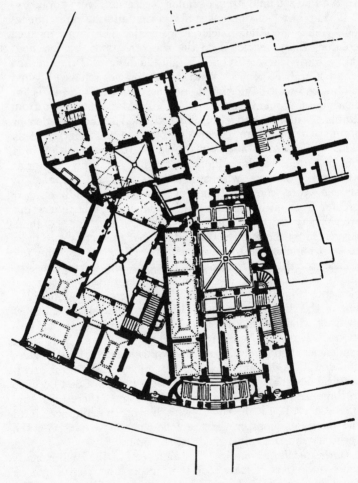

FIG. 203—ROME. MASSIMI PALACES. PLAN

Bramante and Raphael. Thus in Sanmicheli's Palazzo Pompeii in Verona (1530) and Sansovino's Palazzo Corner della
Ca' Grande in Venice (1530), we have a reminiscence of
Raphael's own palace. Sanmicheli initiated a long series of
designs of a still more rugged character by his notable city
gates for Verona (1533 *ff.*), with rusticated columns which

FIG. 204—FLORENCE.   MEDICI CHAPEL AT SAN LORENZO

are the embodiment of military strength.   In the Palazzo
Grimani at Venice (Fig. 205) he restudied the scheme of the
earlier Palazzo Vendramini, eliminating the medieval survivals and endowing all the forms with a truly classical spirit.
Sansovino took the Tabularium of the Capitol in Rome as
his model for the Library of Saint Mark (Fig. 206), which gives
the effect of an open arcade in two stories.   The employment
of subordinate engaged columns to support the imposts of the

upper story, and the wealth of ornamental sculpture, are features of this extreme yet characteristic product of the Renaissance.

Types of buildings. Churches. The longitudinal type. As strands in the general tendency in matters of style ran the individual developments of single types of buildings, which

FIG. 205—VENICE.   PALAZZO GRIMANI

offer some further points of importance. The churches here fall into two groups, those composed about a longitudinal axis and those composed about a central axis. It was the former of these groups which represented the continuance of medieval tradition and thus offered less of novelty. Brunelleschi contributed to it by reviving the basilican scheme of Constantine's day, with a flat ceiling in the nave and the addition of domical vaults over the aisle bays. Although in

San Lorenzo (1425) the T-shaped plan of the first basilicas was adhered to, in Santo Spirito (1435) the full Latin cross of the Middle Ages was adopted, with square ends to the arms and the aisles carried completely around them.   A vaulting of the nave with a barrel vault, then considered the most

FIG. 206—VENICE.   LIBRARY OF SAINT MARK

classical, was possible only with suppression of the aisles.   A membering of the nave walls and a richer spatial effect was furnished in such cases by lateral chapels.   This was the case in the little church of the Badia at Fiesole, completed in 1463, where the chapels were all alike, and in Alberti's Sant' Andrea at Mantua, which initiated the rhythmical system of piers.   In San Salvatore in Venice (1506) this rhythmical scheme was applied to a three-aisled church by the employment of the vaulting scheme of Saint Mark's.   Already in these churches appeared the characteristic tendency of the later long-naved churches. This was toward a development of the crossing, choir, and transepts on the lines of a building of central type with equal arms.

Basilican façades. The façades of the basilican churches also presented a problem. Those of the earliest architects remained in crude brickwork awaiting some ambitious completion. Alberti was the one who established the general type: an order or superposed orders, with the doors and windows in the intervals. Usually there was a pediment and often there were great volutes opposite the aisle roofs, uniting the aisles with the clerestory. In some cases an arcaded portico was prefixed.

Churches of the central type. The church composed on a central axis was perhaps the most characteristic problem of the Italian Renaissance (Fig. 207). The solutions were based either on a central octagon with an octagonal dome or cloister vault, or on a square central space with a dome on pendentives. In the first example—Brunelleschi's Santa Maria degli Angeli (1434)—the eight subordinate spaces are of equal importance. They themselves have minor elements in the form of niches, which are connected by unimportant doors. Similar in their co-ordination of the subordinate spaces are the churches of Greek cross type, beginning with Alberti's San Sebastiano (1459) and finding their ultimate expression in churches by the elder San Gallo. Beginning with the sacristies by San Gallo and by Bramante, however, there is usually an alternation in the subordinate spaces, which tend to become more elaborate, but in general have no connection with one another except through the central space. An intermediate between the square and octagonal schemes was created by Bramante's cutting off the corners below the pendentives in the crossing of Saint Peter's. His further innovations were anticipated somewhat in manuscript studies of Leonardo da Vinci, where he attempted to canvass systematically all possible combinations of domes and subordinate spaces. Here Leonardo progressed to centrally composed buildings of the second degree, that is, to groups in which the subordinate spaces are themselves composed of minor features about a central axis. It was a still more elaborate composition of this sort which

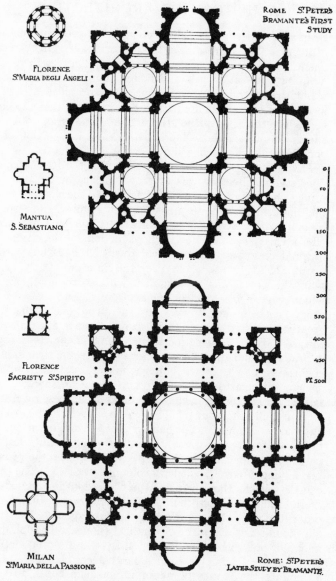

ROME St PETER'S
BRAMANTE'S FIRST
STUDY

FLORENCE
St MARIA DEGLI ANGELI

MANTUA
S. SEBASTIANO

0
50
100
150
200
250
300
350
400
450
FT 500

FLORENCE
SACRISTY St SPIRITO

MILAN
St MARIA DELLA PASSIONE

ROME: St PETER'S
LATER STUDY BY BRAMANTE

FIG. 207—THE DEVELOPMENT OF RENAISSANCE CHURCHES OF
CENTRAL TYPE

Bramante undertook in Saint Peter's.   Between the four arms of a great Greek cross he placed four smaller Greek crosses opening into the arms of the larger one, and having themselves a minor zone of niches.   Although a means of circulation about the central space was incidentally provided, it was not in an aisle of co-ordinated bays, but involved periodic emergence into the arms of the great cross.   The variety of spatial effects was thus greatly increased, while each portion of the church retained a strong individual unity.

Palaces.   The characteristic problem of the Renaissance in domestic architecture was the town palace of the merchant prince, the petty tyrant, or the dignitary of the church.   Such a building had to rise in several stories on a limited site, bounded by one or more streets and usually by party walls, and had to offer security against the turbulent factions of the city.   Like its predecessors of the medieval towns, it had thus to open about a court, and to be closed on the exterior.   In the typical plan the court was rectangular, with surrounding arcades which gave a covered communication at least between the rooms of the ground story.   In general, no one of the rooms greatly surpassed the others in size and importance, although toward the end of the period there was a tendency to introduce a principal hall or gallery.   The façade even then took no cognizance of the internal divisions but retained a uniform spacing of the axes.   All these qualities are summarized in the largest of the Roman palaces, the Palazzo Farnese by Antonio da San Gallo the younger (c. 1520–80).   Without embodying any radical innovations, it had a wide influence in the diffusion of the type (Figs. 208, 209).   It stands free on all sides, with passages to the court at the center of each face, the principal one having a barrel vault with colonnaded aisles.   The square court itself has the scheme of the Colosseum in three stories, Doric, Ionic, and Corinthian, the two lower ones with the arch order, the upper one with pilasters and pedimented windows. On the façade the scheme of Raphael's Palazzo Pandolfini was adopted, but with an additional story and a strong emphasis on the central axis.   In the Roman palaces about the time of Bramante the stories of minor importance began to secure recognition in the façade.   A low uppermost story for the servants was given small windows beneath the entablature of the upper order, as in the Cancelleria, or in the frieze of the main cornice, as in the Farnesina. In stories of which the full height was needed only for certain larger rooms, it became customary to halve the height for the smaller rooms, securing over them a half story or mezzanine. The windows of such mezzanines, which first appear, much subordinated,

FIG. 208—ROME. PALAZZO FARNESE

in the palaces of Raphael, tended to attain increasing independence. In Venice, as we have seen, the inherited palace type was an exception to the rule which prevailed elsewhere. Instead of a monumental court there was a large principal room in the center of the front, extending deep into the building. At the sides were minor suites, and the threefold division was characteristically expressed on the façade.

Villas. The increasing security of the country permitted, even in the early days of the Renaissance, the erection of villas outside the city walls. The earliest of these, the Villa Medicea at Carregi by Michelozzo, is still somewhat irregular in plan, but has projecting loggias which are suggestive of later developments in the union of house and garden. Such projections, however, were relatively infrequent. The house tended to remain a unity by itself, as at Cajano, and the gardens were laid out without much reference to the axis of the building. Only at the end of the period, in the Villa Madama, does the architectural scheme tend to assert itself also in the garden, in the manner so characteristic of the later, baroque villas.

Public buildings. Some further important types were the municipal palaces and the public hospitals. An open loggia on the exterior, as in Brunelleschi's Spedale degli Innocenti, was the symbol that such buildings belonged to the public. An early Renaissance example outside of Florence is the Loggia del Consiglio at Verona, attributed to Fra Giocondo (1476). It has arches descending on small columns, and an upper story of typical north Italian richness of detail. In the Palazzo Comunale at Brescia a similar scheme is realized with more classical forms, the arch order with projecting half-columns below, a second story with pilasters and tabernacle-like window enframements. The series really includes the library in Venice (Fig. 206), where the upper story is also arcaded. A final solution, in which open loggias in two stories completely surround the building—Palladio's "Basilica" at Vicenza (Fig. 225)—stands at the threshold of the following period (1549).

Town planning. The town planning of the Renaissance was limited for the most part to the leveling and straightening of streets in existing towns, with the sweeping away of booths and minor constructions which encumbered the surroundings of churches and public buildings. Open squares before important new buildings, which would permit an appreciation of their symmetry, were early desired, but were obtained in few instances. Where a square was bordered by porticoes these were kept distinct, and were not continuous as they had been in Hellenistic and late Roman times. The buildings themselves formed the unities, and not the square. In the rare cases where new towns or quarters were to be laid out, regularity and symmetry were preferred. The civic group at Pienza (1460–63) is the most notable of the schemes which came to execution. Here the episcopal palace and the palace of the Piccolomini balance on either side of the cathedral piazza, which has its sides converging toward the spectator, as in some of the most famous of the baroque squares.

Individual forms. The forms of Renaissance architecture (Figs. 210, 211), although inspired by those of Rome, were no more literal imitations of them than the Roman forms themselves had been imitations of Greek forms. Partly because of medieval survivals, partly because of inadequate knowledge of antiquity, partly even in criticism of the antique, the architects of the Renaissance modified the classical forms so that they are unmistakably theirs. In simpler buildings, to be sure, there was sometimes scarcely a detail which would betray the dependence of the period on Rome. The façade of the

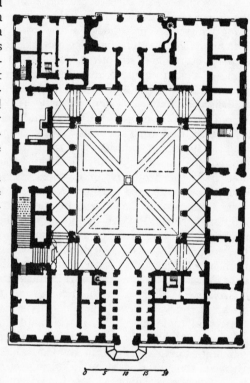

FIG. 209—ROME. PALAZZO FARNESE. PLAN

Palazzo Pitti might seem suggested merely by material and function. In later and richer buildings there is still always some nuance, even aside from the fresh combinations, in which is visible the originality of the Renaissance.

Walls. The continuous wall received much characteristic

treatment both in the early and in the High Renaissance. During the early phase the usual method was that or rustication—an artistic modification of the medieval practice of leaving the stones quarry-faced, with merely the joints dressed. In the Palazzo Pitti there is a gradation in the projection of the stones in successive stories, the lower ones reaching in extreme cases a projection of over two feet. In the Palazzo Medici (Riccardi) there is a more pronounced gradation, with rough blocks in the lower story, rectangular grooving, like that of some Roman examples, in the intermediate story, and smooth ashlar in the upper story (Fig. 192)—a system considerably imitated in later Florentine structures. The buildings mentioned have courses of irregular height and stones of differing lengths. Not until toward 1500, in the Cancelleria and other buildings of the time, was a perfectly uniform system of jointing adopted. Meanwhile another system of exterior wall treatment had been gaining ground, the use of stucco for the main surface, as it had been used from the beginning in interiors. Against this stuccoed surface was contrasted the stonework about the openings, and, later, tiers of rusticated blocks or quoins at the angles of the building. In the Palazzo Pandolfini and the Palazzo Farnese angle quoins were made of alternating lengths, bonding into the wall. In late works of Raphael and his school the stucco itself was modeled into festoons and medallions, still subordinate, however, to the window enframements.

Moldings. As in Roman architecture, the foot and the crown of the wall, as well as minor divisions, were marked by horizontal moldings. The machicolated and battlemented cornices of the Middle Ages gave place to cornices with a bed molding, corona, and cyma on Corinthian lines (Fig. 211). Between the stories were carried string-courses, likewise made up of classical elements. As time went on there was an increasing approximation to the full membering of the orders. Thus, whereas the Palazzo Medici has a cornice only, the Palazzo Strozzi (1489–1507) has also a frieze, and many later buildings, even without columns or pilasters, have a full entablature of classic type. In the same way it became customary to employ in the arch order, in tabernacle windows, and elsewhere. a pedestal with its own cap and base moldings.

FIG. 210—EARLY RENAISSANCE DETAILS. (AFTER GROMORT)

1. Cornice of the Palazzo Medici (Riccardi), Florence. 2. Cornice of the Palazzo Strozzi, Florence. 3. Faience medallion by Della Robbia. 4. Flagstaff bracket from Palazzo del Magnifico, Siena. 5, 6. Capitals from the porch of the Cathedral at Spoleto. 7. Lantern from the Palazzo Strozzi, Florence. 8. Capital and entablature from a tomb in the Badia, Florence. 9. Window from the Palazzo Strozzi, Florence. 10. Cornice of the Palazzo Pitti, Florence.

like those in the upper stories of the Colosseum. The profiles of individual moldings increase in delicacy of line and truth to antique principles until in the works of Raphael and Peruzzi there is a refinement suggestive of Greek models.

Openings. The openings at first were predominantly arched. Medieval traditions preserved a strong influence in the retention of a ring of deep voussoirs, the sinking of the profile in the wall, and the persistence of a central colonnette with tracery-like arches (Fig. 210). In walls of stucco and in interiors, however, the projecting classical architrave early asserted itself, and rectangular and circular-headed windows without subdivisions made their appearance. A more elaborate treatment, which was destined to become normal, was the enframement of openings by an order, often with a pediment. This had been revived during the Middle Ages in the baptistry of Florence and was employed by Brunelleschi in the doors of the sacristy of San Lorenzo. For its use about a window or niche, the tabernacles of the interior of the Pantheon, with their common pedestal, gave the model followed in the Palazzo Pandolfini and others of its type (Fig. 211). The use of ears on an architrave began with Raphael, and consoles to support the cornice in doors and windows came with Michelangelo and Peruzzi.

The orders. The men of the Renaissance distinguished five orders, elaborating the vague suggestions of Vitruvius regarding an Etruscan or "Tuscan" and a composite order. The favorite order of the early Renaissance was the Corinthian. The smaller capitals in this order, although more classical than those of the Middle Ages, were still greatly modified in comparison with ancient examples. Especially frequent was a capital with but a single row of leaves, often with dolphins or other fantastic substitutes for the volutes. In a series of such capitals each one was often individually designed, as in medieval composition (Fig. 210). With Alberti came a wider use of the other orders, due to their superposition as in the amphitheaters, although the strict sequence of Doric, Ionic, and Corinthian was not always followed. From the time of Bramante the Doric order obtained the preference, and the forms of all the orders became more strictly classical. There was also a tendency to increase the scale of the orders

and to subsume more than a single story in the height of one
order.   In the interior of churches the use of a single order
reaching to the spring of the vaults was a legacy from medieval
churches with their vaulting shafts.   It persisted when, in
Bramante's studies for Saint Peter's, he introduced subordi-

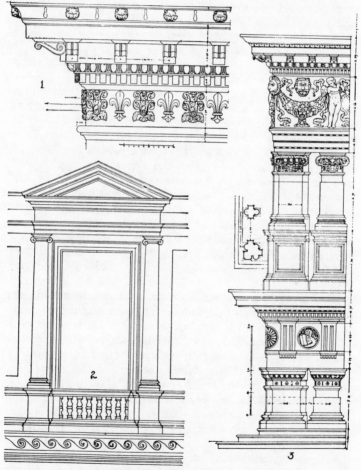

FIG. 211—"HIGH RENAISSANCE" DETAILS.   (AFTER GROMORT)

   1. Cornice of the Palazzo Farnese, Rome.
   2. Window of the Palazzo Pandolfini, Florence.
   3. Corner of the Library of Saint Mark, Venice.

nate superposed orders, and it appeared on the exterior as well. In civil architecture, also, the employment of a single inclusive order was approached, although during the Renaissance proper there was scarcely more than a mezzanine combined with the principal story. At the other extreme from the employment from these "colossal" orders was the use of miniature columns to carry the coping of a parapet (Fig. 210). In the villa a Cajano and later buildings, however, these colonnettes were replaced by the vase-like forms known as balusters (cf. Fig. 211), creations of the Renaissance, which have ever since retained their importance.

Arch, lintel, and column. The architects of the Renaissance rarely made use of the free horizontal lintel, except in loggias where there was no vaulting or superincumbent wall. They preferred at first to spring arches from column to column, later to enframe the arch by an order with pilasters or engaged columns. In this they reversed the sequence of development in Roman architecture. In the last years of the period, however, the desire for richness led them to substitute an entablature for the impost in the arch order and place a minor column below it. Thus was devised the so-called "Palladian motive" of a central arch resting on the entablatures of lateral square-headed bays, which first appeared in the Pazzi Chapel and found its definitive use in Palladio's Basilica at Vicenza (Fig. 225).

Wall membering. In the use of columnar forms for the membering of a wall, the tendency of development was in the same direction as in Roman architecture. Whereas, beginning with Alberti, a subdivision by pilasters and entablatures was usual, after 1500 there was a reversion to wall surfaces without other orders than those of the window enframements. In Bramante's palaces the order is omitted in the ground story, which once more has merely a frank rustication; and in the Pandolfini and many later palaces the effect is dependent entirely on tabernacle-work, as it had been in the late Roman stage backgrounds. In High Renaissance palaces, to be sure, the engaged column was often substituted for the pilaster, but this was followed by the use of columns standing quite free of the wall and thus clearly betraying their decorative character. The scheme of the arch of Domitian (Constantine) was thus repeated in a playful manner in Sansovino's Logetta in Venice (1540).

Proportions. With the revival of classical forms came a revival of classical proportions, and still more of the classical system of proportions. Alberti and others inculcated the use of integral ratios, and the modular system of Vitruvius for determining the members of the orders. However much the architects of the period felt free to depart from such mathematical proportions in actual practice, there can be no question that they gave great attention to geometrical similarity in the designing of masses and openings. There results in many works a musical harmony of forms like that of Periclean architecture.

Ornament. The love of ornament, both in sculpture and in color, which was characteristic of Italy throughout the Middle Ages, persisted in the Renaissance. Classical models were here taken up even more readily than for the larger forms of architecture. Garlands, rosettes, arabesques, candelabra, and acanthus foliage were carved with a knowledge and freedom which showed them to have become true possessions of the Renaissance artist (Fig. 210). Notwithstanding their own abilities as sculptors and ornamentalists, the early Florentine architects kept the carved detail strictly subordinate to the architectural forms. In Lombardy this was less often the case. There even the pilaster itself was paneled to receive an arabesque. In Rome under Bramante the abstract architectural forms tended to supersede floral ornament altogether. The Tempietto of Bramante shows not a leaf on the exterior. Under Raphael and Michelangelo, on the other hand, decorative features once more reasserted themselves in the façade (Fig. 202), and in the loggias of the Villa Madama and of the Vatican they reached perhaps their highest development (Fig. 201).

Spatial forms. The same preoccupation with proportions which appeared in the study of façades showed itself in the determination of the forms of interior space. Except in churches, rectangular shapes were almost the only ones employed. Simple integral ratios were recommended for the relations of the length and height of rooms to their width. In general each element formed a unit completely independent, without any spatial connection with others. The stairs, which might have furnished such a connection, were either based on the spiral stairs of the Middle Ages or were in narrow runs inclosed between walls.

Vaults. The technical difficulties of vaulting, after the vast experience of the Middle Ages, troubled the men of the Renaissance but little. They were free to choose those forms, whether classical or medieval, which comported best with their feeling for the composition of space. The one most preferred was the dome. Except in the attempts of Alberti to imitate Roman examples, this was usually employed over a square plan—either as one of a series of domical vaults supported on cross-arches or as a dome on pendentives at the central point of a plan. From the time of Bramante's studies for Saint Peter's his solution of the problem of a dome on pendentives— with an enlargement of the central space by short diagonal faces below the pendentives—was widely adopted. The barrel vault, which frequently appeared over the arms of cross-plans and elsewhere, was likewise seldom given its unbroken continuity but was banded with cross-arches at each bay after the medieval fashion. Penetrations of the vaulting surface, which might have given light directly in the vault, were as rare as in Roman architecture. The groined vault, too, was little favored, appearing almost solely in the interior arcades of courts, where it was necessary to have a concentrated thrust which might be met by iron rods at each bay. On the other hand the cloister vault, a square or octagonal dome, was widely used, as well as the apse, which might be either semicircular or semi-octagonal. A rich combination of vault forms with supporting members perfectly adapted to them occurs in the loggia of the Villa Madama (Fig. 201), in which appears also a characteristic decoration of arabesques in stucco.

External treatment of the dome. The only one of the vaults which rose above the roofs, and thus required an external expression, was the central dome, usually on pendentives. In the cathedral of Florence this already dominated the exterior in a way which set the model for all the great domes of the period. In minor buildings like the Pazzi chapel the dome might still spring directly from the pendentives and be inclosed in a conical roof, but in more important examples a drum was unfailingly introduced, lighting the space below and raising the dome into prominence. The curve of the dome was then shown on the exterior. Bramante, in his Tempietto, treated the drum with pilaster-like panels inclosing windows and niches alternately. For Saint Peter's he placed around the drum a full exterior peristyle. This rose above the center of the curve, and was surmounted by a pedestal and steps, so that the dome has the saucer-effect of the Pantheon and other Roman examples. This form, however, remained without imitators, for the tendency was rather to increase both the steepness of the curve and the height of the drum. Thus the model made by San Gallo for the dome of Saint Peter's had its base encircled by a Roman arch order in two receding stories, and was crowned with a vast lantern which gave the whole mass an almost conical aspect.

Roofs. The roofs in Italy had relatively little importance in the composition of individual buildings, being either low in pitch or else quite flat and bordered with balustrades. In the general effect of town and landscape, however, their red tiles made a striking contrast with the prevailing whiteness of the walls.

General character of Renaissance forms. Through the spatial forms of the Renaissance, the massing, the forms of detail, runs a consistent character, which might be expressed as the internal unity of each element and the unchangeableness of its impression on the observer. The isolation of each spatial element by bounding arches, the preference for self-centered domical forms and for centrally composed buildings, the self-sufficiency of each story and each bay, the unbroken enframement of openings and gables, the lack of projecting masses which might make transition between a building and its surroundings, and render its effect changeable with changing points of view—all these are manifestations of a definite feeling regarding form, which distinguishes the Italian Renaissance from both preceding and following periods.

France. The country outside of Italy which was earliest and most deeply affected by the Renaissance was France. The Latin element in the population was here predominant, and Latin culture was reassimilated with such readiness as to find a new home. The centralized power of the crown gave opportunity for undertakings on a scale unrivaled elsewhere outside of Rome, and for the calling from Italy of artists of the first class. At the same time it determined the character of the predominant architectural type, the château of the king or the court noble.

Development. Transitional period, 1495–1515. It was the claims of the French kings to Italian territory, leading to a series of invasions by Charles VIII., Louis XII., and Francis I., which revealed to them the splendor and luxury of Italian art, and led to the successful establishment of Renaissance forms in France. The process was a gradual one, occupying a period of twenty years from the return of Charles VIII. in 1495. During this time the predominant character of the buildings remained Gothic, but Renaissance details mingled with the Gothic forms in ever increasing proportions. An early instance of such a mixture is the wing built by Louis XII. in the château of Blois (1503, Fig. 212). Here the classical influence appears in little else but the elliptical form of the arches and the delicate arabesque panels which decorate the piers. At the château of Gaillon pilasters and entablatures imitate the arch order and other classical features.

Early Renaissance, 1515–45. Francis I. With the reign of Francis I. (1515–47) coincides the early Renaissance, in which, although the structure and disposition of buildings were still fundamentally Gothic, they were completely clothed in a garb of pseudo-classical forms. The irregular plans, round towers, and high, steep roofs with dormers persisted, but the stories were treated with superposed orders of delicate pilasters and entablatures, the main cornices were emphasized with an aggregation of Italian elements. The center of activity remained in the royal residences of the Loire valley. The earliest phase of the style is well illustrated in the wing of Francis I. at Blois (1515–19), with the magnificent spiral stairway in classical masquerade (Fig. 212). At the château of Chambord, constructed in 1526–44, the detail was similar, but the plan was for the first time rigidly symmetrical. In the château of Ecouen (1531–40), likewise symmetrical, square towers or angle pavilions took the place of round ones, and the Château Madrid near Paris was lent a truly Italian air by its graceful exterior arcades resting on columns like those of a

Florentine court.   Owing to the conquest of Milan by Francis and to his patronage of north Italian artists, it was the influence of Lombardy which predominated in the detail.   The paneled pilasters and florid ornament of the Loire châteaux are the descendants of those at San Satiro and the Certosa (Fig. 195).

The High Renaissance, 1545–70.   Henry II.   In the last years of Francis and the following reign of Henry II. came a

FIG. 212—BLOIS.   COURT OF THE CHATEAU, SHOWING WINGS OF LOUIS XII (AT BACK) AND FRANCIS I (AT LEFT)

change, due to the assimilation of the style and to the influence of the Roman school of Bramante.   The Italian masters now brought to France represented this tradition—Serlio the pupil of Peruzzi, Primaticcio the pupil of a disciple of Raphael. For the first time, also, Frenchmen assumed the rôle of architect in the modern sense.   Jean Goujon, Pierre Lescot, Philibert de l'Orme, Jacques Androuet du Cerceau, and Jean Bullant were not mere master builders.   Most, if not all, of them had been in Italy and had studied the designs of the Roman masters; some of them held high court appointments. Their buildings show a mastery of the grammar of classical forms and an ability to use them freely to secure new effects which were characteristically national. These depended partly on differing climatic conditions, which required lower rooms, larger windows, and tall chimney stacks, and partly on tradition, which still caused the retention of projecting pavilions with high individual roofs.

First designs. The earliest work to show the characteristics of the High Renaissance is the Hôtel de Ville in Paris, begun from a model by Domenico of Cortona (called Boccador) in 1531. The motive was suggested by Raphael's Palazzo dell' Aquila, with a Roman arch order below and niches between the windows of the main story. By 1535 a Frenchman himself had caught the spirit of classicism, as Goujon showed in his tomb for Louis de Brézé at Rouen. At Ancy-le-France (1538–46) Serlio regularized the scheme of the French château, not only in the strictly rectangular plan but in the uniform intercolumniations of the exterior and the rhythmical bay treatment of the court. At the same time De l'Orme, in Saint Maur-les-Fossés, introduced the rusticated orders of Sanmicheli. At Bournazel in the south, about 1545, the neighboring classical monuments stimulated a treatment of the triumphal arch motive with engaged columns, which was truly classical in its monumentality. The most characteristic design of all was that for the rebuilding of the Louvre in Paris, the work of Lescot and Goujon (Fig. 213). Here there was the subtlest mingling of French and Italian traditions. The lower stories—with their superposed orders, their pedestals and pedimented windows—recall Bramante and Raphael. The projecting motives which mark the end bays and the center suggest those of the Cancelleria, as well as the French tower-pavilions. The delicacy of profiling rivals that of Peruzzi. The great size of the windows, the pediments which terminate the attic, are of northern origin, while the emphasis which results from the use of both pilasters and engaged columns is a novel contribution by Lescot.

Later developments. Still more advanced developments, parallel with contemporary movements in Italy, were the later designs of Primaticcio, Bullant, De l'Orme, and Du Cerceau. In the château of Monceaux the Italian master employed for the first time in France—in the same year that Michelangelo

FIG. 213—PARIS. COURT OF THE LOUVRE. (ORIGINAL CONSTRUCTIONS OF LESCOT AND GOUJON)

designed his palaces on the Capitol (1546)—the "colossal order" rising through two stories to the main cornice. A similar use of free standing columns occurs in the monumental frontispiece erected by Bullant at Ecouen (about 1564) and elsewhere. Domed chapels were built by De l'Orme at Anet (1548) and by Primaticcio at Saint Denis (1559ff.). Finally came the vast symmetrical plans grouped about a multitude of courts, designed by de l'Orme for the Tuileries (1564, Fig. 214), and by Du Cerceau for Charleval (1572), which surpassed anything projected in Italy.

Types of buildings. Châteaux. The Renaissance château developed, as its name implies, from the fortified castle of the Middle Ages. Although no longer planned to withstand a siege, it was still made secure against marauders by a moat and gate-house, and preserved the arrangement about a court and at least a reminiscence of the earlier fortified towers at the angles. The staircases, at first spiral like those of the Middle Ages, were later arranged in straight flights. Access to individual rooms could usually be obtained only by passing through others, for even the open air circulation provided by the arcades of an Italian courtyard was usually absent. A principal hall or gallery for functions of state was provided, often monumental in its size and treatment, like the gallery of Henry II. at Fontainebleau. A forecourt outside the moat accommodated the service functions.

City hôtels. Although at this time the court still resided mostly in the country, town houses of some pretensions were built by officials and wealthy merchants. These, such as the Hôtel d'Assezat at Toulouse, were unlike the Italian town houses which faced directly on the street. They followed the larger medieval houses of France in facing on a court which was separated from the street by a screen wall with an arched carriage entrance.

Churches. During the early Renaissance church architecture remained fundamentally Gothic, with a mere substitution of classical details, poorly understood. Saint Eustache in Paris, a typical example, still has a plan like that of Notre Dame, with groined vaults and flying buttresses. Many of these buildings are not the less effective from their combination of supposedly incongruous elements. The same character

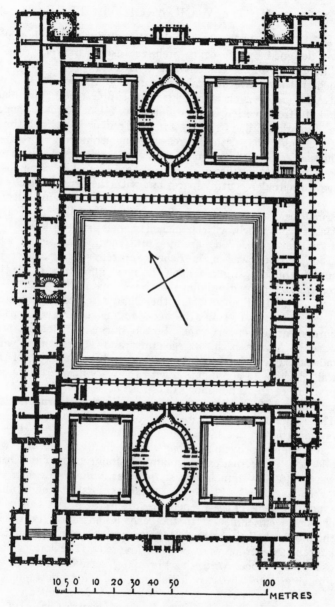

10 5 0   10 20 30 40 50   100
METRES

FIG. 214—PARIS. THE TUILERIES. (DE L'ORME'S PLAN)

persists in most churches of the High Renaissance, but the few designed by the court architects show the new spirit. Thus the façade of Saint Nizier at Lyons (1542) has a great niche with massive half-columns, and the Mausoleum Chapel at Anet (1566) is classical both in its simple rectangular plan and its front with pilasters and attic. De l'Orme's chapel in the park of Villers-Cotterêts had a circular dome with three semicircular chapels and a free-standing pedimented portico— the earliest in France, more advanced in classical character than most Italian designs. His Palace Chapel for Anet had again a circular central space, but with the arms of a Greek cross. For the Mausoleum of the Valois at Saint Denis, Primaticcio adopted a plan like that of Brunelleschi's Santa Maria degli Angeli, with six niched chapels and a gallery about a central dome. The architectural membering here, both inside and out, was of the richest and purest classical forms, and the building ranks among the most important of all the centrally composed buildings of the Renaissance.

Details. In France where the climate scarcely permitted the open loggias of Italy, the free-standing column with either lintel or arch was very rare. So too, during the Renaissance, was the simple wall, for columns and entablatures were indispensable elements of decoration. The membering of the wall, perhaps in combination with rustication, was the major problem of the time among questions of detail. In the solution of it, alternation in some form was the favorite device. The earlier châteaux, treated with pilasters, had windows over one another in one bay, then blank panels in the next bay. Later the true rhythmical bay scheme in all its variants was adopted. The rusticated column introduced by De l'Orme was exalted by him into a sixth order, which he called the "French order" (Fig. 215). Unlike most of the Italian examples, some of the French ones are of the greatest delicacy of carved enrichment. In the early Renaissance the Corinthian order had the same preference which it enjoyed in Italy; later no one order was specially favored. The low ceilings usual in France, with the prevailing secular character of French architecture, gave little opportunity for a development of vaulting. The flat ceilings were treated as in Italy with elaborate coffering. A striking feature of contrast with Italian architecture was the high roof with its dormers, gables, and chimneys. The dormer was treated first with pilasters bearing pinnacles, and with elaborate gables and finials; later it was given merely the form of a pedimented window. The balustrade above the cornice gave place to an ornamental cresting. A common feature making transition between the wall and the roof was a row of pediments which crowned repeating motives below, as in the Louvre. Such elements were sufficient by themselves to endow French buildings, no matter how strictly classical in their ordonnance, with a characteristically national aspect.

Spain. In Spain, as in France and other countries outside of Italy, there was a mingling of Italian forms with those already existing in the native medieval architecture. Here, however, the medieval style itself included a large admixture of Moorish forms. Moriscoes, until their expulsion in 1610, remained prominent among artificers, and thus had their influence on the Renaissance forms as well. Thus arose the Plateresque or silversmith's style, so called from the intricate and delicate ornament abounding in it. This, which corresponds with the early Renaissance, extended from about 1500 to 1560. A notable example is the Town Hall at Seville (Fig. 216), built in 1527–32. Here there is an application of engaged orders in two stories which in its main lines is

FIG. 215—PARIS. DETAIL FROM THE TUILERIES. (PLANAT)

thoroughly grammatical, but which has pilasters, columns, window enframements, and panels alike covered with the richest arabesques and candelabra-like forms. Even more characteristic in its mode of composition is the doorway of the University at Salamanca. Here the ornament is massed in a great panel above the opening, which contrasts with the broad neighboring surfaces of unbroken masonry. Other notable features of the style are open arcaded loggias which often terminate a façade, as in the Casa de Monterey at Salamanca (1530), and the courts or patios surrounded by galleries which are found in all important buildings.   Forms like those of the High Renaissance in Italy first appeared in the palace begun for Charles V. in the Alhambra (1527), by Pedro Machuca.   This building is square in plan with a circular

FIG. 216—SEVILLE.   TOWN HALL

colonnaded court having superposed orders, Doric and Ionic (Fig. 217).   In purity and classical quality the building holds its own with contemporary monuments of Italy.   From this time occasional buildings continued the stricter classical tendency, the most famous examples of which really belong to the succeeding period.

Germany and the Low Countries.   In Germany the multitude of small states resulted in great variety in the degree to which Renaissance principles were assimilated, and in the stage of advancement in different regions.   The Belvedere built at Prague about 1536 shows a full exterior peristyle with arches descending on columns, all of Florentine aspect.   Such designs

were but isolated exceptions, however. In most buildings
the Italian forms were strongly modified, and the medieval
element was much more persistent than in France. The
wing built by the Elector Otto Heinrich (1556–59) in the
castle at Heidelberg shows a combination of elements derived

FIG. 217—GRANADA. PALACE OF CHARLES V. COURT

from Bramante and his school with other elements from
Lombardy (Fig. 218). Three superposed orders, the two lower
ones with pilasters, recall the Cancelleria, but every second
support is replaced by a corbel and a statued niche like those
introduced by Raphael. In the lower story the pilasters are
rusticated, in the following story they have arabesque panels.
The window enframements with their candelabra mullions
recall the Certosa at Pavia. A similar character prevailed
in most buildings of the later sixteenth century, which began
to be influenced by the baroque movement in Italy. The

baroque spirit, as we shall see, was indeed akin to that of the German Renaissance craftsmen, as their ready assimilation of the forms of herms, "cartouches," and broken pediments reveals. The wing at Heidelberg built by Friedrich IV. (1601–07), where such features appear, shows at first glance

FIG. 218—HEIDELBERG.   WING OF OTTO HEINRICH IN THE
CASTLE

but little difference from its predecessor. The Peller house at Nürnberg (1625) shows the continued vitality of the Renaissance as applied to one of the most common problems in Germany, the dwelling of the wealthy town merchant (Fig. 219). Its superposed orders, enframing the windows, run up continuously into the great stepped and ornamented gable, which still proclaims a descent from the Middle Ages. In Flanders and Holland, except for the more frequent use of brick, the general character of the work is similar to that of Germany.

England. Development. The latest of the great Western nations to feel the effects of the Renaissance in architecture was England, isolated and always conservative. Italian sculptors were employed by Wolsey and Henry VIII., and their

FIG. 219—NURNBERG. PELLER HOUSE

influence made itself felt, as at Hampton Court (1515–40), in the carved details of many buildings which remained essentially Gothic. Meanwhile the spirit of classical symmetry was appearing in the plans, and shortly before the accession of Elizabeth in 1558 the forms of the orders began to be imitated and applied to the façades of buildings. The Italians had meanwhile gradually departed, but Flemings and Germans began to take their places, and at least one Englishman, John Shute, went to Italy to study architecture (1550). His *First and Chief Grounds of Architecture* (1563) was based on Vitruvius and gave diagrams of the orders. Sir Thomas Gresham secured from Flanders the design of the Royal Exchange (1567–70), which had a court of Florentine aspect, with arches resting on columns below, pilasters and statued niches above. In Longleat House (1567–80) the whole exterior, in three stories, was treated with superposed orders of grammatical form and proportions, and many porches and doorways from less elaborate houses of just this period show that the classical forms were well understood. It is this phase of style, lasting but a very few years, which really corresponds to the High Renaissance in Italy and France. The tide of baroque ornament which was already inundating the Continent swept over England also before either the medieval or the Renaissance currents had spent their force. The architectural books of De Vries (1559–77) and other Flemings and Germans—full of the new and bizarre combinations of classical elements, scrolls, cartouches, and "strapwork," imitating cut leather—were widely followed.

Types. While in its details the architecture of Elizabeth and James I. thus passed from medieval to post-Renaissance, in its practical problems and types it forms unmistakably a unit, governed by the life of the Renaissance itself—the period of Spenser, Shakespeare, and Raleigh. Although the monarchy was powerful enough to insure peace, the landed aristocracy remained of great wealth and importance. The country houses of nobles and gentlemen, often on a vast scale, were the principal creations of the period. These men were less interested in religious than in mundane things, so that new churches were few and they remained almost purely Gothic.

The house. The Elizabethan and Jacobean houses were developed from the medieval fortified manors by making them more symmetrical and more open, and by ornamenting or overlaying certain portions with classical details. The basic arrangement was a square court, on one side of which, opposite the gate-house, was the great hall, where master and servants ate and mingled. At one end of the hall was the entrance passage or "screens," at the other the dais for the high table, with its fireplace and bay window. Beyond, in either direction, were the kitchens and the private apartments, respectively, and along the sides of the court were lodgings reached only by passing through those intervening or through the open air. In the second story, approached by the principal staircase near the dais, was the long gallery, a luxurious feature first introduced at Hampton Court. This often attained a length of over two hundred feet, with a width of but sixteen to twenty-five. In the earlier examples there was no attempt to secure formal symmetry either in plan or in elevation. At Sutton Place (1523-25) the court was made for the first time rigidly symmetrical, and this later became the rule also for the external façades, so far as they could be appreciated in any single view. The gate-house and "screens"

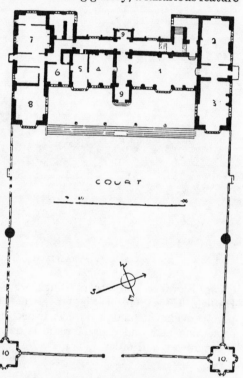

FIG. 220—MONTACUTE HOUSE. (GOTCH)

1. Hall. 2. Drawing-room. 3. Large dining-room. 4. Small dining-room. 5. Smoke-room. 6. Pantry. 7. Kitchen. 8. Servants' Hall. 9. Porch. 10. Garden house.

were centered on the main axis, the bay window of the dais was repeated on the other side of the court. At Montacute (1580) and many later houses, the lodgings inclosing the court were omitted and the house was opened freely in all directions. With the porch and with projections on the garden side the plan thus became E or H-shaped (Fig. 220). Medieval elements remained important in the aspect as well as in the plan, for a multitude of high roofs, gables, dormers, turrets, chimney stacks, and bay windows diversified the skylines and the wall surfaces. Even at Longleat, the most classical of all the houses, the mullioned bays still tell more powerfully than the

FIG. 221—HATFIELD HOUSE

engaged orders. In others which were more typical, like Hatfield House (1611, Fig. 221), the elements are almost purely medieval, and what has transformed the whole into something new and characteristic is only the classical spirit of symmetry and order.

PERIODS OF RENAISSANCE ARCHITECTURE

ITALY

I.   Fifteenth century.
    Florentine School.
        Filippo Brunelleschi, 1379–1446.
        Spedale degli Innocenti, begun 1419.
        San Lorenzo, begun 1419.
        Pazzi Chapel and Sacristy of San Lorenzo, begun 1429.

ITALY—(*Continued*)

Santa Maria degli Angeli, 1434.
Santo Spirito, begun 1435.
Michelozzo di Bartolommeo, 1396–1472.
Palazzo Medici (Riccardi), begun 1444.
Giuliano da San Gallo, 1445–1516.
  Villa Poggio a Cajano, 1480–85.
  Sacristy of Santo Spirito at Florence
    (with others), 1489–96.
  Palazzo Strozzi at Florence (with others),
    1489–1507.
Simone del Pollajuolo (called Il Cronaca),
    1457–1508.
  San Francesco al Monte at Florence, begun
    1475.
Roman School
  Leon Battista Alberti, 1404–72.
    San Francesco at Rimini, 1447.
    Palazzo Rucellai at Florence, 1451–55.
    Palazzo Pitti at Florence, begun 1458.
    Sant' Andrea at Mantua, begun 1470.
    SS. Annunziata at Florence, 1470–71.
  Luciano Laurana, d. 1479.
    Ducal palace at Urbino.
  Other monuments.
    Arcades of Palazzo Venezia and Church of
      San Marco at Rome, 1466–71.
    Palazzo Cancelleria at Rome, 1486–95.
Venetian school.
  Palazzo Vendramin, begun 1481.
  Santa Maria dei Miracoli, .481–87.
Lombard school.
  Fra Giocondo, c. 1433–1515.
    (?) Loggia del Consiglio at Verona, de-
      signed 1476.
  Giovanni Antonio Amadeo, 1447–1522.
    Façade of the Certosa at Pavia (with
      others), begun 1491.
  Donato Bramante, 1444–1514.
    San Satiro, Milan, 1488.
    Choir of Santan Maria delle Grazie, Milan,
      1492–99.
    Santa Maria at Abbiate Grasso, begun 1497.

ITALY—(*Continued*)

II. Sixteenth century.
    Roman school.
        Donato Bramante (1444–1514), from 1499.
          Cloister of Santa Maria della Pace, 1500.
          Tempietto at San Pietro in Montorio, 1501–02.
          Court of the Belvedere at the Vatican, begun 1503.
          Saint Peter's, begun 1506.
          Palazzo Caprini (Palace of Raphael)
        Raphael, 1483–1520.
          Saint Peter's, 1514–20.
          Loggias of the Court of San Damaso at the Vatican, 1514–20.
          Palazzo dell' Aquila, c. 1515.
          Villa Madama, begun, 1519.
          Palazzo Pandolfini in Florence, 1516–1520.
        Baldassare Peruzzi, 1481–1536.
          Villa Farnesina in Rome, 1509–11.
          Palazzo Albergati in Bologna, 1522.
          Palazzi Massimi at Rome, 1535.
        Antonio da San Gallo the elder, 1461 (?)–1534.
          San Biagio at Montepulciano, 1518–37.
        Antonio da San Gallo the younger, 1485–1546.
          Palazzo Farnese in Rome, c. 1520–80.
    Venetian school.
        Michele Sanmicheli, 1484–1559.
          Gates of Verona, 1533 *ff.*
          Palazzo Pompei at Verona, 1530.
          Palazzo Grimani at Venice, completed 1539.
        Jacobo Sansovino, 1486–1507.
          Palazzo Corner della Ca' Grande at Venice, 1530.
          Library of Saint Mark's at Venice, 1536.
          Logetta of the Campanile at Venice, 1540.
        Jacopo Sansovino, 1486–1570.
          Palazzo Cornaro della Ca' Grande at Venice, 1530.
          Library of Saint Mark's at Venice, 1536.
          Logetta of the Campanile at Venice, 1540.

FRANCE

I. Transitional period, c. 1495–1515.
    Invasions of Italy by Charles VIII., 1494–
        95, and by Louis XII., 1499–1504.
    Wing of Louis XII. at Blois, 1503.
    Château of Gaillon, 1497–1510.

II. Early Renaissance, c. 1515–45 (Francis I., 1515–
    47).
    Wing of Francis I. at Blois, 1515–19.
    Château of Chambord, 1526–44.
    Château of Ecouen, 1531–40.
    Château Madrid near Paris, 1528–c. 1565.
    Saint Pierre at Caen, 1518–45.
    Saint Eustache at Paris, begun 1532.

III. "High Renaissance," c. 1545–70.
    Domenico of Cortona (Boccador), d. 1549.
        Hôtel de Ville at Paris, begun 1531.
    Jean Goujon, d. between 1564 and 1568.
        Tomb of Louis de Brézé at Rouen, 1535.
    Pierre Lescot, 1510 (?)–78.
        Court of the Louvre (with Goujon),
          1546–76.
    Sebastiano Serlio, 1475–1554.
        Château of Ancy-le-France, 1538–46.
    Francesco Primaticcio, 1490–1570.
        Château of Monceaux-en-Brie, 1547–55.
        Tomb of the Valois at Saint Denis, 1559 ff.
    Philibert de l'Orme, b. between 1510 and
        1515; d. 1570.
        Château of Saint Maur-les-Fossés, c. 1545.
        Château d'Anet, 1548–54.
        Tuileries at Paris, begun 1564.
    Jean Bullant, c. 1525 (?)–78.
        Château d'Ecouen, porticoes, c. 1564.
    Jacques Androuet du Cerceau, b. c. 1510;
        d. after 1584.
        Château of Verneuil, 1565 ff.
        Château of Charleval, 1572–74.

SPAIN

I. Early Renaissance, "Plateresque," c. 1480–1530.
    Enrique de Egas, c. 1455–1534.
        Portal of the Hospital of Santa Cruz, before 1514.
        Portal of the University in Salamanca, 1515–30.

BIBLIOGRAPHICAL NOTE

Renaissance architecture in general. Aside from series of which the individual volumes are listed below there may be mentioned especially P. Frankl's *Die Entwicklungsphasen der neuren Baukunst,* 1914 (a study of development).

Italy. The most recent and authoritative works are almost exclusively in foreign languages. Scholarly general works are H. Willich's *Baukunst der Renaissance in Italien,* 1914 *(Handbuch der Kunstwissenschaft),* J. Burckhardt's *Geschichte der Renaissance in Italien (Geschichte der neuren Baukunst),* 5th ed., 1912 (both with emphasis on development), and J. Durm's *Baukunst der Renaissance in Italien (Handbuch der Architektur),* 2d ed., 1914 (with emphasis on technical analysis). A. Venturi's *Architettura del Quattrocento,* 2 vols., 1923–24, is specially full on the provincial work. Convenient collections of illustrations are J. Baum's *Frührenaissance,* 1920, and C. Ricci's *High and Late Renaissance Architecture,* 1923. W. J. Anderson's *The Architecture of the Renaissance in Italy,* 4th ed., 1909, and T. G. Jackson's *The Renaissance of Roman Architecture,* are richly illustrated works, which, however, repeat many statements now generally considered erroneous. Among numerous monumental illustrated folios may be mentioned: P. Letarouilly's *Edifices de Rome moderne,* 3 vols., 1868–74, the engravings of which are supplemented by photographs in H. Strack's *Baudenkmäler Roms des XV.–XIX. Jahrhunderts,* 1891; C. Stegmann and H. von Geymüller's *Architektur der Renaissance in Toscana,* 11 vols., 1885–1908; Biagi's *La Renaissance en Italie,* and R. Reinhardt, Raschdorff, and others' *Palast-Architektur von Ober-Italien und Toscana vom XV. bis XVII. Jahrhundert,* 6 vols., 1886–1923. H. Strack's *Central-und Kuppelkirchen der Renaissance in Italien,* 2 vols., 1882; W. Limburger's *Die Gebäude von Florenz,* 1910, and B. Patzak's *Die Renaissance-und Barock-Villa in Italien,* vols. 2 and 3, 1908–12, are careful monographs.

France. The fundamental works are W. Lübke's *Geschichte der Renaissance in Frankreich,* 2d ed., 1885 *(Geschichte der neueren Baukunst),* and H. von Geymüller's *Die Baukunst der Renaissance in Frankreich (Handbuch der Architektur),* 2 vols., 1898–1901. W. H. Ward's *The Architecture of the Renaissance in France,* 2 vols., 1911, embodies Geymüller's researches in English, with numerous illustrations. R. Blomfield's *History of French Architecture, 1498–1661,* 2 vols., 1911, suffers from failure to employ the discussions in German. C. T. Mathew's *The Renaissance under the Valois,* 1893, is still valuable for its fine illustrations. Among the many collections of measured drawings may be mentioned those of Berty, Rouyer and Darcel, Daly, and Sauvageot. Large photographs are provided by C. Martin's *La Renaissance en France,* 2 vols., 1910–12, and the relevant section of C. Gurlitt's *Die Baukunst Frankreichs,* 4 vols.,

1896–1900. The châteaux are treated specifically in two works by Victor Petit (lithographs), in H. Saint Saveur's *Châteaux de France* and in J. Vacquier's *Anciens Châteaux de France*, 1922 *ff.* (photographs). and, for the smaller buildings, in L. C. Newhall's *Minor Châteaux of the XV. and XVI. Century*, 1914. Urban dwellings are covered by P. Vitry's *Hôtels et maisons de la renaissance française*, 2 vols., 1911–12. The field of biography is particularly rich, in the works of Berty (1860), Destailleur (1863), Lance (1872), Bauchal (1887), and Vachon (1910).

Spain and Portugal. A. Byne and M. Stapley's *Spanish Architecture of the Sixteenth Century*, 1917, chiefly devoted to the Plateresque, may be supplemented by the sketch prefixed to O. Schubert's *Geschichte der Barock in Spanien*, 1908. Further illustration is furnished by M. Junghändel's *Die Baukunst Spaniens*, 3 vols., 1889–98; C. Uhde's *Baudenkmäler in Spanien und Portugal*, 2 vols., 1892; and A. Haupt's *Die Baukunst der Renaissance in Portugal*, 2 vols., 1890–95. The *Monumentos arquitectónicos de España*, 1859–81, is a vast series published at the expense of the state.

Germany. The two fundamental accounts are W. Lübke's *Geschichte der Renaissance in Deutschland* (*Geschichte der neueren Baukunst*), 2d ed., 2 vols., 1882, and G. von Bezold's *Die Baukunst der Renaissance in Deutschland, Holland, Belgien und Dänemark* (*Handbuch der Architektur*), 2d ed., 1908. Monumental folios of illustrations are A. Ortwein and A. Scheffer's *Deutsche Renaissance*, 9 vols., 1871–88; K. E. O. Fritsch's *Denkmäler deutscher Renaissance*, 4 vols., 1891; and A. Lambert and E. Stahl's *Motive der deutschen Architektur des XVI., XVII., und XVIII. Jahrhunderts*, vol. 1, 1890. A work in briefer compass is J. Hoffman's *Baukunst und dekorative Skulptur der Renaissance in Deutschland*, 1909.

England. For the Renaissance proper the principal account is J. A. Gotch's *Early Renaissance Architecture in England*, 2d ed., 1914. R. Blomfield's *History of Renaissance Architecture in England, 1500–1800*, 2 vols., 1897, includes a briefer discussion of the period in question. An abridged edition in one volume was issued in 1904. Large photographs are furnished by Gotch's *Architecture of the Renaissance in England*, 2 vols., 1894; C. Uhde's *Baudenmäler in Gross Britanien*, 2 vols., 1894; H. A. Tipping's *English Homes*, vol. 4, and T. Garner and A. Stratton's *The Domestic Architecture of England During the Tudor Period*, 3 vols., 1908–11. Other discussions of the domestic architecture of the Renaissance in England occur in C. F. Innocent: *The Development of English Building Construction*, 1916, Gotch's *The Growth of the English House*, 1909, and H. Muthesius's *Das englische Haus*, vol. 1, 1904. The Renaissance garden is covered by H. I. Triggs's *Formal Gardens of England and Scotland*, 1902, and H. A. Tipping's *English Gardens*, 1925.

CHAPTER XI

POST-RENAISSANCE ARCHITECTURE

By the middle of the sixteenth century the spiritual forces of the Renaissance in Italy were exhausted, and new forces began to determine the cultural development. Men no longer dreamed of a literal resurrection of pagan Rome, but were confronted by the revival of militant Christianity in the Reformation and the counter-Reformation. With the growth of centralized states came absolutism on the part of the monarchs, elaboration of their courts, and the final establishment of domestic security and of modern city and country life.

Architectural changes. Simultaneously with the beginning of these cultural changes, architecture also underwent changes which were not less fundamental. Classic forms, indeed, still remained elements of the design, and conformity to classical canons still remained the ideal in some quarters. The feeling as to what constitutes a classical character, however, was changed, the elements became materials which could be recombined or played with freely, and emphasis was transferred to other qualities than purity of detail and geometrical simplicity. First among these qualities was a heightened unity in the composition of single buildings, and extension of the scope of the composition to include their surroundings, or even whole quarters or whole towns. There was a corresponding decrease in the isolation and self-sufficiency of individual parts of a composition: the subdivisions of interior space tended to melt away; the lines of cornices and string-courses were interrupted, or architraves, pediments, and orders were broken by rustic blocks. Façades no longer conformed to a single plane, but had a boldness of relief which resulted in an aspect varying with every movement of the observer. Practical requirements became more specialized and the forms of rooms began to be differentiated so as to stand in an organic relation with their functions.

Academic and baroque tendencies. Sharing these qualities, which give the fundamental unity to the style of the time, are buildings of two diverse tendencies, opposed to each other in their relations to classical architecture. On one hand was the academic tendency, which perpetuated the striving of the Renaissance for accurate reproduction of classical features and for the establishment of mathematical canons of proportion. On the other hand was the so-called baroque tendency, which was to disregard classical dispositions and theoretic rules alike, and to use the forms of the orders as elements of a plastic modeling of masses. Such tendencies to strictness and to freedom within a style offered nothing new in principle, having been indeed always present in greater or less measure. Only the sharpness of their antithesis was hitherto unusual, and even this did not prevent a great variety of compromises both in individual buildings and in the work of national schools.

An inclusive term. In English the designation baroque has always been applied only to the works of the freer tendency, and not, as in German and Italian, to all the works of the period. The other works, considered as still belonging to the Renaissance, have thus too often been separated from those which were not only contemporary with them, but shared with them most of their fundamental qualities. It has here been thought better to preserve the historical unity of the period, and to adopt a name for it—post-Renaissance—which expresses merely its chronological position and its artistic patrimony.

Centers and diffusion. As in the Renaissance, the new movements first acquired form and momentum in Italy. In northern lands, where the Renaissance itself was associated with the Reformation, they scarcely appeared until the time of the wars of religion. Unlike the Renaissance, however, they produced results elsewhere equal in importance to those in Italy. Spain, France, and England had meanwhile become highly centralized nations, which successively attained world power, while Italy and Germany remained torn by internal struggles. During the central years of the period France dominated European politics and European culture, and it was thus the French version of contemporary ideas which, in later years, had the greatest influence.

Italy. Academic origins. The germs of both academic and baroque tendencies existed in Italy well within the Renaissance period. The forerunners of academicism were Alberti and the early editors and commentators of Vitruvius. All these were concerned largely with the fixing of normal forms and proportions for individual architectural members. After 1500 the editions and translations of Vitruvius multiplied rapidly, and belief in the infallible authority of the Roman writer increased to a fantastic extent best seen in passages in the writings of Serlio, appearing 1537–75. The rules were to be followed even when they were in conflict with the teachings of ancient monuments. By 1542 the adherents of formal theory were sufficiently numerous and self-conscious to found a Vitruvian academy in Rome.

Baroque origins. Michelangelo. Against this academic tendency there arose a powerful champion in Michelangelo. He boldly proclaimed his ambition "to burst the toils and chains" which architecture had suffered to be laid upon itself and his intention to hold himself bound by no rule ancient or modern. Already, in his designs for the façade of San Lorenzo (1514) and for the interior of the Medici chapel in Florence (1521–34, Fig. 204), he had shown a new freedom. In one it was the richer relief of free-standing columns and sculpture, here used for the first time as decorative forms in a Renaissance façade. In the other it was the unconventional use of classical details in the filling of the main architectural framework. Entablatures were broken, architraves and friezes omitted at will, proportions were modified, and a multitude of consoles were introduced. Within the tabernacles above the doors the inner enframement penetrates even the horizontal cornice and rises into the tympanum of the pediment. In the sarcophagi of the Medici chapel Michelangelo even gave a suggestion for breaking the upper cyma of a pediment, which he and others soon proceeded to do. Similar liberties of detail appear in another of his designs at this period, not completed until after his death—the vestibule of the Laurentian

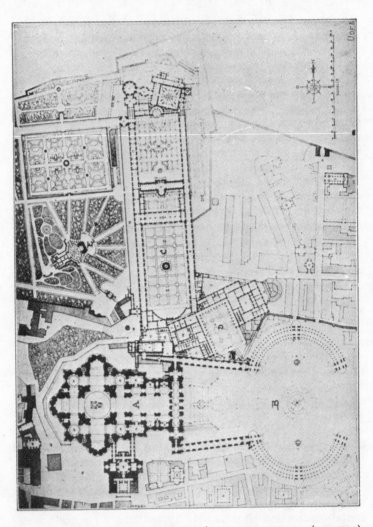

FIG. 222—ROME.   PLAN OF SAINT PETER'S AND THE VATICAN.   (GROMORT)

A. Basilica of Saint Peter
B. Piazza of Saint Peter
C. Court of the Belvedere

D. Court of San Damaso (with the
        Loggias of Raphael)
E. Villa Pia

Library in Florence. An even more striking innovation here was the placing of the stairs, free on all sides, in the center of a room which rose through two stories.

Michelangelo's later work. Saint Peter's. The second and more important period of Michelangelo's architectural work began on the death of Antonio da San Gallo (1546), when he succeeded to the direction of Saint Peter's and the papal build-

FIG. 223—ROME. SAINT PETER'S DOME FROM THE WEST

ings generally. He was already seventy-one years of age, yet he survived and continued to develop for eighteen years more. In Saint Peter's (Fig. 222) he reverted to the centrally composed scheme of Bramante which had been modified as a result of liturgical considerations He omitted the outer aisles and chapels hitherto proposed and restored the single colossal order on the exterior. For the domes proposed by Bramante and San Gallo he substituted one of his own design, embodying many novel features (Fig. 223). It followed the dome of Brunelleschi in having more than a single shell and in having a system of deep ribs with lighter filling. Michelangelo, however, took advantage of the multiplicity of shells to give the exterior of the dome a steeper pitch than the interior, and he gave the ribs a visible expression both inside and out. Instead of a continuous exterior peristyle he placed around the drum a series of buttress-like masses, one at

FIG. 224. ROME. THE CAPITOL

each rib. The result was a dome of new and more soaring aspect, which has remained an almost universal model for the following centuries.

The Capitol. Of scarcely less influence was Michelangelo's work on the Capitoline Hill in Rome (begun 1546). Here on the saddle between the two summits he created a monumental group hitherto unrivaled in its unity (Fig. 224). Taking a suggestion, perhaps, from the square at Pienza, he made the sides of his square diverge toward the Palazzo del Senatore which formed the background for a rich display of ancient sculpture. To right and left were palaces identical with each other, harmonious with the principal one, yet subordinated to it in height and scale. In these, for the first time in a secular building of the Renaissance, the façade was conceived as a whole in the manner of a Roman building, with podium, columns, and entablature. The stories are not individual units superposed on one another, but are created by the division of the larger unity. The horizontal subdivisions are in-

FIG. 225—VICENZA. THE BASILICA

terrupted by the continuous vertical lines of the great pilasters. Another notable feature of the whole composition is the emphasis on the central axes given by features of greater size and relief, or by progressive increase in size. The great double stair of the Palazzo del Senatore which contributes so much to this emphasis was itself novel and influential.

Establishment of the tendencies. Palladio. In the younger generation which surrounded and succeeded Michelangelo the dual tendencies of the day became firmly established. Although the free or baroque tendency had the greater following, the stricter or academic tendency did not yield until its greatest master had created models which later had wide influence. This master was Andrea Palladio of Vicenza (1518–80). He had in his youth given to the Roman remains the most intensive study so far attempted. His earliest building, the Palazzo della Ragione, or Basilica, at Vicenza (Fig. 225), although continuing certain traditions of the

FIG. 226 —VICENZA. VILLA ROTONDA

Renaissance, closely approximates a basilica of Roman times. There is no doubt that he chose this as his model precisely because of the identity in the uses of the buildings. In his subsequent designs there can be traced the influence of Michelangelo as well as of the antique. In some palaces he employed the colossal order, in others, where he still retained an order for each story, he omitted the pedestal between and allowed the lines of the balustrade to be interrupted by the columns. In either case he frequently added an upper story, treated as an attic like those of the Roman triumphal arches. He carried the interruption of the architectural lines even farther than Michelangelo, permitting the windows of the upper story to penetrate into the main entablature, and breaking the entablature at each bay of the great order. While he thus reduced the independence of individual members, he tended to decrease the isolation of the whole building. Instead of emphasizing the corner of the building he often weakened the expression there, making the work not a microcosm, like the Renaissance palaces, but a fragment of the cosmos. Something of the same character appears in Palladio's designs for churches and villas. In the villas, for instance, he treated the service buildings surrounding the house as wide-flung colonnaded wings which unite house and landscape. In both churches and villas Palladio made an attempt to imitate the ancient pedimented temple front. The Villa Almerigo or "Villa Rotonda" near Vicenza has even free-standing porticoes with a front of six columns (Fig. 226). This villa, composed about a central axis, with a domed central salon, served as a prototype for many others in northern lands.

Palladio's writings. Palladio's influence was exercised chiefly through his *Four Books on Architecture* (1570). In these he not only gave a codification of the orders which was widely adopted, but furnished the first considerable body of measured drawings of ancient buildings, and instituted a new custom by publishing engravings of his own works.

Vignola, Vasari, Alessi. Other men who aided in the establishment and diffusion of the new tendencies were Vignola, Vasari, and Alessi, all disciples of Michelangelo. Vignola, who measured ancient fragments in the interest of the Vitruvian academy, and who published perhaps the most influential canon of the orders, showed in his buildings great freedom of invention. At Caprarola (1558) he took a suggestion from new methods of fortification to build a five-sided castle, with a circular court. In the Villa di Papa Giulio (1550) he made a rich use of semicircular forms, and in the church of Sant' Andrea he employed an elliptical dome. Vasari, best known for his biographies of artists, also created in his buildings many new spatial effects. His court of the Uffizi in Florence, built to house the officials of the ducal administration, was opened freely at one end. and partially at the other, in contrast to the inclosed courts of earlier palaces.

Alessi began the creation of modern Genoa by his palaces with their arcaded courts and their elaborate stairways. His Palazzo Marino in Milan (Fig. 227), with its lavish use of panels, masks, garlands, and consoles to organize and enliven the wall surfaces, had the widest influence on Renaissance architecture north of the Alps.   In the works of these three

FIG. 227—MILAN. PALAZZO MARINO. COURT

men rustication commenced to attack the orders and the window enframements.   It broke through the shafts and architraves, which appeared only at the capitals and bases, in the corners, or between the blocks.   Sculptured figures, or herms with a sculptured bust and tapering shaft, began to replace pilasters and enframements, although geometrical forms and classical dispositions still dominated.

   Baroque supremacy.   The years from 1580 to 1730 in Italy were years of undisputed supremacy for the baroque. Buildings in which classical forms were strictly followed did indeed appear occasionally, even among the works of the great masters of the free tendency, but they were exceptional. In general the greatest liberty was assumed in planning and in membering. This liberty, which has so often been conceived as mere caprice or license, resulting in a dissolution or degeneration of Renaissance forms, may better be looked on as a positive, constructive process. It was an effort, thoroughly conscious of its aims and studious of its means, to follow to extreme consequences the search for those qualities of molten unity and variety of aspect which were ideals of the period as a whole. In this striving, geometrical complexity took the place of simplicity, ever-varying diagonal views resulted from curvatures in plan, ever-varying silhouettes resulted from curves and projections in elevation. The substitution of swelling, leather-like cartouches for simple shields and panels, the appearance of twisted columns, the overflowing of architectural lines by sculpture, or the substitution of sculptural forms for the architectural frames themselves, the use of richly veined and colored marbles and of gilding are but several manifestations of a consistent tendency. The aim of the academists was never to surprise; the aim and the achievement of the baroque masters was to surprise continually.

Della Porta, Maderna. Among the first constructions to feel the new spirit were those of the villa gardens, where long before the end of the sixteenth century the architecture lost its formality in a riot of sculpture, artificial rock-work, and broken silhouettes. The penetration of similar motives into monumental architecture soon followed. In the façade of the church of the Gesù in Rome, designed by Della Porta (c. 1573), there are pediments one within another on the same entablature. In the terminal fountain of the Acqua Paola, notwithstanding its severe classical models, the outline is boldly animated by consoles and finials. The façade of Saint Peter's added by Maderna (1606–26) has a graduated increase of relief toward the center and a complexity of rhythm in the setting out and subdivision of its bays which defies any casual analysis. Its skyline dissolves in balustrades, statuary, and cartouches.

Bernini, Boromini. The many-sided artist who dominated

the later years of the baroque movement was Gian Lorenzo Bernini (1598–1680). Equally distinguished in sculpture and in architecture, he broadened the scope of architectural expression to a range hitherto unknown. The canopy over the altar of Saint Peter's (1624–33) with its twisted and floriated columns, its crown of consoles and its bronze hangings (Fig. 199), is at the opposite pole from his colonnades of the square in front (1656–63), unrelieved in their Doric simplicity. A common quality is present, however, in the conception of every part as a fragment, requiring the others to complete it. No part by itself is symmetrical. The twisted columns turn in opposite directions, one half-ellipse of the colonnades demands the other (Fig. 222). Rarely are opposite sides of a motive in a single plane or parallel. The colonnades converge toward the square of Saint Peter's, the faces of the Palazzo Ludovisi (Montecitorio) recede equally on each side, the lines of the Scala Regia of the Vatican converge toward a single vanishing-point. Similar devices appear also in the work of Bernini's contemporary, Francesco Boromini. His façade for San Carlo alle Quattro Fontane at Rome (1638–40) has its lines curved in plan; his plan for Sant'Ivo (1660), an idea of Michelangelo is a combination of triangles and arcs which continually presents something unexpected.

The baroque supremacy outside of Rome. Although Rome itself was the center of the baroque movement, other Italian cities were quick to feel its influence. The extent to which it was welcomed varied greatly with the local traditions or lack of traditions. Thus in Piedmont, in Genoa, and in the south, where the school of Bramante had never become firmly established, the baroque was unrestrained. In Turin especially the works of Guarino Guarini, such as the Palazzo Carignano (1680) with its double reverse curve in façade, went to extremes. In Florence, on the other hand, the baroque scarcely obtained a foothold, and in Venice the tradition of Sansovino restricted it to a few examples. The most notable of these, the church of Santa Maria della Salute (1631–82) by Longhena, by its position at the head of the Grand Canal, has, however, a high importance in the aspect of the city (Fig. 228). Eight-sided, with its central dome buttressed by great scrolls carrying statues, and with a second large dome over its choir, it has captivated successive generations of artists by its ever-changing perspectives.

Compromise: Juvara, Galilei, Vanvitelli.   In the eighteenth century the academic tendency in Italy was strengthened by return influences from France and from England.   A touch of this appears in the work of Filippo Juvara (1685–1735),

FIG. 228—VENICE.   SANTA MARIA DELLA SALUTE

whose buildings in Turin include the great domed church of the Superga (1717–31).   Another of the leading Italian architects of the eighteenth century was Alessandro Galilei (1691–1737), who had worked in England under Vanbrugh and represented the same compromise between academic and baroque tendencies.   His façade for the church of the Lateran in Rome is strict in its use of classical elements and in its geometrical regularity, but has a free skyline and complicated grouping.

The splendor of Versailles under Louis XIV. tempted Italian princes to imitation. The most notable of the resulting country palaces is that of Caserta near Naples by Luigi Vanvitelli, begun in 1752. The plan of building and gardens embodies French elements, the membering of the long façades is dryly Palladian. The cycle through freedom back to strictness was soon to be completed.

Types of buildings. Churches. The Counter Reformation was a period of feverish building of churches, and of a return to a more liturgical conception in their design. The longitudinal type of plan was once more preferred, as in the Middle Ages. Naves were added to some Renaissance churches of central type as ultimately to Saint Peter's itself (Fig. 222). The crossing of nave and transept tended to lose its independence. In new designs the central type was rarely adopted except for votive churches like the Superga and the Salute. In the Salute the radial chapels were no longer isolated, but united to form a single encircling aisle, the first of its kind since Byzantine days. Throughout the churches the self-centered domical vaults gave place to groined vaults with their centrifugal tendency, barrel vaults were interrupted by penetrations, galleries tended to unite the bays at the aisles and even to project into the nave. A broad nave and shallow transepts gave space for a congregation corresponding to the increased importance of the sermon. The whole plan tended increasingly to conform to a single rectangle, usually subdivided, to be sure, but into parts having no strong unity of their own. The façades, too, were treated as units, with little precise relation to the subdivision of the interior. The Renaissance scheme of using superposed orders in the center with consoles to make transition from the lower order at the sides was adhered to in many cases. Even more characteristic, however, was the employment of a single order the full height of the nave, masking the unequal heights of nave and aisles. The bell tower was no longer designed as a separate unit, but was combined with the façade and repeated on either side as in northern church fronts. In the treatment of façades and still more of interiors there was often a lavishness of figure sculpture and of painting which was mundane and theatrical, perhaps, but remarkably facile and decorative

(Fig. 229). The Jesuits, who led in the reactionary religious movement, adhered to florid Italian models in their churches in other countries, and thus gave the baroque an international character as the "Jesuit style."

Palaces. In the town palaces the principal innovations of the post-Renaissance period lay in planning. Vestibule,

FIG. 229—ROME. SAN CARLO A' CATINARI. CHAPEL OF SANTA CECILIA·
(RICCI)

court, and stairs were no longer isolated, but combined in a suite which gave unity to the entire building. Genoese examples, like the University (1623), are the most notable. Many palaces, such as that of the Barberini in Rome, have more than a single file of rooms in a block and a multitude of stairways which permit independent access and privacy. The stereotyped plan with a single central court was no longer followed exclusively, and the courts were no longer always inclosed, but opened on one side toward either street or garden. This was the case, for instance, with the court of the Palazzo Pitti in Florence, executed by Ammanati in 1558–70.

Villas. The characteristic creation of the period in domestic architecture was the villa, in which house and garden were now inextricably combined. Usually on hillside sites, and with an abundant supply of water, the villas included a series of terraces, steps, pools, and fountains, all highly organized in accordance with a unified axial system. The house or casino might be either at the top or at the bottom of the slope, or even part way between; there might be a level parterre of flowers, or terraces only, as the ground permitted. A characteristic example of artful variety within modest dimensions is the Villa Lante near Viterbo, designed by Vignola (begun 1566, Fig. 230). Here a parterre with a central fountain and basins occupies the lower third of the length. To left and right of the first ascent stand the two casinos which provide the living quarters, and above rise terraces of differing widths and heights, connected on the main axis by features in which steps and falling water are ingeniously intermingled. Ramps and stairs offer numerous alternative means of ascent and descent. The Villa Pia in the gardens of the Vatican, with its oval court and curved ramps, is another such unexampled background for the art of living (Fig. 222 E).

Fountains. Fountains occurred not only in the villas but everywhere in the cities, multiplied and diversified as never before. For large volumes of water or small, for high pressures or low alike, treatments were found which gave the water itself the chief place in the design, however rich and free the architecture or sculpture.

Theaters. A novel problem in modern times was to give an architectural treatment to the theater. The classical precedents suggested to Palladio, for his Teatro Olimpico in Vicenza (1580), a close imitation of the interior of a Roman theater, with cavea, encircling colonnade at the rear, and architectural *scænæ frons*. An addition quite in the spirit of the time was that of constructed architectural perspectives visible through openings of the stage. The theater at Parma (1618) has a deeper auditorium and a single wide opening to a stage for movable scenery. Equally significant is the replacing of the rear colonnade by arcades in two stories

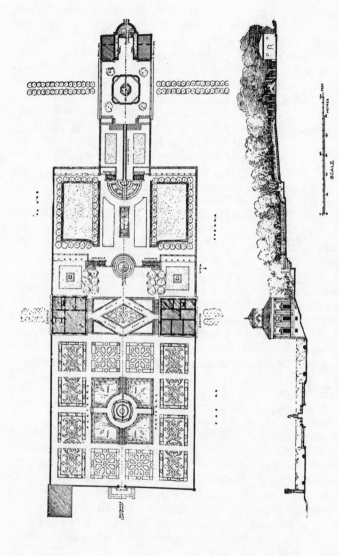

FIG. 230—BAGNAIA. VILLA LANTE. PLAN. (TRIGGS)

From these grew in the eighteenth century the tiers of individual loges which still form the characteristic treatment of the Italian theater interior. No attempt to secure an exterior expression was yet made.

Town planning. An ultimate extension of baroque principles was the inclusion of the whole city in a single architectural composition. Efforts of the sort had mostly to remain in the ideal stage, like the *Città Ideale* of Bartolomeo Ammanati (1511–92) whose Ponte Santa Trinità in Florence inaugurated a new lightness and grace in bridge building. Less fantastic than the cities on paper, but still ambitious, were the corrections undertaken in existing cities, above all in Rome. These, which had been begun in a small way by Julius II., were continued on a vast scale by his successors. They included the Piazza of Saint Peter's and the Piazza del Popolo, both begun by Bernini about 1656, the Spanish Steps, and the port of Ripetta on the Tiber. In all these there appear the grandiose unity and variety of form so characteristic of the period.

Individual forms. The governing conception of the post-Renaissance period in Italy was that each individual element was but a fragment, and that a high degree of unity in the parts was damaging to the unity of the whole. This conception was essentially in conflict with the antique conception of unity, which did not preclude parts sufficient unto themselves. It thus came about that the structural expressiveness of many forms had to yield to the imperative demand for dismemberment and coalescence. Thus as in Roman architecture, by comparison with Greek, purity of detail was rendered less important by the mode of composition.

Walls. The period in Italy was distinguished by a wide use of stucco, not only for wall surfaces, as in the Renaissance, but for all the members of openings and orders. This extension of its use resulted in the first instances from economy, but it was turned to advantage in the execution of luxuriant modeled decoration. Rustication was rarely used except in quoins or about the openings. In interiors the incrustation of walls with marble veneering was revived, inlaid patterns giving a striking contrast.

Openings. In the enframement of the openings few Italian

designers followed the practice of Palladio in retaining a simple rectangular architrave, perhaps with a frieze and cornice. Even Palladio himself multiplied ears and consoles and employed a bulging or pulvinated frieze. His contemporaries were already elaborating enframements with rusticated architraves, broken pediments, and herms or figure sculpture, which soon became the rule.

Columns and wall membering. The general relations of column, arch, and wall remained much the same as in the Renaissance period, except for the frequent use of a "colossal" engaged order. Free-standing colonnades with horizontal lintels appear but seldom, although notably in the Piazza of Saint Peter's. Columns bearing arches remained in favor for courtyards, but the supports were now usually grouped in pairs, a motive especially favored by Alessi. In the membering of façades the tendency toward grouping the members, which had begun with the coupled columns of Bramante, was carried much further. The pilaster was reinforced by slight breaks in the wall at either side, or groups of shafts and pilasters were composed, like the grouped piers of the Middle Ages. In interiors these once more gave individual support to the various members of a vault, on exteriors they served, with the corresponding breaks in entablatures and balustrades, to enliven the silhouette.

Stairs. A special production of the period was the monumental stairway, either inside a building or outside. Michelangelo's stairways at the Laurentian Library and at the Capitol gave the suggestion, which was quickly taken up in many different ways. Thus, in the Villa d'Este at Tivoli (about 1550), the two arms of a symmetrical stairway are bent into semicircles; at the Villa di Papa Giulio, into quadrants. Then followed the stairs with two arms side by side, and with three arms winding up against the walls of a rectangular room as in the Palazzo Barberini (about 1630). Further possibilities lay in a symmetrical doubling of these schemes, best exemplified in the cloister of San Giorgio Maggiore in Venice by Longhena (1644). In the Genoese palaces the stairs through several stories were brought into a single composition by the breaking through of all surrounding walls, and the carrying of the upper flights on bridge-like vaults.

Spain. Academic architecture. The conquest of the Indies made Spain, by the middle of the sixteenth century, the greatest power in Europe. Philip II. gave expression to this

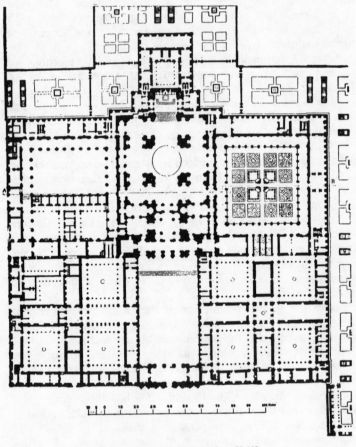

FIG. 231—THE ESCURIAL.   PLAN

power by the building of the Escurial (1563–84), comprising a votive church and mausoleum, monastery, and palace, with every needful dependency for the service of both church and state (Figs. 231, 232). Its building lay chiefly in the hands of

Juan de Herrera (1530–97), whose work, severely academic in its forms, established the post-Renaissance tendencies in Spain. In the Patio of the Evangelists, to be sure, he employed the Roman arch order with equal bays and unbroken entablatures, but elsewhere the membering abounds in the

FIG. 232—THE ESCURIAL

complex grouping of supports, the breaking of horizontal members, the uniting of interior spaces by penetrating vaults, and the multiplication of aspects in perspective by the combination of dome and towers.

Baroque supremacy. Herrera's sobriety was soon superseded by baroque freedom, which ultimately in the hands of José Churriguera (1650–1723) became the boldest license. The national traditions of the Plateresque were reflected in the "Churrigueresque" style, which paid less attention to the creation of new forms of plan and space than to the luxuriant elaboration of detail.   It reached its fullest development in the great portals and altar-pieces, such as the high altar of the church of El Salvador in Seville (Fig. 233).

Reaction.   The accession of the Bourbons in 1714, which marked the end of Spanish domination in politics, brought

also a subordination of Spanish tendencies in art. The palaces of the new rulers at La Granja and Madrid imitated not only the worldliness of Versailles but its architectural formalism.   The baroque tendency, which comported so well with national sympathies, persisted nevertheless, now creating novel forms of interior space, and still filling the framework of the orders with an exuberance of ornament.

France. In France there came first a brief period of baroque supremacy. This was of relatively short duration, however; a compromise was soon reached, and the ultimate victory of the academic tendency came earlier than in Italy and was more complete. Even during the years of compromise the academic tendency predominated, although in the later of them the freer tendency once more asserted itself vigorously, in the phase known as the rococo.   The conventional subdivision

FIG. 233—SEVILLE.   ALTAR OF THE CHURCH OF EL SALVADOR. (SCHUBERT)

of the period in France into phases designated by the names of the kings conforms tolerably well with this development, although the duration of the phases by no means corresponds exactly to that of the reigns. In general the baroque supremacy may be identified with the style of Henry IV. and Louis XIII.; the compromise, in its earlier and stricter form, with the style of Louis XIV., in its later and freer form, with that of Louis XV.; the ultimate victory of the academic, with the style of Louis XVI.

Establishment of academic and baroque tendencies. Already in the later work of native masters of the High Renaissance, as we have seen, there were signs of the appearance of post-Renaissance tendencies. On one hand De l'Orme and Bullant had written treatises discussing the proper form and proportions of classical members. On the other hand De l'Orme and Du Cerceau had employed at the Tuileries and at Charleval many of the forms of the school of Michelangelo, such as the herm, the rusticated architrave, and the broken pediment.

Baroque supremacy. Henry IV. With the resumption of building under Henry IV. after the religious wars (about 1600), the strict classical forms had everywhere yielded to those of the triumphant baroque of the day in Italy. It was rarely, however, that baroque principles governed the whole composition. In the typical buildings of the time of Henry IV., only the details of the baroque were applied to the simplest rectangular masses. A combination of brick and stone came in through the close affiliation with Protestant Holland. Examples of these characteristics are Henry IV.'s additions to Fontainebleau, as well as his buildings about the Place Royale and the Place Dauphine in Paris. All these have a simple treatment of rusticated quoins at the corners and at the openings, with occasional use of consoles, rusticated architraves, and broken pediments at small scale. The internal decoration went much further toward Italian freedom. In the treatment of doors and chimneys, enframements were doubled, members broken and interwoven, consoles and cartouches multiplied. Other developments which recall contemporary Italian movements lay in planning. At Saint Germain, Du Pérac built for Henry a series of vast terraces and steps recalling those of the Villa d'Este. For the improvement

of Paris, which henceforth became the focus of national life
the king laid out the two great squares already mentioned.
They were surrounded by buildings of unified design—the
first of a long series of similar enterprises in town planning.

Louis XIII. Under Louis XIII. (1610–43) the baroque
influence still preponderated, although to a degree which
gradually decreased. A more frequent use was again made of
the orders, and the baroque elements were confined within the
fields marked out by them. The leading architect of the
earlier years of the reign was Salomon de Brosse (d. 1626).
For Marie de' Medici he built the Luxembourg Palace
(1615–20), which she wished to resemble the Pitti Palace in
Florence. The drawings which she secured from Italy did
indeed have their influence, for there were many points of similarity between the work of De Brosse and that of Ammanati.
The open court, the superposed rusticated orders, the
rusticated arches, flat and semicircular, as well as the rigidity
of the architectural framework, all reappeared. The general
grouping and the broken silhouette of the palace, with its
many pavilions and high roofs, were, of course, wholly French.
In De Brosse's façade for the Gothic church of Saint Gervais
he also showed the influence of the freer Italian tendency as
exemplified in the Gesù, which furnished the model for most
later French church façades. The conservative French
tendencies were represented by the earlier designs of Jacques
Lemercier (1585–1654). His enlargement of the court of the
Louvre (1624–30) was on the system established by Lescot,
with the addition of a few baroque elements; his vast symmetrical château of Richelieu depended solely, for its wall
treatment, on rusticated enframements with a filling of stucco.

Reaction. In the later years of the reign of Louis XIII.
there was already a strengthening of the academic tendency
which resulted in compromise. That this should have been so
at the very moment when the baroque in Italy was receiving
its greatest development was due to several causes. Among
these perhaps the strongest was the growing tendency of
France toward absolutism and organization in every field—
the monarchy, the church, the arts in general. An instance
was the founding of the French Academy (1635), having for
its object "to give certain rules to our language and to render

it pure." Similar in its direction was the fundamental French belief in "reason" and "good sense," more sympathetic with the logic of the Italian academists than with the emotional liberty of the baroque masters. The renewed imitation of classical models in the drama, beginning with Corneille about 1635, coincides with the return to the stricter following of classical forms in architecture. The Frenchmen who went to Rome no longer studied contemporary architecture so much as

FIG. 234—BLOIS. WING OF GASTON D'ORLEANS

the work of the High Renaissance masters, with whom they shared a direct interest in Roman buildings. The academic writings of the Italians were diligently read and compared. Fréart de Chambray, who had been sent to Rome in 1640, published the first complete translation of Palladio (1650), and also a parallel of the canons of ten of the principal theorists.

Compromise. François Mansart. Style of Louis XIV. The leader in the return to academic purity in architectural practice was François Mansart (1598–1666). His wing for Gaston d'Orléans in the château of Blois (1635–40) depends for its

effect almost solely on the proportions and the sober membering of the superposed orders (Fig. 234). Except for an
increase in the height of the entrance pavilion and for the
single cartouche in the center, all the architectural lines, even
those of the roofs, carry through without interruption. Rustication and dormers are alike absent, and baroque influence
appears only in the decorative carving. Mansart's purism
in the use of the orders persisted in his work at the church of
the Val-de-Grâce in Paris (begun 1645), although the general
scheme is that of the baroque churches of Italy, and baroque
consoles occur both in the façade and in the dome. Henceforth, throughout the reign of Louis XIV., the compromise
between academic and baroque tendencies prevailed on much
the same terms. On the exterior, and even in the larger
membering of the interior, the academic framework dominated
the design; baroque forms were confined to the decoration.

Le Vau. A step beyond Mansart in the direction of
pronounced post-Renaissance character was taken by Louis
Le Vau (1612–70) who was the court architect after the death
of Lemercier. Whereas Mansart used always an order to
each story, Le Vau rarely failed to introduce a "colossal
order," rising from a low plinth to the main cornice. This
was, indeed, no new thing in French architecture, but it was
a feature which had fallen into disuse during the baroque
supremacy. Le Vau employed it in the château of Vaux-le-
Vicomte, in the south façade of the Louvre (1664), and in the
Collège des Quatre Nations (1660–68). In all these cases,
however, only one or more pavilions have the large order and
the rest of the building is treated with superposed orders or
no order at all.

The Louvre. Perrault. For the principal front of the
Louvre it was felt that something grander was necessary.
After the rejection of many designs by native architects, it
was finally decided to summon Bernini from Rome. His
design, produced in 1665, involved the destruction of much of
the existing building. It proposed the rebuilding of the court
with a single gigantic order rising from the ground, and the
treatment of the exterior with an order of equally large scale,
raised on a rusticated basement. The execution of this
scheme was soon abandoned as impossibly extravagant, and

a new design was prepared by Claude Perrault, a savant who had turned his attention to architecture. He profited by the lesson Bernini had given in unity of design and largeness of scale, but adapted his façade better to the existing work and gave it a more uniform membering and proportions (Fig. 235). Like Bernini he placed a large Corinthian order, in-

FIG. 235—PARIS. COLONNADE OF THE LOUVRE

cluding the two upper stories, over a basement the height of the ground story, and used a flat roof behind a balustrade. Unlike Bernini, however, and indeed for the first time in such a situation, he did not merely decorate the wall with an engaged order, but employed a free standing colonnade in front of it, like that of a peristylar temple. He followed De Brosse and Mansart in employing coupled columns, but gave them larger scale and more Roman detail. He also gave a new impress to the five-part scheme for long façades. This had grown up in France from the medieval castle with its corner towers and central gate-house, and had so far preserved a medieval massing. Perrault treated it with but slight projection to all the pavilions, and with a pediment over the central one—a formula which has remained usual to this day.

The academies. The predominance of principles of law and order based upon the antique was fortified by the formation in 1671 of the Academy of Architecture, to complete the system of organization begun in literature by the founding of the *Académie Française*. A further reinforcement of classical

FIG. 236—VERSAILLES. THE PALACE FROM THE PLACE D'ARMES

influence came through the establishment on a regular footing of the custom of sending promising artists to complete their studies in Rome. Thus arose the French Academy in Rome, chartered in 1677.

Versailles. J. H. Mansart. From the commencement of his personal administration in 1661, Louis XIV. began the development of the château built for his father at Versailles, for which he had a special preference. Ultimately he made it his permanent residence and the seat of his government. The original château, a simple structure of brick and stone, had to be many times enlarged, although it retained much of its original aspect toward the fore-court, and inevitably had an influence on the scale of the later work (Fig. 236). The extensions, begun by Le Vau, were completed by Jules Hardouin Mansart, a great-nephew of François. The system of membering finally adopted for the long unbroken façades

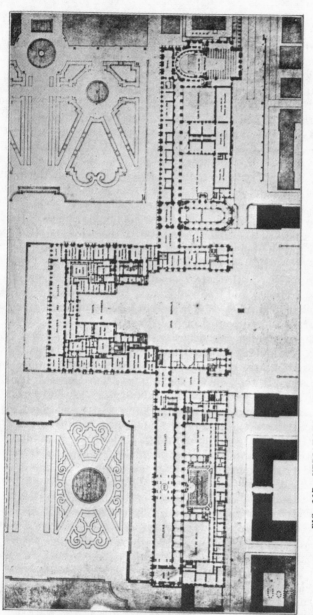

FIG. 237—VERSAILLES. PLAN OF THE PRINCIPAL FLOOR OF THE PALACE. (GROMORT)

toward the garden was that of a rusticated basement, an order, and an attic with balustrade.   The interest of the building, however, lies less in the architectural treatment of the exterior than in the plan, with its multiplicity of functions (Fig. 237). The problem was to provide quarters not only for the king and the princes of the blood, but also for the entire court, with offices for the ministers, provisions for service, immense stables, a chapel, and ultimately a theater.   In addition there were, on one side, the garden and park, on the other side, the town, newly founded—both alike symmetrical on the main axis of the palace.   Never before, even at the Escurial, had there been a single composition on such a vast scale.   The interior decoration was of a corresponding richness.   Here, more than on the exterior, appeared the baroque elements which still characterized contemporary architecture.   Thus in the ceiling of the long Galerie des Glaces, decorated by Charles Le Brun (Fig. 238), there was an abundance of broken pediments, consoles, and free sculpture.   In extent and luxuriousness alike, Versailles established an ideal which every prince in Europe soon dreamed of realizing.

Outbreak of the free tendency. Louis XV. Rococo. The extreme formality imposed on life and art by Louis XIV. provoked a new outbreak of the free tendency under his successor.   It took many suggestions from the late Italian baroque of Borromini and his followers, which had hitherto been little favored in France.   The earliest and most pronounced manifestations of the movement occur in interior decoration.   Curves were multiplied both in plan and in elevation; architectural lines were broken and were overflowed by sculpture.   The pompous apparatus of column and entablature was banished from interiors, and replaced by a more delicate and intimate treatment with panels, cartouches, and floriated scrolls (Fig. 242).   The prevalence of shell-work or *rocaille* led to the designation *rococo*, applied loosely to all the work of free tendencies which resulted from the new movement.   Efforts were not wanting to remodel external architecture on similar lines.   In many of the designs of J. A. Meissonier (1693–1750) vertical and horizontal members are alike abandoned in favor of flowing reverse curves.   In France, however, this extreme was not reached in the exterior of any building actually executed. The orders were retained on the façade, with only a slightly greater liberty of detail. The spirit of freedom showed itself on the exterior mainly by an increased use of curved and angular elements of plan, and by an exuberance of ornament within the bays and above the cornice. All these characteristics are specially well exemplified

FIG. 238—VERSAILLES. THE GALERIE DES GLACES

in the notable group of buildings erected for Stanislas, Duke of Lorraine, at Nancy (1753–57).

Academic victory. Louis XVI. Contemporary with the later years of the rococo and well within the reign of Louis XV, there was a new reaction against the extravagance of the free tendency, associated with the name of his successor. The design for the façade of the Hôtel Dieu by Soufflot at Lyons (1741) showed a classical strictness and majesty unusual at the time. In the work of Anges Jacques Gabriel, falling in the years 1752 to 1770, the tendency won a complete victory, and the academic system received its ultimate development. Gabriel's designs for the Place de la Concorde (Fig. 239), for the Ecole Militaire in Paris, the Palace at Compiègne, the Theater at Versailles, and the Petit Trianon (Fig. 240) form a body of work unrivaled for the purity of academic detail and ornament. In most of them he followed the scheme consecrated by Perrault—an order embracing two stories

FIG. 239—PARIS.   PLACE DE LA CONCORDE

above a high basement.   In the handling of the order itself, in some cases, he secured Perrault's touch of Roman magnificence.   Often he restricted the order to the principal pavilion, and left the remaining walls unbroken except by the slender and elegant window enframements.   Before the accession of Louis XVI. even the interiors of buildings had lost their luxuriant freedom.   At the same time there began a change in character, both within and without, due to the literal imitation of classical motives, which brought rococo and academic movements alike to an end.

Types of buildings. Châteaux.   The close of the religious wars once more made it safe to live in the country, and permitted a new and freer development of the château.   From this time until Louis XIV. made constant residence at court a necessity, the nobility built many châteaux which correspond to the countless manor houses of England. While some of the larger of these retained the inclosed court, the tendency was to omit the block on the fourth side and to shorten the arms, so that in many of the smaller examples only the main

FIG. 240—VERSAILLES. PETIT TRIANON

block was left. On the other hand the main block itself was made thicker, with a double file of rooms, so that it was no longer necessary to traverse private apartments. The main staircase, which in François Mansart's designs still occupied the center, was pushed to one side in favor of a monumental vestibule. The functions of rooms became increasingly specialized. The salon or reception-room now made its appearance, and was accorded the place of honor in the center, facing the gardens. From the time of Le Vau it was given an elliptical form, projecting so that it commanded a view to the sides as well. The régime established by Louis XIV. affected châteaux in two opposite ways. On one hand, at Versàilles, it magnified the château into the modern palace. On the other hand it produced in the neighborhood of the palace a number of small but elegant châteaux serving as retreats for recreation or privacy, like the casinos of the Italian villas. Marly, the Grand Trianon, and the Petit Trianon (Fig. 240) are examples showing the increasing desire for intimacy, which ultimately resulted in the rustic hamlet of Marie Antoinette.

Gardens. The gardens themselves were given a new and magnificent treatment. This was inaugurated by André le Nôtre at Vaux and developed by him at Versailles and the other royal residences. It involved a general increase in scale, the introduction of canals, basins, cascades, and fountains of great size, and an extension of the garden scheme over all the neighboring countryside by means of a system of radiating and intersecting allées. The reaction from splendor apparent in the building of the Trianon had later its expression in the gardens. The informal or landscape garden of England was adopted, as a more fitting milieu for the playful phases of court life.

Hôtels. The development of Paris into a national metropolis gave an impetus to the development of the city residence or hôtel, which often rivaled a château in the extent of its court and gardens. The ambitious examples, large and small alike, preserved the fore-court and screen toward the street, with the living-rooms in a block facing the garden at the rear. The same internal changes in the direction of greater convenience took place in the hôtel as in the château. Great ingenuity was exercised in making separate provision for all the varied functions of the establishment, often on limited and irregular sites. Stables and service quarters were provided with subsidiary courts of their own, where the dimensions at all permitted. The minor houses on narrow lots were also given the architectural expression in classic forms which has governed the aspect of cities to this day. Sometimes whole ranges of houses were treated uniformly as the surrounding walls of a monumental square; at other times there was but a single façade, usually of three bays. In either case the favorite division of height, a basement story with two others above, corresponding to an order, was adopted.

As land values rose, apartment houses in four and more stories were built, conforming to the same architectural scheme, but with mezzanines and attics.

Churches. The church in France during the seventeenth and eighteenth centuries was less significant than either the state or society, yet a certain number of notable religious buildings were undertaken. The parish churches had the basilican plan, as well as the façade in two stories with consoles or twin towers, characteristic of contemporary basilican churches in Italy. The more important churches of the time were those which either had a votive character, like the Val-de-Grâce (begun 1645), or were chapels attached to an institution, like the churches of the Sorbonne (1635–53), the Collège des Quatre Nations (1660–68), and the Hôpital des Invalides (1692–1704). They were thus relatively free from liturgical restrictions and could fulfil their monumental functions through the adoption of a dome. All four of these just mentioned have the high drum and external silhouette inaugurated by Saint Peter's. The Sorbonne and the Val-de-Grâce, both of which have basilican naves, have two-storied façades like those of the basilican churches. In the new chapel of the Invalides this scheme was retained even though the church was a composition of purely central type, without aisles or galleries. Only at the Collège des Quatre Nations was the single order employed. The plans of all these domed churches offer interesting examples of the tendencies of post-Renaissance days toward the multiplying of interrelations between the parts, rather than the preserving of their individual unity. At Versailles there were special reasons why a dome could not be introduced. The palace chapel had to yield the axial position to the state bedroom of the king, and thus could not receive a development which would injure too much the symmetry of the whole group. The solution adopted by Mansart, a basilican plan, with galleries treated as tall colonnades above the low arcaded aisles, was novel in church design, yet quite in accordance with the general formulæ of the period.

Ensembles. Planning. The design of vast unified ensembles, which had begun in French architecture with De l'Orme, was even more characteristic of the post-Renaissance period. The great châteaux like Versailles and the Louvre were not the only examples. The Hôpital des Invalides in Paris, which furnished accommodation for six thousand disabled soldiers, and the Ecole Militaire, also on an enormous scale, were symmetrical compositions about a series of courts. The systems of subordinated axes reached a high degree of organization, as in the vast Roman ensembles. An equal skill was shown in the handling of diagonal axes, and in the union of elements in irregular plans by means of circular and elliptical features.

Town planning. The creation of squares surrounded by private buildings of uniform design, begun by Henry IV., was continued under his successors. His Place Royale and Place Dauphine were both rectangular in plan. A project of his which was never realized, however—the Place de France—involved a semicircular space at the entrance to the city, with avenues radiating to every quarter. A similar conception was embodied by Louis XIV. in the circular Place des Victoires (1684–86). The Place Louis le Grand or Place Vendôme was a rectangle diversified by the cutting off of the corners diagonally, and ornamented by engaged columns and pediments at the axial points. The Place Louis XV., or Place de la Concorde, was conceived, like these last two, primarily as a setting for a monument. Its buildings occupy only one side, but with their free standing colonnades like those of the Louvre they have a richness unapproached in the other examples. In the provincial towns squares and quais were also treated as unified compositions; at Nancy even a whole series of squares was brought into one design, comparable in extent and complexity to the greatest of the Roman fora. Thus was expressed the fondness of the time for order and subordination, as well as for the absorption of individual unities in a larger unity.

Construction. Except for the period of Henry IV., when Dutch influence caused the adoption of brick even in some regions where stone was more easily obtainable, stone was used almost exclusively in monumental constructions. The softness and fine texture of the French limestone permitted carving almost as free and delicate as if in marble. Marble itself was used but seldom, and then only as a precious adornment, for instance, in the shafts which distinguish the central blocks at Versailles and Trianon. The ease of working the stone, as well as the geometrical skill of the French builders, resulted in the use of cut stone for vaulting to an extent nowhere else approached. The science of stone-cutting or stereotemy was thus developed to the highest point.

Details. The conception of general unity in exterior treatment was not often pushed, as in Italy, to the destruction of the unity of single details such as the enframements of doors

FIG. 241—PARIS. PORTE SAINT DENIS. PRINCIPAL FRONT

FIG. 242—VERSAILLES. DETAIL OF THE APARTMENTS OF LOUIS XV.

and windows. After the brief period of baroque supremacy such details followed classical or Palladian models with but little modification, and equaled them in harmony of proportion and profiling. The spirit of the time appeared, nevertheless, in the fondness for the use of ears and consoles, and for the coupling and grouping of supports. It appeared also in the frequent use of transitional members. Thus in the façade of the Petit Trianon (Fig. 240) a subordinate break was introduced on either side of the main projecting portico, and a similar though minute break was made in the architraves of the side windows. The same rationalistic sentiment which found interrupted pediments repugnant sometimes demanded the omission of the orders altogether where the column would not fulfil its original function as an isolated support. An example is the Porte Saint Denis in Paris (Fig. 241), in which the Roman scheme of triumphal arch was expurgated by substituting for the columns large tapering panels decorated with sculptured trophies. This distinctively national tendency, which gradually gained strength during the eighteenth century, was one which bore much fruit in the following period.

Interiors. In interiors the unity of design between wall treatment and furniture was a novel and striking feature. During the prevalence of the rococo, indeed, interior unity was carried to the extreme—the shape of the room, the motives of its paneling and the lines of the furnishings being all based on similar curves, which precluded any individual self-sufficiency in the parts (Fig. 242). Under Louis XV. and Louis XVI. the desire for intimacy led to a reduction in the size and height of the rooms, in which elegance was sought rather than splendor.

England: baroque supremacy. Jacobean architecture. The first of the post-Renaissance forms to reach England were the baroque cartouches and strap-work from Germany, which, as we have seen, were lavished on buildings still fundamentally Gothic in their disposition (Fig. 218). The reign of James I. (1603–25) thus constitutes a period of baroque supremacy, analogous to that of Henry IV. in France. As in France, also, this baroque predominance was brief, and was soon succeeded by a compromise in which academic elements predominated.

Introduction of academic forms. Inigo Jones. The introduction of academic forms into England was essentially the work of one man, Inigo Jones (1573–1652). His architectural career began after a journey to Italy in 1613 and 1614 in which he visited Rome and Vicenza, studied the writings of Palladio and others, and became acquainted with Maderna and the other foremost contemporary architects of Rome. He was thus subjected both to the academic influence and to the baroque, and both affected his work. The resulting compromise, however, was not, as in France, one based on the forms already in use in the country, but one based directly on the forms current in Italy. Thus England was endowed, as early as 1620, with buildings more advanced in point of style than those of any other country than Italy itself. The most noted of Jones's designs was for the palace at Whitehall (1619). The only portion executed, the Banqueting Hall (Fig. 243), had a characteristic Palladian façade with orders in two stories, a flat balustraded roof and an entablature broken about the supports. Jones's free-standing Tuscan portico of Saint

FIG. 243—LONDON. THE BANQUETING HALL, WHITEHALL

Paul's, Covent Garden, his "Queen's House" at Greenwich, as well as his gigantic portico for the old Cathedral of Saint Paul, represent his academic side. The gate at York Stairs, with other minor works and interior designs, shows pronounced baroque characteristics.

John Webb. Jones's disciple, John Webb elaborated a plan for Whitehall, a vast composition resembling De l'Orme's for the Tuileries. His design for King Charles's block at Greenwich Hospital, however, closely follows Maderna's façade of Saint Peter's.

Sir Christopher Wren. With the Restoration of Charles II, began the activity of Christopher Wren (1632–1723), a distinguished mathematician, whose chief training in architexture was derived from books and from a visit to Paris in 1665, the very year of Bernini's triumphant reception there.

It was natural that in him, as in Inigo Jones, academic and baroque influence should mingle, the baroque element being even stronger than in his predecessor. In certain designs, to be sure, such as the Library of Trinity College, Cambridge, with its reminiscence of the Library of Saint Mark, he remained strictly academic; and in the Monument in London, commemorating the great fire of 1666, he anticipated later classical movements by an imitation of the column of Trajan.

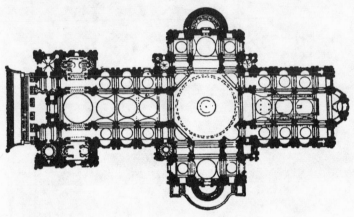

FIG. 244—LONDON. SAINT PAUL'S CATHEDRAL. PLAN

In his towers and spires, however, in his fondness for the combination of brick and stone, and above all in the luxuriant detail of his interiors, he shows the influence of contemporary Italy and the Low Countries.

Saint Paul's. Wren's most important commission was the rebuilding of Saint Paul's, 1668–1710. His first design for it was a great octagonal domed church with an encircling aisle, like Santa Maria della Salute in Venice, but with even greater multiplicity of connections and variety of spatial effect. This proved too radical for the clergy as Bramante's and Michelangelo's central schemes for Saint Peter's had proved, and a longitudinal scheme had to be substituted (Fig. 244). The dome, however, remained a dominant feature, including the whole width of both nave and aisles as in the cathedral of

By courtesy of London Stereoscopic and Photograph Co.

FIG. 245—LONDON. SAINT PAUL'S CATHEDRAL

Florence. Its external form in the earlier projects seems to have been derived from San Gallo's model for Saint Peter's, but in its final form (Fig. 245) it was influenced rather by Bramante's designs. Like Bramante's Tempietto at San Pietro in Montorio, it has a peristyle of free-standing columns with a balustrade, a paneled drum, and flat ribs on the dome proper. The vastly larger scale of Saint Paul's gives the composition a new majesty. For the façade Wren adopted the two-storied scheme of most of the Italian churches of the time, with twin towers similar in composition to those of Sant' Agnese at Rome and other baroque examples. The super-posed porticoes of coupled columns in the center, however, had more of the academic dignity of Palladio and Perrault. The basilican arrangement of the interior, with the flying buttresses made necessary by the clerestory, Wren felt it necessary to mask by carrying his second story order around the exterior. The interior dome also fell far below the exterior one, which was formed of timber framework over a cone of brick supporting the lantern. Thus frankness of construction was sacrificed to gain the complete liberty of design which the post-Renaissance artist demanded for both interior and exterior.

Vanbrugh. The dual tendencies of the period appear in heightened contrast in the work of Sir John Vanbrugh, who took up architecture at thirty-five, after a brilliant success as a writer of comedies. In his vast designs for Castle Howard, Blenheim Palace (Fig. 246), and other houses of the aristocracy, he carried to the limit the scale of orders and rooms, the picturesque composition of masses, and the support of the main mass by subordinate colonnades and dependencies. Baroque features abound in the treatment of the cupolas and the skyline generally, whereas the porticoes and colonnades are often of strictly classical ordonnance. A classical portico of this sort, without any combinations with baroque elements, appears in the Clarendon Press building at Oxford, designed by Vanbrugh and his pupil Nicholas Hawksmoor about 1710.

Academic supremacy. "*The Palladian style.*" The influence of the universities, indeed, was squarely on the side of the classical and academic, and the same was true of the noble amateurs for whose schooling the "grand tour" to Italy had become indispensable. The most influential of these was Lord Burlington (1695-1753) who purchased Palladio's drawings in Vicenza, issued an edition of his writings in 1715-16, and of his restorations of ancient buildings in 1730. He also assisted the architects of Palladian tendencies—Colen Campbell, William Kent, and others—by commissions and by help-

FIG. 246—BLENHEIM PALACE FROM THE FORE-COURT

ing in the publication of their designs. Burlington House in London by Campbell, 1716-17, shows direct following of Palladio's designs. The favorite of these was his Villa Rotonda, which was reproduced both by Campbell and by Burlington himself. For the assembly rooms at York, Burlington adopted an imitation of Palladio's "Egyptian Hall," surrounded by colonnades in two stories. The freestanding portico as used by Palladio became the rule for the great houses of the nobility (Fig. 247) and for churches as well. Henceforth throughout the century in England academic purity of detail was carried to the point of banishing all decorative sculpture from the façades, which depended for their effect solely on abstract composition and proportion. Thus England anticipated by a generation or more the victory of academism and the advent of classicism in other countries, and was in a position to exercise on them a powerful return influence.

Domestic architecture. The great houses. The post-Renaissance period after the Restoration was the heyday of the English landed aristocracy, and it was natural that the characteristic type of the period should have been the great country house. The royal palaces scarcely surpassed many other seats in size and splendor and may well be considered with them. In the development considerations of form took first place, and the interior was arranged as well as possible without disturbing the façades. The first building of the new order was the Queen's House at Greenwich, designed in 1617. It was a solid rectangular block, with a central colonnaded loggia over a high basement, and with a flat roof and balustrade—a revolutionary contrast to the typical Jacobean house, its tall wings, bays, and gables. In his design for Whitehall, Jones employed superposed orders; Webb, for the later buildings at Greenwich, a colossal order and attic. In Somerset House, as executed, Webb adopted pilasters running through two stories, over an arcaded basement. The plans made certain advances in the direction of convenience and privacy— the files of rooms were doubled in many of the blocks, and corridors were often added. Palladio's scheme of dependencies on either side of the fore-court, connected with the house by colonnades, was also adopted. Of the Italian formulæ for façades introduced by Jones, a favorite was the one which had the added prestige of its adoption in the Louvre—the tall order over a basement story. This was used by Wren at Hampton Court (1689–1700), and was reverted to (after Vanbrugh's preference for the colossal order) by the later Palladians. In the larger houses of Vanbrugh, there was a modification of the block-like mass of the main house by wings providing long suites of state apartments toward the gardens, on the model of those at Versailles. At Blenheim, indeed, these wings were also turned forward along the sides of the house; and the kitchens and stables were pushed still farther forward, and grouped about independent courts on either side of a second fore-court like the Cour Royale at Versailles. Unlike Versailles, however, Vanbrugh's houses had an emphasis on the central and terminal masses which makes them much more lively in silhouette (Fig. 246). With the return to Palladianism came the adoption of the great free-standing pedimented portico, often of six Corinthian columns, as at

FIG. 247—PRIOR PARK NEAR BATH

Prior Park near Bath, built in 1734 (Fig. 247). In other Palladian houses the arrangement was still more schematic— even symmetrical on both axes—sometimes with four outlying blocks, as at Holkham. The service quarters were now provided for in the basement story, less frankly confessed but more convenient in their relation to the living-rooms.

Smaller houses. Besides the multitude of great houses with their weight of academic apparatus, there was an even greater number of unpretentious houses in many of which no orders at all were used. Even those attributed to Webb and Wren are

merely straightforward compositions of wall and openings—
of stone, of brick, or of brick and stone—sometimes with
classical architraves, but sometimes without even these.
Leaded and mullioned windows were abandoned for painted
wooden sashes, and classical detail was restricted to the
pilastered doorway and main cornice.   In the simpler examples
there might even be nothing specifically classical except the
general regularity and symmetry, as, for instance, in Clifford

FIG. 248—CLIFFORD CHAMBERS

Chambers (Fig. 248), where the "vernacular" style is seen in
a typically cultivated and luxuriant natural setting.

Gardens.   The earlier gardens of the period in England were
under foreign influence—successively Italian, with terraces,
statues, and fountains; Dutch, with yews clipped in fantastic
shapes; and French, with the long allées and canals of Le
Nôtre.   In the early years of the eighteenth century, under
the leadership of writers like Shaftesbury, Addison, and Pope,
began the modern appreciation of natural landscape, and in
its wake came the creation of the informal landscape garden—
a new type, specifically English.   The great formal gardens
were gradually remodeled until the houses stood immediately

in naturalesque grounds, where every stratagem was employed
to create pleasing vistas and a constant variety of character.
A multitude of minor decorative structures, among which
playful reproductions of classical temples began to appear,
served still further to diversify and enliven the grounds.

Parish churches. Church building was uncommon in England during the post-Renaissance period, except in London.
There the vast growth of the city and the havoc wrought by
the great fire of 1666 made many new structures necessary.
They presented a problem, which even the established church
in England shared with the Protestants of France and Germany: to build in Renaissance forms a church primarily
adapted for preaching. In the first example, the church of
Saint Paul's, Covent Garden (1631), Jones came nearer the
Palladian ideal of a reproduction of the classic temple than
had Palladio himself. It proved an isolated exotic. Wren
solved the problem by the adoption of broad and compact
plans, little encumbered by columns, yet of the greatest
variety and ingenuity of forms. A basilican arrangement
with a barrel-vaulted nave, as in Saint Bride's, is not uncommon in them, and a dome supported on columns and
diagonal arches is occasionally found, as at Saint Stephen's,
Walbrook. Galleries were frequently added to increase the
seating capacity. On the exterior Wren usually retained the
bell tower and subordinated the architectural treatment of the
rest of the church to the rich development of its upper portion.
He sought to retain the expressive effect of the Gothic spire by
facile combinations of classical elements in decreasing stages.
The first and most influential of these steeples was that of
Saint Mary-le-Bow (Fig. 249), which has the transition from
the square belfry stage masked by angle finials, and the further
reduction in diameter accomplished by a range of consoles.
The later development of the type took place through the
elimination of Gothic or baroque elements in the steeple and
through the addition of a portico and other classical members
to the body of the edifice. All these changes best appear in
the churches of James Gibbs, whose church of Saint Mary-le-
Strand has a treatment of the exterior by superposed orders
based on that of Saint Paul's. His design for Saint Martin-
in-the-Fields' has a hexastyle Corinthian portico and a steeple

in which the transition from square to octagonal is even more subtly accomplished than in those of Wren. It became the prototype of many others.

Town planning. The unified planning of many buildings, so characteristic of the period, began in England with Inigo Jones's design for Covent Garden—a square surrounded by open arcades, which are treated as the basement for pilasters running through two stories above. For the rebuilding of London after the great fire of 1666, Wren prepared a plan based on the radiating principle already adopted in France, but the multitude of private interests affected prevented its execution. Unified streets and squares, however, continued to be built by the great landed proprietors, whose system of ground rent favored this method. The ultimate scope of such enterprises is best seen outside of London, at Bath, where the architect John Wood created not only squares, but also "circuses" and "crescents" with coherent academic façades treated with pilasters or superposed columns.

Details. The period of compromise between academic and baroque tendencies in England was generally marked by strict following of the forms and proportions of the orders themselves, but by considerable license in the other details, especially in interiors. Thus, although twisted columns, for example, appear in but few instances (as in the porch of Saint Mary's Church, Oxford, attributed to Inigo Jones), broken and scroll pediments, architraves with rusticated key-blocks, and free combinations of consoles often occur. In the interiors by Wren, such features are combined with the most lavish and exuberant carving, the work of Grinling Gibbons, a spiritual descendant of Bernini and the Italian decorators. In all this work appears the characteristic post-Renaissance feeling for interdependence, transition, and fusion of the parts in an indissoluble whole. With the Palladian movement in the eighteenth century, however, came a tendency to abandon this mode of composition, even to expurgate the works of Palladio himself, who had followed it so far as academic forms permitted. Thus the use of pavilions, the breaking of cornices at engaged columns, the use of ears and consoles, and of string-courses interrupted by pilasters was gradually abandoned. Unbroken cornices and self-sufficient doors and windows

By courtesy of London Stereoscopic and Photograph Co.

FIG. 249—LONDON. SAINT MARY-LE-BOW

tended to rule in buildings themselves standing proudly self-sufficient, with little transition to their environment. Academism thus here first gave place to the new classicism which was destined to succeed it.

Germany. Baroque architecture: c. 1580–1730. In Germany, after the introduction of baroque forms from Italy, about 1580, the baroque spirit maintained a complete ascendancy. At first it was the influence of Alessi and of north Italy which dominated, and which, united with survivals of medievalism, produced such characteristically German buildings as the Friedrichsbau at Heidelberg (1601–07), and the Rathaus at Augsburg (1614–20). The Thirty Years' War (1618–48) with its unparalleled devastation, however, brought all building in Germany to a standstill, and destroyed architectural tradition itself.

FIG. 250—DRESDEN. CENTRAL PAVILION OF THE ZWINGER

Meanwhile, in the south, the Catholic princes had summoned to their aid the Jesuits of Italy, bringing with them Italian architects and their maturer baroque. Thus in 1606 Vincenzo Scamozzi, a disciple of Palladio, prepared a plan for the cathedral of Salzburg, which was executed in 1611–34, with forms reminiscent of Il Gesù in Rome. Italian architects built at Prague the Waldstein

Palace (1621–29) with its great garden loggia of arches on coupled columns; and later, in Munich, the Theatine Church (1663–75) with its two-story façade, its tall dome and Western towers with multiplied consoles. An independent German version of the baroque did not flourish until after 1700, when a group of masters arose who showed a facility in this medium of expression scarcely equaled even in Italy. Andreas Schlüter imbued the royal palace in Berlin with the exuberant decorative spirit of his sculptures, Matthäus Pöppelmann attained in the Zwinger at Dresden (1711–22) the ultimate fusion of all the elements through the incompleteness and mutual dependence of every one (Fig. 250). Georg Bähr brought to a brilliant culmination the development of the Protestant auditorium-church by his Frauenkirche at Dresden (Fig. 251), with its rotunda and storied interior galleries, its unique and successful transition from mass to dome. In Vienna, Johann Fischer von Erlach, the pioneer historian

FIG. 251—DRESDEN. FRAUENKIRCHE

of architecture, showed a more eclectic spirit—as in the employment of a classical portico, and of imitations of the column of Trajan, as elements in his church of San Carlo Borromeo—but in general baroque conceptions dominate wholly.

Rococo. French influence: c. 1730–70. From about 1730, this native growth was submerged, thanks to the overpowering prestige of France, by an influx of French architects and French influence. These men were adepts in the free rococo decorations of Louis XV. and, unlike their fellow extremists who remained in France, were not restrained by academic tradition from carrying over their curvilinear style to exteriors. On the contrary the prevailing native baroque encouraged them to indulge their tendencies in graceful châteaux like the Amalienburg by François de Cuvilliés, which have no counterpart outside of Germany.

Rise of academism. English influence. Frederick the Great (1740–86) turned not only to France but to England, which in the later eighteenth century began to set the mode even for France itself. The Royal Opera House in Berlin (1743) has a pedimented Corinthian portico of six columns, severe classical niches, and almost complete absence of sculpture. The final victory of this academic tendency, presaging that of classicism itself, appears in the decorative towers of the Gendarmenmarkt in Berlin (1780 *ff*.) by Karl von Gontard, in which are mingled reminiscences of the tall domes of Wren and Soufflot.

PERIODS OF POST-RENAISSANCE ARCHITECTURE

ITALY

I. Establishment of academic and baroque tendencies, c. 1540–80.
    Michelangelo Buonarroti, 1475–1564.
        Studies for the façade of San Lorenzo at Florence, 1514 *ff*.
        New Sacristy of San Lorenzo (Medici Chapel), 1521–34.
        Laurentian Library at Florence, 1524–71.
        Saint Peter's at Rome, 1547–64; dome, 1588–92.
        Palaces and square of the Capitol at Rome, 1546 *ff*.
        Santa Maria degli Angeli at Rome, 1563–66.
        Porta Pia at Rome, 1559.
    Andrea Palladio, 1518–80.
        Basilica at Vicenza, 1549.
        Palazzo Valmarana at Vicenza, begun 1556.
        San Giorgio Maggiore at Venice, 1565.
        Il Redentore at Venice, 1577.
        Villa Almerico (Villa Rotonda) near Vicenza, 1552.
        Teatro Olimpico at Vicenza, 1580–84.
    Giacomo Barozzi da Vignola, 1507–73.
        Palace at Caprarola, 1558.
        Villa di Papa Giulio at Rome, 1550–55.

Sant' Andrea at Rome, 1550.
Villa Lante near Viterbo, begun 1566.
Il Gesù at Rome, 1568–84.
Giorgio Vasari, 1511–74.
Court of the Uffizi in Florence, 1560–80.
Galeazzo Alessi, 1512–72.
Palazzo Sauli at Genoa, c. 1550.
Santa Maria di Carignano at Genoa, begun c. 1552.
Palazzo Marino at Milan, 1558–60.
Bartolomeo Ammanati, 1511–92.
Ponte Santa Trinità at Florence, 1567–70.

II. Baroque supremacy, c. 1580–1730.
Giacomo della Porta, 1541–1604.
Design for façade of Il Gesù at Rome, c. 1573.
Domenico Fontana, 1543–1607.
Acqua Paolina, 1585–90.
Carlo Maderna, 1556–1629.
Nave and façade of Saint Peter's at Rome, 1606–26.
Giovanni Lorenzo Bernini, 1598–1680.
Baldachino of Saint Peter's at Rome, 1624–33.
Colonnades of Saint Peter's, 1656–63.
Scala Regia in the Vatican, 1663–66.
Palazzo Ludovisi (Montecitorio), 1642–1700.
Francesco Boromini, 1599–1667.
Remodeling of Palazzo Spada at Rome, 1632.
San Carlo alle Quattro Fontane, 1638–40.
Guarino Guarini, 1624–83.
Palazzo Carignano at Turin, 1680.
Baldassare Longhena, c. 1604–82.
Santa Maria della Salute, 1631–82.

III. Compromise, c. 1730–80.
Filippo Juvara, 1685–1735.
The Superga near Turin, 1717–31.
Palazzo Madama at Turin, 1718.
Alessandro Galilei (1691–1737).
Façade the Church of the Lateran, 1734.
Luigi Vanvitelli, 1700–73.
Palace at Caserta. 1752 ff.

SPAIN

I. Academic architecture, c. 1570–1610.
Juan de Herrera, c. 1530–97.

The Escurial, 1563–81.
Cathedral in Valladolid, 1585 ff.
Exchange in Seville, 1584–98.

II.   Baroque supremacy, c. 1610–1750.
Juan Gomez de Mora, d. 1647.
Jesuit college and church in Salamanca, 1614 (–1750).
José Churriguera, 1650–1723.
Catafalque for Queen Maria Luisa, 1689.
Town Hall of Salamanca.
Pedro Ribera.
Façade of the Hospicio Provincial in Madrid, 1772 (–1799).
Ventura Rodriquez, 1717–85.
San Marcos in Madrid, 1749–53.
San Francisco el Grande in Madrid, 1761.

III. Reaction, c. 1730.
Filippo Juvara and Giovanni Battista Sacchetti, d. 1766.
Royal Palace at La Granja, 1721–23.
Royal Palace at Madrid, 1734 ff.
Pedro Caro, d. 1732.
Palace at Aranjuez, 1727 (–78).

FRANCE

I.   Baroque supremacy, c. 1590–1635.
Henry IV., 1589–1610.
Etienne du Pérac, c. 1540–1601.
Palace at Saint Germain, 1594, terrace 1672.
Claude Chastillon, 1547–1616.
Place Royale at Paris, 1604.
Louis XIII., 1610–43.
Salomon de Brosse, b. between 1552 and 1562, d. 1626
Luxembourg Palace, 1615–20.
Façade for Saint Gervais in Paris, 1616–21.
Jacques Lemercier, 1585–1654.
Enlargement of the Court of the Louvre, 1624–30.
Château de Richelieu, 1627–37.
Church of the Sorbonne, 1635–53.

II.   Compromise, c. 1635–1745.
Stricter phase, c. 1635–1715.
François Mansart, 1598–1666.
Wing of Gaston d'Orléans at Blois, 1635–40.
Château of Maisons near Paris, 1642–51.
Church of the Val-de-Grâce in Paris, begun 1645.
Louis XIV., 1643–1715.

Louis le Vau, 1612–70.
  Château of Vaux-le-Vicomte, c. 1657–60.
  Collège des Quatre Nations at Paris, 1660–68.
  Continuation of the Louvre, 1664–70.
  Remodeling of Versailles (Cour de Marbre), 1665–70.
Claude Perrault, 1613–88.
  Colonnade of the Louvre, 1665.
Jules Hardouin Mansart, 1646–1708.
  Second remodeling of Versailles, 1678–88; chapel, 1699–1710.
  Dome of the Invalides at Paris, 1675–1706.
François Blondel, 1617–86.
  Porte Saint Denis at Paris, 1673.
Freer phase, rococo, c. 1715–45.
Louis XV., 1715–74.
  J. Aubert, d. 1741.
    Stables at Chantilly, 1719–35.
    Hôtel Biron at Paris, 1728.
  Giardini, dates uncertain.
    Palais Bourbon at Paris, 1722.
  Germain Boffrand, 1667–1754.
    Hôtel d'Amelot at Paris, begun 1695.
  Emmanuel Héré de Corny, 1705–69.
    New quarter at Nancy, 1753–57.
III. Academic victory, 1745–80.
Louis XVI., 1774–92.
  Jacques Germain Soufflot, 1709–80.
    Façade of the Hôtel Dieu at Lyons, 1741.
  Anges Jacques Gabriel, 1698–1782.
    Ecole Militaire in Paris, 1751–1787.
    Palace at Compiègne, 1751–75.
    Theater, etc., at Versailles, 1748–70.
    Petit Trianon, 1762–68.
    Palaces of the Place de la Concorde in Paris, 1755–63.
  Jacques Denis Antoine, 1733–1801.
    The Mint in Paris, 1768–75.

ENGLAND

I. Baroque supremacy, c. 1600–20.
  (See English Renaissance architecture, under James I.)
II. Compromise, c. 1620–1720.
  Inigo Jones, 1573–1652.

Queen's House in Greenwich, 1617–35.
Banqueting Hall of Whitehall Palace in London, 1619–22.
Square and church of Saint Paul, Covent Garden, 1631.
Portico of old Saint Paul's Cathedral in London, 1633 *ff*.
John Webb, 1611–1672.
Plans for Whitehall Palace, 1643–61.
King Charles's Block at Greenwich, 1663–70.
Somerset House in London.
Sir Christopher Wren, 1632–1723.
Sheldonian Theater at Oxford, 1663–68.
Plan for rebuilding of London, 1666.
Saint Paul's Cathedral in London, 1668–1710.
The Monument in London, 1671.
Temple Bar in London, 1671.
City churches in London, 1670–1711.
Saint Stephen's, Walbrook, 1672–79.
Saint Mary-le-Bow, 1680.
Saint Bride's, 1680–1702.
Buildings at Greenwich, 1676–1716.
Library of Trinity College, Cambridge, 1678.
Hampton Court, 1689–1703.
William Talman, *fl.* 1670–1700.
Chatsworth, 1687–1706.
Sir John Vanbrugh, 1666–1726.
Castle Howard, 1702–14.
Blenheim Palace, 1705–24.
Nicholas Hawksmoor, 1661–1736.
Clarendon Press at Oxford (with Vanbrugh), c. 1710.
III. Academic supremacy, c. 1720–70.
Richard Boyle, Earl of Burlington, 1695–1753.
General Wade's house in London, 1723.
Villa at Chiswick, 1729.
Assembly rooms at York, 1730–36.
Colen Campbell, d. 1729.
Burlington House in London, 1717.
Wanstead, 1720.
Mereworth Castle, 1723.
James Gibbs, 1682–1754.
Saint Martin-in-the-Fields' in London, 1721–26.
Radcliffe Library at Oxford, 1737–47.
William Kent, 1684–1748.
Holkham, 1734–61.
Horse Guards in London, begun 1742.

John Wood, c. 1704–54.
  Prior Park near Bath, 1734.
  The Circus at Bath, 1754 *ff*.
George Dance the elder, 1698–1768.
  Mansion House in London, 1739–53.
James Paine, 1725–89.
  Worksop Manor House, 1763.
Sir William Chambers, 1726–96.
  Rebuilding of Somerset House in London, 1776–90.

GERMANY

I. Baroque architecture, c. 1580–1730.
    Michaelskirche in Munich, 1583–97.
    Friedrichsbau at Heidelberg, 1601–07.
  Elias Holl, 1573–1646.
    Rathaus in Augsburg, 1614–20.
  Vincenzo Scamozzi, 1552–1616.
    Design for the Cathedral of Salzburg, 1606, executed
      1611–34.
  Andrea and Pietro Spezza.
    Loggia of the Waldstein Palace at Prague, 1629.
  Enrico Zuccali, 1643–1724.
    Theatine Church in Munich, 1663–75.
  Andreas Schlüter, 1664–1714.
    Royal Palace in Berlin, 1698 *ff*.
  Johann Bernard Fischer von Erlach, 1658–1723.
    Palace of Prince Eugene at Vienna, 1703.
    Church of San Carlo Borromeo in Vienna, 1716–37.
  Matthäus Daniel Pöppelmann, 1662–1736.
    Zwinger in Dresden, 1711–22
  Georg Bähr, 1666–1738.
    Frauenkirche in Dresden, 1726–40.
  Balthasar Neumann, 1687–1753.
    Schloss Bruchsal, 1720–43 (partly rococo).
II. Rococo, c. 1730–80.
    François de Cuvilliés the elder, 1698–1768.
      Amalienburg near Munich, 1734–39.
    Philipe de la Guêpière.
      Schloss Monrepos near Ludwigsburg, 1760–67.
      Schloss Solitude near Stuttgart, 1763–67.
    Georg von Knobelsdorff, 1699–1753.
      Neues Schloss at Charlottenburg, 1740–42.
      Sanssouci, begun 1745.

III. Rise of academism, c. 1740–80.
   Georg von Knobelsdorff, 1699–1753.
   Royal Opera House at Berlin, 1743.
   Karl von Gontard, 1738–1802.
   Communs at Potsdam, 1765–69.
   Towers in the Gendarmenmarkt in Berlin, 1780.

BIBLIOGRAPHICAL NOTE

General works covering the period are G. Ebe's *Die Spät-Renaissance*, 2 vols., 1886; C. Gurlitt's *Geschichte des Barockstiles, des Rococo und des Klassizismus (Geschichte der neueren Baukunst)*, 3 vols., 1887–89, of which the individual volumes are listed below, and P. Frankl's *Die Entwicklungsphasen der neueren Baukunst*, 1914. Further illustrations are provided by R. Dohme's *Barock- und Rococo-Architektur*, 3 vols., 1892. Books dealing with but one of the complementary tendencies of the times are P. Klopfer's *Von Palladio bis Schinkel: eine Charakteristik der Baukunst des Klassizismus (Geschichte der neueren Baukunst)*, 1911, and M. S. Briggs's *Baroque Architecture*, 1914. Discussions of the relation of the tendencies are H. Wölfflin's *Renaissance und Barock*, 1888, 2d ed., 1907; A. Schmarzow's *Barock und Rokoko*, 1897, and K. Escher's *Barock und Klassizismus*, 1910.

Italy. A. E. Brinckmann's *Baukunst des XVII. und XVIII. Jahrhunderts in den romanischen Ländern*, 1919, supersedes Gurlitt's volume. It may be supplemented by the photographs reproduced in C. Ricci's *Baroque Architecture in Italy*, 1912, 1922; and Magni's *Il barocco a Roma*. Specially concerned with Rome are A. Riegl's *Die Entstehung der Barockkunst in Rom*, 1908, and Escher's *Barock und Klassizismus*. For the villas and gardens see M. L. Gothein's *Geschichte der Gartenkunst*, 2 vols., 1914, Chapter VII; H. I. Triggs's *The Art of Garden Design in Italy*, 1906, and G. Lowell's *Smaller Italian Villas and Farmhouses*, 2 vols., 1916 *ff.*, A. T. Bolton's *The Gardens of Italy;* L. Dami's *Italian Gardens;* and J. C. Shepherd and G. A. Jellicoe, *Italian Gardens of the Renaissance*.

France. The principal accounts are those of Brinckmann, listed above, and of Blomfield. The works of Geymüller and of Ward on Renaissance architecture cover the post-Renaissance period as well. Topographical works with large photographic reproductions include those of L. Deshairs on Bordeaux, Dijon, and Aix, and those of R. le Nail and C. Gurlitt on Lyons. Contet's and Vacquier's *Les vieux hôtels de Paris*, 15 vols., 1908–24, covers Paris in a similar way, while each of the great royal palaces has several works devoted especially to it. Three works by P. Planat and E. Rümler: *Le style Louis XIV.*, *Le style Louis XV.*, and *Le style Louis XVI.*, 1907, give similar plates for the periods indicated by their titles. Garden architecture is treated in M. Fouquier's *De l'art des jardins du XVe au XXe siècle*, 1911, and in H. Stein's *Les jardins de France*. The general biographical works covering French architects are supplemented by E. F. Dilke's *French Architects and Sculptors of the XVIII Century*, 1900.

England. The principal work is R. Blomfield's *History of Renaissance Architecture in England, 1500–1800*, 2 vols., 1897, of which the major part is devoted to the period after 1615. It includes a full bibliography of contemporary and modern works. A series of large photographs and measured drawings is furnished by J. Belcher and M. E. Macartney's *Later Renaissance Architecture in England*, 2 vols., 1897–1901. Domestic architecture is specially treated in J. A. Gotch's *The English Home from Charles I to George IV*, 1918; H. A. Tipping's *English Homes*, vols. 4 and 5; M. E. Macartney's *English Houses and Gardens in the XVII. and XVIII. Centuries*, 1908; H. Field and M. Bunney's *English Domestic Architecture of the XVII. and XVIII. Centuries*, 1905 (smaller buildings); T. V. Sadlier and P. L. Dickinson's *Georgian Mansions in Ireland*, 1915; M. A. Green's *The Eighteenth Century Architecture of Bath*, 1904; and A. E. Richardson and C. L. Gill's *London Houses from 1660–1820*. For individual biography see E. B. Chancellor's *The Lives of the British Architects*, 1909.

Spain. O. Schubert's *Geschichte des Barock in Spanien* (*Geschichte der neueren Baukunst*), 1908, is the authoritative discussion. Further illustrations are furnished by the works of Uhde, Junghändel, and others listed under the Renaissance in Spain.

Germany. M. Wackernazel's *Baukunst ces XVII. u. XVIII. Jahrhunderts in den Germanischen Ländern*, 1915, supersedes the pioneer work of C. Gurlitt, 1889. Ample illustration is furnished by Dohme's work, mentioned above; by Lambert and Stahl's *Motive der deutschen Architektur*, vol. 2, 1892; P. Schmoll and G. Staehelin's *Barockbauten in Deutschland*, 1904; O. Aufleger's *Süddeutsche Architektur . . . im XVIII. Jahrhundert*, 2 vols., 1891–95; and, in more convenient compass, in H. Popp's *Architektur der Barock und Rokokozeit in Deutschland und der Schweiz*, 1914. J. Braun's *Die Kirchenbauten der deutschen Jesuiten*, 2 vols., 1908–10, covers a notable series of churches. C. Gurlitt's *Historische Städtebilder*, 11 vols., 1901–09, is largely devoted to German cities important in this period.

CHAPTER XII

MODERN ARCHITECTURE

The mid-eighteenth century witnessed the beginnings of a series of changes, political and cultural, scarcely less important than those of the fifteenth century. Although many of these movements were extensions or logical consequences of those of the Renaissance, their importance and approximately simultaneous appearance justify the idea that they constitute the beginning of a new era, specifically modern. The freedom of inquiry applied in the Renaissance to letters and art, and in the Reformation to religion, was now applied to history, politics, and science. A multitude of individual tendencies combined to initiate the age of archeological discovery and historical research, of revolution and democracy, of natural science and invention, of capitalism and colonial empire. These were destined to affect not only the stylistic aspect of architecture, but equally the nature of the prevailing types of buildings and methods of construction, as well as the extent to which these were diffused over the world.

General characteristics. Although the kaleidoscopic interplay of forces makes it difficult to generalize regarding the architectural characteristics of the period, they may be conceived broadly as the result of a synthesis of retrospective and progressive tendencies, which exist side by side, not unlike the academic and baroque tendencies in the previous period. In matters of form and detail it is the newly won historical understanding of previous styles which has been chiefly influential, resulting in a series of attempted revivals followed by a season of eclecticism. In matters of plan and construction, however, the growth of material civilization and the development of new forms of government and commerce have produced a multitude of novel types of buildings as well as constant changes in the form and importance of the old types, making every supposed revival unconsciously a new creation. A conscious movement to give the new functional types and structural systems an expression that shall also be novel and characteristic contends today with a return to pure form.

Complexity of development. It thus comes about that, within a century and a half of coherent development in practical matters, there is a series of subordinate phases distinguished by very different forms of detail. Although a greater or less number of these phases might be distinguished, the principal ones may be considered as four, corresponding generally to literary and cultural phases: classicism, romanticism, eclecticism (all outgrowths chiefly of the historical attitude), and functionalism (primarily an outgrowth of natural science). As each of these phases, like the academic and baroque movements, varies in character and duration in different countries, it becomes even more difficult to preserve a strictly chronological and local order during the discussion of the most modern architecture than it is during the discussion of the architecture immediately preceding. In view of the fundamentally international character of the architectural tendencies, and their uniform order of predominance in all countries, it is more fruitful to consider the individual movements in their general sequence rather than individual countries one by one. The continuity of development in any given individual type, and the simultaneous existence and interplay of movements in any given country, scarcely less characteristic, may be indicated by the way.

Classicism: study of classical monuments. The first of the modern movements to affect architectural forms was the flood of archeological discovery and publication in the middle of the eighteenth century. Hitherto the fund of knowledge concerning ancient buildings, aside from the details of the orders, was surprisingly small. Writers and engravers, in general, had been chiefly concerned with the construction of academic theories, or the representation of the buildings of their own day—both supposedly based on the antique, but really departing from it with the greatest freedom. Palladio, to be sure, had published rationalized restorations of the

Roman temples as early as 1570, and in 1682 Desgodetz had issued his far more accurate drawings of the monuments of the city of Rome.   These were but isolated forerunners, however, of the multitude of works which now commenced to appear, many of them illustrating buildings hitherto unregarded or entirely unknown.   In 1730 Lord Burlington brought out many of Palladio's drawings of Roman buildings which had lain a century and a half in manuscript.   In 1741 the engraver Piranesi issued his first plates, the commencement of a colossal series of views of ancient ruins and fragments, which placed before the public the great wealth of Roman architecture in Italy, and, with their striking artistic qualities, powerfully stimulated the vogue of the antique. In the fifties there began to appear illustrated works dealing with Herculaneum, and later with Pompeii, the buried Campanian cities which exhibited Roman art in a way so much more lively and intimate than the ruined and despoiled monuments of the capital.   The knowledge of Roman architecture was further enriched by the study and publication of the temples at Palmyra and Baalbek by Wood and Dawkins (1753 and 1757) and of the palace at Spalato by Robert Adam and Clérisseau (1764)—buildings differing widely in composition and detail from the conventional conceptions of the academic theorists.   Scarcely later came the revelation of Greek monuments, hitherto known only by the vague accounts of a few travelers.   In 1750 and 1751 Cochin and Soufflot were drawing and measuring at Pæstum;   Stuart and Revett were at Athens.   A few years later publications regarding these and other sites began to pour forth.   Leroy's *Athens* appeared in 1758, the first volume of Stuart and Revett's *Antiquities of Athens* in 1762, Major's *Pæstum* in 1768, Chandler's *Ionia* in 1769, with a stream of successors of the same character reaching well into the nineteenth century.   At the same time the Comte de Caylus and Winckelmann were laying the foundations of archeology and of the history of art, Winckelmann asserting for the first time the superiority of Greek architecture and sculpture over those of the Romans.

Reaction against the baroque and against academic formulæ. The increasing appreciation of antiquity was coincident with independent tendencies, already visible in contemporary architecture. The rationalistic advocacy of the primitive orders by Laugier in 1752, the appeal for a "noble simplicity and quiet grandeur" which Winckelmann made in 1755, were based rather on antithesis to contemporary art than on a real knowledge of the art of the ancients. The reaction from the extreme crescendo of the baroque had already begun, even in Italy, in such works as the Superga and the façade of the Lateran. In France the manner of Soufflot prevailed over the rococo, while in England the reversion from Wren and Vanbrugh to strict Palladianism was universal. It was felt that, in the striving for animation, picturesqueness, and originality, dignity and earnestness had been lost. It was these sober qualities, which so many were seeking, that were now found superlatively exemplified in certain of the works of antiquity.

Characteristics and development of classicism. The result was that the current of practice was turned toward the closer imitation of classical forms, and ultimately even of classical dispositions and ensembles. Architects approached the antique directly, and not through Palladio or Vitruvius. Hitherto the orders had been used principally in the decoration of wall surfaces; columns and pilasters had been freely grouped and often placed above a high basement. The temple portico, except in England, where the example of Palladio was directly followed, had been used very rarely or not at all. Now, on the other hand, it became almost essential, its columns closely and equally spaced, rising directly from the ground. The membering of walls was renounced in favor of the simplest jointing or rustication. Forms like those of the rectangular temple and the Pantheon, determined for the most part in advance, had now to be employed to meet not only the traditional problems of the church, the school, and the dwelling, but also a multitude of new problems in the legislative and other governmental buildings, the banks, exchanges, and commercial structures, the museums and theaters, assembly and concert halls, the prisons and institutions which great political, economic, and social changes were bringing into being. Academic conservatism, especially in France, however, hindered the literal imitation of ancient precedent, just in proportion as it differed from the currently accepted canons.   Thus, although the Roman and the Greek tendencies ran side by side almost from the beginning, the Roman remained predominant until shortly before 1820. Even then, when Greek forms surpassed the Roman in popular favor, important monuments of Roman character still continued to be built.

Roman supremacy. The beginnings in England.   The classical revival in architecture developed first in England, where the work of Burlington and Kent gave a point of departure for that of Robert Adam and his brothers (1759 *ff.*).   Although they created no building of such monumental quality as Sainte Geneviève in Paris, they gave a powerful stimulus to the employment of more strictly Roman forms, especially for the treatment of interiors.   Free-standing columns, coffered vaults and domes, statued niches and bas-reliefs marked the principal rooms even of private dwellings (Fig. 255), while a delicate surface decoration of vases, griffins, and garlands in stucco, with Wedgwood medallions and slender furniture designed in harmony, lent the rest an air of unusual distinction.   Although Piranesi and others had anticipated many of these features or assisted the brothers Adam with them, it was the skill of the Adams which first welded them into a coherent style.   Simultaneously came the first work inspired by Greek models, in a few designs by Stuart and by Revett.   The details of the Greek orders, the employment of antæ and anthemia, the purity of decoration, refinement and severity, with a preference for the heavier orders, gradually permeated the academic style of buildings, which still long continued.

The beginnings in France.   In Sainte Geneviéve, in Paris (1759–90), Soufflot thought to imitate the portico and dome of the Pantheon in Rome (Fig. 252).   For the first time in France there is a free-standing portico of the full height of the façade, its Corinthian columns no less than sixty-two feet high. This soon had its successors in such buildings as the Grand Thêâtre at Bordeaux (1777–80), by Victor Louis, with its colossal portico of twelve columns, and in the urban dwellings of Roman cast.   The characteristic features of these houses, a peristylar *cour d'honneur* with a triumphal arch at the grille, a temple portico at the door, and a saucer dome over the circular projecting salon toward the garden, are well combined in the Hôtel de Salm (1782–86), now the Palace of the Legion of Honor. The interiors lost the flowing lines of the rococo and turned to the delicate, simple paneling and refined

FIG. 252—PARIS. CHURCH OF SAINTE GENEVIEVE. (THE PANTHEON)

imitation of antique motives under Adam influence which mark the style of Louis XVI.

Literal imitation of classical models. Monuments. Meanwhile, however, a more strict imitation of classical examples was beginning, extending not merely to individual details and elements, but to whole monuments. This appeared first in the sentimental or landscape gardens, which were decorated with miniature classic temples of ruins. Stuart enriched the repertoire with the Monument of Lysicrates and other Athenian types. Ledoux, in his octroi gates and stations for Paris (1780–88), made liberal use of classical motives—the

triumphal column, the exterior peristyle, the circular temple—
even using the Greek Doric column without a base. Lang-
hans took the Propylæa at Athens as his model for the Brandenburg Gate in Berlin (1788–91), although he used a more
Roman type of column and introduced other notable changes
which resulted in an original creation (Fig. 253). The French

FIG. 253—BERLIN.   BRANDENBURG GATE

Republic and its successors, with their studied imitation of
Rome, naturally reproduced its monuments also; and Napoleon outdid all others with the column of the Place Vendôme
(1805–10), modeled on that of Trajan, the Arc du Carrousel
(1806), modeled on the Arch of Domitian ("Constantine"), and
finally the colossal Arc de l'Etoile by Chalgrin (Fig. 254). In
contrast to most of its predecessors this showed great freedom
in the rendering of the antique motive, with a puristic tendency
very characteristic of French architects of the revival period.

Other literal imitations. Even in buildings intended for
practical use, the literal following of classical prototypes began,
on the initiative of rulers and statesmen. Catharine II.
commissioned Clérisseau in 1780 to design her a dwelling
which should be strictly Roman. For his Temple of Glory,

now the church of the Madeleine, Napoleon insisted on the
selection of the design by Vignon (1807), a peristylar Corinthian
temple with its interior treatment suggested by the halls of
the thermæ.   The design of the Bourse (1808–27) also included
an external peristyle, but its great breadth did not permit a
pediment.   In all these works Roman forms were employed,

FIG. 254—PARIS.   ARC DE TRIOMPHE DE L'ETOILE

although in the interiors of the Empire style—developed by
Percier and Fontaine on the lines of the Adams and Louis
XVI.—Greek decorative elements were abundant, and even
Egyptian forms became popular as a result of Napoleon's
Eastern campaign.

The Greek supremacy.   The Greek supremacy began after
the Napoleonic wars, with important works first in England
but later especially in Germany.   Again, as in the case of
the Roman revival, the use of Greek orders and larger elements preceded the bodily imitation of the temple.   Among
British buildings the High School at Edinburgh (1825–29), by

FIG. 256—LONDON. THE BANK OF ENGLAND, LOTHBURY ANGLE. (RICHARDSON)

FIG. 255—KEDLESTON. THE DOMED SALOON

Thomas Hamilton, is especially noteworthy, no less for its plastic handling of Greek forms in the wings and terraces than for its reproduction of the portico of the Theseum in the central feature (Fig. 257). In Germany a great personality, Friedrich Schinkel, succeeded in combining classical spirit with modern requirements in a series of works of which the Royal Theater in Berlin (1818–21) is perhaps the most notable (Fig. 258). Later, under the patronage of Ludwig I. of Bavaria, Leo von Klenze carried still further the imitation of classical ensembles, culminating in the Walhalla at Regensburg (1830–42), a reproduction of the Parthenon, raised on a mighty terraced substructure. The idea of such a reproduction had long captivated designers: Gilly had proposed it as early as 1797 for a memorial to Frederick the Great; the National Monument in Edinburgh had been begun in accordance with it in 1829.

Reaction from literal classicism. With these buildings, most of them, to be sure, commemorative monuments without exacting practical functions, the high tide of classicism was reached, and a reflux set in toward more rationalistic use of classical forms. The temple portico was abandoned, and the Greek suggestion appeared only in the fondness for the Doric order, the delicacy of the projections, the elegance of the profiles. In France, where the Roman tendency was strongest and the academic resistance to actual copying was most tenacious, this last phase of the classical movement was the first in which Greek influence was really much felt, and it thus received the name of néo-grec. By other tendencies which they incorporate, however, as well as by their date, the néo-grec buildings belong, in spite of the name applied to them, less with the revivalist movement than with the following phases of eclecticism and functionalism.

Types of buildings during the classical movement: administrative. Counter to the extreme formal tendency of classicism —to assimilate all buildings to a single classical type—there had constantly been the utilitarian tendency to differentiate types of buildings more and more in accordance with their increasingly specialized functions. This had already begun under the old régime, but it was powerfully stimulated by the Revolution, which detached many governmental functions

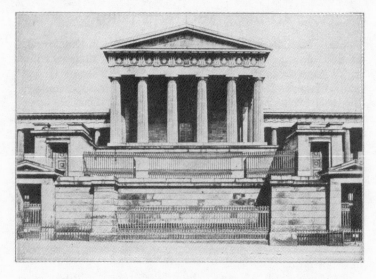

FIG. 257—EDINBURGH. THE HIGH SCHOOL. (RICHARDSON)

FIG. 258—BERLIN. ROYAL THEATER

from the palace, and threw theaters and museums open to all. The earliest of modern administrative buildings, distinct from the palace, were developed in Great Britain, where the Admiralty, Somerset House, and a number of other buildings fall quite within the period of academic supremacy. Even in France, however, specialized governmental functions had also commenced to find monumental expression, in the Mint (1771–75) and in the rebuilding of the Palace of Justice after 1776. All of these buildings, however, are essentially on the scheme of the palace, as their multitude of small rooms permits; and even the latest of them have merely a Doric solidity and earnestness to suggest this specific character. A more pronounced suggestion of governmental functions was first given in the grandiose façade of the Four Courts in Dublin, with its commanding portico and classical dome, built by James Gandon in 1784–96.

Legislative buildings. Such a new expression for governmental functions was soon found also in legislative buildings, where one or more large deliberative halls forced the adoption of a great scale. The Parliament House at Dublin had led the way as early as 1730–39, with an arcaded portico and a domed hall suggested by the Pantheon, but carried out with Palladian forms. The seats were arranged in a semicircle in one-half the octagonal room. For the meeting of the States-General at Versailles in 1789, an impressive basilican room with Doric columns was improvised within an indifferent building. Here at first the throne was at one end, the seats along the other three sides; but when the body was reconstructed as the National Assembly the chair was moved to the center of a long side and the seats arranged in a double horseshoe. The hall with semicircular form, on the lines of a Roman theater, was afterward developed in the deliberative halls of the Palais Bourbon in Paris, 1795–1833, and was widely followed on the Continent. For the unicameral legislative building a powerful external expression was found in the Corinthian portico of twelve columns prefixed to the Palais Bourbon in 1807.

Prisons. Related to political movements was the agitation for the reform of methods of punishment, first by the substitution of imprisonment for the death penalty in many cases, and later by the improvement of the prisons which this new order had caused to multiply.   Characteristic of the first phase was Newgate Prison in London (1770–82), designed by George Dance, which, with its vast rusticated walls and narrow doorways, was the very embodiment of force (Fig. 259).   Humanity, sanitation, or reformation of the prisoners, however, had little consideration until well into the nineteenth century, and the form of prison which then resulted was very different. Ideas of correction through solitary confinement or disciplined labor ultimately caused, about 1835, the universal adoption of individual cells and of a highly organized system of separate workrooms and yards for various classes of prisoners.

Banks, exchanges, and commercial structures.   Other novel structures were called into being by the commercial and capitalistic developments of the age, and proved to find congenial garb in the prevailing classical mode.   The monumental portico placed before the bank or exchange suggested the power of finance or the stability of credit, while the blank walls which classical purism had made its own exactly met the necessities of vast docks and warehouses.   In the rebuilding of the first and greatest of the modern financial institutions, the Bank of England (1788–1835), Sir John Soane had to design a windowless exterior, with a multitude of great halls and light courts.   Although the general external treatment with columns and blank windows is less frank than some other solutions of similar problems, certain features, like the Lothbury Angle (Fig. 256) or the Lothbury Courtyard, are masterpieces of free composition with classical forms, while the interiors are full of dignity.   The Bourse in Paris and the Royal Exchange in London (1840–44), with their colossal porticoes, continued the monumental tradition.   The utilitarian side of commerce had its most notable embodiment in the Halle au Blé in Paris (1783), a circular, domed market-hall, destitute of extraneous adornment, but effective by its very simplicity and adaptation to purpose.

Theaters.   Not less novel were the theaters, museums, and concert-halls, which responded to the growth of democracy as well as to the development of music and of archeology. Such features had hitherto usually been adjuncts of the palace; now they became detached, and subjects for special treatment. The first of the independent theaters to receive a monumental exterior had been the Royal Opera in Berlin (1741–42), for which Frederick the Great had insisted on an English Palladian form. The Grand Théâtre at Bordeaux (1777–80), with its still more classical treatment, was followed in the Odéon in Paris (1799–1802) and in many others, especially in France and England. All these were cubical masses, into

FIG. 259—LONDON. OLD NEWGATE PRISON. (RICHARDSON)

which stage, auditorium, foyer, and vestibule were fitted. A more varied form made its appearance in Schinkel's Royal Theater in Berlin (1818–21), with which a concert-room, ball-room, and refreshment-rooms had also to be incorporated (Fig. 258). Wings containing these adjuncts were added to the main mass, which dominates them by its high-gabled clerestory, its monumental steps, and its Ionic portico, all treated with Hellenic forms of slight relief and with severely classical ornaments. The ultimate classical solution of the theater problem in Germany was a different one, for which, not the temple portico, but the ancient theater itself served as a model. In this scheme the circular end of the auditorium, with its surrounding corridor, formed the façade, clearly indicating the nature of the building, but involving considerable sacrifices in the vestibules, foyers, and stairs which had become such prominent features of the modern theater. The most notable example, the old Court Theater in Dresden (1838–41), shows the persistence of this type even when strict classical forms were not employed (Fig. 264).

Museums and concert-halls. In giving the museum an independent form Germany led the way, even in the eighteenth century. In the early nineteenth it created two notable monuments, the Glyptothek in Munich by Von Klenze (1816-30) and the Old Museum in Berlin by Schinkel (1824–28). These were both severe compositions in the Greek Ionic order, which was used also in the British Museum (1825–47), designed by Sir Charles Barry. For the problem of the concert-hall, Schinkel had given a solution of the greatest elegance in connection with the theater in Berlin. An auditorium for vast popular concerts is the principal feature of Saint George's Hall in Liverpool (1838–54) which includes also a smaller recital-hall, two court-rooms, and public offices. The exterior—by the gifted and youthful Elmes—with its two vast Corinthian porticoes, its commanding attic, its magnificent terraces and approaches, is justly famous as among the most monumental of all modern structures (Fig. 260).

Other types. Churches. For the problems already consecrated by time—the church, the college, the house, or palace—classicism did not achieve new solutions of the same importance. This was partly because the satisfactory solutions already attained in the previous period tended to be followed, partly because the problems themselves were becoming secondary to the new ones of the age, and partly because other forces tended before long to take these very problems entirely out of the hands of the classical architects. In the church, as elsewhere, the imitation of classical models was attempted, both the rectangular-temple type and the Pantheon type being followed. One of the most notable of the revivalist churches was Saint Pancras in London, in which the beautiful details of the Erechtheum were imitated—the North Porch for the entrance portico, the Porch of the Maidens for the sacristies, with the Athenian Tower of the Winds, twice repeated, for the steeple. Chalgrin, in the church of Saint

Philippe du Roule in Paris, was inspired by the Christian-Roman basilica, initiating a notable series. Others, however, followed the established academic types, with a tall central dome or two western towers, merely adopting a more classical portico and details.

Domestic architecture. Few palaces were built during the period which classicism shared with revolution. Even Napoleon contented himself with remodeling the interiors of three among the many palaces left by the old régime. The

FIG. 260—LIVERPOOL.   SAINT GEORGE'S HALL.   (RICHARDSON)

great country mansions henceforth likewise multiplied less rapidly, although magnificent town houses continued to be built. Like the hôtels under Louis XVI., already described, all these had usually a portico of Roman or Greek detail, and often a circular salon suggested by the Pantheon. The less ambitious town houses, solidly built up in blocks, had usually a most restrained treatment, depending on the proportions of stories and openings alone. Often the town-planning traditions of the previous period were continued by the unified design of the houses in whole streets and squares, as in the Adelphi and Regent's Quadrant in London, or the Rue de Rivoli in Paris. Colonnades or arcades were now sometimes adopted in the lower story, to shelter the foot passengers and to increase the effect of Roman magnificence. In the minor European country houses, a type most frequent in England, there was some attempt, about 1820, to imitate the temple, although not without breaking its unity by projections or wings. All these types of domestic architecture, however, as well as the classical types of churches, were gradually swept away by the rise of romanticism, which for a time even bade fair to prevail in modern architecture as a whole.

Romanticism: cultural changes. Romanticism in architecture, like classicism, had its precursors and companions in cultural and literary movements. Their origins in some cases were quite as early as those of the neo-classical tendency. The modern appreciation of landscape and the idea of the landscape garden had begun early in the eighteenth century. Sentimentalism came in toward the middle of the century with Richardson and Gray, and on the Continent, in the sixties, with Rousseau, who also transplanted and quickened the cult of nature. At the same time England and Germany awakened to an appreciation of their northern, national heritage, the mythology and legend, the history and art of the Middle Ages. The importance of the Goths for the cultural development of Europe was affirmed in the dialogues of *The Investigator* in 1755; the principle of nationalism in history, literature, and art was announced by Herder and his friends in *Von deutscher Art und Kunst* in 1773. The ideas thus implanted, however, did not bear their full fruit, even in literature, until the beginning of the nineteenth century, with Wordsworth and Coleridge, Byron and Scott, with the German romanticists who influenced Madame de Staël, and, through her, made way for Hugo and the French of the thirties. With all these men the emotion and enthusiasm of the individual, rather than the following of academic rules, were proclaimed as the springs of artistic success. The emotional upheaval was naturally accompanied by a revival of religious faith, which found its expression both in the glorification of traditional Christianity by Chateaubriand and the leaders of the Oxford movement and in the preaching of a personal and naturalistic belief by Schleiermacher.

The medieval revival in architecture. Picturesqueness and

naturalness, nationality and religion, all seemed embodied, not in classic architecture, but in Gothic, then a synonym for the art of the Middle Ages.   A revival of medieval architecture in northern lands thus grew out of racial and contemporary conditions, as the renaissance of classic architecture had developed in the Italy of the fifteenth century.   Moreover, just as classic architecture had never quite died out in Italy during the Middle Ages, but had lingered to provide a con-genial soil for the revival, so Gothic architecture had never quite ceased to be practised, especially in England. Traditional survivals of Gothic had continued in country churches and in the Oxford colleges until the time of the Restoration, and the reconstruction and repair of buildings in the old style went on under Sir Christopher Wren and even in the middle of the eighteenth century.   At the same time a historical interest in the heritage of medieval monuments was evidenced by antiquarian works such as the *Monasticon Anglicanum* (1655–73) and publications dealing with individual towns and cathedrals.   Neither the books nor the buildings show any very accurate knowledge of medieval forms of detail or prin-ciples of construction, yet they furnished a living stock on which the romantic idea could be grafted.   It thus came about that England, where the romantic movement in litera-ture was earliest and strongest, was also essentially the home of romanticism in architecture.

Origins.   Pseudo-Chinese and Gothic designs.   The earliest purely voluntary departures from classical architecture in the eighteenth century had scarcely the serious motives of later efforts, being suggested rather by search for novelty and modishness, in the sportive, trivial structures which the taste of the time demanded for garden shelters and the assemblage of intimate parties.   The reports of Eastern travelers had aroused enthusiasm for things Chinese, and as early as 1740 designs for porticoes and pavilions supposedly Chinese were being executed side by side with miniature classic temples, both in France and England.   By 1750 others supposedly Gothic appeared in England, as similar to the pseudo-Chinese in their fantastic flourishes as they were dissimilar to their prototypes, still so imperfectly understood.   In the land-scape gardens which were already universal in England, such buildings now began to acquire a sentimental significance, as expressing to the beholder different moods which the scenes were designed to evoke. The Gothic, symbolizing the ideals of rusticity and unworldliness which were then fashionable, rapidly gained ground.

The Gothic revival in England. First phase, c. 1760–1830. The castellated style. The first to extend the imitation of Gothic to a building of more important type was Horace Walpole, in the remodeling of his villa, Strawberry Hill (1753–76). He was inspired by the same enthusiastic admiration of the Middle Ages which appears in his pioneer historical romance *The Castle of Otranto* (1764), and he hoped to give a model of pure Gothic in contrast to the ignorant perversions which were in vogue. With this idea he imitated porches and battlements, doors, ceilings, and chimney-pieces from old work, but with complete unconsciousness of their inconsistency in periods of origin, and even with utter disregard for the original purposes of the designs. The resulting "castellated style," as it was called, was widely adopted in country seats, on many of which such well-known academic architects as George Dance and Sir William Chambers were employed. At the same time the first churches with similar forms were undertaken.

Ecclesiastical influence. In the last quarter of the eighteenth century new forces furthered the movement, while giving it a more ecclesiastical cast. A new generation of antiquaries poured forth works on the medieval churches, at once more numerous and more adequately illustrated than those of a century earlier. Attention was attracted to the repair of the structures themselves, and restorations were attempted, although with insufficient knowledge and often with disastrous results. James Wyatt, the chief of the restorers, had also a great vogue as an architect of domestic buildings. Ecclesiastical names were often given to these, and the details of their windows, buttresses, and towers were derived rather from churches than from the old manorial halls. Fonthill Abbey (1796–1814), the extravagant creation of the romancer William Beckford, was the most famous of these; Eaton Hall (1803–14) was another noteworthy example (Fig. 261). Although religious feeling in England at this time was still at a low ebb, and new churches were few, an increasing number of these followed the Gothic style, as it was then understood.

Literal imitation of medieval models. A great improvement in grammatical accuracy of detail, as well as an appreciation of chronological consistency of style, followed the publication, in 1819 and 1820, of Rickman's *Attempt to Discriminate the Styles of English Architecture,* and of Pugin and Willson's

FIG. 261—EATON HALL BEFORE ALTERATION IN 1870.   (EASTLAKE)

Specimens of Gothic Architecture. These books, which provided for the first time a tolerable historical account of the development of the style, and accurate geometrical drawings of its examples, opened an era of literal copying of whole features, conscientiously culled from this or that period, most frequently the later Perpendicular.   The inclusion of drawings of domestic work helped bring about an abandonment of the ecclesiastical forms previously adopted for dwellings, in favor of a domestic treatment dependent on the grouping of masses, gables, and chimneys—the so-called "baronial style."   In planning, which was still dominated unconsciously by classical ideals, a strict symmetry was preserved; while in construction and decoration lack of means and of sympathetic craftsmen prevented a reproduction of the spirit of the rich medieval work chosen for imitation.

Second phase, 1830–70. Pugin. The second and far more important phase of the revival opened with the work of Augustus Welby Pugin, a son of the elder Pugin. He displayed at once a freedom and fertility of invention with Gothic forms which had hitherto been unknown, and a zeal for their exclusive adoption which had the force of religious fanaticism. In his designs, 1830–52, he sought and attained a medieval picturesqueness of plan and mass; in his studios he trained carvers and metal-workers to execute the details of his facile designs; in his writings he preached the revival of Christian architecture, as he called it, for civil as well as for religious and domestic buildings. At the same time began the revival of ritual in the Anglican church, and the study of church architecture in relation to ritual arrangements. As a result of all this, Gothic became the accepted style not only for country residences but for churches, which recovered alike their medieval functions and their medieval form. Architects, many of whom henceforth devoted themselves exclusively to Gothic, began to design, within the accepted English Gothic modes, with greater confidence in themselves.

The Houses of Parliament. Simultaneously with the first of Pugin's publications (1836), the cause of medievalism achieved a triumph in the retention of the Gothic style in the rebuilding of the palace at Westminster—the new Houses of Parliament, executed between 1840 and 1860 (Fig. 262). The architect, Sir Charles Barry, was a man experienced in design with classical as well as with Gothic forms, and the building was currently described as having Tudor details on a classic body. The emphasis in massing, however, is by no means of a classical type, for it is laid not on the essential components of the plan, the two chambers, but on towers which mark the royal entrance and support the clock. Notable qualities of the design are the practical solution of extremely complex problems in plan, including accommodation to portions of the old structure still remaining, and the picturesque employment of the magnificent river site. The employment of medieval forms in a national monument of such importance, of course, gave the revival another great impetus.

Ruskin. An impulse of different sort, yet equally or more powerful, was given meanwhile by the writings of John Ruskin. In his *Seven Lamps of Architecture* (1849) and his *Stones of Venice* (1851) he urged a return to the methods as well as the forms of the Middle Ages, and this not simply on grounds of religion or of ritual, but even of morality. The emancipation

FIG. 262—LONDON. HOUSES OF PARLIAMENT

of the individual craftsmen from the modern industrial system was to be at once an end in itself and a means to the attainment of true beauty in architecture. This was proclaimed to lie not in abstract qualities, such as proportion, but in honesty of materials and of structure, and in evidence of human devotion and thought, appearing above all in the sculptured and painted details. Such an animation of detail and color he found especially in the marble capitals and polychrome walls and mosaics of Italy, to which his admirers soon turned for inspiration. It was at the moment when architects were wearying of the restrictions of antiquarian national precedent, and seeking a greater liberty of invention. Thus many who were impatient with Ruskin's principles took advantage of this or that individual suggestion.

Victorian Gothic. The result of all these forces was the so-called Victorian Gothic, distinguished by great elaboration of detail, polychromy of materials, including marble, brick, and encaustic tiles, and a leaning toward Italian forms of "surface Gothic" rather than the northern "linear Gothic." Among the leading exponents of the style were Sir Gilbert Scott (1811–78) and his pupil George Edmund Street (1824–81), who in long and active careers ran through a number of its phases; and William Butterfield (1814–1900) who strove to create a novel development with a variety of Gothic and modern elements. Scott and others of the group even extended their practice beyond the bounds of England by successful competition against Continental architects of all schools.

"The battle of the styles." By 1855 the adherents of Gothic were strong enough to challenge the supremacy of classic architecture in secular buildings generally. To the growing conviction that each style was exclusively appropriate to certain uses—the Gothic to churches, colleges, and rural architecture, the classic to public buildings and urban dwellings—they opposed the traditional belief that a single style must prevail, and maintained that the Gothic was superior for all purposes. Thus the "battle of the styles," which had enkindled over the Houses of Parliament, continued to be fought in a wider field, and with a zeal unknown outside of England. The Gothicists were not without their successes, for although Lord Palmerston finally forced Scott to substitute a classical scheme for his accepted Gothic design for the Foreign Office (1858–73), victories soon followed in the Manchester Assize Courts (1859–64) and Town Hall (1868–69), both by Alfred Waterhouse. In the sixties the influence of Viollet-le-Duc and of French Gothic, with its greater structural logic, gave the movement a fresh element of strength as well as fresh material. With the adoption of Street's design for the national Law Courts in 1868, the adherents of Gothic felt their cause vindicated. The building proved, however, to mark the end of their supremacy. By the time of its completion, 1884, it met little but condemnation, and the conclusion was outspoken that Gothic was unfit for public

buildings. The fundamental cause lay less in certain defects in the building than in the gradual change of public taste. The belated enthusiasm of the revivalists could no longer withstand the eclecticism which elsewhere prevailed so widely, and which had steadily gained strength even in England.

Romanticism in Germany; Gothic and Romanesque. On the Continent the medieval revival was most vital in Germany, where, as in England, it was associated with a nationalistic movement. Goethe's youthful panegyric on the cathedral of Strasburg (1773) long remained alone, however, and it was not until after the Wars of Liberation that the brothers Boisserée awakened a general interest in the artistic monuments of the German past. Pseudo-Gothic buildings had appeared as accessories to the landscape gardens on English models since their introduction about 1770, but the Gothic style was not seriously considered for important buildings before the time of Schinkel, who made a Gothic project for the cathedral of Berlin in 1819. Of his two projects for the Werderkirche (1825), the Gothic and not the classical one was chosen. The exterior, as was to be expected, was Gothic rather in detail than in spirit and constructive principle. The interior was conceived with an insight in advance of the day. Henceforth the style was frequently employed, with steadily increasing knowledge, in the building of churches, and occasionally in other buildings, although it never became universal, and even as the medium of romantic expression had to share honors with the still more national Romanesque. The strongest supporter of the Romanesque was Friedrich von Gärtner in Munich (1792–1847), whose buildings, however, show a large measure of Italian influence. The most notable modern Gothic church in German lands, which may still be considered an outgrowth of the revival, is the Votive Church in Vienna, built by Ferstel in 1853–79, on the scheme of a cathedral with western towers and spires.

Romanticism in France. In France before the romantic outburst of the thirties the strength of classical architecture was so great that, although the "hamlets" of Trianon and Chantilly initiated, as early as 1775, garden architecture on English models in a style supposedly Gothic, the mode long remained without serious adoption. Meanwhile, however, the Musée des Monuments Français, collected by Alexandre Lenoir from the churches and châteaux destroyed by the Revolution, was revealing to the French the glories of their own medieval art; and the *Histoire de l'art* of Seroux d'Agincourt (1811–23), the first general work devoted to the arts of the Middle Ages, registered a new appreciation of them. By 1825 such a work as the chapel at Les Herbiers in Vendée could be constructed, with tolerable knowledge of the details of French Gothic, although still with rigid classical symmetry. A more popular appreciation was stimulated by Victor Hugo's *Notre-Dame de Paris* in 1831, and a more scientific understanding was created by the archeologists De Caumont and Lassus, and above all by the architect Viollet-le-Duc (1814–79), who developed, in the years following 1840, a wide activity as a restorer of medieval buildings and as a writer on the art of the Middle Ages. In his great *Dictionnaire de l'architecture française du XI. au XVI. siècle* (1854–68) he emphasized the idea that the principles of Gothic architecture were essentially structural, and thus his influence tended to make current designs in the style more logical and organic. By Louis Napoleon's appointment of Viollet-le-Duc to a professorship at the Ecole des Beaux-Arts the Gothic movement received an official sanction in the very citadel of the academic forces, but the opposition was so strong that even the Emperor was forced to abandon his attempt. On the whole, few new buildings resulted from the Gothic movement, and these were almost exclusively churches. The most striking of them is Sainte Clotilde in Paris (Fig. 263), built in 1846–59 by the architects Gau and Ballu, with twin spires and fourteenth century detail. This church, however, is relatively frigid compared with some examples from the last days of the movement, after 1860.

Influence of the romantic movement on the development of types of buildings. The types of buildings to which the romantic movement contributed were almost exclusively those having direct precedents in the Middle Ages—such as churches, schools, town halls, and dwellings. Even in these types the development was largely a formal one, the dispositions remaining close to those of medieval times, as the national character of the precedents and the relative stability of the problems permitted. It was, indeed, precisely the superiority of medieval dispositions in fulfilling the needs of modern life which the Gothicists maintained as one of their chief theses. Their innovations respecting plan and structure were thus, for the most part, novel only in relation to the classical forms which had immediately preceded them, since medieval dispositions and modes of construction were generally followed as well as medieval forms of detail. So in the church Catholic, and even beyond it, the long aisled naves and chancels of the Middle Ages supplanted the domes and halls of the Renaissance and of Protestantism. Other types were influenced in certain lands only. In England the flexible scheme of the Tudor or Elizabethan manor, with its freedom in the fenestration and in the treatment of service quarters, replaced the strict symmetry of the Palladian house. The old residential col-

leges of Oxford and Cambridge were followed in the further development of these institutions and of the English boarding schools. In Germany the late Gothic town halls and guild halls of the country and of Flanders were taken as models for new constructions devoted to similar uses.

Eclecticism: conditions and ideals. Long before the force of the romantic movement had spent itself, it had become but one of many forces influential in architectural style, united only as emanations of a general eclecticism. This freedom of selection from a number of styles was just as surely grounded in the conditions of the time as the uniform adherence to a single style had been in some earlier times. A choice between two styles, to be sure, had often been offered to architects before, as when Gothic art was introduced into Italy in the thirteenth century or Renaissance art into the north in the sixteenth. The mere alternative of neo-classic or revived Gothic was thus of itself nothing new in kind; the novelty was that the struggle between them did not end, as it had always done before, in the triumph of either one, but that both continued, subdivided further, and received the addition of still others. The reason lay in the growth of historical knowledge, one of the most characteristic creations of modernity, which, for the first time, made the forms of many styles thoroughly familiar to a single generation. This had already contributed largely to the growth of classicism and romanticism, and to their increasing differentiation into Greek and Roman phases, Gothic and Romanesque phases, with further alternatives offered by subordinate chronological and local varieties—constituting in themselves a field for the exercise of a certain measure of eclecticism. To these the historical spirit now added other styles unconnected with the neo-classic and romantic programs, and soon created among designers the conscious principle of complete freedom of choice between the various historical styles. This expressed itself first in the sheer desire to create a collection of historical imitations; it passed to the adoption of a given style on grounds of personal preference or supposed appropriateness to the problem in hand, later sometimes to the combination of elements from a number of styles and the creation of a hybrid which might serve as a personal medium of expression.

Origins of eclecticism in architecture. The beginnings of this wider knowledge and wider eclecticism themselves can be found quite early in the eighteenth century, when the Viennese architect, J. B. Fischer von Erlach, published his pioneer *Entwurff einer historischen Architektur*, 1721, including illustrations, systematically arranged, of pre-classical, Eastern, and Greek buildings, as then understood, besides those of Rome and of contemporary France and Germany. The eighteenth-century gardens at Kew and elsewhere contained imitations of Moorish pavilions and Turkish mosques, as well as their Greek, Roman, Gothic, and Chinese structures. Such exotic models were obviously unsuited for any wide adoption, however, and the same was true of the Egyptian motives made popular by Napoleon's Eastern campaigns.

The "Italian style." Serious productions outside the classical and romantic movements resulted first from the study of the Italian styles of the Renaissance. Appreciation of these was a by-product of the Italian sojourn which formed part of the traditional education for clients as well as for architects. The classicists appreciated first the buildings of the High Renaissance, at once most classical and most in view in the tourist centers, Rome and Venice. Percier and Fontaine, in two works devoted to the Roman palaces (1798) and villas (1809), were among the earliest to call attention to the style and to make drawings available for imitation. The romanticists, a little later, extended their admiration from the medieval buildings of Italy to those of the earliest Renaissance in Florence. Fruits of these appreciations were as usual a decade or two in appearing in current practice. By 1820, however, the old Opera House in Paris was built in the style of the Basilica at Vicenza, and numerous other buildings recalled the arch orders or columnless façades of the Italian palaces. Germany took the lead in 1825–30, with buildings by Klenze and Gärtner in Munich—the Pinakothek with its pilastered arches, the Königsbau, the Ministry of War, and the Royal Library, with their novel suggestion of the Pitti Palace and other Florentine designs. In England the Italian manner came in with Barry, who adopted it as the most suitable expression for the London clubs, of which his Travelers' Club, 1829–31, initiated a long series.

Later developments. With the advent of the "Italian" style, as it was called, the field was open for imitations and inspirations of the greatest variety. The material was furnished not only by individual observation but by a multitude of special publications concerning monuments of the most diverse styles. In practice a general tendency to follow more and more recent styles, like the baroque, academic, and rococo, may perhaps be discerned—following the repetition of history already begun by the successive imitation of classic, Gothic, and Renaissance; but the development is neither a universal nor a regular one. It thus becomes necessary to sketch the trend of subsequent developments in each country singly, rather than to seek to follow this or that stylistic thread, often confusedly interwoven with others even in the work of an individual architect. Although manifestations of the eclectic movement appear in all countries, there are marked differences in its strength. Germany, whose scholars took the lead in historical study of architecture, gave itself freely to experiment with varied historic modes of expression, whereas England, torn by its furious struggle between classicism and romanticism, came late to a really eclectic standpoint, and France, more than the others, remained true to the classical tradition. In proportion to the adoption of eclectic practice there appeared another general phenomenon which may be noted here once for all. This was the increasing gulf between the few designs of trained architects and the great mass of buildings erected by men who were no longer sustained by a traditional knowledge of any one or even two sets of forms, and who could not adequately master others even if they would.

Germany: Munich. In Germany, eclecticism dominated architectural practice from 1825 to 1890. Within this time falls the phenomenal growth of German cities, which thus bear deeply the impress of the movement. The first of them to receive it was Munich, essentially the creation of Ludwig I. (1825-48), under whose personal inspiration Klenze and Gärtner turned now to Greece, now to Italy, now to the Middle Ages. Ludwig's successor, Maximilian II. (1848-64), gave his eclecticism a different form, wishing to create a new style by a combination of elements from the older ones. The task fell to the architect Bürklein, whose buildings are effective in their balanced yet picturesque composition and in their rhythmical subdivision into bays, but suffer so much from their poverty of execution as to have discredited the attempt.

Dresden and Vienna. A man of powerful personality, Gottfried Semper (1804-79), had meanwhile turned the scale in favor of the Italian Renaissance by his buildings in Dresden, especially the Court Theater (1838-41, Fig. 264). Semper was also one of the creators of modern Vienna, in the vast

buildings of the magnificent Ringstrasse on the lines of the
fortifications removed in 1858–60. A beginning had been
made in Ferstel's Votive Church and in the Opera House
built by Van der Nüll and Siccardsburg in 1861–69, with forms
reminiscent of the French Renaissance under Francis I.
Semper, in his designs for the extension of the Imperial Palace,
with the Court Theater (1871–89) and the Museums of Art
and of Natural History (1870–89), continued to draw his

FIG. 264—DRESDEN.   OLD COURT THEATER.   (SEMPER)

suggestion from the Italian styles, but now with a strong
leaning toward the grandiose effects of the baroque.   Among
the later buildings of the Ringstrasse are the Rathaus (1873–
83), built by Friedrich Schmidt with German Gothic forms,
the University and the Palace of Justice, with a mixture of
French and Italian Renaissance forms, and the Houses of
Parliament (1874–83) with the forms of neo-Hellenism.

Berlin, Leipzig, and Strasburg.   With the founding of the
German Empire began a period of predominance for Berlin,
distinguished especially by the building for the Reichstag
(1882–94) by Wallot, and of the cathedral (1888–95) by
Raschdorff.   The architectural forms adopted as a basis

sometimes academic, sometimes Renaissance, were as a rule greatly modified by the influence of the baroque, and showed the study of German even more than of Italian examples. This style, backed by the influence of the court, has remained in favor for governmental buildings in spite of the efforts of the modernists.   One of its principal contemporary adherents is Ludwig Hoffmann, who achieved success with the Imperial Supreme Courts in Leipzig (1884–95) and still retains the leadership of the conservatives.   A third monumental creation of the new German Empire is the imposing group of buildings erected in Strasburg about 1890, in academic and baroque forms.   For religious buildings the medieval styles have continued to be generally preferred, while for town halls late Gothic or German Renaissance forms have been frequently employed.

Eclecticism in England.   In England eclecticism remained for a long time less the result of conscious tolerance than the unintentional product of warring factions, each of which insisted on the universal superiority of its chosen style.   The classical side was chiefly maintained, after 1840, by adherents of a somewhat free rendering of antique or Italian motives, allied to the French néo-grec.   Their principal representatives were Cockerell, best known for his restrained designs for branches of the Bank of England, and Pennethorne, whose University of London (1869), originally designed in Gothic forms, retains a vertical movement in its rich Venetian garb. Although Victorian Gothic also had its wide variety of proto-types, final acceptance of the principle of general liberty of choice scarcely came before 1870.   The style which then obtained the preference was no one of those previously favored, but the so-called "Queen Anne."   This took its suggestion from the vernacular, half-classic English domestic architecture of the late seventeenth and early eighteenth centuries, but sought a free adaptation to practical requirements and left considerable liberty to the personality of the individual architect.   Such individuality was also exercised in certain experiments with other styles, while the Gothic, on the whole, remained the rule for churches, as it remains in England even to the present day.

"Queen Anne" and "Free Classic."   The creators of the

Queen Anne were Eden Nesfield, in his lodges at Regent's Park (1864) and Kew (1866), and Norman Shaw in his office building, New Zealand Chambers (1873, Fig. 265). These buildings had the frank expression of a variety of materials which the Gothic school had initiated, forms recalling the Dutch character which reigned in the English architecture of William and Anne, and an individuality of combination which was modern.   The union was timely, and buildings in the same general manner multiplied.   They included not only residences, to which the founders of the style and many others devoted themselves with results of uncommon livableness, but also more ambitious buildings such as banks and theaters, in which its residential origin and smallness of scale rendered it less monumental than picturesque.   A higher degree of monumentality began to be sought during the nineties through the reintroduction of Palladian elements.   Thus was produced the so-called "Free Classic" — a species of baroque in which individual liberty continued to hold a large place — which has dominated the public and urban architecture of England until very recently.   Among its adherents may be mentioned John Belcher, whose Institute of Chartered Accountants, 1895, was the manifesto of the school, and Sir Aston Webb. Within the last five years a tendency has been visible to return to more strictly academic forms, encouraged by the teaching of the Ecole des Beaux-Arts and the reversion to classical architecture in America.   The façade of the Royal Automobile Club (1911), modeled on the buildings of the Place de la Concorde, and Bush House are among the striking instances.

FIG. 265—LONDON.   NEW ZEALAND CHAMBERS. (MUTHESIUS)

Other styles.   Beside this main tide of eclecticism in England has run a continuance of the medieval tradition—now no longer regarded as a counter-current—in the building of country houses and churches. Here Sedding, Bodley, Pearson, and others have worked within a chosen range of historic national forms, scrupulously respecting honesty of materials and workmanship. They have contrived to give their designs a personal impress and at the same time to come nearer the spirit of the

FIG. 266—LONDON.   WESTMINSTER CATHEDRAL

old masters than had their predecessors whose imitations were more literal (Fig. 267). The simple country parish churches especially they have endowed with a devotional character and a suitability to the landscape which had hitherto escaped modern architecture (Fig. 268). As the Anglican church has appropriated the medieval architecture of England, the Roman church there has turned to other styles. Thus, since 1895, in the cathedral of Westminster, J. F. Bentley has employed forms predominantly Byzantine, securing an interior of vast spatial effect and deeply religious character (Fig. 266). The various dissenting sects have continued their traditions by following mainly the current classical or baroque styles. Until recently it was not wholly unusual to find more exotic styles essayed in secular architecture as well as in religious. Thus Alfred Waterhouse employed a personal variety of Romanesque in his monumental Museum of Natural History at South Kensington, and Aston Webb and Ingress Bell made use of a modified French Renaissance in the Law Courts at Birmingham. Of late years, however, eclecticism in England has become less personal, and the individualists have ceased to be of much importance.

Eclecticism in France. Secular buildings. In France, where congruity with a taste developed on classical architecture is the criterion of every experiment in other styles, eclecticism

FIG. 267—FLETE LODGE, NEAR HOBLETON. (MUTHESIUS)

was relatively a matter of nuances, except in churches and country villas. The Italian manner of the thirties was followed by a mingling of Italian and Greek influences in the so-called néo-grec. Labrouste, Duc, and Duban, the first pensioners of the French Academy to study the temples of Pæstum and other Greek monuments, were the leaders of the movement in France. It found expression in Duban's Bramantesque work at the Ecole des Beaux-Arts (1832–62) and Labrouste's refined façade of the Library of Sainte Geneviève (1843–50, Fig. 269), where Greek delicacy of profiling was employed in a façade reminiscent of the Tuscan palaces. The contemporary interest in things romantic and national led to a revival of the style of the French Renaissance, stimulated especially by the enlargement of the Hôtel de Ville in Paris (1836–54) and its rebuilding after the Commune. Under the Second Empire a powerful impulse toward the baroque, which so well expressed a luxurious society, was given by a genius of the first order, Charles Garnier. In the Paris Opéra (1861–74, Fig. 270) he took suggestions from the late Venetian forms, in the Casino at Monte Carlo, from the

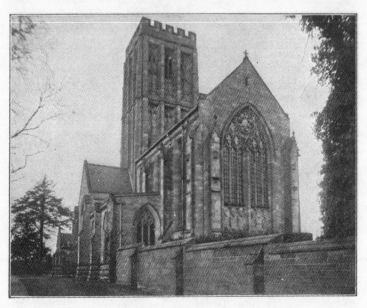

FIG. 268—HOARCROSS. CHURCH OF THE HOLY ANGELS

Roman baroque, employed with a technical facility and a profusion of detail which were his own. In the widened conception of the classic which still dominated French architecture on its formal side, the influence of Garnier has long continued to be felt. Thus the Musée Galliéra by Ginain, the Petit Palais des Beaux-Arts by Girault (1900), in the main perpetuate his traditions.

Churches. In the building of churches the identification of Christianity with the Middle Ages led to wider departures from the classic than in secular buildings, even where romanti-

cism did not dictate the adoption of Gothic. The Romanesque
was chosen as a compromise even before 1840, and after that
date churches in that style multiplied in the metropolis as
well as in the provinces. The variant which came to be
preferred was one reminiscent of the buildings of Angoulême
and Aquitaine, with their suggestion of Byzantine forms.
The most conspicuous example is the great church of the

FIG. 269—PARIS. BIBLIOTHEQUE SAINTE GENEVIEVE

Sacred Heart at Montmartre by Abadie and Daumet, begun
in 1873 (Fig. 271). Its elevated site, lofty domes, and gleam-
ing whiteness make it a striking object in the panorama of
Paris. In other churches of the latter half of the century,
such as Saint Augustin and Sainte Trinité, Renaissance forms
have reasserted themselves, although rarely without being
tinged by Byzantine or other medieval influences. Finally
in the commemorative chapel for the victims of the Charity
Bazaar fire, Guilbert has expressed the devotions of the
fashionable world in the facile modern baroque.

Domestic architecture. Domestic architecture has also had
its experiments with Gothic and other styles, but, so far as
urban dwellings are concerned, has tended to revert to the
French urban architecture *par excellence*, that of the eighteenth

century, which still responds almost completely to needs which have changed but little. The small country villa or cottage, however, has presented a problem relatively new to the French, which they have tried, with less success, to solve by picturesque designs suggested by English or Swiss examples.

FIG. 270—PARIS. OPERA HOUSE

Other European countries. Belgium. Italy. In other European countries there are certain buildings which must not be overlooked, the products of national movements of importance. Thus in Belgium the prosperity experienced under Leopold II. (1865–1909) resulted in a sumptuous rebuilding of Brussels. The most notable of the new constructions was the huge Palais de Justice (1866–83), by Poelaert. Here an eclectic modification of classic forms by an admixture of elements suggesting the Orient has produced effects of the most monumental character (Fig. 272). Italy, on its achieving liberty and unity in 1861, entered a period of development which had also its consequences in the arts. The monument to Victor Emmanuel II. in Rome by Count Giuseppe Sacconi, begun in

FIG. 272—BRUSSELS. PALAIS DE JUSTICE

FIG. 271—PARIS. CHURCH OF THE SACRED HEART, MONTMARTRE

1884 and dedicated in 1911, was designed to symbolize the triumph of Italian nationality. Rivaling the work of Poelaert in vastness, it also shows his influence in the forms of detail, at once classic and novel (Fig. 273). The two buildings are the most notable examples of the younger phase of eclecticism, which, not content to adopt historical styles in their integrity, has wished to make new syntheses of historical elements.

Contributions of the eclectic movement to the development of types of buildings. The specific contributions of the eclectic movement to the development of types of buildings were necessarily formal, and, to a large degree, second-hand. Thus the movement in general placed the seal of its approval on the types already created by the classical movement for government buildings, banks, exchanges, and theaters, on the types created by the romantic movement for churches, town halls, and rural dwellings. In such buildings the changes introduced by eclecticism were relatively slight, such as the tingeing of classicism by Palladian or baroque forms, or the replacing of Gothic forms by those of the northern Renaissance. For certain types, to be sure, these eclectic molds have become very firmly established. The French town hall has become almost uniformly an adaptation of national Renaissance forms as found in the old Hôtel de Ville of Paris. Administrative buildings for government departments, which have multiplied during the period all over the world, have acquired an international physiognomy of Renaissance or post-Renaissance motives. Many types but newly created, such as modern universities, public libraries, baths and welfare institutes, railway stations and hotels, received their first treatment in these preferred styles of eclecticism, and have tended to retain the impress. In one young and notable group, the museums of history and art, a peculiar appropriateness has been felt in employing forms characteristic of the age or region from which objects exhibited come, and the same tendency has manifested itself in the national and local buildings at international expositions. In buildings, the exteriors of which are clothed in one or another garb of historic form, the plans often show, of course, the most novel adaptation to purely modern requirements. The striving to make this adaptation and to bring it to expression in the massing and subdivision of the exteriors is, however, really opposed to the underlying ideas of eclecticism and may best be considered as manifestations of the movement toward functionalism.

Functionalism. Fundamentally different in direction from the eclectic movement, which forms part of the historical tendency of modern times, there has developed in architecture another movement, which is part of the tendency toward

FIG. 273—ROME.   MONUMENT TO VICTOR EMMANUEL II.

natural science.   It is at one with the biological concept of the adaptation of form to function and environment.   Adaptation in both these respects conforms to the philosophical concept of function—the dependence of a variable trait on other variables.   The conscious endeavors in modern architecture to make the forms of individual members correspond to their structural duties, to make the aspect of buildings characteristic of their use and purpose, to make the style of the time expressive of the distinguishing elements in contemporary and national culture, may thus be inclusively designated by the name functionalism.

Early structural purism. In its narrower meaning, as a striving for truth and frankness of expression in structure, the functionalist tendency has been present in many earlier styles, like the Greek and Gothic. It is thus not incompatible with the modern use of historic forms. Such a structural purism indeed has been, as we have seen, a notable characteristic of French architecture since the seventeenth century—a rule of "reason" and "good sense." It manifested itself in the restriction of the column by Soufflot and Chalgrin to its original function as an isolated support, in rationalization of the Roman triumphal arch at the Porte Saint Denis and the Arc de l'Etoile. The same tendency appeared among the partisans of Gothic architecture, who claimed a superiority for their style in functional expressiveness. The writings of Pugin, indeed, state the structural theory in completeness: "There should be no features about a building which are not necessary for convenience, construction, or propriety," and "All ornament should consist of enrichment of the essential construction of the building." The conclusion drawn by Pugin, however, was that Gothic forms should be employed, and this was the burden also of the early rationalistic writings of Viollet-le-Duc. Likewise content with an inspiration from historical forms were Gottfried Semper and William Morris, although their writings were contributing powerfully to the idea of a purely modern style based on considerations of material and technique.

The theories of environment and evolution. Reaction against historical tendencies. For the development of such a modern style a broader cultural foundation had gradually been in process of creation since the later days of the eighteenth century. Herder and Madame de Staël enunciated the principle of national individuality and organic evolution in literature; Hegel generalized the doctrine into a philosophy of history and art; Schnaase made concrete application of it in his *Geschichte der bildenden Künste* (1843–64), where he traced for the first time the relation of the art of different countries to environment, race, and beliefs. Taine gave the idea its ultimate formulation and a wide popularity. Parallel with all this there came recognition of the importance of evolution and environment in the natural world, culminating in the biological theories of Darwin, and also the application of the principle of nationalities in political affairs, in the unification of Italy and Germany. The reaction against historical tendencies of all sorts showed itself likewise in creative art, in the radicalism of Nietzsche, Zola, Ibsen, and Tolstoi in literature, of Courbet, Manet, and Monet in painting, of Meunier and Rodin in sculpture, and Wagner in music.

Modern material civilization. At the same time came the marvelous material development of the nineteenth century, depending on utilitarianism and applied science, which has changed with ever increasing rapidity the existing social conditions, the prevailing types of buildings, the materials, and the structural systems. Everything has contributed to the concentration of population in cities, which, especially in America and in Germany, have had the most fabulous and sudden growth. While the middle class has multiplied and reached a degree of comfort hitherto unknown, there has developed on the one hand an aristocracy of wealth and on the other an organized proletariat. Capitalism has brought with it vast factories, stores, and office buildings, steam transport has created railroad and dock buildings, palatial hotels for travelers, and great international expositions. Sanitation and altered social theories have revolutionized the building of schools, hospitals, asylums, and prisons, as well as the housing of the working classes. Philanthropy has endowed free libraries, settlements, and welfare institutions of all sorts. Economic pressure has led to a striving for the most efficient employment of space, time, and technical resources. The generous excess of strength characteristic of most earlier styles has become often impractical. The employment of iron and steel has brought new possibilities in the spanning of openings and interior space, and a new statical theory, which has fundamentally altered esthetic principles as well. Other new materials have multiplied daily, while cheap transportation has made them available everywhere and tended to break down local peculiarities.

Characteristics of functionalism in architecture. Since the middle of the nineteenth century all these forces have produced a body of architecture which, in spite of its variety, has a fundamental unity in its striving for functional expression. Sometimes the attempt has been to give to new materials like steel or glass, or new systems of construction like reinforced concrete, a form suggested by their own properties. Sometimes the effort has been to express on the exterior of buildings the function of each of their component elements, and to endow each building as a whole with a specific character in

FIG. 274—PARIS.   READING-ROOM OF THE BIBLIOTHEQUE NATIONALE

conformity with its purpose.   More recently there has been a tendency not to remain satisfied unless all the forms employed, even in the solution of time-honored problems, owe as little as possible to the historic styles, and thus are peculiarly and emphatically modern.

Development of functionalism. Expression of structure. At the outset of the development of functionalist architecture its principles were broadly stated, but the application made of them was relatively limited. With the conviction that the historic styles of architecture were outgrowths of contemporary conditions of race, climate, religion, and society, there had arisen a belief that imitation of those styles in modern buildings was inappropriate, and that a wholly new style must be developed, suggested by modern conditions and modern problems. This was the later gospel of Viollet-le-Duc in his *Entretiens sur l'architecture* (1863–72), and of Fergusson in his *History of Architecture* (1865–67). The scientific and utilitarian tendency of the day, however, made the criterion of style primarily a matter of structural system, and the hope of the advocates of modernity of style thus lay in the effort to find suitable expression for new methods of construction.

Construction in iron. The novel constructive material of the day was, of course, iron, whether cast or wrought, which had been coming into use for utilitarian constructions since the early years of the century. The dome of the Halle au Blé in Paris had been reconstructed in iron in 1811, the Menai Suspension Bridge, with its unprecedented span, had been built in 1819–26. Although the elaborate mathematical calculations of strength in the new material tended to withdraw such constructions from the architect's domain, efforts were not lacking on the part of architects, even before the theoretical writings just mentioned, to employ iron in a manner at once frank and artistically satisfactory. The most notable instances of this were the great reading-rooms of the Library of Sainte Geneviève (1843–50) and of the Bibliothèque Nationale (1855–61, Fig. 274) where Labrouste employed iron columns, very slender and widely spaced, supporting spherical vaults of metal plates. In these buildings the façades were of masonry, with no exterior expression of the iron work. In the great market buildings known as the Halles Centrales, by Ballu (1851–59), the exterior also displayed its construction of iron columns covered with zinc. It was arid, yet in harmony with the practical character of the buildings. Of metal alone, and only made possible by metal, have been the more recent suspension, arch, and cantilever bridges, with their enormous spans, as well as the gigantic Eiffel Tower in Paris (1889), which, like many of the bridges, combines grace with absolutely frank confession of structure.

Glass and iron. For inclosed buildings wider possibilities were secured by the use of glass as a filling between the supports. Structures of glass and iron had early been introduced for the cultivation of plants, and a similar structure was suggested by the horticulturist Paxton for the international exposition at London in 1851. There resulted a sort of vast conservatory, which was made permanent in the Crystal Palace at Sydenham, 1852–53, and was widely influential in stimulating construction in glass and iron or steel. In some later buildings the roof only was of glass, as at the Palais de l'Industrie for the Paris Exposition of 1855 and a multitude of later museum buildings, consisting in effect of vast covered courts. In other buildings the roof was largely solid, the walls almost entirely of glass, as in the buildings of the Paris Exposition of 1878. There has been a general tendency, owing to excess of sunlight, heat and cold, to recede from the extreme areas of glass at first employed, but in urban shop fronts where light and exhibition space are often the great desiderata, the glass has been kept at a maximum. A notably successful solution of such a problem with visible structural steel work is the Grand Bazar de la rue de Rennes, in Paris (Fig. 276).

Stone and iron. Experiments to devise novel structural systems with materials long in use, or with a combination of old and new materials, have also not been wanting. In the Vestibule de Harley (1857–68) at the Palais de Justice in Paris, J. L. Duc employed a system of ribbed stone vaulting which was neither Gothic nor classical, but resulted from an independent analysis of his structural problem. Viollet-le-Duc himself made designs showing the frank employment of iron in connection with walls and vaults of masonry and tile, which were a good deal followed, although mainly in utilitarian constructions.

Ferro-concrete. A further application of steel has been in connection with concrete. The employment of Portland cement as a building material, which rapidly increased in the later years of the nineteenth century, gave to concrete a much greater compressive strength. During the same time inventors were attempting to strengthen the concrete still further by building in a network of iron rods. This composite construction, popularized by the Frenchman Joseph Monier after 1868, has received the names ferro-concrete, armored concrete, or reinforced concrete. Its merit consists in that it employs steel and concrete in such a way that each material contributes the elements of strength for which it is best fitted—the concrete, compressive strength and indifference to fire, the steel, tensile strength and resistance to shearing. Theoretical study and practical experience have kept pace in the design and construction of piers, girders, floor slabs, and arches of the new material, which combines the possibility of wide spans with cheapness and security. The method of execution is the pouring of the freshly mixed, semi-liquid concrete in temporary forms of wood or metal, within which have first been placed the reinforcing bars, in the position where tensile or shearing stresses may occur. The temporary forms constitute one of the greatest items of expense, and, since they cannot be eliminated, current experiments are now directed to the devising of forms which may be used over and over. Owing to the fact that the steel reinforcement of each member is already incorporated in a protecting mass of concrete, and owing to the difficulty of casting thin walls of the material, there is less temptation with ferro-concrete than with other fireproof systems to disguise the essential members of the framework with enveloping walls. Aside from this frank articulation of structure, a variety of characteristic decorative treatments has been devised, such as the embedding of tile patterns in the surface of the concrete, and the creation of grooves by blocks nailed inside the forms. Thus, especially for utilitarian buildings, some highly interesting results have already been attained both in light and in massive construction.

Other materials. Independent of the novel structural systems, and earlier than the latest developments just described, came a revival of certain neglected materials, especially brick and terra cotta. Philip Webb initiated the movement by using brick in William Morris's "Red House" at Bexley Heath (1859). In the architecture of England and America during the following period it has received a variety of interesting treatments through the use of different bonds, the varying of the width, depth, and color of the mortar joints, and the employment of a variety of colors and patterns. Terra cotta, hitherto used mainly for friezes and ornamental detail, became available, as a result of improved methods of manufacture, for whole buildings, the Museum of Natural

506 A HISTORY OF ARCHITECTURE

History at South Kensington (1868–80) being a notable early example. The possibilities ultimately reached—impervious white structural terra cotta, besides a wide range of permanent colors—with the advantages of cheapness, resistance to fire, and ease of reproducing ornament—have given the material an ever increasing popularity. Efforts to give it also a characteristic expression, through frank recognition of its differences from stone masonry, have produced many interesting results.

Expression oj use and character. Deeply rooted, like the striving for structural expression, has been the attempt to secure expression for the use and character of buildings. Goethe had praised the expression of character as the highest merit in architecture; the Italian critic Milizia, with Ruskin and Viollet-le-Duc, had applied this principle specifically to the expression of the central purpose and determining conditions of the building in hand. The eclectics already recognized the principle in part when they chose for different types of buildings the several historic styles which seemed most appropriate to their general purposes. The pioneers of structural functionalism inevitably gave to many types of structures, especially those with exacting utilitarian requirements, an impress which was characteristic of their uses. The desire for expression of function has gone much farther, however, influencing the plan and massing as well. It has become the object of architects not merely to make the interior elements adapted to their purpose in extent, in height, and in relation to one another, but also to emphasize the existence of each of these elements on the exterior and to indicate their nature and relationships in such a way that the purpose and arrangement of the building might be unmistakable. For the functionalist movement the practical development and the formal development of types of buildings have thus become logically inseparable.

Contributions of the functionalist movement to the development of types. Theaters. With the multiplication and specialization of requirements and types of buildings, it becomes impossible even to mention all those of importance. It must suffice to discuss one or two which are representative of the transformations which have taken place in types already

existing and of the creation of wholly new ones. The theater is a type which, already highly developed during the
classical movement, has retained its importance and undergone characteristic modifications. The first of these was in
external expression. Semper felt that the stage, with its
fundamental importance and immense extent, should no
longer be kept under a single roof with the auditorium, but
deserved independent recognition, which the growing practical
necessity for great height has made permanent. In the
Paris Opéra (1861–74) Garnier carried still further the idea
of characterization, emphasizing on the exterior the form of
the auditorium as well, so that foyer, auditorium, and stage
form an ascending series, while the stage entrance, dressingrooms, and administrative offices are all given a frank and
suitable expression (Figs. 270 and 275).

Inner modification of the theater. The internal elements, the
auditorium and the stage, have likewise been modified, especially in those theaters unconnected with court functions and
not intended for the production of operas of a conventional
sort. Democratic conditions have here tended to do away
with the tiers of private loges grouped in a horseshoe, and to
make the house more nearly fan-shaped, so as to give all as
favorable a view as possible of the stage. A similar arrangement has been introduced, for somewhat different reasons, in
the theaters specially built for performance of the music-
dramas of Richard Wagner at Bayreuth and Munich. In
these, as in an ancient theater, the seats rise in a single slope.
The technical apparatus of the stage, where traditional arrangements had retained their hold until the last quarter of the
nineteenth century, was suddenly transformed by the substitution of metal for wood and of electric motive power for
manual strength. The revolving stage has made possible a
hitherto unhoped for rapidity in the change of scenes, while
electric lighting has opened the way for a thousand new optical
effects.

Railway stations. Railway stations had their origin only
in the thirties; they at once assumed, of necessity, the two
fundamental forms which still exist—terminal stations and
way stations. For both, if they were of sufficient importance,
a single train-shed spanning tracks and platforms was soon

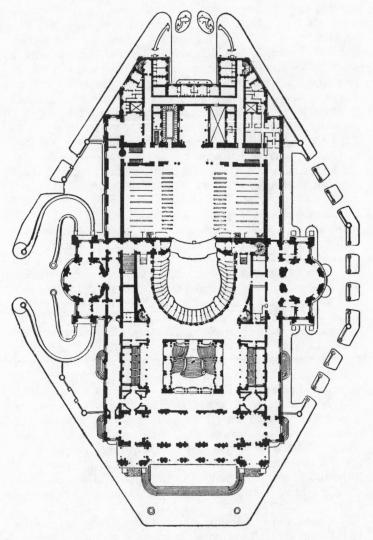

FIG. 275—PARIS. OPERA HOUSE. PLAN

adopted, and, with the multiplication of tracks and the employment of iron trusses, spans of over two hundred feet were reached early in the fifties. The part of the station containing the waiting-rooms and offices gave opportunities for monumental treatment which architects were quick to realize, as in the classic hall of Euston Station in London, built by Hardwick in 1847. In the Gare de l'Est in Paris (1847–52) a great gable containing a single arched window expressed on the façade the form of the train-shed behind, and a similar motive received magnificent treatment on a larger scale in the Gare du Nord (1862–64). At terminal stations with the main building at the head of the tracks the two sides have generally been used in Europe for arrival and departure, respectively, with specialized conveniences for passengers of a number of different classes. In way stations, and in terminal stations where space has not permitted the main building to be at the end, a depression or elevation of the tracks has made possible direct access to all the platforms. Where steam is the motive power the smokiness of the inclusive train-sheds has led increasingly to the substitution of low individual "umbrella-sheds" with long narrow slots close above the stacks. Where electric power has been adopted, on the other hand, there has been a reversion to the more monumental single hall, as in the Gare du quai d'Orsay, Paris, opened in 1901 (Fig. 278). In the giving of expressive form to such practical requirements, often far from the traditional domain of architecture, lie a great number of the problems presented by the multiplicity of modern types of buildings.

Expression of modernity and nationality. Although the endeavor to find appropriate expression for new types and new systems of construction has inevitably given a modernity of character to much current architecture, the forms of detail in traditional materials have long continued to be drawn from historical precedent, and many conventional types have retained a historical imprint—whether classical, medieval, or Renaissance. The broad principle enunciated by Semper, "The solution of modern problems must be freely developed from the premises given by modernity," has not yet been pushed, any more than it was by its author, to its ultimate conclusions. During the last decade of the nineteenth

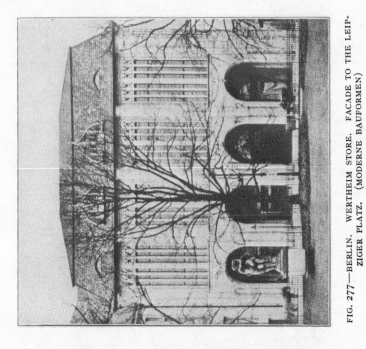

FIG. 277—BERLIN. WERTHEIM STORE. FACADE TO THE LEIP-
ZIGER PLATZ. (MODERNE BAUFORMEN)

FIG. 276—PARIS. GRAND BAZAR DE LA RUE DE
RENNES. (LA CONSTRUCTION MODERNE)

century, however, the conviction has deepened that, as Otto
Wagner has expressed it, "Modern art must yield us modern
ideas, forms created by us, which represent our abilities, our
acts, and our preferences."

In forms based on material and structure. Within the movement there are two diverse tendencies, having otherwise little

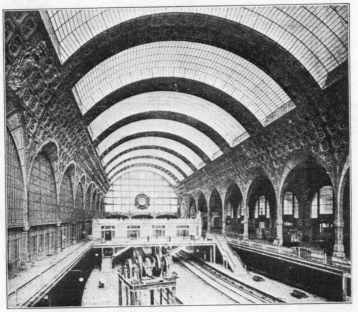

in common. One, represented by Wagner and his followers
in Germany, by Sullivan in America, and by the spiritual
descendants of Morris and Viollet-le-Duc in England and
France, holds to the belief that "The modern architecture of
our time seeks to derive form and motives from purpose, construction, and materials. If it is to give clear expression to
our feelings it must also be as simple as possible. Such
simple forms are to be carefully weighed against one another, so
as to secure beautiful proportions, on which almost solely
the effect of our architectural works depends." In the works

of these men only the traditional emphasis on base and cornice is retained. The enframement of windows and the demarcation of individual stories is generally avoided, and the forms of detail at the bases and crowns of the piers, at the doors and cornices, are individual ones suggested by the natural properties and technical treatment of the materials.

In plastic forms to which construction is subservient. The other modernist school holds quite a different view. Its fundamental theory, stated by L. A. Boileau as early as 1889, is that, "instead of constructing first, without preoccupation with the final appearance, promising oneself to utilize the ingeniousness of the construction as the decoration, one should relegate the ingenuities of structure to a position among the secondary means, unworthy of appearing in the completed work." This school attributes to a material a degree of artistic value in proportion as it is more plastic, more susceptible of receiving the impress of the personal sentiment of the artist. To this branch of modernism belonged the early phase known specifically as *l'art nouveau*, in which curved lines suggested by plant forms played so great a rôle. To it belong also the current works of Van de Velde and others, who treat their forms almost like flesh, with cartilage-like formations at the points of junction. These might be described as baroque without the classical elements. At the Ecole des Beaux-Arts in Paris, although classical forms are retained, much sympathy prevails for the scenic theory of this school of modernists, with which, indeed, most modern classic architecture has really much in common. Thus at the Paris Exposition of 1900 the bizarre masking of the structural forms, which at earlier French expositions had themselves been taken as the basis for decorative treatment, was less a retrograde movement, from the modernist standpoint, than the triumph of a different phase of modernism.

Besides the consistent followers of these two systems there is, as always, a multitude of practitioners whose convictions are a mixture of elements not wholly concordant, and who are united only in the rebellion against historical forms.

Development of modernist forms. The origins. England. The forerunners of modern individual treatment in architecture were the disciples of Morris in England, who in 1888 instituted the Arts and Crafts Exhibition for the display of works of handicrafts and interior decoration in forms created by their own makers.   The first attempts to make use of original forms on the exterior of buildings were made almost simultaneously in 1892 and 1893 by C. Harrison Townsend in London, Paul Hankar and Victor Horta in Brussels, and

FIG. 279—BROADLEYS ON LAKE WINDERMERE (MUTHESIUS)

Louis Sullivan in Chicago.   Townsend took his departure from the Romanesque forms of the American, Richardson, and transformed them by novel treatment of the projections, by fertile original ornament, and by a rich use of color.   In England the new departure has proved too radical for popular taste, in spite of the preparation made by the craft guilds, and few architects have pursued its ideals.   The chief of them, C. F. A. Voysey, however, has had much success in his chosen field of the dwelling (Fig. 279), in which he has adhered most strictly to the idea of economy, yet has secured interesting effects by his employment of rough cast, woodwork painted in broad but unhackneyed colors, and individual designs for hangings, furniture, and hardware.

Belgium and France. The Belgians introduced somewhat fantastic combinations of curved lines, and experimented at the same time with steel work in connection with brick, concrete, mosaic, and colored glass. They gave the first impulse in both France and Germany, although English models

FIG. 280—VIENNA. STATION OF THE METROPOLITAN RAILWAY. (LUX)

were followed in rural domestic architecture and independent creations soon outweighed all external contributions. The Belgian influence made its way to France about 1896 under the name of *l'art nouveau*. First felt in the minor arts, it soon invaded architecture in the light and graceful structures of glass and steel designed since 1898 by Hector Guimard to serve as entrances to the Paris underground—"the Metro." After the first enthusiasm for the new forms, however, few buildings in France have shown so pronounced a break with tradition. The new leaven appears mainly in a greater freedom within the academic style itself, which France, with its Latin elements and its faithfulness to classical tradition during the nineteenth century, regards, not without some reason, as a national style of its own.

Germany: Vienna. It is in Germany that the movement has taken deep root, so that, in spite of its foreign origins, it is already regarded by artists, if not by the government, as an expression of the Teutonic spirit in rebellion against the Latin domination of classic architecture. The pioneer has been Otto Wagner in Vienna, whose inaugural address as professor at the Academy in 1894 was a declaration of independence from the historical styles. His stations for the Metropolitan Railway (1894-97) were frankly developed from purpose, environment, and modern materials, with little ornament, and that freely invented (Fig. 280). The formation of the Viennese "Secession" in 1897, for which Wagner's pupil, Joseph Olbrich, designed an exhibition building of novel type and fresh decorative conception, inaugurated an analogous tendency in painting and in handicraft, which gave the architectural movement much support. Joseph Hoffman, another pupil, founded in 1903 the "Viennese Workshops" on the lines of Morris's establishment, and has had wide influence in domestic architecture and interior decoration. Although Wagner achieved in the Postal Savings Bank (1905) a notable expression of steel construction and marble veneering, official conservatism has prevented the execution of other monumental projects of the first order, and the buildings in Vienna which are most advanced in functionalist tendencies have hitherto been due to private initiative.

North Germany. The same has been generally true in North Germany, where the first striking success of the movement was in the Wertheim department store in Berlin, built by Alfred Messel at intervals from 1896 to 1904 (Fig. 277). Although historic forms—at first baroque, later Gothic—here furnished the suggestions, all have been so transformed that the impression is predominantly modern. Active official encouragement was first given the movement by Grand Duke Ernst Ludwig of Hesse-Darmstadt, who called Olbrich, Peter Behrens, and others to Darmstadt, and gave them a free hand. Their initial exposition of domestic architecture and handicraft in 1901 was the beginning of a widespread reform in these fields, largely on English lines, but less affected by medievalism and saturated with new decorative conceptions. Free from historic suggestion, and thus pronounced in its modernity, is the expression of the nature of the factory found in 1909 by Behrens in his turbine factory for the General

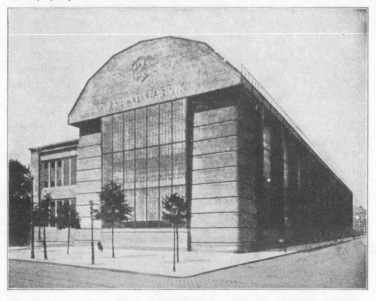

FIG. 281—BERLIN.   TURBINE FACTORY OF THE GENERAL ELECTRIC COMPANY (AEG).   (HOEBER)

Electric Company (AEG) in Berlin (Fig. 281).   The single vast hall has its great areas of glass confined between angular masses of concrete, and the forms of its trusses and steel columns are expressed with unusual frankness and skill. With the great majority of professional architects in Germany now participating in the modernist movement, only the personal intervention of the Emperor in the case of public works has prevented it from prevailing there almost universally.

After, as before, cessation of architectural activity in Europe due to the great war, two contrary tendencies are struggling for mastery in matters of style. One emphasizes the elements of continuity with the past, the other the elements of novelty in modern civilization. In the Germanic countries it is the radical emphasis on novel elements which has secured the advantage, in France and England it is the conservative emphasis on continuity which on the whole retains the supremacy. In view of the currently intensified nationalism, it is natural to expect that these national differences will be cultivated and perpetuated at least for a time. The underlying elements of internationalism existing in the community of practical problems, materials, and structural systems, and the essentially international character of both the conservative and the radical movement, however, may seem to indicate that this particularism will be relatively temporary. Whether the present conservative or the present radical tendency may ultimately be victorious, we may be sure that change in architectural style is bound to be constant, and that architecture will remain a living art, not less expressive of the complicated texture of modern life than it has been of the life of earlier and simpler periods.

PERIODS OF MODERN ARCHITECTURE

FRANCE

I. Classicism, c. 1780–1830.

Jacques Germain Soufflot, 1709–80.
Sainte Geneviève (the Panthéon) at Paris, plan 1755, execution 1764–90.

Victor Louis, 1735–c. 1807.
Grand Théâtre at Bordeaux, 1772–80.
Colonnades of the Palais Royal in Paris, 1781–86.

Charles Nicholas Ledoux, 1736–1806.
Gates of Paris, 1780–88.

Pierre Rousseau, b. 1750, d. after 1791.
Hôtel de Salm (Palace of the Legion of Honor) in Paris, 1782–86.

Jean François Thérèse Chalgrin, 1739–1811.
Saint Philippe du Roule in Paris, 1768–84.
Arc de l'Etoile, 1806–36.

Barthélemy Vignon, 1762–1829.
Madeleine at Paris, 1807–42.

Alexandre Brongniart, 1739–1813.
  Bourse in Paris, 1808–27.
Charles Percier, 1764–1838, and Pierre Fontaine, 1762–1853.
  Arc du Carrousel in Paris, 1806.
  Chapelle Expiatoire in Paris, 1815–26.
II. Romanticism, c. 1830–65.
  Chapel of Les Herbiers in Vendée, 1825.
  François Christian Gau, 1790–1854.
    Sainte Clotilde in Paris, 1846–59 (with Théodore Ballu. 1817–85).
  Eugène Emmanuel Viollet-le-Duc, 1814–79.
    Restoration and flèche of Notre Dame in Paris, 1857 ff.
III. Eclecticism, c. 1820–1900.
  Italian phase.
    Old Opera House in Paris, 1820.
  Néo-grec phase.
    Jacques Félix Duban, 1797–1870.
      Ecole des Beaux-Arts, 1832–62.
    Théodore Labrouste, 1799–1875.
      Bibliothèque Sainte Geneviève in Paris, 1843–50.
    Joseph Louis Duc, 1802–79.
      Completion of the Palais de Justice at Paris, 1857–68.
  French Renaissance phase.
    Jean Baptiste Leseur, 1794–1883.
      Enlargement of the Hôtel de Ville at Paris, 1836–54.
  Baroque phase.
    Charles Garnier, 1825–98.
      Opera House in Paris, 1861–74.
      Casino at Monte Carlo.
    Paul Ginain, 1825–98.
      Musée Galliéra in Paris, 1878–88.
    Charles Girault, 1851–.
      Petit Palais des Beaux-Arts in Paris, 1900.
  Byzantine phase.
    Paul Abadie, 1812–84.
      Church of the Sacred Heart, Paris, 1873–date.
IV. Functionalism, c. 1850–date.
  Théodore Labrouste, 1799–1875.
    Reading-rooms of the Bibliothèque Sainte Geneviève, 1843–50, and Bibliothèque Nationale, 1855–61.
  Joseph Louis Duc, 1802–79.
    Vestibule de Harley in the Palais de Justice at Paris. 1857–68.

Victor Baltard, 1805–74.
  Halles Centrales in Paris, 1852–59.
Buildings of the Paris Expositions of 1878 and 1889.
Alexandre Eiffel, 1832–.
  Eiffel Tower at the Paris Exposition of 1889.
Hector Guimard, 1867–.
  Stations of the Paris Underground Railway ("Metro")
  1898 ff.
Auguste Perret, 1874–, and Gustave Perret, 1876–.
  Théâtre des Champs Elysées, 1912.

ENGLAND

I. Classicism, c. 1760–1850.
    Roman phase.
        Robert Adam, 1728–92, and James Adam, 1730–94.
          Screen for the Admiralty in London, 1759.
          Remodeling of Kedleston, 1760–68.
          Record Office in Edinburgh, begun 1772.
          The Adelphi in London, begun 1768.
          University Buildings in Edinburgh, designed c. 1785.
        Sir John Soane, 1753–1837.
          Bank of England in London, 1788–1835.
        Harvey Lonsdale Elmes, 1814–47.
          Saint George's Hall in Liverpool, 1838–54.
    Greek phase.
        James Stuart, 1713–88.
          Temple at Hagley, 1758.
          Chapel at Greenwich Hospital.
        Thomas Harrison, b. 1744.
          "The Castle" at Chester, 1793–1820.
        Thomas Hamilton, 1785–1858.
          High School at Edinburgh, 1825–29.
        Sir Robert Smirke.
          British Museum in London, 1825–47.
II. Romanticism, c. 1760–1870.
    First phase, c. 1760–1830.
        Strawberry Hill, 1753–76.
        Fonthill Abbey, 1796–1814.
        Eaton Hall, 1803–14.
    Second phase, c. 1830–70.
        Augustus Welby Pugin, 1813–52.
          Church of Saint Augustine, Ramsgate, 1842.

Sir Charles Barry, 1795–1860.
  Houses of Parliament in London, 1840–60.
Sir Gilbert Scott, 1811–78.
  Church of Saint Giles in Camberwell, 1842–44.
William Butterfield, 1814–1900.
  All Saints', Margaret Street, in London, 1849.
George Edmund Street, 1824–81.
  Law Courts in London, 1868–84.
Alfred Waterhouse, 1830–1905.
  Assize Courts in Manchester, 1859–64.
  Museum of Natural History in London, 1868–80.
III. Eclecticism, c. 1830–date.
  Italian and néo-grec phase.
    Sir Charles Barry, 1795–1860.
      Travelers' Club in London, 1829–31.
    Charles Robert Cockerell, 1788–1863.
      Taylor and Randolph Buildings, Oxford, 1840–45.
      Branch Bank of England, Liverpool, 1845.
    Sir James Pennethorne, 1801–71.
      University of London, 1866–70.
  Queen Anne phase.
    Eden Nesfield, 1835–88.
      Lodges at Regent's Park, 1864, and Kew, 1866.
    R. Norman Shaw, 1831–1912.
      New Zealand Chambers in London, 1873.
IV. Functionalism, c. 1850 to date.
  Sir Joseph Paxton, 1803–65.
    Crystal Palace in London, 1851.
  C. Harrison Townsend.
    Bishopsgate Institute in London, 1893–94.
    Horniman Museum in London, 1900–01.
  C. F. A. Voysey, 1857–.

GERMANY

I.   Classicism, c. 1770–1840.
  Roman phase, c. 1770–90.
    Abbey Church at Saint Blasien, 1770–80.
    Deutschhauskirche in Nürnberg, 1785.
  Greek phase, c. 1790–1840.
    Karl Gottfried Langhans, 1733–1808.
      Brandenburg Gate in Berlin, 1788–91.

Friedrich Gilly, 1771–1800.
  Proposed memorial for Frederick the Great in Berlin, 1797.
Karl Friedrich Schinkel, 1781–1841.
  Royal Theater in Berlin, 1818–21.
  Old Museum in Berlin, 1824–28.
Leo von Klenze, 1784–1864.
  Glyptothek in Munich, 1816–30.
  Walhalla at Regensburg, 1830–42.
II. Romanticism, c. 1825–50.
  Karl Friedrich Schinkel, 1781–1841.
    Gothic project for the Cathedral of Berlin, 1819.
    Werderkirche in Berlin, 1825.
  Friedrich von Gärtner, 1792–1847.
III. Eclecticism, c. 1830–1900.
  Italian Renaissance phase.
    Leo von Klenze, 1784–1864.
      Pinakothek in Munich, 1826–33.
      Königsbau in Munich, 1826–35.
    Friedrich von Gärtner, 1792–1847.
      Royal Library in Munich, 1832–43.
    Gottfried Semper, 1804–79.
      Old Court Theater in Dresden, 1838–41.
  Gothic and northern Renaissance phase.
    Heinrich von Ferstel, 1828–83.
      Votive Church in Vienna, 1853–79.
    Friedrich von Schmidt, 1825–91.
      Rathaus in Vienna, 1873–83.
  Baroque phase.
    Gottfried Semper, 1804–79.
      Extension of the Imperial Palace in Vienna, 1870 *ff*.
      Court Theater in Vienna, 1871–89.
    Paul Wallot, 1841–1912.
      Reichstag Building in Berlin, 1882–94.
    Ludwig Hoffmann, 1852–.
      Imperial Supreme Courts at Leipzig, 1884–95.
IV. Functionalism, c. 1850–date.
  Otto Wagner, 1841–.
    Stations of the Stadtbahn in Vienna, 1894–97.
    Postal Savings Bank in Vienna, 1905.
  Alfred Messel, 1853–1909.
    Wertheim store in Berlin, 1896–1907.

Joseph Olbrich, 1867–1908.
   Secession gallery in Vienna, 1897.
   Tietz store in Düsseldorf, 1906–08.
Peter Behrens, 1868–.
   House in Darmstadt, 1901.
   Turbine factory in Berlin, 1909.

BIBLIOGRAPHICAL NOTE

The two final volumes of D. Joseph's *Geschichte der Baukunst*, 1902, bear the title *Geschichte der Baukunst des XIX. Jahrhunderts*, and constitute the only historical work devoted to modern architecture as a whole. One may also consult the modern section of K. O. Hartmann's *Die Baukunst in ihrer Entwicklung . . . bis zur Gegenwart*, vol. 3, 1911. Both of these are naturally fullest on work in Germany. L. Magne's *L'architecture français du siècle*, 1889, covers France to its date. For the development of special types, in general, or in single countries, see A. G. Meyer's *Eisenbauten: ihre Geschichte und Æsthetik*, 1907; H. Multhesius's *Das englische Haus*, 3 vols., 1904–05, and his *Die neuere kirchliche Baukunst in England*, 1906.

Classicism. P. Klopfer's *Von Palladio bis Schinkel* (*Geschichte der neueren Baukunst*), 1911, gives a general survey of the movement, with accounts of the development of individual types of buildings. L. Hautecœur's *Rome et la renaissance de l'antiquité à la fin de XVIIIe siècle*, 1912, which discusses the genesis of the movement, and its beginnings in France, may be supplemented by F. Benoit's *L'art français sous la révolution et l'empire*, 1897. A. E. Richardson's *Monumental Classic Architecture in Great Britain and Ireland During the XVIII. and XIX. Centuries*, 1914, with A. T. Bolton's *Adam*, 2 vols., 1922, and H. A. Tipping's *English Homes*, vol. 6, covers the period in England; and P. Mebes's *Um 1800. Architektur und Handwerk . . .*, 2 vols., 1908, gives a partial survey of the work in Germany.

Romanticism. The history of the romantic movement in architecture has received special treatment only in the case of England, in C. L. Eastlake's *History of the Gothic Revival*, 1872; in H. Muthesius's *Die neuere kirchliche Baukunst, Das englische Haus*, vol. 1, 1904, and *Die englische Baukunst der Gegenwart*, 1900, vol. 1. The early transplantation of the movement to the Continent best appears although incidentally, in M. L. Gothein's *Geschichte der Gartenkunst*, 1914, vol. 2, chap. 15. For its later progress there one must turn to the general histories of Hartmann and Joseph.

Eclecticism. Two works devoted to illustrations of German buildings of this phase are H. Licht's *Architektur Deutschlands . . . der Neuzeit*, 2 vols., 1882, and H. Rückwardt's *Façaden und Details moder-*

ner Bauten, 1892. A similar work for England is Muthesius's *Die englische Baukunst der Gegenwart*, 2 vols., 1900, supplemented by his other works listed above. For France one may consult the works of César Daly or R. Selfridge's *Modern French Architecture*, 1899, a collection of photographs of buildings from the period, largely domestic.

Functionalism. The theories of "character" and structure developed by Ruskin, Viollet-le-Duc, and others are discussed, although rather unsympathetically, in G. Scott's *The Architecture of Humanism*, 1914. Some of the applications made in practice appear in F. Billerey's paper, *Modern French Architecture*, in the *Journal of the Royal Institute of British Architects*, 1912–13, 3d series, vol. 20, pp. 317–45. The influence of iron in architecture is most fully discussed in A. G. Meyer's *Eisenbauten: ihre Geschichte und Æsthetik*, 1907. The pioneer works of "modernist" character in England and Belgium are described in Muthesius's *Die englische Baukunst der Gegenwart* and in H. Fiérens-Gervært's *Nouveaux essais sur l'art contemporain*, 1903. The manifesto of the movement in Germany was Otto Wagner's *Moderne Baukunst*, translated by N. C. Ricker, 1901. Its later development there may be traced in Karl Scheffler's *Moderne Baukunst*, 2d ed., 1908, and in the biographies of Wagner, by J. A. Lux, 1914, and of Peter Behrens, by F. Hoeber, 1913. For the work in America see the note to Chapter XIII.

CHAPTER XIII

AMERICAN ARCHITECTURE

Pre-colonial architecture. Yucatan. Long before European explorers and colonists crossed the Atlantic there flourished in America civilizations which, although still ignorant of iron or even of bronze, had a highly developed architecture. The first, and in some respects the greatest, of these was that of the Maya, whose center was in modern Yucatan. They flourished in the early centuries of the Christian era, and their great buildings were in ruins long before the arrival of the Spanish conquerors. Their colossal structures at Palenque (Fig. 282), Chichen Itza, and elsewhere reveal an ability to transport and work stones of great size, to employ the column and the corbeled vault, and to devise symmetrical plans of some complexity. Religious structures came first in importance; even the royal palaces were secondary. A characteristic feature was the raising of all buildings of importance on great substructures, often with sloping faces or in the form of a stepped pyramid. A broad and steep staircase on the principal face led to the upper platform. Here stood the building proper, of massive rubble-concrete faced with stone (Fig. 283). The arrangement of the plan was conditioned by the use of the corbeled vault to cover all interior spaces. This resulted in narrow rooms which could be extended indefinitely in length, but which had to be multiplied one behind the other to secure greater depth. Openings to the exterior or between the chambers were spanned with lintels of wood or stone, or by smaller corbeled arches. On the exterior a belt course marked the line of the impost within, and the space opposite the tall vault was often treated as a broad frieze with relief decoration. A unique feature was the "roof comb," a long pierced wall rising along the center of the terraced roof. Most of the principal buildings were temples, although monasteries and palaces on a large scale were also erected.

Mexico. Successive invading tribes, less civilized than the Maya, fell heir to their art, and diffused their own versions of

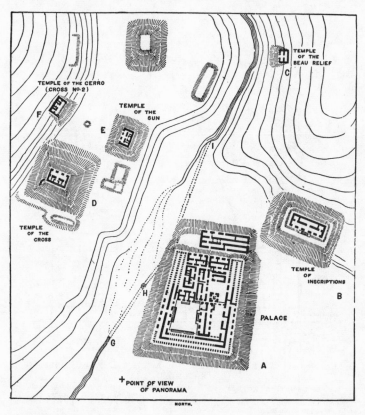

FIG. 282—PALENQUE. SKETCH PLAN OF THE PALACE AND TEMPLES. (HOLMES)

it throughout Mexico. The buildings of the Toltec and later the Aztec were on an equal scale with those of the older civilization, but show less refinement and constructive skill. The terrace and pyramid substructures, the relief decoration, the general types of plan with long, narrow rooms, were retained. Often the building or rooms were grouped around quadrangles and courts. In general the corbeled vault was abandoned, and the terrace roofs of concrete were supported by wooden

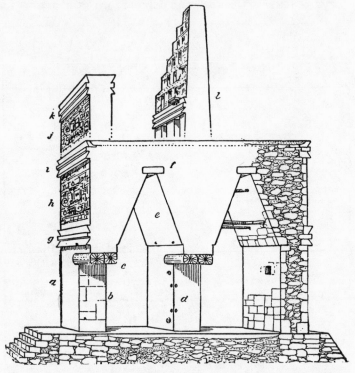

FIG. 283—TRANSVERSE SECTION OF A TYPICAL MAYA BUILDING.
(HOLMES)

The upper part of the pyramid is shown with the stairway at the left. *a.* Lower wall-zone pierced by a plain doorway. *b.* Doorway showing squared and dressed stones of jamb. *c.* Wooden lintels cut midway in length. *d.* Doorway connecting front with back chamber and showing position of cord holders. *e.* Inner face of arch dressed with the slope. *f.* Ceiling, or cap-stones of arch. *g.* Lower line of molding, a survival of the archaic cornice. *h.* Decorated entablature zone. *i.* Upper moldings and coping. *j, k.* False front with decorations, (occasionally added). *l.* Roof-crest with decorations, (occasionally added).

beams. The varied character of the materials available resulted in many local differences in construction. At Mitla, for instance, large stones could be had for columns and lintels; in some other places stone could scarcely be found suitable for facing, and mud brick or *adobe* had to be used, decorated with stucco and color.   These native developments came to an end with the conquest of Mexico by the Spaniards beginning in 1519.

Peru.   In Peru the Spaniards, on their conquest of the Inca empire in 1532, found another well-developed style of architecture, with an independent development of many centuries.   Palaces, fortresses, and cities rivaled one another in importance.   Polygonal walls of vast blocks, rising in many terraces, guarded the pass of the Andes at Ollentaitambo. Houses and palaces were built around courts, sometimes with a second story receding from the first and supported on corbeled vaults.   Windows and niches with inclined jambs were notable features.

Colonial architecture.   With the coming of the European colonists to the New World a problem new and unique in modern times was created for architecture;   civilized men had to face conditions which were absolutely primitive and to struggle against odds for the attainment of traditional ideals of building.   As a result there was everywhere a pioneer stage, in which the settlers seized the first means at hand—adobe, logs, or even turf—and built as simply as would serve primary needs of shelter and worship.   Later they sought to replace such modes of building by those of their mother country, but these were inevitably modified to a greater or less degree by differences in the materials available, and in economic and social conditions.   The duration of the pioneer period itself varied greatly with the character and support of the colonists, and with the resources and climate of the country.

Spanish colonial architecture. Development.   In the conquered empires of Mexico and Peru, where wealth and a large civilized native population already existed, the Spanish were soon able to establish their own architecture, and even to erect monuments rivaling those of the mother country in size and number.   Desire to implant the Catholic faith gave prominence from the very beginning to churches.   The earliest ones, including doubtless the small church erected in 1524 on the foundations of the great Aztec temple in Mexico City, showed reminiscences of the Plateresque and even of Gothic and Moorish details.   Such buildings were soon replaced by more elaborate structures, designed either by the court architects in Spain or by others of scarcely less ability who emigrated to the New World. Thus, for the cathedral of Mexico, two successive designs were sent from Spain, in 1573 and 1615, the second by Juan Gomez de Mora (Fig. 284). The cathedral at Lima (1573) and many other buildings were designed on the spot by Francisco Becerra, a disciple of Herrera. The successive transformations of style in Spain

FIG. 284—MEXICO CITY. CATHEDRAL, WITH SACRISTY (RIGHT)

were faithfully reflected in the Spanish colonies, usually a few years later, with baroque tendencies naturally predominating. In 1749, when Lorenzo Rodríguez began the great sacristy of the cathedral of Mexico, he employed a most luxuriant aggregation of baroque details for the façades (Fig. 284). By 1797, however, when the towers of the cathedral were added, the academic reaction was supreme; and the work of the last of the great colonial architects, Francisco Eduardo Tresguerras (1745–1833), shows a handling of academic elements reminiscent of that of Chalgrin.

Types of buildings. The dominant type of church was the basilican, as in the cathedral of Mexico—a solid rectangle with a barrel-vaulted nave and transepts, having penetrations at each bay, domed compartments in the aisles, and chapels between the buttresses. Twin western towers, as here, were frequent elsewhere, and a dome over the crossing was a general feature. Domed churches of central type were also not wanting. A special development of the central type occurs in the sacristy of the cathedral of Mexico, the *Sagrario Metropolitano.* This consists of a Greek cross inscribed in a square, with an octagonal dome over the crossing, barrel-vaulted arms, and minor domes in the angles of the cross. Secular and domestic buildings followed those of the mother country in being composed about an arcaded court or patio.

Florida. The outpost of Spain in North America, Saint Augustine, founded in 1565, was not without structures of some architectural pretensions, although these were of relatively utilitarian character. The old fort, with its rusticated bastions, and the molded and paneled posts of the city gate still stand, as well as a simple house or two with whitewashed walls and wooden balconies.

New Mexico. In the remote interior of New Mexico architecture was still more primitive. Here the native population was sparse and relatively poor, so that little tempted the Spaniards to the region except missionary zeal. The first mission church, at San Juan de los Caballeros, was built in 1598, and the country was well covered by 1630. These buildings were merely cubical structures of adobe, or mud brick, perhaps with a simple belfry, built by the natives under supervision of the Franciscan fathers. Even the cathedral of Saint Francis at Santa Fé (1713-14) differed from these chiefly by its larger scale. Its doorway and its twin western towers were alike destitute of classical details, and ornament was reserved for the altar, a distant reminiscence of the lavish examples of Spain and Mexico.

California. In Alta California colonization was not attempted until 1769, when Padre Junipero Serra established at San Diego the first of the series of missions which ended in 1823 with San Francisco Solano, north of San Francisco Bay. The first chapels of brush and the wooden frames for bells were soon replaced by adobe structures of a single nave, with roofs of poles covered with clay or reeds. As the missions flourished and the number of Indian converts who worked under the direction of the fathers increased, larger and more imposing buildings replaced these. Thus at Santa Barbara the first chapel, dedicated in 1787, was enlarged in 1788, re-built in 1793 and again in 1815–20, when the present church,

FIG. 285—SANTA BARBARA. MISSION AND FOUNTAIN

the largest and best constructed in the province, was built (Fig. 285). In it the baroque survivals which appear in the crude façades of the earlier churches are superseded by an attempt at classical elegance—the low pediment with the six engaged Ionic columns. Single or twin towers, pierced belfry walls, as at San Gabriel, long arcaded corridors or cloisters, as at San Juan Capistrano, are characteristic features of the California buildings, which are otherwise dependent for their effect on the broad surfaces and massive buttresses of their walls.

French and Spanish colonial architecture in Canada and Louisiana. The French pioneers in North America were in general hunters and traders rather than settlers, and they built correspondingly little. At Quebec, which was founded in 1608, a considerable town gradually developed, however, with churches, monastic and collegiate buildings, and palaces for the intendant and the archbishop. These had for the most part the simple wall surfaces and detail of the period of Louis XIII., although in the more elaborate interiors there was the rich pilaster treatment of the following reign. New Orleans was not founded until 1718. The typical house

Copyright, American Architect and Building News Co.

FIG. 286—NEW ORLEANS.   THE CABILDO

there was one surrounded by roofed verandas with light supports, sometimes in a single story, sometimes in two stories. The cession of Louisiana to Spain in 1764, almost simultaneous with the loss of Canada to England, made the later architecture of these French colonies fall under foreign domination. Thus in New Orleans after the great fire of 1788 the buildings about the Place d'Armes were rebuilt on a coherent plan, in the contemporary style of Spain. The Cabildo or city hall (1795, Fig. 286) had two stories of open arcades, with the arch order and a pediment, all originally of quite a classical aspect.

Dutch colonial architecture in New Netherlands. 1624–64.

The Dutch, who founded Albany in 1624 and settled on Manhattan Island in 1626, naturally tended to follow the mode of building of their mother country, still full of medieval reminiscences. Although the majority of buildings long remained of wood, thatched with reeds, a few houses of stone were soon built, and later bricks were frequently used. In these masonry structures the stepped gable toward the street, so common in Holland, was adopted, as well as the tile roof. The most conspicuous building, the "Stadt-Huis"—erected for the city tavern in 1642 and converted into a city hall in 1653—conformed to this type. It had vertical banks of small segmental-headed windows in pairs, and a simple open cupola to contain the bell. Although architecture had thus made little progress before the English conquest of 1664, there were the seeds of an independent growth which developed later under English rule.

Architecture in the English colonies. Seventeenth century. The English colonies in America were at first widely separated, as well as very different in their character and purposes, so that there was much diversity of architecture even in those where the settlers were mainly of English birth. Certain general characteristics hold for all, however, among them the essentially medieval nature of all the buildings of the seventeenth century. This could scarcely have been otherwise, in view of the fundamental medievalism of most building in England during the century, outside of London and of court circles. England had been one of the last countries to adopt Renaissance forms of detail, and was much later still in adopting classical types of plan and mass. Throughout the seventeenth century in England the country churches built were Gothic, and the rural cottages and minor country seats were medieval in all but a few applied details and a tendency to symmetry. Even in London, we may recall, the first classical church was not built until 1630, and it had no imitators until after 1666. Small wonder, then, if the colonists, themselves largely from the rural districts, erected buildings which, stripped of almost every detail not structurally indispensable, revealed their basic medievalism. A corollary of this, and of the relatively primitive state of society, was the general absence of professional architects and the dependence of the craftsmen builders on tradition in matters of style and workmanship. Another general trait in the seventeenth century was the almost universal prevalence of wood as a building material, even in regions where the later monuments which are preserved are of masonry. In contrast with England the new continent was densely forested, so that in clearing land for cultivation timber was felled ready to hand. The immediate introduction of sawmills in populous centers made plank still less expensive than otherwise, so that for years, and even to this day, brick and stone have stood at a disadvantage in cost far greater than anywhere in Europe.

Virginia and the South. Virginia had at the start the backing of a powerful trading company and the advantage of a unique staple crop, tobacco, which soon became enormously valuable for export. With the outbreak of the civil war in England, the colony, with Maryland, became a refuge for the royalists, many of them possessing some means. Nevertheless architectural progress was very slow. From the founding of Jamestown in 1607 the home authorities made constant efforts to establish towns and require buildings of brick. The absolute necessity of a plantation system, however, forced the inhabitants to scatter along the navigable rivers and made mechanics of any kind scarce. Framed houses only began about 1620 and were still uncommon in 1632. Clay and some brick makers there were, yet the first house wholly of brick does not seem to have been built until 1638. The typical Virginia house of the seventeenth century was a rectangular framed building of very moderate size, devoid of any architectural ornaments, and with a great chimney of brick at each end. The buttress-like form of these chimneys, with the steepness of the roof, proclaimed the medieval basis of the design. This is even more pronounced in the oldest of the Virginia churches still remaining, at Jamestown, rebuilt 1639, and in Saint Luke's, Smithfield, on the model of which the Jamestown church has been restored. With its pointed and mullioned windows this is unmistakably an English parish church of the outgoing Gothic, in spite of the quoins of its tower. In Maryland and Carolina the same general history was later repeated, bricks of local manufacture being gradually adopted by the wealthier planters. Although Carolina was not settled until after 1660, and large houses were not built until near 1700, one or two of them still show the fantastic curved gables of the Jacobean manors.

New England.   In New England buildings entirely of brick and stone were especially rare, but permanent framed buildings of wood were erected almost immediately after the founding of Plymouth (1620), Boston (1630), and Hartford (1636), with no long period of makeshifts.   The earliest settlers included carpenters, and, under the conditions of town life which prevailed, artisans were numerous throughout the colonial period.   They brought with them the medieval English traditions of framing houses with overhanging upper stories, and of filling up the frame, where possible, with brick. The changeable climate did not favor the exposure of such half-timber work to the weather, and from the start, in most instances at least, the exteriors were covered with clapboards.   The windows were small leaded casements, essentially medieval, as were the clustered form of the chimneys and the ornamental drops at the corners of the overhangs. Several different types of plan may be distinguished, each characteristic of certain localities.   In Massachusetts Bay and the Connecticut colony the usual type was one having two rooms upstairs and down, with an entry and a great chimney between, and often with a lean-to added at the back.   **Later the lean-to was included from the start, as in the Parson Capen** house at Topsfield, Massachusetts, well preserved and restored. The typical house of the ordinary artisan was one of a single room below, with a great chimney at one end, sometimes a "stone-end house."   Occasionally, as later in the William Browne house at Beverly, Massachusetts, the Elizabethan U or H plan, with a central "hall," was preserved.   In interiors the cavernous fireplaces, the wainscot sheathing, and the occasional paneling were devoid of any Renaissance detail. Toward 1700 the framed overhang was abandoned, but medieval details and methods lingered well into the eighteenth century.   The churches or "meeting-houses" in New England likewise retained survivals of medieval forms, but their disposition was fundamentally affected by the extreme Protestantism of the settlers there.   After the passing of the earliest simple cabins they tended to conform to the prevailing Protestant type of England and the Continent—a squarish, hall-like room, with galleries around three sides and the pulpit against the fourth, which was generally one of the longer sides. There was no tower; the belfry was merely placed astride the ridge at one end or

Courtesy of the White Pine Bureau

FIG. 287—IPSWICH.   WHIPPLE HOUSE

on a deck in the center when the roof was hipped, as in the "Old Ship" Meeting House at Hingham, Massachusetts.

Pennsylvania.   Philadelphia was not founded until 1682, so that colonial architecture in Pennsylvania has mostly the post-Renaissance detail of the eighteenth century.   Before leaving the medieval survivals, however, one must consider the buildings of the German sects of Pennsylvania, although the earliest of any pretensions were not built until well after 1700, and others not until about 1750.   The monastic halls of religious communities like that at Ephrata, with their whitewashed walls and small windows, their steep roofs and ranges of little dormers, are unmistakable offshoots of the Middle Ages in Germany.

Eighteenth-century colonial architecture. With the eighteenth century came greater means and comfort, wider use of permanent materials, and the adoption of classical forms of detail. The whole seaboard was now under English rule, and local diversity was subject to uniform English influence. By this time in England the style of Jones and Wren was every-- where established, and the small provincial towns abounded with doorways and interior woodwork in which the favorite post-Renaissance motives of broken pediments, consoles, and rich carving were conspicuous. Still more important for the colonies was the codification of current architecture in books, great and small, which reproduced both formulæ for the orders and other details and designs for whole buildings. These were imported very freely and will be found to have had the greatest influence on single buildings and on the prevailing style. In the early part of the century the colonists merely adopted classical details for the individual features of their buildings—the cornice, the doorway, and perhaps a cupola—without any general classical treatment beyond a symmetrical arrangement. Later the churches and public buildings, and finally even the dwellings, began to assume a monumental character. During the later years of the colonial régime there also appeared some tendency toward the Palladian strictness which had carried the day in England, and had dominated the later architectural publications. In these movements, as was also the case in England, cultivated amateurs played the leading rôle, although the builders themselves were quick to master the teaching of the books and to assume also the functions of architects.

Houses. The first signs of the transition at the opening of the eighteenth century were the adoption of less steep roofs, the substitution of sash windows for the leaded casements, and the tendency to employ a uniform cornice with a hip roof, or a pedimented gable instead of a gable of medieval type. When cornice and door were given rich detail—of modillions and of pilasters with a pediment—one had the scheme exemplified about 1730 in Westover, Virginia (Fig. 288), and in the finest houses of that day throughout the colonies. The ample and symmetrical dependencies seen at Westover were characteristic of Virginia and of Maryland and used at Mount Pleasant in Philadelphia. Frequent use of the curved and the broken pediment and of rusticated enframements shows that the baroque element of Wren's work was still current. In many instances, one even before 1700, tall pilasters were applied

FIG. 288—WESTOVER, VIRGINIA

to the corners of the house. As most of these were only associated with an individual pedestal and a fragment of entablature, however, they create no general architectonic treatment. An exceptionally important house in which a more academic scheme was attempted was Mount Airy in Virginia (1758), where two loggias—one arched, the other colonnaded—were the axial features of a group with balanced outbuildings, taken apparently from James Gibb's published designs. It was not until 1765 or later that the free-standing portico with a pediment was applied to dwellings, and this did not become at all common until after the Revolution. In a few instances, notably the Miles Brewton house in Charleston, South Carolina (c. 1765), there were superposed porticoes on the general scheme of many of Palladio's villa designs, although with much freedom in proportions and detail.   Strict following of Palladian canons in residence work only began with Thomas Jefferson's design for Monticello in 1771, on the very eve of the Revolution.   The interior of houses, owing partly to the prevalence of wooden paneling, was much richer and often more coherent in architectural treatment than the exterior. The subdivision of walls by pilasters was by no means uncommon, although more often, as in the Brewton house, each essential element, such as a doorway or chimneypiece, was elaborated individually.   Baroque features persisted even after they had vanished from the exterior.

Churches.   The buildings in which the more advanced tendencies were first manifested were the churches.   Old Saint Philip's, Charleston, consecrated in 1723, had a portico of four columns in front of its tower, only a few years after the great London churches with a similar general *parti*.   The nave of Christ Church, Philadelphia, built 1731–44 under the direction of Dr. John Kearsley, has an architectonic treatment of the Roman arch order with pilasters in two stories.   Both of these buildings had the basilican interior treatment of Saint Bride's and other London churches, which became the favorite system for the more elaborate colonial examples. The exterior portico, which in Saint Philip's had only the width of the tower, was enlarged in Saint Michael's, Charleston (1752–61), and in Saint Paul's Chapel, New York (1764–66, Fig. 289), to embrace almost the full width of the church. The steeples followed English examples, among which that of Saint Martin-in-the-Fields' and other designs reproduced in Gibbs's published works attracted the most imitators.

Public buildings.   The earliest public buildings of any pretensions, such as the older New York City Hall (c. 1700) and the old Virginia Capitol at Williamsburg (1702–04), still betrayed a lingering medievalism in their H plans, in spite of the round arches or the columns of the connecting loggias.   Even in buildings where all medieval character has vanished, like the old State House (Independence Hall) in Philadelphia (1732–52), the architectural character remains fundamentally domestic, and the public functions are suggested on the exterior only by the greater size of the building and its possession of a cupola.   In the interior of Independence Hall, indeed, there is a monumental treatment by an arch order with engaged columns, which was almost unique in the colonial

FIG. 289—NEW YORK.   SAINT PAUL'S CHAPEL

period.   The first attempt at academic design was Faneuil Hall in Boston (1742), by the painter Smibert, with the arch order in two stories, the lower one forming an open market. A series of buildings of unique architectonic character was designed by Peter Harrison of Newport, Rhode Island.   Though he seems not to have had professional training in England, he was certainly the most distinguished Colonial architect in North America. His Redwood Library in Newport (1748–50) has a Roman Doric portico of four columns, united to the body of the building by a single unbroken entablature (Fig. 290). Originally only the small wings flanking the façade prevented the building from conforming entirely to the temple

FIG. 290—NEWPORT.   REDWOOD LIBRARY

type, already imitated in the garden temples in England. The Market at Newport, 1761, represents a more advanced academic phase than Faneuil Hall, in that it involves an engaged order running through two stories, over an arched basement. Harrison's work remained exceptional however, even among the more ambitious buildings on the eve of the Revolution. The greater number even of public buildings meanwhile still retained not only the modest materials, brick and wood, but also the simple wall surfaces and isolated details of the early part of the century.

Architecture of the national period. Its origins. During the Revolution (1775–83) building was almost completely suspended. At its close, although some craftsmen continued their work in the same style as before, the leaders were inspired by very different ideals.   They recognized that the colonial style, whatever its merits, was provincial, and they sought to establish an architecture worthy of the new, sovereign, republican States and of the great nation soon welded from them.   In all types of buildings connected with political and social institutions, moreover, the republican and humanitarian ideals of America demanded solutions very different

FIG. 291—RICHMOND.   VIRGINIA CAPITOL.   ORIGINAL MODEL

from those which were traditional in Europe.   For government buildings, prisons, asylums, and other types new dispositions had to be found.   The pioneer in both these movements was Thomas Jefferson, whose political career gave him an unexampled opportunity for the realization of his architectural conceptions.   He felt that even the forms of detail should not be borrowed from contemporary European styles, although they should command the respect of foreign observers.   In this situation he turned to what he felt to be the unimpeachable authority of the ancients, in whose republics the new States were felt to have their closest analogy.   In his design for the Capitol of Virginia at Richmond (1785, Fig.

291), the first of modern republican government buildings, he boldly took as his model the Maison Carrée at Nîmes. The Ionic order was substituted to save expense, windows were necessarily pierced in the cella walls, and the interior was subdivided in conformity with the balance of legislative and judicial functions, if not exactly in accordance with the expression of the exterior. It is little realized that this design considerably antedated anything similar abroad. Classical examples had indeed been imitated in garden temples and commemorative monuments, but never on such a large scale and never in a building intended for practical use. Even Gilly's proposed temple to Frederick the Great (1791) and Vignon's Napoleonic Temple of Glory (1807) were monuments simply, and not until the Birmingham Town Hall (1831) was there anything in Europe really analogous to this first monument of American national architecture.

Academicism and classicism. Public buildings. The seed of a literal classic revival thus implanted required time to bear its fruit. Meanwhile many buildings of less advanced character evidenced none the less the change from colonial ideas. Engineers, builders, and amateurs, both of native and of foreign birth, united to infuse them with largeness of scale and academic character. James Hoban of Dublin, in his South Carolina Capitol at Columbia (1786–91), and L'Enfant, the French military engineer, in his remodeling of Federal Hall in New York, the first Capitol of the United States (1789), both employed the favorite academic formula of a columnar central pavilion over a high basement. William Thornton's Philadelphia Library (1789), and Samuel Blodget's marble façade of the Bank of the United States (Girard's Bank) in Philadelphia (1795), had similar frontispieces rising the full height of the building. The competitive drawings for the Capitol at Washington (1792–93) showed a determined effort to secure a monumental result. The design of Thornton, which received first prize, was based on the great Palladian layouts of England. More advanced still were the competitive designs of Stephen Hallet, a French architect of the highest professional training, who was placed in charge of the work. In his first study he had adopted the scheme, since so popular in legislative buildings, of a tall central dome with balancing

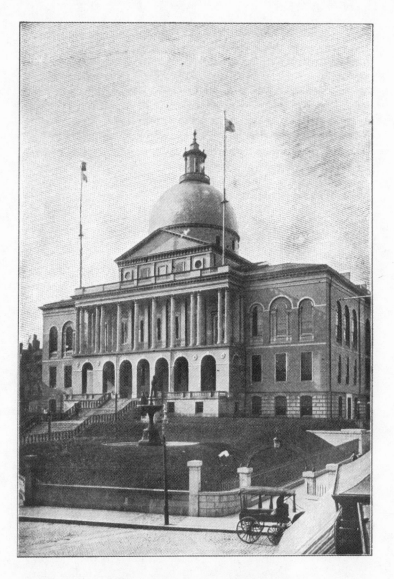

FIG. 292—BOSTON.   STATE HOUSE

wings, similar in form to the Collège des Quatre Nations in Paris. Various later studies, under Jefferson's influence, were based on the peristylar temple, the Panthéon in Paris, and the motive of the Pantheon in Rome, which remained the accepted central feature. In these studies, also, Hallet anticipated the foreign instances of legislative halls of semicircular form. Charles Bulfinch showed both the classical and the academic influences, in the Beacon column in Boston (1789), based on

FIG. 293—NEW YORK.   CITY HALL

Roman examples, and in the Massachusetts State House (1790–98), with its tall dome and its colonnade above an arched basement (Fig. 292).   Pure French academism of the mid-eighteenth century appears in the New York City Hall (1803–12, Fig. 293), designed by the French engineer, Joseph Mangin, in partnership with John McComb. Here for the first time in America appears an academic façade with angle pavilions, with a sophisticated wall treatment of superposed orders, of archivolts and rustication. The complete victory of classicism, even in its Roman phase, did not ensue until after 1815. It was Jefferson, the initiator of the movement, who crowned its triumph with the design of the University of Virginia group. Here long colonnades connecting classical pavilions of varied design lead up to the central Rotunda or library, based on the Roman Pantheon.

The Greek revival. Latrobe. Long before classicism had carried the day the Roman revival had been reinforced by a Greek revival. The introduction of Greek forms, already used in England and Germany, was due to Benjamin Henry Latrobe,

FIG. 294—PHILADELPHIA. BANK OF THE UNITED STATES (CUSTOM HOUSE)

an architect who had the professional training of both these countries. He came to America in 1796, and in his first monumental work, the Bank of Pennsylvania, 1799, employed a Greek Ionic order in two hexastyle porticoes which gave access to the domed banking-room. In the conduct of the work on the national Capitol, with which he was charged from 1803–17, his principal opportunities lay in the interior, where he created the great semicircular Hall of Representatives (now Statuary Hall), with its Corinthian colonnade employing

Greek capitals of the Lysicrates type. His last design was for the second Bank of the United States in Philadelphia (1819–24), in which—encouraged doubtless by the philhellene Nicholas Biddle, later its president—he adopted the octastyle Doric form of the Parthenon itself (Fig. 294). The need for additional space in the interior, indeed, led to the suppression of the side colonnades, but even then the building approached the ultimate Athenian ideal more nearly than any modern building which had so far been erected in Europe.

The later classicists. Hellenic influence dominated American architecture until nearly 1850. A pupil of Latrobe, Robert Mills, rivaled his master in advanced classicism by employing a Greek Doric column, nearly a hundred feet in height, as the motive of his Washington Monument in Baltimore (1815), and an obelisk of five hundred feet in the Washington Monument in Washington (1836 *ff.*). The temple form was followed in a series of State capitols, and notably in the one-time Custom House of New York (1834–41), now the Sub-Treasury —another and more literal version of the Parthenon. The latest and richest example was the main building of Girard College in Philadelphia (1833–47), for which Nicholas Biddle forced the adoption of the temple form, carried out with the Corinthian order of the Lysicrates type by Thomas U. Walter. For State capitols, however, the type having a dome and wings, with the prestige given it by the completion of the national Capitol (1829), found thenceforth more adherents. Another favorite motive was the long unbroken colonnade, as used in the original (Fifteenth Street) façade of the Treasury in Washington by Robert Mills (1836–39), and in the Merchants' Exchange in New York (now forming the lower story of the National City Bank), by Isaiah Rogers (1835–41). A novelty was the great semicircular portico of the Merchants' Exchange in Philadelphia, by William Strickland. When the Capitol at Washington was enlarged to its present form (Fig. 295) by Walter in 1851–65, he had naturally to follow the academic-Roman ordonnance of the exterior, and thus helped to give the later buildings of the classical movement a less Hellenic stamp. By all these designs, the States and the nation were endowed with a tradition of monumental and dignified government architecture which has been continued with but slight interruptions to the present day.

Domestic architecture. In domestic architecture after the Revolution the colonial style was resumed by the craftsmen with little change, so that a large group of buildings may well be described as "post-colonial." An early example is the Peirce-Nichols house in Salem (c. 1790), by Samuel McIntire.

Copyright by the American Architect and Building News Co.

FIG. 295—WASHINGTON.   UNITED STATES CAPITOL

The façade differs little from that of the Royall house in Medford, built many years earlier, except in the substitution of a heavy Doric order in the corner pilasters and in the bolder treatment of the doorway (Fig. 296).   Classical influence soon showed itself in two quite different ways.   One, which still involved no break with the past, was the employment of Adam forms of detail, both in exteriors and interiors.   Thus were developed the attenuation of proportions and the delicacy of ornament so characteristic of the later work of McIntire in Salem, typical of New England in the early nineteenth century, and occasionally seen elsewhere.   The appropriateness of these forms to execution in the prevailing material, wood, lent them a special attraction.   The other classical tendency, which dominated the southern States, was quite different in its inspiration and direction. It took its departure from Palladianism and from French models, and ultimately sought to assimilate the house also to the ideal form of the temple. From the start the portico or frontispiece of tall columns was common, a prominent example being the White

FIG. 296—SALEM.   PIERCE-NICHOLS HOUSE

House in Washington (1792 ff., Fig. 297). The tall portico became especially popular in Virginia and the South through Jefferson's numerous designs, in which he sought, where possible, to give the effect of a single story, as in the French houses of supposedly Roman cast. In remodeling his own house, Monticello (1796–1809), he introduced a dome over the projecting salon, to secure a still further resemblance to such buildings as the Hôtel de Salm in Paris. The professors' houses of the University of Virginia, which he designed as "specimens for the architectural lectures," included imitations of the prostyle temple, and these were widely copied where there were no didactic motives. Nicholas Biddle, with his customary enthusiasm for things Greek, adopted the model of the Theseum, peristyle and all, for his country seat "Andalusia" on the Delaware. Even in New England the prostyle temple with Greek forms finally carried the day, while in the South the peristyle, with its manifest suitability to the climate, was widely adopted. Such magnificent specimens as Arling-

FIG. 297—WASHINGTON. WHITE HOUSE. (HOBAN'S ORIGINAL DESIGN)

ton in Virginia, where the ponderous columns of the great temple of Pæstum were imitated, as the Bennett house in New Bedford, with its hexastyle Ionic main portico and tetrastyle wings, as Berry Hill in Virginia, with two octastyle Greek Doric porticoes and balancing outbuildings of the same order, or as the Hill House in Athens, Georgia, with a Corinthian peristyle eight columns wide in front, show extremes of classicism which have no parallel abroad. City houses in blocks showed the same tendencies as houses which stood isolated. In 1793 Bulfinch erected for the first time in America a block of unified design, the Franklin Crescent in Boston, with pavilions of academic scheme and Adam detail. Some coherent treatment of the block remained an ideal, although one seldom realized. The most notable later example was Colonnade Row in Lafayette Place, New York (1827), which had a free-standing Greek Corinthian order carried throughout its length. The interiors of the classical houses lost in richness through the abandonment of paneling, and through the chaste purism which confined all detail to essential structural elements. The tall, cool rooms, with their occasional screens of columns, served now as neutral backgrounds to rich furniture and hangings.

Churches. Post-colonial buildings, differing but little from the more advanced buildings erected before the Revolution, were also common among the churches of the early republic. Here, too, slender proportions came in with Adam detail. Nevertheless more monumental effects, parallel to those attained in public buildings, made their appearance soon after the opening of the nineteenth century. The fundamental work was Latrobe's Catholic Cathedral in Baltimore (1805–21), the first cathedral undertaken in the United States—where it was as novel in its size and ritualistic arrangement as in its classical forms. The plan was a Latin cross, vaulted throughout, with a low dome over the crossing, a western portico of Greek detail, and twin belfries, Hellenized as best they might be. In 1816 Latrobe employed the Greek cross form for Saint John's Episcopal Church in Washington. Robert Mills developed the auditorium type of octagonal or circular form in the Monumental Church in Richmond, Virginia (begun 1812), and others. The temple form was only adopted later, for instance in Saint Paul's Church, Boston (1820), with an Ionic prostyle portico of six columns.

Prisons and asylums. With its new departures in all branches of government, America soon took the lead in the reform of methods of punishment and of the treatment of the insane. The New York State Prison, built by Joseph Mangin in 1796–98, included provision for the separation of the sexes and of classes of criminals, and the Virginia Penitentiary, built by Latrobe in 1797–1800, was based on the principle of solitary confinement. Later these ideas were more fully applied, and embodied in radial plans, by the architect John Haviland, of English birth. By 1835 the American prisons were so favorably known that commissions from England, France, and other European countries came to study them and to introduce their principles abroad.

The Gothic revival in America. Although Jefferson, with his underlying vein of romanticism, had proposed imitations of Gothic models as early as 1771, Latrobe was the first to execute a Gothic design, in Sedgeley, a country house near Philadelphia (1800). For the cathedral in Baltimore he submitted an alternative scheme, the first revived Gothic church design in America. In 1807 Godefroi, a French engineer and architect, carried out the chapel of Saint Mary's Seminary in Baltimore with Gothic forms. Other architects soon essayed occasional buildings in Gothic, still inspired less by a conscious principle of eclecticism than a romantic interest in the style, of which neither the structural principles nor the decorative forms were much understood. A new period in the Gothic revival was opened by the building of Trinity Church in New York, by Richard Upjohn (1839-46, Fig. 298). Here the design was carefully studied from English examples. These long remained the favorite models, although James Renwick in Saint Patrick's

FIG. 298—NEW YORK.   TRINITY CHURCH

Cathedral, New York (1850-79), adopted the traditional French scheme with twin western towers. In the sixties the influence of Ruskin led to the adoption of Italian Gothic detail, and to a moral fervor in the advocacy of medievalism which had hitherto been absent in America. Meanwhile, in the forties, the imitation of temples in domestic architecture had been attacked as absurd and impractical, and cottages and villas of Gothic, Elizabethan, Swiss, or "Italian" style had taken their places, as more flexible and convenient, more domestic, and more in harmony with the landscape. Individual Greek forms, however, had continued to be employed for the details of other houses, especially in the towns, and thus both romanticism and classicism were gradually replaced by an eclecticism which chose for each building the style which seemed most appropriate to its use and surroundings.

Eclecticism. In America, where there were so few trained architects or accessible models, the supplanting of traditional knowledge of forms by unrestrained eclecticism had even more disastrous results for the common run of buildings than it had in Europe. The Civil War (1861–65), with the materialism of the resulting era of economic reconstruction, accentuated the difficulty, and subjected government architecture to a mechanical system. Nevertheless there was no period of years in which competent and thoughtful men did not seek to uphold the ideals of their art, in buildings which worthily represented contemporary movements in Europe. Most notable of the earlier men was Richard Morris Hunt (1827–95), the first American to study at the Ecole des Beaux-Arts in Paris, who brought with him to New York in 1855 the rationalistic training of the school and a preference for French Renaissance forms, then dominant under the Second Empire. In the Lenox Library, New York (1870–77), he followed the tendencies of Labrouste; while in the houses for the Vanderbilts in New York and at Biltmore, in the Astor residence, and in "cottages" at Newport, he exploited every phase of his favorite style, only adopting a more classical tendency in the last years of his life, under the influence of younger men. The older architects of English training, meanwhile, were attempting to establish the supremacy of Victorian Gothic, and in churches, at least, medieval forms were employed as a matter of course.

Richardson and the Romanesque. When Henry Hobson Richardson, another American of French academic training, chose the Romanesque style for his accepted project for Trinity Church in Boston (1872), he was influenced primarily by the slight depth of the site, which was unfavorable to a Gothic nave. He clothed the broad cruciform naves and great central tower with a rugged mantle of polychrome sandstone reminiscent of Auvergne and Salamanca (Fig. 299). By the time the building was completed in 1877, however, he saw in Romanesque forms a far-reaching adaptability to American

needs, which would permit the development of a truly
national style. Their simplicity and ruggedness seemed suited
alike to materials readily available, to the general limitation
of funds, and to the relative lack of skilled carvers. In
subsequent buildings, like the Allegheny Court House at

FIG. 299—BOSTON. TRINITY CHURCH, AS ORIGINALLY BUILT. (VAN
RENSSELAER)

Pittsburgh (1884), he expressed freely, with a personal vocabulary of Romanesque elements, the ideal character and practical conditions of a great number of contemporary types—
the town library, the country railroad station, even the vast
warehouse. Richardson's mannerisms, however, such as the
fondness for towers and for broad low arches, were more
easily acquired by others than his power of picturesque yet
logical composition. Thus, after his untimely death in 1886,
his style was quickly discredited by imitators, while the abler
architects continued their independent development.

"Queen Anne" and the beginnings of the colonial revival.
Simultaneously with the building of Trinity had come the
founding of the Queen Anne movement in England, with its

wide program of frankness and colloquialism, and the revelation of foreign arts and crafts to America through the Centennial Exposition in 1876. These inspired many attempts at imitation, and some free and original creations, such as the Casino at Newport, built in 1881 by the firm of McKim, Mead, and White. The attention of these men and some others, hitherto attracted by the French Renaissance or the Roman-

FIG. 300—BOSTON. PUBLIC LIBRARY

esque, was naturally drawn to the American buildings of the seventeenth and eighteenth centuries which correspond to the prototypes of the Queen Anne style abroad. Thus began a direct revival of colonial architecture, in many houses of the eighties, with a richness of delicate detail on the exterior very different, to be sure, from the general simplicity of the old examples.

The adoption of Renaissance forms. It was this adaptation of native Renaissance forms which prepared McKim, Mead, and White for the adoption of those of the Italian Renaissance. These were employed for the first time by one of their associates, Joseph M. Wells, in the Villard houses in New York (1885), where the arched windows of the Cancelleria furnished the motive. The decisive work, however, was the Boston Public Library (1888–95, Fig. 300), in which McKim, taking his departure from the Bibliothèque Sainte Geneviève, gave the

scheme the warmer and more robust character of Alberti's
San Francesco at Rimini.   In the interior each element of the
building was sympathetically studied from Italian examples
which showed the structural use of classical elements, and
executed with a characteristic treatment of each material and
a harmony of decoration hitherto unknown in America.

FIG. 301—ROCKVILLE.   GARDEN OF "MAXWELL COURT"

McKim's purism of detail in the library was complemented
by the luxurious elaboration of Renaissance ornament by
White and Wells in the Century Club and Madison Square
Garden in New York (1889).   The effect on current practice
was electrical. Almost overnight Romanesque and Queen
Anne gave way to Renaissance forms, which more nearly
approached universal acceptance than those of any style since
the Greek revival.   There were variants, to be sure,.   Fresh
arrivals from the Ecole des Beaux-Arts tended to follow French
Renaissance and academic architecture rather than Italian.

For domestic buildings many preferred more literal imitations of the "Georgian" houses of the colonies in the eighteenth century. The Italian tendency received a powerful reinforcement, however, in the work of Charles A. Platt, who introduced the Italian formal garden into America (Fig. 301), and has steadily widened the scope of his architectural activity without departing far from his favorite style. It has furnished the medium for many current abstract compositions.

Neo-classicism. The Chicago Exposition. The crucial test between the partisans of a free and modern interpretation of motives chiefly medieval and the partisans of a strict following of some form of classic architecture came in the buildings of the Columbian Exposition in Chicago in 1893. The studies of John W. Root, the original consulting architect of the exposition, were of a free semi-Romanesque character, with some recognition of the steel construction and the temporary nature of the buildings. These conceptions might well have dominated the ensemble had not the death of Root on the eve of the undertaking left the group of Eastern architects, headed by Hunt, to whom had been confided the buildings of the Court of Honor, free to carry out their own ideas. These were that the mutual dependence of their buildings, and the formal character of the court, demanded a consistent style of generally Roman classical character, with a uniform cornice height fixed at sixty feet. This did not preclude a treatment of merely academic cast, with details tinged by Italian or Spanish influence, so that within the classical scheme there was a considerable diversity of style. The buildings which attracted the most admiration, however, were those in which the main cornice was reached by a single order of strictly Roman character—namely, the Agricultural Building by McKim, the Fine Arts group and the "Peristyle" toward the lake, both by Charles B. Attwood (Fig. 302). Attwood, in the Fine Arts Building, followed Besnard's project for the Grand Prix de Rome, with its central portico with an attic and a saucer dome behind; McKim was also greatly influenced by the same design, although he followed it much less closely. True to the hopes of their designers, the classical buildings produced a cumulative effect of harmony and magnificence which was deeply stamped on the memory of the whole nation.

FIG. 302—CHICAGO EXPOSITION. COURT OF HONOR, WITH AGRICULTURAL BUILDING (AT RIGHT) AND PERISTYLE (AT BACK)

Neo-classicism. Later developments. Although the leading architects of the exposition had hoped to give a striking object-lesson of the value of classical and academic formulæ, they hardly expected the result which ensued. Whereas, earlier, there had been one or two isolated experiments with strictly classical forms, such as the Grant Mausoleum in New York (1891), the whole public architecture of the country was now turned into a monumental and classical channel. The first fruit of the movement was McKim's unified classical design for Columbia University in New York, with its great domed library (1895). A fresh impulse came through the restoration of the University of Virginia by White after the fire of 1896, and the activity of McKim—with D. H. Burnham, Olmsted, and Saint-Gaudens—on the commission for the improvement of Washington. The character of the early buildings of the republic thus gave a nationalistic sanction to the classical tendency, and the style of new government buildings was henceforth established. Milestones in the progress of the movement were the Knickerbocker (Columbia) Trust Company in New York, with its single rich Corinthian order including the whole height of the building, and the Pennsylvania Terminal Station, with its long Doric façades, and its great hall, literally copied from the Roman thermæ, almost devoid of practical functions. From the start the orders used frequently included Greek forms, and these have been employed increasingly. A notable recent instance is the Lincoln Memorial in Washington, a peristylar cella in which the old revivalist enthusiasm for an abstract architectonic ideal has prevailed over any suggestion of individual character. The mass composition of high buildings, stimulated by the New York "zoning law" of 1916, has generally followed classical principles of balance, whether or not they are classical in detail. This second classical revival in America has little contemporary parallel abroad except in England, which has itself been influenced in the matter by developments across the ocean. While the rest of the world is seeking, in one way or another, new forms expressive of the novel elements of modern life, this insistence on the traditional authority of the past can be adequately explained only by the unparalleled heritage of classical monuments from the formative period of the nation.

Thus the founders of the republic might seem for the moment to have achieved their aim of establishing classical architecture as a permanent national style.

Gothic survivals.   In spite of the overwhelming victory of classical forms, the Gothic tendency has been kept alive, largely through the enthusiasm and artistry of two men, Ralph Adams

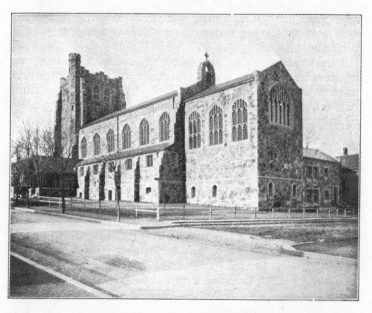

FIG. 303—ASHMONT.   CHURCH OF ALL SAINTS

Cram and Bertram Grosvenor Goodhue, who practised in partnership for many years.   Their initial success was the church of All Saints, Ashmont, Massachusetts (1892, Fig. 303), which embodied the same free tendencies as the designs of Sedding in England.   These tendencies have been perpetuated in Goodhue's later work, such as the chapel and other buildings of the Military Academy at West Point, with their picturesque adaptation to the rugged site.   Cram has tended to follow precedents more strictly, and to range more widely among the medieval styles, as in his "Early English" features of the New York cathedral, the late Byzantine administration building for the Rice Institute at Houston, Texas. Even in its last strongholds, ecclesiastical and collegiate architecture, the Gothic has had to yield ground, especially to the colonial revival. Nevertheless, although both the Protestant sects and the Roman Catholic church now prefer the styles unequivocally associated with their past, the preference of the Anglican episcopate for Gothic forms, and the personal prestige and ability of the Gothic leaders, have still maintained the Gothic tendency.

Functionalism. The striving for characteristic expression, which is the principle of functionalism in architecture, appeared subordinately—in America as in Europe—in all the movements of the nineteenth century. Structural purism was a quality of Latrobe's designs, as it was, more pronouncedly, of those of the Gothicists. The lessons of Ruskin and Viollet-le-Duc were not forgotten in the early years of the Renaissance revival and of neo-classicism, when it was felt that the column must be used only in its original function of an isolated support. Even in the later years of these movements, when structural purism has yielded to the expression of monumental character, this very character itself is felt to be but one of a number of ideals which govern the different phases of architecture—civic, religious, and domestic. Moreover, in spite of eclectic inclination—so strong in America, especially in McKim's work—to model the exterior of a building on an individual prototype selected in advance, there has been a steady development of logical planning and expression of plan, under the leadership of the Beaux-Arts men. McKim and White themselves were the pioneers in a characteristic use of materials which has produced such interesting results as the "Harvard" and "tapestry" brickwork, the modeled and polychrome terra cotta, and the local ledge-stone revival of Philadelphia.

Expression of structure. A new problem. In the expression of structure a new problem has been presented by the steel-frame building. The absence of legal restriction permitted real estate owners in the crowded districts of New York and Chicago, about 1880, to increase the number of stories in new office buildings by supporting the floors entirely on iron or steel columns, leaving the wall with only its own weight to

carry. The development of elevators or lifts made the upper
stories as desirable as the lower ones, and made possible
"skyscrapers" like the World Building in New York, with a
height of three hundred and seventy-five feet. Here, however,
the self-supporting walls reached a thickness of nine feet at the
base, and injured the value of the lower stories. It soon

Copyright by the American Architect and Building News Co.

FIG. 304—BUFFALO. (PRUDENTIAL) GUARANTY BUILDING

occurred to the designers that the wall itself might be supported
on the steel frame at intervals, and be reduced to a mere veneer,
with great resulting economy. Thus buildings of twelve to
twenty stories have become commonplace in every considerable city, and such extreme heights as that of the Woolworth Building in New York (779 feet) have been reached.
The retention of a shell of masonry, which differentiates these
buildings from the steel and glass shop fronts abroad, was
originally due to a natural adherence to tradition. It has
been perpetuated for a far more vital reason—the extreme
necessity of rendering such tall buildings secure against fire,

before which exposed steel work proved to twist and bend with disastrous results. The only adequate protection proved to be that furnished by casing all the structural members in

FIG. 305—NEW YORK. WOOLWORTH
BUILDING

masonry, preferably brick or terra cotta, which had already been through fire. Aided by experience in the great conflagrations in Baltimore (1904) and San Francisco (1906), the technique of such fireproof construction has developed so that with the aid of metal interior trim, wire glass, composite floors resting on steel beams, and other devices, a building can now be made not only non-combustible, but absolutely proof against fire, whether arising within or sweeping the surroundings without. The manifest practical advantages of the system have led to worldwide adoption of many of its features. Its employment in façades, however, involves a new and delicate problem of expression.

The solutions. A visual indication that the masonry was no longer self-supporting but depended on the steel frame, was achieved

FIG. 305—NEW YORK. WOOLWORTH
BUILDING

about 1895 by Louis Sullivan, notably in the Guaranty (Prudential) Building in Buffalo (Fig. 304). He abandoned a wall surface of ashlar in favor of a simple casing of the members of the frame, with glass filling the whole of the space between. The greater weight carried by the vertical members he recognized by emphasizing the vertical lines. To avoid any structural suggestion in the casing he used terra cotta having a delicate surface pattern. The principle of his

designs has been widely fol-lowed by architects of tall buildings, irrespective of the style employed, although few have carried it through with such logical completeness. To Cass Gilbert the emphasis on the vertical lines sug-gested the employment of Gothic forms, which the éclat of his employment of them in the Woolworth Building (Fig. 305) has popularized to some extent. In many very recent build-ings, however, a reactionary tendency, based on the over-whelming predominance of classicism in other depart-ments of architecture, has resulted in a reversion to plain wall surfaces and ap-plications of the orders.

Modernist forms. The origins. America, with its freedom from the restraint of tradition, was also natu-rally one of the first coun-tries to experiment with novel forms, consciously pre-

FIG. 306—CHICAGO EXPOSITION. TRANSPORTATION BUILDING. DETAIL

ferred to those of the past as expressive of modernity. The old desire for an "American style" could not be satisfied merely by the general adoption of any group of historic forms, even if, as in the case of Richardsonian Romanesque, its adoption was purely an American movement.   In Richardson's work itself there was, as we have noted, a strong tendency to modification and originality of detail, and this tendency was taken up with special aptitude by Harvey Ellis, Root, and

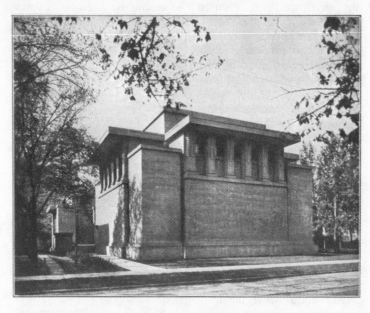

FIG. 307—OAK PARK.   CHURCH OF THE UNITY

others in the Middle West.   The manifesto of a truly independent progressive tendency was the Transportation Building of the Chicago Exposition by Louis Sullivan (1893, Fig. 306), contemporary with the earliest similar attempts abroad.   Here, side by side with the first monuments of neo-classicism, was a building in which there were indeed some reminiscences of Romanesque and Saracenic motives, but in which the essential effort was to express the modernity and novelty of the type of building, its materials, and its structural system.   The plain stuccoed wall surfaces, with their unbroken, block-like cornices enriched by bands of fertile original relief ornament, the arch and column with novel yet expressive forms, anticipated by many years corresponding treatments in the German "Secession." In spite of the overpowering influence of the classical ensemble of the exposition on America at large, this building made some converts, chiefly in Chicago itself. Through Sullivan's pioneer expression of the veneered steel frame the movement had an influence far beyond its own circle of devotees.

Later developments. That participation in the movement did not involve mere imitation of its leader was early established by one of Sullivan's pupils, Frank Lloyd Wright. In his designs for residences he has employed broad ramified plans, wide eaves, novel fenestration, and a harmonious use of abstract motives of ornament, which have a suggestion of the Japanese. The appropriateness of these houses to the landscape of the lakes and the plains has been widely recognized, and they have profoundly influenced the architecture of the Middle West. More ambitious applications of similar forms have not been wanting. In the Midway Gardens in Chicago Wright has embodied the spirit of gaiety in forms of exuberant yet delicate fantasy. In his Church of the Unity at Oak Park (Fig. 307), he has evolved a monumental and characteristic house of worship for disciples of modern rationalism. To the present time, however, the movement has received more appreciation abroad than at home.

It remains to be seen whether the wide acceptance and nationalistic basis of the neo-classical tendency will enable it to surmount the elements of weakness which aided the downfall of the earlier classical revival, or whether the international forces of functionalism will ultimately cause a wider adoption of modernist forms.

PERIODS OF ARCHITECTURE IN THE UNITED STATES

I.   Colonial period, to 1776 (or later in Spanish colonies).
    Spanish colonies.
        Florida (Saint Augustine founded 1565).
            Fort San Marco (Fort Marion) at Saint Augustine, completed 1756.
            Cathedral at Saint Augustine, begun 1793 (rebuilt 1887).

New Mexico (Santa Fé founded 1605).
　Cathedral of Saint Francis at Santa Fé, 1713-14.
California (San Diego founded 1769).
　San Carlos Mission, present church, 1793-97.
　San Juan Capistrano Mission, later church, begun 1797.
　San Gabriel Mission, present church, 1794-1806.
　Santa Barbara Mission, present church, 1815-20.
Louisiana (under Spain 1764-1800).
　Cathedral at New Orleans, 1792-94
　Cabildo at New Orleans, 1795.
Dutch colonies, 1624-64.
　"Stadt Huis" at New Amsterdam, 1642 (demolished).
English colonies.
　Seventeenth century.
　　Virginia (Jamestown founded 1607).
　　　Saint Luke's, Smithfield, about 1650.
　　　Bacon's Castle, before 1676.
　　Massachusetts (Plymouth founded 1620; Boston, 1630).
　　　"Scotch House," Saugus, 1651.
　　　Tufts house, Medford, 1677-80.
　　　"Old Ship" Meeting House in Hingham, 1681.
　　Carolina (Charleston established on its present site 1680).
　　　Yeoman's Hall, Goose Creek, c. 1693.
　　Pennsylvania (Philadelphia founded 1682).
　　　William Penn (Letitia) house in Philadelphia, 1683.
　Eighteenth century.
　　Houses.
　　　The Mulberry, South Carolina, c. 1714.
　　　Westover, Virginia, c. 1730.
　　　Royall house in Medford, Massachusetts, c. 1737.
　　　Mount Airy, Virginia, 1758.
　　　Whitehall, Maryland, 1764-68.
　　　Mount Pleasant in Philadelphia, c. 1761.
　　　Brewton house in Charleston, 1765-69.
　　　Monticello, Virginia (Thomas Jefferson), begun 1771.
　　Churches.
　　　Old Saint Philip's, Charleston, 1723 (since rebuilt).
　　　Christ Church, Philadelphia (John Kearsley), 1727-44.
　　　King's Chapel, Boston (Peter Harrison), 1749-54,
　　　　portico 1790.
　　　Saint Michael's, Charleston, 1752-61.
　　　Saint Paul's Chapel, New York (McBean), 1764-66,
　　　　steeple 1794.

Public buildings.
Old City Hall in New York, 1700 (demolished).
Old Virginia Capitol in Williamsburg, 1702–04 (demolished).
Andrew Hamilton (1676–1741).
Old State House (Independence Hall) in Philadelphia, 1732–52.
John Smibert (1684–1751).
Faneuil Hall in Boston, 1742 (since twice rebuilt).
Peter Harrison (1716–75).
Redwood Library in Newport, R. I., 1748–50.
Brick Market in Newport, R. I., 1761.

II. National period, 1776–date.
Classicism, c. 1785–1850.
Thomas Jefferson, 1743–1826.
Virginia Capitol at Richmond, 1785–98 (remodeled).
Remodeling of Monticello, 1796–1808.
University of Virginia, 1817–26.
Pierre Charles L'Enfant, 1754–1825.
Federal Hall in New York, 1789 (demolished).
Plan of the city of Washington, 1791.
Robert Morris house, Philadelphia, 1792–95 (demolished).
Stephen Hallet.
Designs for the Capitol at Washington, 1792–94.
James Hoban, c. 1762–1831.
South Carolina Capitol at Columbia, 1789 (destroyed).
White House in Washington, 1792–1829.
William Thornton, 1759–1828.
Philadelphia Library, 1789 (demolished).
Designs for the Capitol at Washington, 1792–1802.
Charles Bulfinch, 1763–1844.
Beacon column in Boston, 1789.
Massachusetts State House in Boston, 1790–98.
Massachusetts General Hospital in Boston, 1818–21.
Completion of the Capitol at Washington, 1818–29.
Samuel Blodget, 1759–1814.
Bank of the United States (Girard's Bank) in Philadelphia, 1795–97.
Benjamin Henry Latrobe, 1766–1820.
Bank of Pennsylvania in Philadelphia, 1799 (demolished).
Works at the Capitol at Washington, 1803–17.
Cathedral in Baltimore, 1805–21.
Exchange, Bank, and Custom House at Baltimore (with Godefroi), 1815–20 (demolished).

(Second) United States Bank at Philadelphia, 1819–24.

Joseph Mangin, and John McComb, 1763–1853.

New York City Hall, 1803–12.

Saint John's, Varick Street, New York, 1803–07.

Robert Mills, 1781–1855.

Washington Monument in Baltimore, 1815–29.

East colonnade of the Treasury in Washington, 1836–39.

Washington Monument in Washington, 1836–77.

William Strickland, 1787–1854.

Merchants' Exchange in Philadelphia, 1832–34.

Tennessee Capitol at Nashville, begun c. 1850.

Ithiel Town.

Former Connecticut Capitol at New Haven, 1829 (demolished).

Custom House (Sub-Treasury) in New York (with A. J. Davis), 1834–41.

Isaiah Rogers.

Merchants' Exchange (Old Custom House) in New York, 1835–41 (remodeled).

Thomas U. Walter, 1804–88.

Girard College in Philadelphia, 1833–47.

Wings and dome of Capitol in Washington, 1851–65.

Romanticism, c. 1800–50.

Benjamin Henry Latrobe, 1766–1820.

Sedgeley near Philadelphia, 1800 (demolished).

Gothic project for cathedral in Baltimore, 1805.

Maximilian Godefroi, c. 1760–1833.

Chapel of Saint Mary's Seminary in Baltimore, 1807.

Richard Upjohn, 1802–78.

Trinity Church in New York, 1839–46.

James Renwick.

Grace Church in New York, 1843–46.

Saint Patrick's Cathedral in New York, 1850–79.

Eclecticism, c. 1850–date.

French Renaissance phase.

Richard Morris Hunt, 1827–95.

Residence of W. K. Vanderbilt in New York, 1878–83.

Lenox Library in New York, 1870–77 (demolished).

Biltmore, North Carolina.

Romanesque phase.

Henry Hobson Richardson, 1838–86.

Trinity Church in Boston, 1872–77 (west towers with porch, 1896–98).

Allegheny County buildings in Pittsburgh, 1884.

Classical phase.
  Charles B. Attwood, 1849–95.
    Fine Arts Building, Chicago Exposition, 1893.
  Charles F. McKim, 1847–1909; William R. Mead, 1846–,
      and Stanford White, 1853–1906.
    Casino at Newport, 1881.
    Residence of Henry Villard in New York, 1885.
    Boston Public Library, 1888–95.
    Agricultural Building, Chicago Exposition, 1893.
    Columbia University Library in New York, 1895.
    Pennsylvania Station in New York, completed 1910.
  John M. Carrère, 1858–1911, and Thomas Hastings, 1860–.
    Ponce de Leon Hotel at Saint Augustine, 1887.
    New York Public Library, 1897–1910.
  Cass Gilbert, 1859–.
    Minnesota State Capitol in Saint Paul, 1898–1906.
    Woolworth Building in New York, 1911–13.
  Charles A. Platt, 1861–.
    Larz Anderson Garden at Brookline.
    Leader Building at Cleveland, 1912.
Gothic phase.
  Ralph Adams Cram, 1863–; Bertram Grosvenor Good-
      hue, 1869–1924.
    All Saints', Ashmont, Massachusetts, 1892.
    United States Military Academy at West Point, 1003.
    Saint Thomas's, New York, 1906.
    Calvary Church in Pittsburgh, 1907.
    Rice Institute in Houston, 1909.
Functionalism, c. 1893–date.
Louis Sullivan, 1856–1924.
    Transportation Building, Chicago Exposition, 1893.
    Prudential (Guaranty) Building in Buffalo, c. 1895.
  Frank Lloyd Wright, 1869–.
    Larkin Building in Buffalo, 1904.
    Church of the Unity in Oak Park, Illinois, 1908.

BIBLIOGRAPHICAL NOTE

Pre-colonial architecture. A general view of the major part of the
field is afforded by three handbooks by T. A. Joyce: *South American
Archæology*, 1912; *Mexican Archæology*, 1914; and *Archæology of
Central America and the West Indies*, 1916. For North America see
S. D. Peet's *Prehistoric America*, 5 vols., 1890–1905; W. H. Holmes:
Handbook of Aboriginal American Antiquities, 1919. Among impor-

tant works on special regions are W. H. Holmes's *Archæological Studies among the Ancient Cities of Mexico*, 1895–97, and H. J. Spinden's *Maya Art*, 1913, W. Lehmann's *Art of Old Peru*, 1923. For others consult the bibliographies in Joyce's handbooks and, on Mexico, in W. Lehmann's *Methods and Results in Mexican Research*, 1909.

Colonial architecture: Spanish colonies. S. Baxter's *Spanish-Colonial Architecture in Mexico*, 10 vols., 1901, is an elaborate work; L. LaBeaume and W. B. Papin's *The Picturesque Architecture of Mexico*, 1915, a slighter book, composed primarily of views. For California see especially P. Elder's *The Old Spanish Missions of California*, 1913, and R. Newcomb's *The Franciscan Mission Architecture of Alta California*, 1916, and *Old Mission Churches and Historic Houses of California*, 1925; for New Mexico, L. B. Prince's *Spanish Mission Churches of New Mexico*, 1915.

English colonies. A popular general survey is afforded by H. D. Eberlein's *Architecture of Colonial America*, 1915; F. Kimball's *Domestic Architecture of the American Colonies and of the Early Republic*, 1922. A full bibliography is given by R. Bach in *The Architectural Record*, vol. 59, 1926, pp. 265 *ff*. Only the more important works are listed below. General collections of drawings and photographs are *The Georgian Period*, 3 vols., 1898–1902; Frank E. Wallis's *Old Colonial Architecture and Furniture*, 1887, and *American Architecture, Decoration, and Furniture*, 1896; G. H. Polley's *The Architecture, Interiors, and Furniture of the American Colonies During the XVIII. Century*, 1914; and D. Millar's *Measured Drawings of some Colonial and Georgian Houses*, 2 vols., 1916. Among regional works with important texts are N. M. Isham and A. F. Brown's *Early Rhode Island Houses*, 1895, and their *Early Connecticut Houses*, 1900; B. C. Trowbridge's *Old Houses of Connecticut*, 1924, and J. F. Kelly's *Early Domestic Architecture of Connecticut*, 1924; H. C. Wise and H. F. Biedleman's *Colonial Architecture . . . in Pennsylvania, New Jersey, and Delaware*, 1913; R. A. Lancaster's *Historic Virginia Homes and Churches;* Huger Smith's *Dwelling Houses of Charleston*, 1917; Eberlein's *Historic Homes of the Hudson Valley*, 1924. Regional works of large photographs are J. E. Chandler's *Colonial Architecture of Maryland, Pennsylvania, and Virginia*, 1882; J. M. Corner and E. Soderholz's *Domestic Colonial Architecture in New England*, 1891, *Domestic Colonial Architecture in Maryland and Virginia*, 1892; E. A. Crane and E. Soderholz's *Examples of Colonial Architecture in South Carolina and Georgia*, 1898; L. C. Coffin and A. Holden's *Brick Architecture in Maryland and Virginia*. Regional works of measured drawings are W. D. Goforth and W. J. McAuley's *Old Colonial Architectural Details in and around Philadelphia*, 1890; L. L. Howe and

C. Fuller's *Details from Old New England Houses*, 1913; R. C. Kingman's *New England Georgian Architecture*, 1913; J. P. Sims and C. Willing's *Old Philadelphia Colonial Details*, 1914; H. F. Cunningham and others' *Measured Drawings of Georgian Architecture in the District of Columbia*, 1914. J. F. Kelly: *Early Connecticut Architecture*, 1924. Among the works treating generally of single classes of buildings are A. Embury's *American Churches*, 1914; F. R. Vogel's *Das amerikanische Haus*, 1910; and J. E. Chandler's *The Colonial House*, 1916.

National architecture: United States. No adequate general work has hitherto been attempted. J. Gréber: *L'architecture aux Etats-Unis*, 2 vols., 1920, richly illustrated, deals mainly with contemporary work as does W. Hegemann and E. Peets' *American Vitruvius* L. Mumford's *Sticks and Stones* is a pessimistic social interpretation. Brief sketches which supplement one another are those of H. Van Brunt: *Development and Prospects of Architecture in the United States* (in N. S. Shaler's *United States of America*, 1894, vol. 2, pp. 425–51) and C. F. Bragdon: *Architecture in the United States*, in the *Architectural Record*, 1900, vol. 25, p. 426, and vol. 26, pp. 38, 84. The development of certain types through successive periods may be followed in *A History of Public Buildings Under the Control of the Treasury Department*, 1901; in F. R. Vogel's *Das amerikanische Haus*, 1910; and in J. W. Dow's *American Renaissance: a Review of Domestic Architecture*, 1904. For the post-colonial and classical period see M. Schuyler's *The Old Greek Revival*, in the *American Architect*, 1910–11, vol. 98, pp. 121, 201; vol. 99, pp. 81, 161. This may be supplemented by G. Brown's *History of the United States Capitol*, vol. 1, 1900; and the biographies *Thomas Jefferson, Architect*, 1916, by F. Kimball; *The Life and Letters of Charles Bulfinch*, 1896, by E. S. Bulfinch, and the *Journal of Latrobe*, 1905. For the later periods apart from the general works mentioned above the most important books are the individual studies of Richardson by M. G. Van Rensselaer, 1888; of Root by Harriet Monroe; of Burnham by Charles Moore; of McKim by A. H. Granger, 1913; and of Wright by C. R. Ashbee, 1911. There are also illustrated monographs on the work of McKim, Mead and White, 4 vols., Platt, Goodhue, and others.

CHAPTER XIV

EASTERN ARCHITECTURE

The East is a world which, as we now realize, long surpassed Christian Europe in enlightenment, as well as in wealth and extent. With its great religions and philosophies, there have flourished architectural styles of corresponding duration and complexity. In comparison with Western styles generally, these have been less concerned with problems of structure and more with abstract problems of repetition and combination of forms. A notable characteristic is the degree to which each Eastern people has held fast to its own artistic traditions under the most varied political and religious supremacies. Nevertheless artistic influences have not failed to pass back and forth between the Eastern peoples, as well as between the Orient and the Occident, so that there has been everywhere a varied historical development. Two main currents may be distinguished, one in the Far East embracing India, China, and their dependent countries, the other in the Near East, embracing Persia and the other countries which ultimately came under the sway of Mohammedanism.

Development of architecture in the Near East. Sassanian art. In return for its heritage from the preclassical civilization of the Levant, Greece endowed the Asiatic empires of Alexander and his successors with a Hellenistic art, which extended even beyond their borders. When the Parthian rulers (130 B.C.— 226 A.D.) overran Mesopotamia, they adopted the Greek columnar system. With the rise of the new Persian empire under the Sassanian dynasty (227–641 A.D.), however, the tide of art once more began to flow from East to West. The subterranean vaults and occasional domes of ancient Mesopotamia were taken as the basis of a consistently vaulted style.

In such instances as the palace at Ctesiphon (Fig. 308), with its great elliptically arched hall and façade of blank arcades, this achieved new effects both monumental and decorative. In other cases the dome, supported over a square room by means of diagonal arches or squinches, was a notable feature. In its westward expansion this virile art contributed largely,

FIG. 308—CTESIPHON. ROYAL PALACE. (DIEULAFOY)

as we have seen, to the formation of the Byzantine systems of construction and ornament.

Mohammedan architecture. General development. The Sassanian empire was brought to an end by the sudden expansion of Mohammedanism. In a few years from the flight of its prophet from Mecca (622), his followers, obeying his injunction to spread their faith by the sword, conquered Mesopotamia (637), Egypt (638), Persia (642), northern Africa and Spain (711). At first Mohammedan architecture in these regions was little else than the art of the different conquered peoples adapted to the worship and the customs of the conquerors. In Syria, in Egypt, and in Spain the Romano-Byzantine column and arch were employed for the construction of buildings such as the mosque of Amru at Cairo (642), or the great mosques of Damascus and Cordova (785–848). In Mesopotamia and Persia the domed and vaulted halls of the Sassanians were adopted as prominent features of the designs. Besides the uniformity of the programs, however, a certain community of artistic character between different regions soon developed—a character pronouncedly Oriental. This was due in part to the taste and the traditions of the Arabs themselves, but more largely to the earlier conquest of the Eastern lands, the prestige of these as the seat of the early caliphates of Damascus and Bagdad, and the vitality of Eastern art as the general source of inspiration in the early Middle Ages. Thus the lace-like incised carving of Mschatta in Syria, which had earlier contributed to Byzantine development, now appeared in the earliest Arab monuments of Africa and Spain. Thus, too, the pointed arch, common in Persia from the eighth century, appeared in Syria and Egypt from the beginning of the ninth. The tall dome of pointed silhouette, and the court with vaulted halls abutting it—also Persian features—penetrated Egypt in the thirteenth and fourteenth centuries. The conquest of northern India and its conversion to Mohammedanism opened the way for Persian influence there in the fourteenth and fifteenth centuries, while Persia itself then borrowed from India the ogee arch and the bulbous dome. With the conquest of Constantinople by the Ottoman Turks (1453), finally, began a new return influence of Byzantine architecture in their Oriental empire, through the imitation of Hagia Sophia, which became the chief mosque of the Turkish caliphs. The development of the various schools which resulted from the mingling of local traditions and distant influences continued uninterruptedly until the eighteenth and even the nineteenth century, and has been checked only by internal disorganization and by the conquests of European powers.

Mosques. The outward observances of the Mohammedan religion are simple—prayer, made facing in the direction of Mecca, and preceded by purifying ablution. For their formal places of worship, the mosques, the early believers naturally adopted the peristylar court—the universal scheme of the Levant—the porticoes of which furnished shelter from the tropical sun. The *mirhab*, a small niche in the outer wall, indicated the direction of Mecca, and on this side of the court the porticoes were deepened and multiplied. This fundamental scheme is seen in the first great mosque built after the conquest of Egypt, the mosque of Amru at Cairo (Fig. 310).

FIG. 309—CORDOVA. INTERIOR OF MOSQUE

The tendency was to develop the deeper side of the court into an inclosed building—often of vast extent, as at Cordova (Fig. 309)—with aisle after aisle of columns and arcades, carrying wooden beams and a terrace roof. In later western mosques the aisle leading to the mirhab was widened, and a special sanctuary was created in front of it. In Persia a great domed sanctuary preceded by a vast open nave or niche was early adopted, and corresponding features were introduced at the other cardinal points of the court.   The Egyptian mosques based on Persian models, such as the mosque of Sultan Hassan (1377), have a court so reduced that these features occupy the greater part of each side, and the scheme becomes

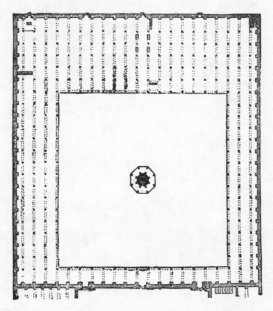

FIG. 310—CAIRO.   MOSQUE OF AMRU.   PLAN

cruciform.   On the capture of Constantinople, Hagia Sophia— with its atrium, its main building to the east, its great central nave, and its eastern apse—was found perfectly adapted to Mohammedan worship.   It was copied almost literally in the Mosque of Suleiman at Constantinople (1550).   In other Ottoman mosques the possible variants were used, especially the scheme of a central dome with four abutting half domes, which the Byzantines themselves had not developed.   Among minor elements of the mosques, which are yet among their most striking features, are the minarets, or slender towers, with corbeled balconies from which the muezzin gives the

FIG. 311—GRANADA. THE ALHAMBRA. COURT OF LIONS

call to prayers. These were erected at one or more of the corners of the buildings, ingeniously incorporated with it. Their forms varied much in different regions, the Ottoman form, with a very tall cylindrical shaft ending in a slender cone, being especially daring.

Palaces. The enjoyment of worldly goods and pleasures was not despised by Mohammedanism, and the absolute power

FIG. 312—AGRA.   THE TAJ MAHAL

and vast revenue of the caliphs enabled them to gratify their taste for splendor and luxury by the construction of magnificent palaces. In these the customs of the Orient demanded a jealous seclusion from the outer world, and a strict separation of the men's quarters and reception-rooms from the private apartments of the women and children, the harem. The rooms were distributed about one or more courts, the façades made as blind as possible, except for loggias and balconies high above the ground and guarded by latticed screens. To relieve the heat of the climate, the courts were surrounded by shady porticoes and provided with basins and fountains. A complex axial system governed the relations of the principal rooms and the courts. The luxurious elegance sometimes attained is well seen in the Alhambra at Granada, built by the last Mohammedan rulers of Spain, chiefly in the fourteenth and fifteenth centuries. The Court of Lions (Fig. 311), with its slender columns, its delicate stalactite decoration in stucco, colored and gilded, shows Mohammedan architecture in the final development of one of its local schools, when the elements of diverse origin had been fused in a characteristic whole.

Tombs. In Egypt, in Persia, and especially in India, the tombs of great monarchs rival the palaces and mosques. The Indian type was a domed mausoleum, set in the midst of a garden. The most noted example is the Taj Mahal at Agra (Fig. 312), built by Shah Jahan in 1630, in which the central dome is flanked by four smaller domes, and the principal, minor, and diagonal axes are marked on the exterior by great arches expressively and harmoniously proportioned.

Forms of detail. The Mohammedan builders were confronted by few structural problems for which solutions had not already been found by late Roman, Byzantine, and Sassanian architecture. At first, like the early Christian builders, they employed borrowed classical columns and capitals, supporting impost blocks and stilted arches. Their early domes rested on squinches. Later their treatment of fundamental structural elements, such as the arch and the vault, was governed by decorative conceptions. In Spain and Africa arches were given a horseshoe shape or were cusped; in Persia, Egypt, and Spain vaults were treated with a multitude of small squinches resembling stalactites. Stalactite motives were also used in some capitals, although in others modified Corinthian motives were used, much as in the most expressive Gothic examples. The ornamentation depended little on effects of bold relief, but greatly on effects of line, of material, and, above all, of color. The prohibition against representing man and animals, with the mathematical bent of the Arabs, resulted in a geometrical ornament of interlacing figures, extraordinarily fertile and intricate. Precious materials were freely used; in Persia whole buildings were faced with colored and glazed faience in patterns suggested by rugs and textiles.

Development of architecture in the Far East. Long before the Christian era, the Chinese and the Aryan population of India had each adopted the basic constructive elements and the religious symbolism of architectural systems, which persistent conservatism, coupled in China with ancestor-worship, has preserved to this day. Each employed at the start a structure of wood, with posts, beams, and brackets—the Indian roofs being of thatch, the Chinese roofs of curved tile. In China wooden construction has remained typical; in India there early developed a stone construction, likewise based on the beam and bracket, with the similar devices of the corbeled arch and vault. Characteristic of both countries was the multiplication of similar decorative elements, graduated in size and subtly varied in arrangement, in combinations of overwhelming decorative effect. As dynasties rose and fell, as foreign conquerors of less developed culture established themselves, as religious systems—Brahmanist, Jain, and Buddhist in India, or Confucianist, Taoist, and Buddhist in China—succeeded or transformed each other, the native architectural systems were steadily adapted to the prevailing programs, without fundamental changes of style. Inner historical growth there was, indeed, and influence of one system or another. Mohammedan India adopted the pointed arch with radiating joints from Persia, and China modified the pagoda, in some instances, on suggestions from the Indian spire or *sikhara*. In the main, however, these changes and influences were not bound by creed or dynasty, so that shrines of different sects were built simultaneously and side by side, in a style essentially one—not Buddhist, Brahmanist, or Mohammedan, but Indian or Chinese. The outlying regions were dominated by the influence of the great cultural centers. Thus Java developed in the eighth to the thirteenth centuries a notable art based on Indian models, and had its own influence on the art of the Khmers in Cambodia. Japan was inspired by China, and, undisturbed by invasion, carried on and preserved tendencies which succumbed in China itself.

India. The basic feature of Indian religious buildings was the *stupa*, a hemispherical tumulus or dome, which was first used as a grave monument and thus gained religious associations. In the early Buddhist chapter-houses at Ajanta (second and first centuries B.C.), the stupa served as an altar or reliquary, standing in the apse-like end of a hall, with a colonnade following the sides and encircling the apse. The domical form of the stupa was also employed as the crowning feature of the shrines of Siva, the destructive aspect of the Brahmanist trinity, while for those of the complementary

FIG. 313—KHAJURAHO. TEMPLE OF VISHNU

preservative aspect, Vishnu, the form adopted was the spire-like sikhara. These are the principal elements of the great medieval temples of India, of which the shrine of Vishnu at Khajuraho (Fig. 313) with its vast bud-like sikhara, its vestibule and symbolic porches, its wealth of carved ornament, is a typical example. When the Mohammedans conquered India their art had already absorbed Indian elements, and no radical change was necessary in methods of construction and composition. The Siva dome, stripped of its sculptured symbolism, became the dome of the mosque. The temple platform was preserved, and the small sikharas which marked

its corners became minarets, as in the Taj Mahal. Thus the
traditions of Indian craftsmanship remained unbroken until
the importation of European ideals by the English.

  Java.   Java felt the influence of Indian movements at later
dates than India itself, so that its Buddhist monuments date

FIG. 314—JAVA. THE CHANDI MENDOOT. (SCHELTEMA)

from the eighth to the twelfth centuries, its Brahmanist
shrines mostly from the subsequent period.   Both were composed of the typical Indian elements.   Sometimes the ensemble
was also of Indian character, as there was a pyramidal chapel
with a porch in front, like the Chandi Mendoot (Fig. 314).
Sometimes, however, the general arrangement was more
characteristically Javan, depending on the repetition, around
a central monument, of small shrines all alike, often in great
numbers.   This was the system at the great temple of Boro-
Budur (ninth century), where the large central stupa, of bell
shape, was surrounded by smaller bells in three terraces,
themselves supported on a pyramid of six steps with many
hundreds of niche-like shrines.

Cambodia. In Cambodia there arose, under Indian and Javan influence, the civilization of the Khmers, whose empire flourished especially from the ninth to the thirteenth centuries. Although it borrowed certain forms, such as the Javanese system of an assemblage of satellite shrines, its developed architecture was markedly different from anything in India and Java. As seen in the city and palace of Angkor Thom or

FIG. 315—ANGKOR WAT. SOUTHWEST ANGLE OF THE PORTICOES

in the temple of Angkor Wat (Fig. 315), the style involved vast ensembles governed by an elaborate system of rectangular axes, with lakes and moats, causeways of approach, tall straight stairways leading to elaborate gateways flanked by long porticoes, and a multiplication of sikhara-like towers with rich pointed silhouettes. The fine limestone freely available was laid up with exquisite precision, without mortar, and carved with endless sculptures in relief and in the round, in which the serpent-head motive was conspicuous. Especially characteristic was the fine restraint and sense of structural fitness in the piers and capitals of porticoes and gateways, which accord with the classical canons of the West as do few other structures of the Orient.

China.   Unlike the West, and even unlike India, China has steadily retained wood as a material for monumental structures.   The single hall of wood has remained the fundamental

element of even the largest temples.   As a result China has carried construction in wood to a degree of elaboration and expressiveness comparable with that of the great systems of masonry construction elsewhere. The essential scheme consists of columns, with arm-like brackets, supporting a beam system and widely overhanging hip-roof, which by the mode of its construction acquires naturally a slight upward curve at the angles. If the span is great, one or more lines of interior supports are

FIG. 316—PEKIN.   THE TEMPLE OF HEAVEN

introduced, creating an encircling aisle or series of aisles, each with its own roof and section of vertical wall (Fig. 316).   A similar effect was produced by buildings in more than one story, for each story was shaded by overhanging eaves.   When the stories were multiplied there was produced the pagoda, often erected as a feature of a temple, but usually as a commemorative monument.   Pagodas were also built of stone, in which case the roofs between the stories were reduced to decorative string-courses, and sometimes the whole structure was given more the character of an Indian sikhara.   The Chinese houses and palaces, of isolated halls grouped in an

FIG. 317—UJI. THE PHENIX-HALL. (CRAM)

inclosure, were accompanied by gardens of a naturalistic style, with miniature mountains, lakes, and bridges. Note-worthy also are the vast works of fortification, the walls and gates of the cities, and, above all, the Great Wall of China, twelve hundred miles long, first erected as an earthen rampart in the third century B.C., and rebuilt in the fifteenth and sixteenth centuries with walls and towers of stone.

Japan.   Chinese architecture was brought to Japan by the Buddhist missionaries of the seventh century. The hall and pagoda of the period at Horiuji are purely Chinese. Soon, however, the Japanese were able to make characteristic modifi-cations, in the direction of greater discretion and elegance.   In the Fujiwara period (898–1186), these qualities were at their height, as may be seen in the subtle and delicate Phenix-hall at Uji with its sanctuary flanked by porticoes and pavilions (Fig. 317).   Later the system of bracketing became more complex, but carving was still almost wholly absent until the Tokugawa period (1587–1867), when ostentatious exuberance replaced the simplicity and dignity of earlier times. Sculpture, lacquered and gilded, disguised the structural members; the roofs were given fantastic curvatures and loaded with orna-ment.   Such was the prevailing style when the opening of the ports to European trade (1854) brought the flood of Western artistic ideas, which have tended, for the moment at least, to submerge the native art of Japan.

PERIODS OF EASTERN ARCHITECTURE

The Near East.
    Sassanian architecture, 227–641 A.D.
        Palace at Firouzabad.
        Palace at Sarvistan.
        Palace at Ctesiphon.
    Mohammedan architecture, 622 A.D.–date.
        Syria and Egypt.
            Mosque of Amru at Cairo, 642.
            Mosque at Damascus, begun 707.
            Mosque of Ibn Touloun at Cairo, 878.
            Mosque of Sultan Hassan at Cairo, 1356.
            Tomb of Kaït Bey at Cairo, 1472–76.

EASTERN ARCHITECTURE 587

Spain.
Great mosque at Cordova, begun 770.
Alcázar at Seville, 1199–1200, restored 1353.
Alhambra at Granada, begun 1230: Gate of Justice, 1337;
Court of Lions, 1354.
Mesopotamia and Persia.
Cathedral mosque at Ispahan, 760–70, remodeled in sixteenth
century.
Tomb of Zobeide at Bagdad, 831.
Imperial Mosque at Ispahan, 1612–28.
India.
Qutb Minar at Delhi, c. 1200.
Buildings at Fathpur-Sikri, 1560–1605.
Taj Mahal at Agra, 1630.
Ottoman Empire.
Mosque of Suleiman at Constantinople, 1550.
Mosque of Sultan Ahmed I. at Constantinople, 1608–15.
Mosque of Mehemet Ali at Cairo, 1815.
The Far East.
Indian architecture.
Cave temples at Karle and Ajanta, second and first centuries
B.C.
Kailasa temple, Ellora, eighth century after Christ.
Temples at Khajuraho, tenth and eleventh centuries.
Javan architecture.
Temple of Boro-Budur, ninth century.
Cambodia, Khmer architecture.
City and palace of Angkor Thom, ninth century.
Temple of Angkor Wat, twelfth century.
Chinese architecture.
Great Wall, third century B.C., rebuilt in fifteenth and six-
teenth centuries.
Rock temples of Lungmen, seventh century.
Pagoda of Porcelain at Nankin, 1412–31.
Temple of Heaven, Pekin, eighteenth century, rebuilt in
nineteenth century.
Japanese architecture.
Early temple buildings at Horiuji, beginning of seventh
century.
Phenix-hall at Uji, eleventh century.
Temple of Iyeasu, Nikko, seventeenth century.

BIBLIOGRAPHICAL NOTE

The most comprehensive general work on Eastern architecture is F. Benoît's *L'architecture: l'orient médiéval et moderne*, 1912, which is provided with very full bibliographical lists.   H. Saladin's volume, *L'architecture*, 1907, in the *Manuel d'art musulman* (vol. 1), covers Mohammedan architecture in more detail as do G. T. Rivoira's *L'architettura Musulmana* and U. Tarchi's work of the same name devoted to Egypt and Palestine.   Works in English covering Mohammedan architecture in special regions are S. L. Poole's *The Art of the Saracens in Egypt*, 1886; A. F. Calvert's *Moorish Remains in Spain*, 1906, and *The Alhambra*, 1904; and E. B. Havell's *Indian Architecture . . . from the First Mohammedan Invasion to the Present Day*, 1913.   The art of the Far East is dealt with generally in J. Fergusson's *History of Indian and Eastern Architecture*, revised by J. Burgess and R. Phené Spiers, 2 vols., 1910.   This should be supplemented by special works embodying more recent views, such as E. B. Havell's *The Ancient and Mediæval Architecture of India*, 1915; O. Münsterberg's *Chinesische Kunstgeschichte*, 2 vols., 1910–12, and *Japanische Kunstgeschichte*, 3 vols., 1904–07; J. F. Scheltema's *Monumental Java*, 1912; and R. A. Cram's *Impressions of Japanese Architecture*, 1905. Most recent are M. S. Briggs' *Muhammadan Architecture in Egypt and Palestine;* E. La Roche's *Indische Baukunst*, 6 vols., 1921; K. Doehring's *Buddhistische Tempelanlagen in Siam*, 3 vols., 1920; N. J. Krom's *Inleidung tod de Hindoe-Javaansch Kunst;* E. Boerschmann's *Die Baukunst der Chinesen*, 2 vols., 1911–14.

GLOSSARY

Abacus. The chief or uppermost member of a capital.

Absidiole. A small, apse-like structure frequently used as a chapel.

Acanthus. An ornament derived from the conventionalized leaves of the acanthus plant.

Acroterion. In classic architecture, an ornament placed upon the corners and the peak of a pediment.

Adobe. Unburnt, sun-dried brick.

Adyton. An inner sanctuary in some Greek temples, housing the image.

Agora. A Greek public square or market-place.

Aisles. One of the divisions in a building divided longitudinally by colonnades or lines of piers, especially one of the side divisions, often lower than the central division.

Allée. A garden path or avenue, usually bordered by trees.

Alternate system. A term applied to an architectural system wherein a simpler pier alternates with a more complex one.

Ambone. A pulpit, especially that found in basilican churches.

Ambulatory. A passageway in a building, especially the passageway around the apse.

Amphiprostyle. A term applied to a temple having columns across both front and rear, but not along the sides.

Amphora. A long pot with a narrow neck, usually of terra cotta.

Annular vault. A ring-shaped vault.

Anta (pl. *antæ*). The end of a wall which carries a lintel, treated with a pilaster-like projection.

Anthemion. The Greek honeysuckle ornament.

Apodyterium. The dressing-room of a Roman bathing-establishment.

Apse. A recess of semicircular or polygonal plan, covered by a semi-dome or other vault; especially the semicircular termination of the choir of a church.

Aqueduct. A conduit or channel for conducting water, especially one supported on masonry arches.

Arabesque. An ornament of a capricious or fanciful character, consisting of foliage, flowers, figures, etc.

Arcade.   A series of arches resting on piers or columns.

Arch.   A structural device to span an opening by means of small stones or brick.   In the "true" arch these are wedge-shaped blocks, or voussoirs.

"Arch order."   In classic architecture, the system of enframing arches by columns and entablatures.

Archiepiscopal cross.   A cross with two transverse arms, the longer one nearer the center.

Architrave.   A lintel, usually with horizontal bands or moldings.

Archivolt.   A molded band like an architrave, carried around a curved opening.

Ashlar.   Squared and finished building-stone.

Atlas (pl. *Atlantes*).   A male figure used as a support.

Atrium.   In Roman architecture, the principal room in the early house.   In more elaborate buildings, a court partly open to the sky.   In Christian ecclesiology, the open court before the narthex of a basilica.

Attic.   A pedestal-like feature or story above the cornice of a building.

Attic base.   A molded column base consisting of two convex moldings, or toruses, with a hollow, or scotia, between.

Axis.   The central line of a symmetrical or other balanced composition.

Baluster.   An upright member used to support a railing; usually urn-shaped or with some other swelling contour.

Bar tracery.   Tracery composed of thin bars of stone, joined together on the principle of the arch.

Barrel vault.   A semi-cylindrical vault, or one approaching this shape.

Basilica.   In Roman architecture, an oblong covered hall, often subdivided by columns or piers, devoted to the transaction of business and the administration of justice.   In Christian architecture, an early Christian church of similar form, composed with reference to a longitudinal axis.

Basilican.   Like a basilica in having longitudinal rows of columns, or a raised clerestory.

Battlement.   An indented parapet behind which archers could shelter themselves.

Bay.   Originally an opening between two columns or piers.   By extension one compartment or division of a building which consists of several such divisions.

Bed-molding.   The molding or suite of moldings supporting a cornice.

Beffroi.   In France and Flanders, the civil or communal bell tower as opposed to the *clocher* of the church.   In medieval military parlance the term is sometimes applied to the movable towers used in attacking walled fortifications.

Belt-course. See *String-course.*

Bema. The rudimentary transept which gave the T-shaped form to the early Christian basilica.

Billet mold. A molding consisting of short, broken, cylindrical members, arranged with their axes parallel to that of the molding. Especially common in Norman Romanesque architecture.

Blind arcade. An arcade applied to the face of the wall so that no actual openings appear.

Bouleuterion. The Greek council-house.

Broken pediment. A pediment in which the raking cornice is broken through.

Buttress. A support against lateral thrust; especially, a member projecting at right angles to a wall, designed to receive such a thrust.

Caldarium. The hot-room in a Roman bathing-establishment.

Campanile. A word applied in Italy to a bell tower, engaged or free standing.

Capilla mayor. The great chapel, nearly filling the apse and blocking the view of the ambulatory, commonly found in Spanish churches.

Capital. The topmost member of a column, distinguished from the shaft by distinct architectural treatment.

Cartouche. An ornament of irregular or fantastic form, inclosing a field sometimes decorated with armorial bearings, etc.

Caryatid. A female figure used as a support.

Casino. A small pleasure-house, especially in an Italian villa.

Catacombs. Extensive underground burial passages and vaults.

Cathedra. The bishop's chair in the early Christian church, commonly placed at the back of the apse on the longitudinal axis of the building.

Catholicon. In Greek, a bishop's cathedral church.

Cavetto. A molding having the form of a quarter-hollow.

Cella. The essential or principal chamber of a temple.

Centering. A timber framework on which the masonry of an arch or vault is supported until the key is in place, rendering the whole self-supporting.

Chamfer. The cutting away of the square edge of an ordinary architectural member.

Chancel. The portion of a church in the east end, railed, and set apart for the use of the clergy.

Chapel of the Virgin. A chapel, dedicated to the use of the Virgin, and usually extending beyond the apse on the long axis of the church.

Chevet. A term applied to the complicated east end of the French cathedral.

Chevron. A V-shaped, or zigzag ornament.

Choir. Primarily the part of the church where the singers are accommodated. The arm of the cross between the transept and the apse.

Ciborium. A canopy, generally of marble and supported on columns, over the altar of an early Christian church. The term is often applied in Italy, however, to the chiseled receptacle in which the consecrated wafers are kept.

Circus. In Roman architecture, a course for horse and chariot races; in England a circular or semicircular open space surrounded by houses.

Clerestory. A part of a building which rises above the adjacent roofs, permitting it to be pierced with window openings.

Cloister. A court surrounded by an ambulatory, usually arcaded.

Cloister vault. A square or polygonal dome.

Coffer. A sunk panel or compartment in a ceiling, vault, or soffit.

Collegiate church. A church that has a college or chapter, with a dean, but not a bishop's see.

Colonnade. A series or range of columns, usually connected by lintels.

Colonnette. A diminutive column.

"Colossal order." An order running through more than one story of a building.

Column. A circular supporting member, usually with a base and capital.

Concrete. An artificial stone composed of an aggregate of broken stone or other small materials, held together by a binding material or cement.

Console. A bracket or corbel, usually in the form of a scroll of reverse curvature.

Corbel. A bracket of masonry, projecting from a wall and used as a support.

Corbel table. A projecting course of masonry carried on corbels, often connected by arches.

Corbeled arch. An arch built up of horizontal courses, each projecting over the one below.

Cornice. A projecting horizontal member which crowns the wall of a building; any molded projection of similar form.

Coro. The elaborate choir, at times almost an independent building, commonly placed to the west of the transept in a Spanish cathedral.

Coupled. A term applied to columns or pilasters grouped in pairs.

Cour d'honneur. An entrance court, open on one side.

Court. An inclosed space within a building or connected with it.

Crocket. A projecting piece of carving, usually foliate, commonly used to decorate the edge of a gable or the sloping ridges of a spire in Gothic architecture.

Cromlech. A type of prehistoric monument composed of a circle of stones.

Crossing. The space in a cruciform church at the intersection of nave and transepts.

Crypt. A story beneath the pavement of a church, commonly used for the keeping of relics.

Cupola. A dome or lantern.

Curia. The building in which the Roman Senate held its deliberations.

Cusp. A point of the small arcs or foliations decorating the intrados of an arch, or of tracery.

Cyclopean. A term applied to early masonry of very large blocks, unhewn or irregular.

Cyma. A molding having a reverse curve in profile. In the cyma recta the thin concave portion projects; in the cyma reversa, the convex portion.

Dado. A continuous pedestal or wainscoting around the base of a wall.

Dentils. Small projecting blocks, suggesting teeth, forming part of the support of a cornice.

Diaconicon. Originally the place where the deacons kept the vessels for the church service. A room on the south side of the building which became the sacristy of the later church.

Dog-tooth. An angular, tooth-like molding, commonly found in Norman Romanesque architecture.

Dolmen. A pair of stone blocks with a covering slab, used of prehistoric monuments.

Dome. A hemispherical vault; an exterior feature based on such a vault.

Domed basilica. The term applied to the form of basilica, especially in the East, when one or more bays are covered with a dome.

Donjon. A tower-like structure, usually free standing, the strongest part of the European medieval castle.

Dormer. A window projecting from the slant of a roof.

Drum. The cylindrical or polygonal vertical wall on which a dome or cloister vault frequently is placed.

Ear. A projecting corner of a molded architrave.

Echinus. The convex member of a capital, supporting the abacus and having a parabolic or hyperbolic profile.

Enceinte. In military architecture, the wall or rampart, usually with bastions or towers and curtain walls, which surrounds a fort or city.

Engaged column. A column-like member projecting from a wall and frequently actually a part of the wall masonry.

Entablature. That part of a lintel construction which rests on the columns and extends upward to the roof or to the beginning of a story or attic above.

Entasis. A slight swelling in the profile of a column.

Exedra. In classical architecture, an open platform, often semicircular, provided with seats: in Christian architecture an apse or niche.

Extrados. The external surface of the voussoirs or stones composing an arch or vault.

Façade. One of the fronts of a building, especially the principal front.

Fascia. A long flat band or belt, usually forming part of a suite of moldings, of which it is usually the widest member.

Fan vault. The vault, in English Perpendicular Gothic, shaped like an inverted, concave cone, and suggesting by its spreading ribs the appearance of an open fan.

Fenestration. The disposition of windows in a building.

Fillet. A narrow flat member accompanying a molding or suite of moldings.

Finial. In Gothic architecture, the bossy, knob-like ornament, of foliate design, usually placed at the point of a spire or pinnacle.

Flèche. A very lofty and slender spire-like structure, used especially in France to mark important parts of a building, like the crossing.

Flute. A groove, usually segmental or semicircular in plan.

Flying buttress. A buttress composed of an arch or a series of arches, which carries the thrust of a vault over the aisle or aisles of a church to a solid pier built at the outer wall.

Forum. The market-place of a Roman city.

Foyer. A lobby or saloon for promenade in a theater.

"French order." An order with rusticated, fluted columns.

Fresco. Wall painting, in mineral colors, applied to a plaster wall while the plaster is still moist, and permitted to dry in with the plaster.

Fret. An ornament of continuous bands or fillets arranged in rectangular forms.

Frieze. A longitudinal band of extended length, often decorated with sculpture; specifically, such a band in an entablature, between the architrave and cornice.

Frigidarium. The cool-room of a Roman bathing-establishment, containing the cold plunge-bath.

Gable. The end of a ridged roof, with the generally triangular wall between its eaves and the apex.

Gargoyle. A water spout, usually grotesquely carved, designed to carry water from the gutter and throw it clear of the wall of the building.

Greek cross. A cross of four equal arms meeting at right angles.

Grille. A grating of any sort, but most commonly of iron work or perforated stone slabs.

Groin. The edge, or arris, formed by the intersection of two barrel vaults.

Groin vault. A compound vault, in which two barrel vaults intersect, forming edges or arrises which are called groins.

Gutta. A drop; one of a series of pendent ornaments generally in the form of a frustum of a cone, but sometimes cylindrical, attached to the under side of a mutule or other architectural feature.

Gynacæa. The galleries, usually in the triforium, commonly arranged in basilicas of Eastern character, for the segregation of women.

Half-timber. A type of construction consisting of a framework of timber with a filling of brick or clay.

Hallenkirche. A type of German Gothic church in which the aisles are as high as the nave, eliminating the clerestory and giving the building the appearance of a great hall.

Herm. A head or bust supported on a quadrangular base corresponding roughly in mass to the absent body.

Hexastyle. Having six columns across the front.

Hippodrome. In Greek architecture, a place in which horse and chariot races were run.

Hip-roof. A roof in which the ends as well as the sides are inclined, so that its planes meet in diagonal lines or hips.

Hypæthral. Roofless—a term applied to some temple cellas.

Hypostyle. Having its ceiling supported by columns.

Impost. A horizontal member at the springing of an arch or vault.

In antis. A term applied to columns embraced between the ends of two walls or antæ.

Intercolumniation. The space or distance between two columns of a colonnade.

Interlacing arches. Two series of arches arranged to intersect each other.

Intrados. The inner face of an arch or vault.

Keystone. The term applied to the topmost, wedge-shaped stone or voussoir in an arch, usually the last to be placed, which renders the whole secure.

Khan. The service quarters of an Oriental dwelling; also an Oriental inn.

Laconicum. A vapor bath in a Roman bathing-establishment.

Lantern. A cupola or tower-like structure rising above a dome or the roof of a building, and having openings in its faces by which the interior is lighted.

Lanterne des morts. An ornamental stone shaft erected in the Middle Ages to signalize the presence of a cemetery.

Lararium. A small shrine in a Roman dwelling where the Lares, or household gods, were worshiped.

Latin cross. The commonest form of cross, in which one arm is considerably longer than the other three.

Lierne. A small subordinate rib, inserted between two main ribs of a vault.

Lintel. A horizontal beam spanning an opening.

Loge. A box or compartment in the auditorium of a theater.

Loggia. A gallery in a building open on at least one side, on which side is an arcade or colonnade.

Machicolation. An opening in the floor of a projecting gallery for the purpose of dropping missiles, etc.

Mastaba. A flat-topped, bench-like Egyptian tomb used by the nobles of the Old Kingdom.

Mausoleum. A large and elaborate tomb.

Meander. See *Fret.*

Megalithic. Composed of very large stones.

Megaron. The large hall of an Ægean or Greek dwelling, generally oblong in shape and sometimes subdivided by one or more longitudinal ranges of supports.

Menhir. A single standing pillar of stone, used of prehistoric monuments.

Metope. The space between two triglyphs in a Doric frieze.

Mezzanine. A story of diminished height introduced between two higher stories or created by subdividing a high story.

Minaret. In Mohammedan architecture, a slender and lofty turret, having one or more projecting balconies.

Mirhab. The niche in a mosque which indicates the direction of Mecca.

Modillion. A bracket, often carved with spiral scrolls, serving to support a cornice.

Module. A unit or common divisor of the dimensions of a building.

Monolithic. Composed of a single stone.

Mosaic. Decoration composed of tesseræ or cubes of glass or marble, set in mortar, in geometric or pictorial designs.

Mosque. A Mohammedan place of worship.

Mullion. A slender, vertical, intermediate upright, forming part of a framework, dividing an opening, and commonly helping to support the glass.

Mutule. A projecting block on the soffit of a Doric cornice.

Naos. The essential or principal chamber of a Greek temple; the cella.

Narthex. A covered vestibule of one or more stories, usually open and colonnaded at the front, placed before a building, and especially common in the early Christian period.

Nave. That part of a church nearest the entrance, constituting the long arm in a Latin cross, appropriated to the laity. The chief central division of the building, the central space between the colonnades, as opposed to the aisles.

Niche. A recess in a wall, usually semicircular and semicircular-headed, often used for the reception of statuary.

Obelisk. A tapering shaft of rectangular plan, generally with a pyramidal apex.

Octastyle. Having eight columns across the front.

Odeion. In Greek architecture, a covered building for musical and oratorical contests.

Ogee curve. A double S curve especially common in Flamboyant Gothic architecture.

Opisthodomos. An open vestibule at the rear of a temple cella.

Opus alexandrinum. An elaborate geometrical mosaic of marble slabs and tesseræ.

Opus francigenum. "French work," the word first applied by the Germans to Gothic architecture.

Opus incertum. A Roman method of facing concrete walls with irregular fragments.

Opus reticulatum. A Roman method of facing concrete walls with small square blocks standing on their corners in diagonal lines.

Opus spicatum. A Roman method of facing concrete walls with kernel-shaped fragments laid in herring-bone pattern.

Orchestra. In Greek theaters, the circle of the dance; in modern theaters, the space for the musicians, or the parquet.

"Order." In classical architecture, a recognized system of forms for the column and entablature.

"Organic architecture." A vaulted architecture in which the vaults are supported by ribs, piers, and buttresses arranged with direct reference to the needs of supporting the vaults and opposing their thrusts.

Ovolo. A convex molding approaching a quarter-circle in profile.

Pagoda. In Chinese and Japanese architecture, a sacred tower in several stories.

Palæstra. A building or inclosure devoted to wrestling, boxing, and kindred gymnastic exercises.

Palladian motive. A central arch resting on the entablatures of lateral square-headed bays.

Parapet. A breast wall placed at the edge of a platform, terrace, balcony, etc.

Parterre. A garden of beds with intervening gravel or turf.

Patio. In Spain or Spanish America, a court in a house, open to the sky.

Pavilion. A central, flanking, or intermediate subdivision of a monumental building or façade, accented architecturally by projection or otherwise.

Pedestal. A base or support for a column or building, usually having its own capital and base moldings.

Pediment. A low triangular gable bounded by a horizontal cornice and raking cornices.

Pendentive. An inverted, triangular, concave piece of masonry, placed upon a pier to support a section of a dome. In mathematical terms, a segment of a hemisphere the diameter of which is equal to the diagonal of the square or polygon to be covered.

Penetration. In vaulting, a surface intersecting the main vaulting surface to permit lateral openings to be raised above the line of its springing.

Peristyle. A continuous surrounding colonnade, either around the exterior of a building or the interior of a court.

Piano nobile. The principal floor of an Italian house, above the ground story.

Pier. A masonry member acting as a support, distinguished from a column by greater massiveness, by a shape other than circular, or by being built of coursed masonry.

Pier buttress. A solid pier of masonry built immediately adjacent to a vault to resist its thrust.

Pilaster. A flat rectangular member, projecting slightly from the face of a wall, and furnished with a capital, base, etc., in the manner of a column.

Pilaster strip. A slender engaged pier-like member in a wall, used in medieval architecture as a stiffener or rudimentary buttress.

Pillar. A loosely used term denoting an isolated vertical mass of masonry, used as a support. In architecture, applied to a support which is neither a pier nor a column in the strict sense of those words.

Plate tracery. Tracery composed of openings pierced in a thin tympanum of stone, as contrasted with bar tracery.

Plinth. A rectangular block usually serving as a base.

Podium. A continuous pedestal.

Portcullis. A sliding barrier or grating to cut off access to a gate or passage.

Portico. An open porch or vestibule having its roof supported by columns or piers.

Presbyterium. That part of a church devoted to the clergy, in which the high altar is placed and which forms the eastern termination of the choir. It is generally raised a few steps above the rest of the church.

Pronaos. A vestibule in front of the cella of a Greek temple.

Propylæum (pl. *propylæa*). In Greek architecture, an elaborate entrance gateway with a portico or porticoes.

Proskenion. In the Greek theater, a wall or series of piers before the skene, carrying a platform which served as a stage for some or all of the actors.

Prostyle. A term applied to a temple or pavilion having columns across the front only.

Prothesis. A chapel or room on the north side of the early Christian church; the prototype of the vestry.

Pulvinated. Swelling or bulging out; a term applied to a frieze of curved section.

Pylon. A monumental gateway to an Egyptian temple; any gate-tower of classical design.

Pyramid-mastaba. An Egyptian tomb having the form of a mastaba with a small pyramid on top.

Quadriga. A chariot drawn by four horses.

Quadripartite vault. A groin vault, generally ribbed, composed of four cells.

Quoins. Stones or blocks reinforcing the angle of a building.

Raking cornice. The sloping moldings of a pediment.

Ramp. An inclined plane rising from a lower to a higher level, taking the place of steps.

"Rhythmical bay." A term applied to a continuous alternation of wide and narrow bays.

Rib. A masonry arch, generally salient from the vault surface and molded, forming part of the skeleton structure on which the vault rests.

Ribbed vault. A vault of masonry with a comparatively thin web supported by ribs.

Rocaille. The shell-work or scroll ornament characteristic of rococo decoration.

Roof comb. In Maya architecture, a pierced screen-wall rising above the roof of a building.

Roundel. A circular medallion.

Rubble. Masonry of stones irregular in shape and size.

Rusticated stone. Stone masonry distinguished from smooth ashlar by having the joints sunk, and sometimes the surface of the stone roughly or bossily finished.

Sarcophagus. A stone coffin, usually ornamented with sculpture.

Saucer-dome. A dome showing on the exterior only the upper zone of its surface.

Scænæ frons. The front wall of the skene, forming the background of the stage, usually decorated with columns.

Scale. The effect of size produced by a building or its members.

Scotia. A concave molding of circular plan.

"Screens." The passage across one end of the hall in an English manor house.

Sexpartite vault. A groin vault, usually ribbed, and provided with a transverse rib to the crown of the vault, which divides the whole into six cells.

Shaft. The main, cylindrical member of a column. An upright member, tall and comparatively small in horizontal dimensions, engaged or free standing, and generally used as a support.

Short and long work. Stones embedded alternately horizontally and vertically in the masonry at a wall angle, used to reinforce the angle and especially common in early Saxon architecture.

Sikhara. An Indian spire, used in the shrines of Vishnu.

Skene. In the Greek theater, the building containing the dressing-rooms, the front of which served as a background for the action.

Soffit. The under side of an architectural member, such as a lintel or arch.

Spina. The barrier dividing a race-course longitudinally into two tracks.

Spire. A lofty, slender, generally octagonal member used to crown a medieval tower.

Splay. A sloped surface, which makes an oblique angle with another, a large chamfer.

Squinch. A slab or small arch thrown across the angle of a square or polygon to render its shape more nearly round, to receive the base of a dome.

Stadion. A course for foot racing, six hundred Greek feet in length.

Staged tower. A tower built in several receding platforms or stages.

Stalactite vaulting. Vaulting composed of small squinches one above another, giving the appearance of stalactites.

Steeple. A lofty structure attached to a church or other building.

Stele. An upright stone employed as a monument.

Step-pyramid. A pyramidal structure consisting of diminishing terraces, forming a series of large steps.

Stereotomy. The science of stone-cutting.

Stilt. To raise the point of springing of an arch above the level of a capital or impost.

Stilt-block. A block above a capital serving to support an arch or vault.

Stoa. In Greek architecture, a long, narrow hall, usually divided longitudinally by columns, and having an open colonnade in place of one of the side walls.

Strap-work. Ornament consisting of fillets, or bands, imitating leather, folded or interlaced.

String-course. A horizontal course of masonry, usually molded, marking an architectural subdivision of a building.

Stucco. Plaster or cement used as a coating for walls.

Stupa. A hemispherical tumulus or dome characteristic of Indian architecture.

Stylobate. A continuous plinth or step serving as a common base to columns, especially those of the Greek Doric order.

Tabernacle. A pedimented or canopied niche.

Tablinum. A recess or apartment at the back of the atrium in a Roman house.

Tepidarium. An apartment in a Roman bathing-establishment intermediate in temperature between the caldarium and the frigidarium.

Terrace-roof. A roof either flat or with barely perceptible inclination.

Tesseræ. Small cubes of marble or glass, used in the composition of designs in mosaic.

Tholos. In Greek architecture, a circular structure or temple.

Thrust. The outward horizontal force exerted by an arch or vault.

Tie-rod. A rod, usually of iron, set in the masonry of an arch or vault to resist its outward thrust.

Tierceron. A secondary or intermediate rib in a vault, springing from the pier on either side of the diagonal rib.

Torus. A molding of convex profile, approaching a semicircle, used especially in bases.

Trabeated architecture. Literally, beamed architecture, the term is applied to the post and lintel or horizontal architectural system, as opposed to the arched or arcuated system.

Transept. A large division of a church lying at right angles to the long axis of the building. It developed probably from the early Christian bema.

Transom window. A window divided horizontally by a bar of stone or iron.

Triclinium. In Roman architecture, the dining-room, furnished with three couches.

Triconch plan. A plan ending in a trefoil or clover-leafed shape, common in Syria, and later in Carolingian and German architecture.

Triforium. A blind space between the ceiling and the lean-to roof over an aisle; any corresponding division below a clerestory.

Triglyph. A projecting block in a Doric frieze, marked by vertical grooves.

Trophy. A monument or memorial of victory, especially one consisting of arms and other spoils, or sculptures representing them.

Truss. A combination of timbers or ironwork so arranged as to constitute an unyielding frame for spanning an opening, etc.

Tudor arch. A four-centered, pointed arch, common in English Tudor architecture.

Tumulus. A sepulchral mound.

Vault cell. A subdivision of a vault, the part defined by adjacent groins or ribs.

Vault web. The thin infilling of masonry composing the main expanse of a rib-vault, supported by ribs.

Velarium. An awning stretched over the seats of a Roman theater or amphitheater.

Veneer. A thin facing of wood or other material which has ornamental qualities and overlays the structural material of a building.

Volute. A spiral scroll.

Voussoir. One of the wedge-shaped stones used in the construction of an arch or vault.

Wall shaft. A shaft, in the thickness of a wall, dividing an opening into two or more parts. Characteristic of early Saxon architecture.

Wheel, or rose, window. The circular window, divided by tracery, which was commonly placed in the west end of a Gothic cathedral.

Ziggurat. A Mesopotamian religious structure, consisting of a tall staged tower or stepped pyramid, with ramps giving access to the top.

BIBLIOGRAPHICAL NOTE

GENERAL WORKS RELATING TO THE HISTORY OF ARCHITECTURE

(For works covering special periods see the note at the end of each chapter.)

Among earlier comprehensive histories of architecture may be mentioned especially the following:

F. Kugler's *Geschichte der Baukunst*, 5 vols., 1859–72. Continued by J. Burkhardt, W. Lübke, and C. Gurlitt as *Geschichte der neueren Baukunst*, 4 vols. in 6, 1887–1911.

J. Fergusson's *History of Architecture*, 2 vols., 1865–67; 2d ed., 4 vols., 1873–76; 3d ed., revised by R. P. Spiers and R. Kerr, 5 vols., 1891–93.

J. Durm's *Handbuch der Architektur, Teil II. Die Baustile*, 7 vols. in 12, 1881 to date. Volumes generally listed singly above.

A. Choisy's *Histoire de l'architecture*, 2 vols., 1899. (A study of the history of constructive methods.)

For the monuments in their geographical setting see the guidebooks of Baedeker, Murray, etc. Fuller topographical treatment is afforded by the official inventories of monuments published by most European countries, such as the *Survey of London*, the publications of the Royal Historical Monuments in England, etc. These are particularly complete for the various Germanic states: a convenient recent list of these is given in Wackernagel's *Baukunst des. XVII. und XVIII. Jahrhunderts*, 1915, pp. 21–23. For the history of the excavations, etc., see A. Michaelis's *A Century of Archæological Discoveries*, 1908.

A superb biographical dictionary of architects is afforded by U. Thieme and F. Becker's *Allgemeines Künstlerlexikon*, which affords the fullest references to individual biographies.

The best general guide to the literature of the subject is furnished by the references in historical works such as those just named, especially the *Handbuch der Architektur*. Mention may also be made of the classified catalogues of special libraries or general libraries having large collections on architecture, especially those of the Royal Institute of British Architects, London, with supplement, 1898; the libraries of Manchester and Salford (by H. Guppy and G. Vine), 1909; and the Boston Public Library, 2d ed., 1914. The most complete collection of books on architecture is that of the Avery Library of Columbia University, New York, of which an alphabetical catalogue was published in 1895. Similar works for Continental libraries, fuller on the work of their respective countries, are E. Vinet's *Catalogue de la bibliothèque de l'Ecole de Beaux-Arts*, Paris, 1873; C. v. Lützow's *Katalog der Bibliothek der Akademie der bildenden Künste in Wien*, 1876; Dobbert and Grohmann's *Katalog der Bibliothek der Kgl. Akademie der Künste zu Berlin*, 1893.

INDEX

Note: The index covers references in the text and illustrations, the presence of an illustration being indicated by a page reference in Italic type. All buildings are listed alphabetically under the towns and cities where they are located.

THE END